pwc

UK illustrative IFRS corporate consolidated financial statements for 2011 year ends

UK Accounting Consulting Services
PricewaterhouseCoopers LLP

Bloomsbury Professional

Bloomsbury Professional, an imprint of Bloomsbury Publishing Plc, Maxwelton House, 41–43 Boltro Road, Haywards Heath, West Sussex, RH16 1BJ

ISBN 978 1 84766 908 7

British Library Cataloguing-in-Publication Data.
A catalogue record for this book is available from the British Library.

Printed in Great Britain.

Preface

This publication provides example sets of financial statements for the year ended 31 December 2011. These model financial statements will assist you in preparing financial statements by illustrating the required disclosure and presentation for UK groups and UK companies, whether reporting under IFRS or UK GAAP.

IFRS GAAP plc
An example annual report including the consolidated financial statements of IFRS GAAP plc group of companies. The annual report has been prepared to show the disclosures and format that might be expected for a group of its size that prepares its financial statements in accordance with IFRS, UK law and listing rules requirements, for a fictional corporate entity (IFRS GAAP plc).

GAAP UK Group Limited
An example annual report including the consolidated financial statements of the GAAP UK Group Limited. The annual report has been prepared to show the disclosures and format that might be expected for a group of its size that prepares its financial statements in accordance with the Companies Act and UK Accounting Standards. GAAP UK Group Limited is a fictional unlisted company that is incorporated in the UK. It has a number of UK and overseas investments, including subsidiaries and joint ventures.

GAAP UK Limited
An example set of financial statements for UK GAAP Limited. These financial statements have been prepared to show how an unlisted UK company might prepare its financial statements in accordance with the Companies Act and UK Accounting Standards.

Peter Holgate
Senior Technical Partner
PricewaterhouseCoopers LLP
London
October 2011

Contents

Introduction

This publication provides an illustrative set of consolidated financial statements, prepared in accordance with International Financial Reporting Standards (IFRS), UK Company Law and Listing Rule requirements, for a fictional manufacturing, wholesale and retail group (IFRS GAAP plc).

IFRS GAAP plc is an existing preparer of IFRS consolidated financial statements; IFRS 1, 'First-time adoption of International Financial Reporting Standards', is not applicable.

This publication is based on the requirements of IFRS standards and interpretations for financial years beginning on or after 1 January 2011.

PwC commentary has been provided, in grey boxes, to explain the detail behind the presentation of a number of challenging areas. These commentary boxes relate to the presentation in: the income statement, statement of comprehensive income, balance sheet, statement of changes in equity, statement of cash flows, statement of significant accounting policies and financial risk management.

Additional PwC guidance is presented in *italics*.

Areas in which we have made significant changes to presentation since 2010 have been highlighted in pink.

We have attempted to create a realistic set of financial statements for a corporate entity. However, by necessity we illustrate disclosures that for many entities may be immaterial. Determining the level of disclosure is a matter of judgement, and naturally disclosure of immaterial items is not required. Certain types of transaction have been excluded, as they are not relevant to the group's operations. The example disclosures, if material, for some of these additional items have been included in appendix III. The forthcoming IFRS requirements are outlined in a table in appendix III.

The example disclosures should not be considered the only acceptable form of presentation. The form and content of each reporting entity's financial statements are the responsibility of the entity's management. Alternative presentations to those proposed in this publication may be equally acceptable if they comply with the specific disclosure requirements prescribed in IFRS.

These illustrative financial statements are not a substitute for reading the standards and interpretations themselves or for professional judgement as to fairness of presentation. They do not cover all possible disclosures that IFRS requires. Further specific information may be required in order to ensure fair presentation under IFRS. We recommend that readers refer to the 2011 version of GAAP Checker (our automated checklist), as well as our publication *IFRS disclosure checklist 2011*.

Abbreviations

IFRS1p37	=	International Financial Reporting Standard [number], paragraph number.
7p22	=	International Accounting Standards [number], paragraph number.
SIC – 15p5	=	Standing Interpretations Committee [number], paragraph number.
DV	=	Disclosure Voluntary. Disclosure is encouraged but not required and therefore represents best practice.
CA06 s992	=	Companies Act 2006, section number.
LR 9.8.6R(1)	=	The Listing Rules of the Financial Services Authority, paragraph number.
RS (OFR) p19	=	Reporting Statement: Operating and Financial Review, paragraph number.
CC A.2.1	=	Combined Code, paragraph number.
TR 35	=	Internal Control Guidance for Directors on the Combined Code, paragraph number (also known as the Turnbull Report).
APB 2002/2	=	Auditing Practices Board Bulletin, number.
APB DB 2005/4	=	Auditing Practices Board, Draft Bulletin, number.
GC 45	=	FRC Guidance, 'Going concern and liquidity risk: Guidance for Directors of UK Companies 2007', paragraph number.
ISA 720p20	=	International Standard on Auditing (UK & Ireland) [number], paragraph number.
SI 2008/410 8 Sch 4	=	Statutory Instrument [year/number], schedule number, paragraph number.
TG 33	=	Turnbull Guidance on Internal Control, paragraph number.
Smith 2.2	=	FRC Guidance on Audit Committees (formerly known as the Smith Guidance), paragraph number.
DTR 7.1.1R	=	Disclosures Rules and Transparency Rules, paragraph number.

IFRS GAAP Plc

Example annual report for the year ended 31 December 2011

Contents

Contents

Operating and financial review

DV, 1p13 Many entities present, outside the financial statements, a financial review by management that describes and explains the main features of the entity's financial performance and financial position and the principal uncertainties it faces.

RS (OFR)
DV The ASB has published 'Reporting statement: Operating and financial review' ('RS (OFR)'), which is a statement of best practice on the OFR. It is written with quoted companies in mind but is also applicable to any other entity that produces an OFR. Where an entity includes an operating and financial review in the financial statements, it is recommended that it complies with the RS (OFR).

Group operating and financial review for the year ended 31 December 2011

Principles

CC C.1
RS (OFR) p15 The board should present a balanced and understandable assessment of the group's position and prospects. Where non-GAAP historical numbers are disclosed, they should be clearly identified as such and reconciled to the statutory numbers, with sufficient prominence being given to the statutory numbers and to the reconciliation. The operating and financial review should give a balanced picture of performance; non-statutory numbers should be presented in a manner that achieves this objective. They should supplement and not replace statutory numbers, and their purpose should be clearly stated. The descriptions of non-GAAP historical numbers should not imply any representation about future performance.

For example, terms such as 'normalised', 'sustainable' or 'maintainable' earnings could be taken to imply an element of forecasting. Instead, 'adjusted' or more specific terms (such as 'profit before tax and exceptionals') can be used.

RS (OFR) p4 The OFR should set out an analysis of the business through the eyes of the board of directors.

RS (OFR) p5 The OFR should reflect the directors' view of the business. The entity should disclose appropriate elements of information used in managing the entity, including its subsidiary undertakings. Where appropriate, the review may give greater emphasis to those matters that are significant to the entity and its subsidiary undertakings taken as a whole. Such matters may include issues specific to business segments where relevant to the understanding of the business as a whole. The presentation of the OFR should complement the format of the annual report as a whole.

RS (OFR) p6 The OFR should focus on matters that are relevant to the interests of members.

RS (OFR) p7 Members' needs are paramount when directors consider what information should be contained in the OFR. Information in the OFR will also be of interest to users other than members — for example, other investors, potential investors, creditors, customers, suppliers, employees and general society. The directors should consider the extent to which they should report on issues relevant to the other users where, because of the influence on the performance of the business and its value, they are also of significance to members. The OFR should not, however, be seen as a replacement for other forms of reporting addressed to a wider stakeholder group.

RS (OFR) p8 The OFR should have a forward-looking orientation, identifying those trends and factors relevant to the members' assessment of the current and future performance of the business and the progress towards the achievement of long-term business objectives.

RS (OFR) p9 The particular factors discussed should be those that have affected development, performance, and position during the financial year and those which are likely to affect the entity's future development, performance and position.

RS (OFR) p10 Given the nature of some forward-looking information, in particular elements that cannot be objectively verified but have been made in good faith, directors may want to include a statement in the OFR to treat such elements with caution, explaining the uncertainties underpinning such information.

RS (OFR) p11 The OFR should comment on the impact on future performance of significant events after the balance sheet date.

RS (OFR) p12 The OFR should discuss predictive comments, both positive and negative, made in previous reviews whether or not these have been borne out by events.

RS (OFR) p13 The OFR should complement as well as supplement the financial statements, in order to enhance the overall corporate disclosure.

RS (OFR) p14 In complementing the financial statements, the OFR should provide useful financial and non- financial information about the business and its performance that is not reported in financial statements but that the directors' judge might be relevant to the members' evaluation of past results and assessment of future prospects.

RS (OFR) p15 In supplementing the financial statements, the OFR should, where relevant:

- provide additional explanations of amounts recorded in the financial statements; and
- explain the conditions and events that shaped the information contained in the financial statements.

Where amounts from the financial statements have been adjusted for inclusion in the OFR, that fact should be highlighted and a reconciliation provided.

RS (OFR) p16   The OFR should be comprehensive and understandable.

RS (OFR) p17   Directors should consider whether the omission of information might reasonably be expected to influence significantly the assessment made by members.

RS (OFR) p18   The recommendation for the OFR to be comprehensive does not mean that the OFR should cover all possible matters: the objective is quality not quantity of content. It is neither possible nor desirable for a reporting statement to list all the elements that might need to be included, as these will vary depending on the nature and circumstances of the particular business and how the business is run.

RS (OFR) p19   Directors should consider the evidence underpinning the information to be included in the OFR. Where relevant, directors should explain the source of the information and the degree to which the information is objectively supportable, to allow members to assess the reliability of the information presented for themselves.

RS (OFR) p20   Directors should consider the key issues to include in the OFR that will provide members with focused and relevant information. The inclusion of too much information may obscure judgements and will not promote understanding. Where additional information is discussed elsewhere in the annual report, or in other reports, cross-referencing to those sources will assist members.

RS (OFR) p21   The OFR should be written in a clear and readily understandable style.

RS (OFR) p22   The OFR should be balanced and neutral, dealing even-handedly with both good and bad aspects.

RS (OFR) p23   The directors should ensure that the OFR retains balance and that members are not misled as a result of the omission of any information on unfavourable aspects.

RS (OFR) p24   The OFR should be comparable over time.

RS (OFR) p25   Disclosure should be sufficient for the members to be able to compare the information presented with similar information about the entity for previous financial years. Comparability enables identification of the main trends and factors, and their analysis, over successive financial years. Directors may wish to consider the extent to which the OFR is comparable with reviews prepared by other entities in the same industry or sector.

RS (OFR) p79   No disclosure of information should be made about impending developments or about matters in the course of negotiation that would, in the opinion of the directors, be seriously prejudicial to the interests of the entity.

Disclosure framework

RS (OFR) p27   The OFR should provide information to assist members to assess the strategies adopted by the entity and the potential for those strategies to succeed. The key elements of the disclosure framework necessary to achieve this are:

- the nature of the business, including a description of the market, competitive and regulatory environment in which the entity operates, and the entity's objectives and strategies;
- the development and performance of the business, both in the financial year under review and in the future;
- the resources, principal risks and uncertainties and relationships that may affect the entity's long-term value; and
- the position of the business, including a description of the capital structure, treasury policies and objectives and liquidity of the entity, both in the financial year under review and the future.

Details of particular matters

RS (OFR) p28   To the extent necessary to meet the requirements set out in paragraph above, the OFR should include information about:

- environmental matters (including the impact of the business of the entity on the environment);
- the entity's employees;
- social and community issues;
- persons with whom the entity has contractual or other arrangements that are essential to the business of the entity;
- receipts from, and returns to, members of the entity in respect of shares held by them; and
- all other matters the directors consider to be relevant.

RS (OFR) p29   The OFR should, in particular, include:

- the entity's policies on environmental matters, the entity's employees and social and community issues; and
- the extent to which those policies have been successfully implemented

If the OFR does not contain information and analysis of each type mentioned above, it should state which of those types of information and analysis it does not contain.

The nature, objectives and strategies of the business

1p9(a)
RS (OFR)
p30, 31
The OFR should include a description of the business and the external environment in which it operates as context for the directors' discussion and analysis of performance and financial position. This description is recommended in order to provide members with an understanding of the industry/industries in which the entity operates; its main products, services, customers, business processes and distribution methods; the structure of the business; and its economic model, including an overview of the main operating facilities and their location.

RS (OFR) p32
Every entity is affected by its external environment. Depending on the nature of the business, the OFR should include discussion of matters such as the entity's major markets and competitive position within those markets and the significant features of the legal, regulatory, macro- economic and social environment that influence the business.

RS (OFR) p33-35
CC C1.2
The OFR should discuss the objectives of the business to generate or preserve value over the longer-term. Objectives will often be defined in terms of financial performance; however, objectives in non-financial areas should also be discussed where appropriate. The nature of the industry will affect the directors' determination of an appropriate time perspective for reporting in the OFR.

RS (OFR) p36
CC C1.2
The OFR should set out the directors' strategies for achieving the objectives of the business.

RS (OFR) p38-40
It should include the key performance indicators, both financial and, where appropriate, non- financial, used by the directors to assess progress against their stated objectives. The KPIs disclosed should be those that the directors judge are effective in measuring the delivery of their strategies and managing their business. Regular measurement using KPIs should enable an entity to set and communicate its performance targets and to measure whether it is achieving them. Comparability will be enhanced if the KPIs disclosed are accepted and widely used, either within the industry sector or more generally.

RS (OFR) p41-42
Directors should also consider the extent to which other performance indicators and evidence should be included in the OFR. These could be narrative evidence describing how the directors manage the business or quantified measures used to monitor the entity's external environment and/ or progress towards the achievement of its objectives.

Current and future development and performance

RS (OFR) p44-46
Trends and factors in development and performance suggested by an analysis of the current and previous financial years should be highlighted. Development and performance should be described in the context of the strategic objectives of the business. The OFR should cover significant aspects of the statements of financial performance and, where appropriate, should be linked to other aspects of performance. It should set out the directors' analysis of the effect on current development and performance of changes during the financial year in the industry, or the external environment in which the business operates and of developments within the business.

RS (OFR) p43, 47-49
The OFR should describe the significant features of the development and performance of the business in the financial year covered by the financial statements, focusing on those business segments that are relevant to an understanding of the development and performance as a whole. It should analyse the main trends and factors that directors consider likely to impact future prospects. The main trends and factors likely to affect the future development and performance will vary according to the nature of the business; they might include the development of known new products and services or the benefits expected from capital investment. The OFR should discuss the current level of investment expenditure together with planned future expenditure and should explain how that investment is directed to assist the achievement of business objectives. Any assumptions underlying the main trends and factors should be disclosed. Directors should consider the potential future significance of issues in deciding whether or not to include an analysis of them in the OFR.

Resources

RS (OFR) p50-51
The OFR should include a description of the resources available to the entity and how they are managed. It should set out the key strengths and resources, tangible and intangible, available to the business, that will assist it in the pursuit of its objectives and, in particular, those items that are not reflected in the balance sheet. Depending on the nature of the business, these may include: corporate reputation and brand strength; natural resources; employees; research and development; intellectual capital; licences, patents, copyright and trademarks; and market position.

Principal risks and uncertainties

RS (OFR) p52-56
The OFR should include a description of the principal risks and uncertainties facing the entity, together with a commentary on the directors' approach to them. Different industries and entities use different risk models or approaches for identifying and managing risk, although all entities face and should disclose strategic, commercial, operational and financial risks where these may significantly affect the entity's strategies and development of the entity's value. The principal risks and uncertainties facing entities will vary according to the nature of the business; some risks, such as the risk to reputation, are likely to be common to all.

RS (OFR) p55-56
The description of the principal risks and uncertainties should cover the exposure to negative consequences as well as potential opportunities. The directors' policy for managing principal risks should be disclosed. The OFR should cover the principal risks and uncertainties necessary for an understanding of the objectives and strategies of the business, both where they constitute a significant external risk to the entity, and where the entity's impact on other

parties through its activities, products or services, affects its performance. Directors should consider the full range of business risks.

Relationships

RS (OFR) p57-58 The OFR should include information about the significant relationships with stakeholders other than members that are likely, directly or indirectly, to influence the performance of the business and its value. In deciding what should be included in the OFR, directors should take a broad view in considering the extent to which the actions of stakeholders other than members can affect an entity's performance and value.

RS (OFR) p59 Where necessary for an understanding of the business, the OFR should describe receipts from, and returns to, shareholders in relation to shares held by them. This should include a description of any distributions, capital raising and share repurchases.

Financial position

RS (OFR) p60-62 1p13(b) The OFR should contain an analysis of the financial position and a discussion of the capital structure of the entity. This should include the sources of funding and may include targeted ratio of liabilities to equity. The analysis, while based on the financial statements, should comment on the events that have impacted the financial position of the entity during the financial year and future factors that are likely to affect the financial position going forward. The analysis should supplement the disclosures required in accounting standards — in particular, those required by IFRS 7, 'Financial instruments: Disclosures'. The OFR should highlight accounting policies set out in the notes to the financial statements. It should discuss those accounting policies that are critical to an understanding of the performance and financial position of the entity, focusing on those which have required the particular exercise of judgement in their application and to which the results are most sensitive. In addition, it should draw attention to the accounting policies that have changed during the financial year under review.

RS (OFR) p65-67 The OFR should set out the entity's treasury policies and objectives. It should also discuss the implementation of these policies in the financial year under review. The purpose and effect of major financing transactions undertaken up to the date of approval of the financial statements should be explained. The effect of interest costs on profits and the potential impact of interest rate changes should also be discussed.

RS (OFR) p63-64 The OFR should contain a discussion of the capital structure of the entity. This could include the balance between equity and debt, the maturity profile of debt, the type of capital instrument used, currency, regulatory capital and interest rate structure. The discussion should include comments on short and longer-term funding plans to support the directors' strategies to achieve the entity's objectives. In addition, the discussion should comment on why the entity has adopted its particular capital structure.

Cash flows

RS (OFR) p68 The OFR should discuss the cash inflows and outflows during the financial year, along with the entity's ability to generate cash, to meet known or probable cash requirements and to fund growth.

RS (OFR) p69-70 Any discussion should supplement the information provided in the financial statements by, for example, commenting on any special factors that have influenced cash flows in the financial year and those that may have a significant effect on future cash flows. Where entities have cash that is surplus to future operating requirements and current levels of distribution, the discussion should include future plans for making use of the excess cash. Analysis of profit by segment might be indicative of the cash flow generated by each segment, but this will not always be so — for example, because of fluctuations in capital expenditure and depreciation. Where segment cash flows are significantly out of line with segment revenues or profits, this should be indicated and explained.

Liquidity

RS (OFR) p71 The OFR should discuss the entity's current and prospective liquidity. Where relevant, this should include commentary on the level of borrowings, the seasonality of borrowing requirements (indicated by the peak level of borrowings during that period) and the maturity profile of both borrowings and undrawn committed borrowing facilities.

RS (OFR) p72-74 The discussion on liquidity should discuss the ability of the entity to fund its current and future operations and stated strategies. It should cover internal sources of liquidity, referring to any restrictions on the ability to transfer funds from one part of the group to meet the obligations of another part of the group where these represent, or might foreseeably come to represent, a significant restraint on the group. Such constraints would include exchange controls and taxation consequences of transfers. Where the entity has entered into covenants in financing contracts that could restrict the use of financing arrangements or credit facilities, and negotiations with the lenders on the operation of these covenants are taking place or are expected to take place, this fact should be indicated in the OFR. Where a breach of a covenant has occurred or is expected to occur, the OFR should give details of the measures taken or proposed to remedy the situation.

Key performance indicators

RS (OFR) p75 The entity should provide information that enables members to understand each KPI disclosed in the OFR.
RS (OFR) p76 For each KPI disclosed in the OFR:

- the definition and its calculation method should be explained;
- its purpose should be explained;

- the source of underlying data should be disclosed and, where relevant, assumptions explained;
- quantification or commentary on future targets should be provided;
- where information from the financial statements has been adjusted for inclusion in the OFR, that fact should be highlighted and a reconciliation provided;
- where available, corresponding amount for the financial year immediately preceding the current year should be disclosed; and
- any changes to KPIs should be disclosed, and the calculation method used compared to previous financial years — including significant changes in the underlying accounting policies adopted in the financial statements — should be identified and explained.

RS (OFR) p77 Quantification or commentary on future targets is about communicating the direction the entity is taking by, for example, setting out future strategies and goals.

Other performance indicators

RS (OFR) p78 Where a quantified measure other than a KPI is included, the OFR should disclose:

- the definition and its calculation method; and
- where available, the corresponding amount for the financial year immediately preceding the current year.

RS (OFR) p80 DV Entities are encouraged to include a statement as to whether the OFR is prepared in accordance with this Reporting Statement and contain particulars of, and reasons for any departure.

By order of the Board

AB Smith
Company Secretary 24 February 2012

6

Directors' report

Group directors' report for the year ended 31 December 2011

CA06 s415(1) The directors present their report and the audited financial statements for the year ended 31 December 2011.

CA06 7 Sch 1 *Note: The directors' report should also comply with the relevant requirements of Schedule 7 to SI 2008/410.*

Principal activities

1p138(b)
CA06
s416(1)(b)
The narrative should cover the principal activities of the entity, including any significant changes in activities, and its subsidiary undertakings included in the consolidation during the year.

1p138(a) and (c) In addition, there should be disclosure of the:

- domicile and legal form of entity;
- country of incorporation;
- address of the registered office or principal place of business, if different[1]; and
  the name of the parent and the ultimate parent of the group.

Review of business[2]

CA06 s417(3)(a), (4) The report should contain a fair review of the development and performance of the group's business during the year and of its position at the year end.

DV Where non-statutory numbers are disclosed, it should be clear that these differ from the statutory numbers; the equivalent statutory number should be disclosed; and there should be a reconciliation between the statutory and non-statutory numbers.

The review of the business should include:

CA06 s417(3)
- a fair review of the business of the company; and
- a description of the principal risks and uncertainties facing the company.

CA06 s417(4) The review is required to give a balanced and comprehensive analysis of:

- the development and performance of the business of the company during the financial year; and
- the position of the company at the end of the year,

consistent with the size and complexity of the business.

CA06 s417(6) The review should, to the extent necessary for an understanding of the development, performance or position of the business of the company, include:

- analysis using the financial key performance indicators; and
- where appropriate, analysis using other key performance indicators, including information relating to environmental matters and employee matters.

CA06 s417(5) The review should, to the extent necessary for an understanding of the development, performance or position of the business of the company include:

- the main trends and factors likely to affect the future development, performance and position of the business;
- information about:
  - environmental matters (including the impact of the company's business on the environment),
  - the company's employees, and
  - social and community issues, including information about any policies of the company in relation to these matters and their effectiveness; and
  - information about contractual and other arrangements that are essential to the business of the company, although nothing need be disclosed about a person if, in the opinion of the directors, such disclosure would be seriously prejudicial to that person or contrary to the public interest.

CA06 s417(8) The review should, where appropriate, include references to, and additional explanations of, amounts included in the financial statements of the company.

Branches outside the UK

SI 2008/410 7 Sch 7(1)(d) The directors' report should disclose the existence of any branches that operate outside of the UK.

---

[1] This disclosure can be given in the note to the accounts and not in the directors' report.
[2] The information that is required to be included in the business review section of the directors' report is often included in the OFR or other document published together with the directors' report. This is permitted, provided that specific cross-references are included in the directors' report to where the information is disclosed.

Future developments

SI 2008/410 7 Sch 7(1)(b) The directors' report should contain an indication of the likely future developments in the group's business.

This disclosure is likely to fit well with the business review. It might therefore be appropriate to combine them.

Dividends

CA06 s416(3) Details of the recommended dividend should be provided.

Research and development

SI 2008/410 7 Sch 7(1)(c) The directors' report should provide an indication of the group's research and development activities.

DV It is recommended that a statement is included with regard to the charge to the income statement for the year (which should be separately disclosed in the notes to financial statements).

Political donations and political expenditure

SI 2008/410 7 Sch 3 If the company and/or any of its subsidiaries made any donations to a registered political party, other political organisation in the EU (including the UK) or any independent election candidate, or if it incurred EU political expenditure exceeding £2,000 in the financial year, the directors' report should disclose:

- EU donations – the name of the political party and total amount given per party, by the entity and each subsidiary that has donated such expenditure individually.
- EU political expenditure – total amount incurred in the financial year by the company and each subsidiary that has incurred such expenditure individually.

SI 2008/410 7 Sch 4 Total contributions to non-EU political parties should be disclosed for the group as a whole in aggregate. (There is no threshold for this disclosure.)

Charitable donations

SI 2008/410 7 Sch 5 If the company and/or any of its subsidiaries has given money in excess of £2,000 in aggregate for charitable purposes during the year, the total amount given for each such purpose should be disclosed.

Land and buildings

SI 2008/410 7 Sch 2 If significant, the directors' report should indicate the difference between market value and book value of land and buildings for the company or any of its subsidiary undertakings.

Post balance sheet events

SI 2008/410 7 Sch 7(1)(a) The directors' report should include particulars of any important events affecting the company or group since the year end.

Like the disclosure on future developments, this disclosure is likely to fit well with the business review. It might therefore be appropriate to combine them.

Directors and directors' interests

CA06 s416(1)(a) The names of all persons who were directors during any part of the period should be provided.

DV (see also CC A.7.1 and CC A.7.2) Changes in directors since the end of the financial year and the dates of any appointments and/ or resignations of directors occurring during the financial year should be provided.

DV Information regarding the retirement of the directors at the AGM and whether they offer themselves for election should be disclosed.

LR9.8.6R(1) All interests in respect of which transactions are notifiable to the company under DTR 3.1.2 R[1], including spouse and children's interests for individuals who are directors at the end of the period under review, should be disclosed.

LR 9.8.6R(1) (a) (b) All changes in directors' interests that have occurred between the end of the period under review and a date not more than one month prior to the date of the notice of the annual general meeting should be disclosed. If there is no change, a statement to that effect is required.

Further information about the directors' interests is provided in the remuneration report.

---

[1] In accordance with DTR 3.1.2R, 'interests' includes shares of the issuer, or derivatives or any other financial instruments relating to those shares. A definition of financial instruments is available in DTR 3.1.23R.

Directors' third-party and pension scheme indemnity provisions

CA06
s236(2)(1) – (5)

The directors' report needs to include a statement if a qualifying third-party indemnity provision and/or qualifying pension scheme indemnity provision (whether made by the company or otherwise) has been in place for one or more directors of the company or of an associated company at any time during the financial year or at the date of approval of the directors' report.

Employees[1]

SI 2008/410
7 Sch 10(1),
11(3)

A statement is required describing the action that has been taken during the period to introduce, maintain or develop arrangements aimed at involving UK employees in the entity's affairs. This statement should discuss the group's policy on:

- systematic provision of relevant information to employees;
- regular consultation with employees or their representatives so that the employees' views may be taken into account in making decisions that are likely to affect their interests;
- encouragement of employees' participation in the group's performance by employee share schemes or other means; and
- achieving awareness on the part of all employees of the financial and economic factors affecting the group's performance.

SI 2008/410
7 Sch 10(3)

A statement should be included as to the UK policy for giving full and fair consideration to applications for employment that disabled people make to the company, the policy for employment, training, career development and promotion of disabled people and for the continuing employment and training of employees who have become disabled while employed by the company.

Policy and practice on payment of creditors[2]

SI 2008/410
7 Sch 12(2)(3)

The company's policy and practice on payment of creditors should be disclosed. This should include a policy statement for the following financial year and the number of days (calculated in the prescribed manner) taken to pay bills in the current financial year. The statement should include whether:

SI 2008/410
7 Sch 12(2)(a)

- in respect of some or all of its suppliers, it is the company's policy to follow any code or standard on payment practice and, if so, the name of the code or standard and the place where information about the code or standard can be obtained; and/or

SI 2008/410
7 Sch 12(2)(b)

- in respect of some or all of its suppliers, it is the company's policy:
  - to settle the terms of payment with those suppliers when agreeing the terms of each transaction;
  - to ensure that the suppliers are made aware of the terms of payment; and
  - to abide by the terms of payment.

SI 2008/410
7 Sch 12(2)(c)

Where the statement does not cover all suppliers, the policy for the other suppliers should be disclosed.

Financial instruments

SI 2008/410
7 Sch 6

Where material for the assessment of the assets, liabilities, financial position and profit or loss of the group, the directors' report must contain an indication of:

- the financial risk management objectives and policies of the entity, including the policy for hedging each major type of forecasted transaction for which hedge accounting is used; and
- the exposure of the entity to price risk, credit risk, liquidity risk and cash flow risk.

Purchase of own shares and sale of treasury shares

SI 2008/410
7 Sch 7,8
SI2008/410
7 Sch 8, 9

Where a company purchases or places a charge on its own shares, there are specific disclosures to be made. These disclosures are:

- the number and nominal value of the shares purchased, the aggregate amount of the consideration paid by the company for such shares and the reasons for their purchase;
- the number and nominal value of the shares acquired by the company, acquired by another person in such circumstances and charged during the financial year;
- the maximum number and nominal value of shares that — having been acquired by the company, acquired by another person in such circumstances or charged (whether or not during that year) — are held at any time by the company or that other person during that year;
- the number and nominal value of the shares acquired by the company, acquired by another person in such circumstances or charged (whether or not during that year) that are disposed of by the company or that other person or cancelled by the company during that year;

---

[1] The requirements only apply if the company employed on average more than 250 employees in the UK each week during the financial year (7 Sch 10(1), 11(1)).

[2] An additional statement regarding the group's policy and practice and number of days for the company and its UK subsidiaries, whilst not mandatory, is considered best practice.

- where the number and nominal value of the shares of any particular description are stated in pursuance of any of the preceding bullet points, the percentage of the called-up share capital that shares of that description represent;
- where any of the shares have been charged, the amount of the charge in each case; and
- where any of the shares have been disposed of by the company or the person who acquired them in such circumstances for money or money's worth, the amount or value of the consideration in each case.

LR 9.8.6R(4)(a), (b), (c), (d)   Details of any shareholders' authority for the company's purchase of its own shares still valid at the end of the period under review. Where any such purchases are made or are proposed to be made, other than through the market or by tender to all shareholders, details should be given of the names of the sellers of such shares purchased in the period. In respect of purchases, made other than through the market or by tender to all shareholders, or options or contracts to make such purchases entered into since the year end, the information listed above should be given. Details should be given of the names of the purchasers of treasury shares sold or proposed to be sold for cash (other than through the market or in connection with an employees' share scheme, or where sales are not pursuant to an opportunity available to all holders of the company's securities on the same terms) during the period under review.

Substantial shareholdings

LR 9.8.6R(2)(a), (b)   Particulars, as at a date not more than a month prior to the date of the notice of the general meeting, should be given of substantial shareholdings (material interests of three per cent or more and non-material interests of 10 per cent or more) disclosed to the company, in any part of the company's share capital. Where there have been no such disclosures, this fact should be stated.

Placing of shares

LR 9.8.4R(9)   Where a listed company is a subsidiary undertaking of another company, particulars should be given of the participation by its parent company in any placing made during the period under review.

Waiver of dividends

LR 9.8.4R (12), (13) LR 9.8.5R   Details should be disclosed of any arrangement under which a shareholder has waived or agreed to waive any dividends or future dividends. Waivers of less than one per cent of the total value of any dividend are not required to be disclosed provided that some payment has been made on each share of the relevant class during the relevant calendar year.

Contracts of significance

LR 9.8.4R(10)(b) LR 9.8.4R(11)   Particulars should be given of any contract of significance (including contracts for the provision of services) between the company (including subsidiary undertakings) and controlling shareholder subsisting in the period. 'Significance' is defined as one per cent or more of the relevant transactions for the group.

LR 9.8.4R(10)(a)   Disclosure is required of the particulars of any contract of significance to which the company or one of its subsidiaries is a party and in which a director of the company is or was materially interested.

LR9.8.4R (3) LR 11.1.10R (2)(c)   Details should be disclosed of small related-party transactions notified to the Financial Services Authority.

Takeover Directive requirements

DTR 7.2.6   The following information should be disclosed:

SI 2008/410 7 Sch 13(2)(a)
- The structure of the company's capital including:

   (a) the rights and obligations attached to each class of shares; (b) where there are two or more classes, the percentage of the total share capital represented by each class.and
   (b) where there are two or more classes, the percentage of the total share capital represented by each class.

A company's capital includes any shares or debentures in the company that are not admitted to trading on a regulated market.

SI 2008/410 7 Sch 13(2)(b)
- Details of any restrictions on the transfer of securities (shares or debentures) in the company, including limitations on the holding of securities and requirements to obtain the approval of the company or of other holders prior to a transfer of securities.

SI 2008/410 7 Sch 13(2)(c)
- In respect of each person with a significant direct or indirect holding of securities in the company, the identity of the person, the size of the holding and the nature of the holding.

SI 2008/410 7 Sch 13(2)(d)
- In the case of each person who holds securities carrying special rights with regard to control of the company, the identity of the person and the nature of the rights.

SI 2008/410 7 Sch 13(2)(e)
- Where the company has an employees' share scheme and shares to which the scheme relates have rights with regard to control of the company that are not exercisable directly by the employees, details of how these rights are exercisable.

| SI 2008/410 7 Sch 13(2)(f) | ■ Details of any restrictions on voting rights, including limitations on voting rights of holders of a given percentage or number of votes; deadlines for exercising voting rights; and arrangements by which, with the company's co-operation, financial rights carried by securities are held by a person other than the holder of the securities. |

| SI 2008/410 7 Sch 13(2)(g) | ■ Details of any agreements between holders of securities that are known to the company and may result in restrictions on the transfer of securities or on voting rights. |

| SI 2008/410 7 Sch 13(2)(h) | ■ Details of any rules that the company has about the appointment and replacement of directors, and details of any rules about the amendment of the company's articles of association. |

| SI 2008/410 7 Sch 13(2)(i) | ■ Details of the powers of the company's directors, including in particular any powers in relation to the issuing or buying back by the company of its shares. |

| SI 2008/410 7 Sch 13(2)(j) | ■ Details of any significant arrangements to which the company is a party that take effect, alter or terminate upon a change of control of the company following a takeover bid, and the effects of any such agreements. This does not apply if disclosure would be seriously prejudicial to the company and the company is not under any other obligation to disclose it. |

| SI 2008/410 7 Sch 13(2)(k) | ■ Details of any agreements between the company and its directors or employees providing for compensation for loss of office or employment (through resignation, purported redundancy or otherwise) that occurs because of a takeover bid. |

| SI 2008/410 7 Sch 14 | ■ Details of any other information and explanations required in respect of the details included above. |

By virtue of DTR 7.2.6R, the information required by 7 Sch 13(2)(c), (d), (f), (h) and (i) may be in a separate report (for example, a corporate governance statement) published with the annual report.

AGM notice

LR13.8.8R Where the shareholders of a listed company are sent a notice of a meeting (which includes any business other than routine business at an AGM) and an explanatory circular does not accompany the notice, an explanation of the non-routine business to be conducted at the AGM should be included in the directors' report.

Auditor and disclosure of information to auditor

CA06 s418(2) The report should contain a statement to the effect that, in the case of each of the persons who are directors at the time when the report is approved, the following applies:

- As far as the director is aware, there is no relevant audit information of which the company's auditor is unaware; and
- The director has taken all the steps that he/she ought to have taken as a director in order to make him/herself aware of any relevant audit information and to establish that the company's auditor is aware of that information.

DV CA06 s489(1) The auditors, PricewaterhouseCoopers LLP, have indicated their willingness to continue in office, and a resolution that they be re-appointed will be proposed at the annual general meeting.

DTR 7.2.1, 7.2.9 ### Corporate governance

The company's statement on corporate governance can be found in the corporate governance report on pages 26 to 38 of these financial statements. The corporate governance report forms part of this directors' report and is incorporated into it by cross-reference.

DTR 7.2.10R states that an issuer that is required to prepare a group directors' report must include in that report a description of the main features of the group's internal control and risk management systems in relation to the process for preparing consolidated financial statements. This may be included in the corporate governance statement, where the corporate governance statement is incorporated into the directors' report by cross-reference.

DTR 7.2.10R states that an issuer which is required to prepare a group directors' report must include in that report a description of the main features of the group's internal control and risk management systems in relation to the process for preparing consolidated financial statements. This may be included in the corporate governance statement (see pages 26-34).

CA06 s419(1) By order of the board

CA06 s419(1) AB Smith

Company Secretary[1]
24 February 2012

---

[1] The directors' report has to be signed by the company secretary or a director after it has been approved by the board of directors. The copy of the directors' report that is delivered to the Registrar of Companies must be manually signed by the company secretary or a director.

Remuneration report

Requirements for the directors' remuneration report – policy section of the remuneration report (unaudited)

CA06 s420-421 The remuneration report should include the following:

Remuneration committee

SI 2008/410 8 Sch 2(1)(a) Names of the members of the remuneration committee (at any time when directors' remuneration for the year is considered)[1].

Advice to the remuneration committee

SI 2008/410 8 Sch 2(1)(b) ■ The names of any person(s) providing advice to the remuneration committee that has materially assisted the committee with their decisions.

SI 2008/410 8 Sch 2(1)(c) ■ For any adviser to the remuneration committee who is not a director, disclosure of the nature of any other services performed by the adviser to the company during the year and whether the adviser was appointed by the remuneration committee.

Remuneration policy

SI 2008/410 8 Sch 3(1) LR 9.8.8R(2(b)) ■ A statement of the company's policy on executive directors' remuneration for the year following the financial year under review and future years.

LR9.8.8R(10) ■ Explanations and justifications of any departure from the policy in the period under review and any changes in the policy from the preceding year.

SI 2008/410 8 Sch 3(3) ■ For each director, an explanation of the relative importance of those elements that are related to performance and those elements that are not related to performance.

Share options/long-term incentive schemes

SI 2008/410 8 Sch 3(2)(a) ■ A summary of the performance conditions attaching to share option or long-term incentive entitlements (including matching awards under deferred annual bonus schemes) by director.

SI 2008/410 8 Sch 3(2)(b) ■ An explanation for the choice of performance conditions.

SI 2008/410 8 Sch 3(2)(f) ■ If share options or long-term incentive awards are not subject to performance conditions, an explanation of why that is the case.

SI 2008/410 8 Sch 3(2)(c) ■ A summary of the methods for assessing whether performance conditions have been met and the reasons for choosing these.

SI 2008/410 8 Sch 3(2)(d) ■ For comparative performance conditions, a summary of the external factors used for comparison.

SI 2008/410 8 Sch 3(2)(d) ■ For comparative performance conditions, the identity of the companies in the comparator group or index.

SI 2008/410 8 Sch 3(2)(e) ■ A description and explanation of any proposed amendments to the terms and conditions of outstanding share options or LTIS awards.

Statement of consideration of conditions elsewhere in the company and group[2]

SI 2008/410 8 Sch 4 ■ A statement of how the pay and employment conditions of employees of the company and elsewhere in the group were taken into account when determining directors' remuneration for the relevant financial year.

Performance graph

SI 2008/410 8 Sch 5(1)(a)(b) ■ A performance graph showing the company's total shareholder return compared with a broad equity market index chosen by the company over the five preceding financial years (including the financial year covered by the report), and the name of and reasons for the choice of broad equity market index.

Directors contracts

SI 2008/410 8 Sch 3(4) ■ The company's policy on the duration of service contracts for directors and notice periods and termination payments under such contracts.

SI 2008/410 8 Sch 6(1) ■ In relation to individual directors' service contracts:
  ■ the date of the contract;
  ■ the unexpired term;
  ■ the contractual notice period;

---

[1] The board should establish a remuneration committee of at least three (smaller companies: two) independent, non-executive directors. The chairman may also be a member, but not chair, of the committee if he/she is considered to be independent. The committee should make available its terms of reference. The committee should be responsible for setting remuneration for all executive directors and the chairman and also monitoring the remuneration for senior management. The board should determine the remuneration of non-executive directors. Shareholders should be invited to approve all new long-term incentive schemes. [CC B.2.1-2.4].

- any provision for compensation payable upon early termination of the contract; and
- details of any other arrangements that are necessary to enable investors to estimate the possible liability of the company upon early termination of the contract.

LR 9.8.8R (8)-(9)
- Details of any director's service contract that has a notice period in excess of one year, or with provisions for pre-determined compensation on termination that exceeds one year's salary and benefits in kind, including the reasons for such a notice period.

LR 9.8.8R (8)-(9)
- Details of the unexpired term of any director's service contract for a director proposed for election or re-election at the forthcoming annual general meeting.

LR 9.8.8R(8)-(9)
- If any director proposed for election or re-election at the forthcoming annual general meeting does not have a director's service contract, a statement to that effect.

Awards to past/former directors

SI 2008/410 8 Sch 6(2)
- An explanation of any significant award made to past directors during the year.

SI 2008/410 8 Sch 15 LR 9.8.8R(2)(c)
- Details of any significant award made in the year to any person who was not a director of the company at the time the award was made but had previously been a director of the company.

External appointments

UKCGC D1.2
- Where a company releases an executive director to serve as a non-executive director elsewhere, a statement as to whether or not the director will retain such earnings, and if so, what the remuneration is.

SI 2008/410 8 Sch 16
- For each director who served as a director at any time during the year, the aggregate amount of consideration paid to or receivable by third parties for making available the services of the director.

APB 2002/2 p 12-16
- Where the remuneration report does not clarify which parts of the report have been audited, such clarification in the audit report.

Corporate governance requirements

The details of compliance and policy are usually set out as a remuneration committee report. Section 422(1) of the Companies Act 2006 requires this to be approved by the board, as it is the board's responsibility to report to shareholders. Schedule 8 to SI 2008/410 and paragraph 9.8.8R of the Listing Rules contain information to be included in the report.

CA06 s439(1) The board should put an ordinary resolution to shareholders for the approval of the remuneration report.

UKCGC D.1.1 In designing schemes of performance-related remuneration, remuneration committees should follow the provisions of Schedule A to the UKCorporate Governance Code.

UKCGC D.1.3 The remuneration of all non-executive directors should reflect the time commitment and responsibilities of the role. Their remuneration should not include share options or other performance related elements.

UKCGC D.1.4 The remuneration committee should carefully consider what compensation commitments (including pension contributions and all other elements) its directors' terms of appointment would entail in the event of early termination. The aim should be to avoid rewarding poor performance. They should take a robust line on reducing compensation to reflect departing directors' obligations to mitigate loss.

UKCGC Main Principle D.2 There should be a formal and transparent procedure for developing policy on executive remuneration and for fixing the remuneration packages of individual directors. No director should be involved in deciding his or her own remuneration.

UKCGC D.2.1 UKCGC D.2.2 To avoid potential conflicts of interest, boards of directors should set up remuneration committees of independent non-executive directors to make recommendations to the board, within agreed terms of reference, on the company's framework of executive remuneration and its cost; and to determine on their behalf the level and structure of remuneration for senior management, including pension rights and any compensation payments. The remuneration committee's terms of reference , explaining its role and the authority delegated to it by the board, should be publicly available (that is, available on request and on the company's web site).

UKCGC D.2.1 The remuneration committee should consist of at least three, or in the case of smaller companies two, independent non-executive directors. The company chairman may also be a member of, but not chair, the committee if he or she was considered independent on appointment as chairman.

UKCGC D.2.2 The definition of senior management is determined by the board but would normally include the first layer of management below board level.

UKCGC D.2 Supporting principle The chairman of the board should ensure that the company maintains contact as required with its principal shareholders about remuneration.

Remuneration report for the year ended 31 December 2011[1]

This part of the remuneration report is unaudited.

Remuneration committee

The members of the remuneration committee during the year were:

- R Graham (Chairman).
- Lord Callender.
- N Chamois.
- A Cartwright.

All the members of the remuneration committee are non-executive directors and are considered to be independent.

UKCGC D.2.2
UKCGC D.2.3
The remuneration committee is responsible for setting all aspects of executive directors' remuneration and for monitoring the remuneration of senior management. The terms of reference of the remuneration committee are available on the group's website at [*group's website address*]. The remuneration of non-executive directors is determined by the board within the limits set by the company's Articles of Association.

Advice to the remuneration committee

During the year, the following parties were appointed by the remuneration committee to provide advice that materially assisted the remuneration committee:

- Accounting Services Limited.
- E F Logan (HR Director).
- NS Watkins (Group senior payroll manager).

Accounting Services Limited also provided advice on personal tax issues to the group.

Remuneration policy

UKCGC Main
Principle D.1
The company's policy on remuneration of directors is to attract, retain and motivate the best people, recognising the input they have to the ongoing success of the business.

SI 2008/410
8 Sch 3(1)
UKCGC Main
Principle
D.1LR 9.8.8R(1)
Consistent with this policy, the benefit packages awarded by IFRS GAAP plc to directors are intended to be competitive. They comprise a mix of performance-related and non-performance- related remuneration designed to incentivise directors and align their interests with those of shareholders.

The remuneration consists of the elements outlined below.

Base pay

SI 2008/410
8 Sch 3(1)
LR 9.8.8R(1)
Executive directors' base pay is designed to reflect individual's capabilities and role within the business. Salary levels are reviewed annually and targeted at the median position against similar industries and the FTSE 100.

Annual bonus and deferred shares

SI 2008/410
8 Sch 3(1)
LR 9.8.8R(1)
LR 9.8.8R(10)
All executive directors participate in the company's annual bonus scheme. Subject to the achievement of individual and company performance targets, the remuneration committee may award bonuses of up to 50% of the director's basic salary. Financial targets represent 75% of the bonus award and include EPS, turnover and operating profit measures, each given equal weighting; the remaining 25% of the bonus is awarded on the satisfaction of individual targets. Half of each director's bonus is awarded in cash, with the remainder taking the form of deferred shares in IFRS GAAP plc, which are held in trust for a period of three years before they are released to the director. In the event that the director leaves the company, these shares may be immediately released to the director at the discretion of the remuneration committee. Dividends accrue to the directors from the date the bonus is awarded.

There have been no changes to the policy from the preceding year and no departures from this policy in the current year. The current policy is expected to remain in place through the next financial year, during which a detailed review of the remuneration policy is to be undertaken for the year 2011.

Long-term incentive scheme

SI 2008/410
8 Sch 3(1), (2)
LR 9.8.8R (10)
The long-term incentive scheme (LTIS) rewards future performance of the directors by linking the size of the award to the increase in shareholder return. Share options under the LTIS are granted at the discretion of the remuneration committee, up to a maximum value of 100% of salary. For the current year, shares were awarded under the long-term incentive scheme at the maximum level.

Shares vest after three years, subject to the achievement of the performance conditions attached to the share options. The vesting condition is dependent on the company's 'total shareholder return' (TSR) compared with the TSR of all companies in the FTSE 100 over the three-year period from the date of grant. If the company's cumulative TSR over the three year period is in the upper quartile of the comparator group, the options will vest in full. If the company's TSR over that period is in the second quartile, 50% of the options will vest. If the company is in the third or fourth quartiles,

---

[1] The content of the remuneration report is not intended to illustrate good practice in executive pay arrangements.

(Amounts in C thousands unless otherwise stated).

the options will lapse. Share options that vest must be exercised within five years of the vesting date, otherwise the shares will lapse. The committee has selected the TSR performance condition, as the committee believes that this best aligns the interests of the directors with those of the shareholders.

In the event that a director resigns, any options that have not vested or have not been exercised will lapse.

Share option scheme

It is the board's intention to continue to award shares to all executive directors under the group's share option scheme. The shares awarded will vest after a period of three years if the performance condition attached to the share options is met and the director is still in employment. Vesting will be dependent on an average annual increase in earnings per share (as reported in the financial statements) of at least the growth in the UK retail price index plus 4%. The committee considers that this scheme rewards the directors for their contribution towards the long-term profitability of the group. In the event that a director resigns as a director, the awards will lapse. The value of shares notionally awarded to a director under this scheme in any year will not exceed that director's salary.

DV, p2.1 of ABI guidelines Dec 2006 The remuneration committee has reviewed the current policy on how both the long-term incentive scheme and the share option scheme operate, including how discretion has been exercised and including grant levels, performance criteria and vesting schedules during the year. The committee considers that the current policy remains appropriate to the company's current circumstances and prospects.

There have been no changes to the policy from the preceding year and no departures from this policy in the current year. The current policy is expected to continue in place through the next financial year, during which a detailed review of the remuneration policy is to be undertaken for the year 2011.

SI 2008/410 8 Sch 3(3) UKCGC Main Principle D.1 If the TSR growth under the long-term incentive scheme is on target – such that 50% of the LTIS options will vest – and assuming that 100% of the share options under the group's share option scheme will vest, the composition of each executive director's remuneration will be as follows:

	Non-performance-related	Performance-related	
	Basic salary	Bonus	LTIS and share option scheme
C D Suede	36%	11%	53%
G Wallace	36%	11%	53%
F Leather	37%	8%	55%
E F Logan	36%	10%	54%

SI 2008/410 8 Sch 4 *Statement of consideration of conditions elsewhere in the group[1]*

In determining remuneration, consideration will be given to reward levels throughout the organisation as well as in the external employment market. The remuneration committee aim to reward all employees fairly based on their role, their performance and salary levels in the wider market.

In the year under review, the average base salary increase for the executive directors was 5%; for all other staff, 2%.

Director pension schemes

All executive directors are members of the final salary defined benefit pension arrangements. Mr C D Suede and Mr G Wallace also participate in the US defined contribution pension arrangement.

Non-executive directors remuneration

UKCGC D.1.2 UKCGC D.1.3 Non-executive directors receive a fee of C10,000 per year. Mr R Graham receives an additional fee of C2,000 per year for chairing the remuneration committee, reflecting the additional responsibilities of that role. Non-executive directors do not participate in the company's share option scheme, long-term incentive scheme or pension schemes.[1]

External appointments

UKCGC D.1.2 During the year, Mr E F Logan has served as a non-executive director with E Group plc. He has retained his earnings in respect of this service of C15,000 (2010: C12,500).

Directors' service contracts

UKCGC D.1.5 SI 2008/410 8 Sch 3(4) It is IFRS GAAP plc's policy that executive directors' service contracts have a notice period of not more than one year. There are no contractual termination payments.

---

[1] If options are granted to non-executive directors on an exceptional basis, shareholder approval should be sought in advance. Any shares acquired by the exercise of options should be held for at least one year after the non-executive leaves the board. Holding of share options could be relevant in determining a non- executive director's independence.

Non-executive directors are appointed for an initial period of three years. Their service contracts are terminable by either the company or the directors themselves with six months' notice. It is IFRS GAAP plc's policy that non-executive directors may serve a maximum of a three-year term. They are reappointed annually thereafter.

The details of the service contracts of those who served as directors during the year are:

SI 2008/410
8 Sch 6
LR 9.8.8R (9)

	Contract date	Notice period
Executive directors		
C D Suede	27 May 07	1 year
G Wallace	15 Sep 07	1 year
F Leather	07 Jan 06	1 year
E F Logan	26 Feb 06	9 months
D Scott[1]	02 Oct 06	6 months
Non-executive directors		
R Graham[2]	08 Sep 11	6 months
Lord Callender	24 Jun 09	6 months
N Chamois[2]	03 Dec 11	6 months
A Cartwright	13 Oct 10	6 months

Performance graph

SI 2008/410
8 Sch 5(1)

The graph provided below shows the group's TSR performance against the FTSE 100 over the past five years. In the opinion of the directors, the FTSE 100 is the most appropriate index against which the total shareholder return of IFRS GAAP plc should be measured, as it is an index of similar-sized companies to IFRS GAAP plc. The calculations assume the reinvestment of dividends.

Source: Date Limited

Requirements for directors' remuneration report – remuneration package (audited)

LR 9.8.8R (2)
(a), (b)

Amounts of each element of the remuneration package should be given for each director (executive and non-executive) by name from all sources, and in total for both current and prior years, including but not restricted to:

SI 2008/410
8 Sch 7(1)

- Basic salary and fees.
- Estimated money value of benefits in kind other than those disclosed in other bullet point headings.
- Bonuses.
- Total amount of expense allowances that are (or would be if the director was an individual) chargeable to UK income tax.
- Compensation for loss of office/payments for breach of contract/other termination payments.

SI 2008/410
8 Sch 7(2)

- Total remuneration for each director for current and corresponding accounting period.

SI 2008/410
8 Sch 7(3)-(4)
LR 9.8.4R
(5),(6)

Such details should be in tabular form, and the nature of any non-cash element of a remuneration package should be stated. Disclosure should be made of any arrangements to waive any emoluments (both current and future).

LR 9.8.8R(7)
UKCGC
Sch A

In general, only basic salary should be pensionable. There should be explanations and justifications given for any elements of remuneration that are pensionable, except basic salary. The remuneration committee should consider the pension consequences and associated costs of basic salary increases and any other changes in pensionable remuneration, especially for directors nearing retirement.

SI 2008/410
8 Sch 15
LR 9.8.8R(2)(a)

Significant payments to former directors made during the current accounting period that have not been included in the table should be disclosed separately.

[1] Mr D Scott resigned on 29 March 2011 and, consequently, his contract was terminated.
[2] Mr R Graham and Mr N Chamois will retire by rotation and seek re-election at the AGM. As non- executive directors both R Graham and N Chamois have service contracts with the company. The agreements require that the company give them 6 months notice of termination. Biographical details of the directors standing for re-election are given in the corporate governance report. LR 9.8.8R (8).

LR 9.8.8R(1), (2)(d) SI 2008/410 8 Sch 8	Information on share options including SAYE options should be given for each director, by name. Such details should be in tabular form; explanations should be given where necessary.
UKCGC Sch A	There should be an explanation and justification where share options are awarded in large blocks rather than phased.

LR 9.8.8R(3) Details of long-term incentive schemes should be provided, including the following, for each director, by name:

- Interests at the start (or date of appointment, if late) and end of the period (or date of cessation, if earlier).
- Details of entitlements/awards granted and commitments made to each director during the period, showing which crystallised in the same period or later periods.
- Number of shares, with award date and market price on that date and on vesting date, performance conditions, cash payments and value of other assets receivable by each director under such schemes during the period.
- Dates when qualifying conditions have to be fulfilled and any variation in terms and conditions of scheme interests.

Notes:

LR 9.4.3R
- *Additional disclosures are required in the first annual report published following the date on which the relevant director becomes eligible to participate in an arrangement in which that director is the only participant and the arrangement is established specifically to facilitate, in unusual circumstances, the recruitment or retention of that director.*

UKCGC Sch A
- *There should be an explanation and justification where incentives are awarded in large blocks rather than phased.*

UKCGC D.2.4
- *Shareholders should be invited specifically to approve all new long-term incentive schemes (including share option schemes) that potentially commit shareholders' funds over more than one year or dilute the equity, except as permitted by LR 9.4.2R and significant changes to existing schemes.*

UKCGC Sch A Executive share options should not be offered at a discount save as permitted by LR 9.4.4R.

The remuneration report should include the following for defined benefit pension schemes for each director by name:

LR 9.8.8R(12)
- Amount of the increase in accrued benefit during the year (excluding inflation).
- The accrued benefit as at the year end.
- The transfer value of the relevant increase in accrued benefit as at the year end or specific information to enable this value to be calculated.

SI 2008/410 8 Sch 13
- The change in accrued benefits during the year under the scheme.
- The accrued benefit at the end of the year.
- The transfer value at the end of the year of the accrued benefits.
- The transfer value of accrued benefits at the previous year end in respect of qualifying services.
- The increase in the transfer value in respect of qualifying services in the year less the director's contributions.

Notes:

It should be made clear that the transfer value represents a liability of the company, but not a sum paid or due to the individual; and that it cannot meaningfully be added to annual remuneration.

Where the group makes provisions in respect of unfunded pensions of a defined benefit type, it should take the related benefits provided to directors into account when determining the amounts to be disclosed in respect of directors' pension entitlements under defined benefit schemes.

SI 2008/410 8 Sch 13(3) LR 9.8.8R(11)	The details of the contribution or allowance payable or made by the company for money purchase (that is, defined contribution) schemes should be disclosed for each director, by name. Disclosure includes provisions for unfunded money purchase benefits as well as actual contributions paid or payable to a scheme.
LR 9.8.8R(12)(c)	No disclosure of voluntary contributions and benefits for defined benefit schemes is required.

LR 9.8.4R(5)(6) Details should be given of any arrangement under which a director has waived or agreed to waive any emoluments from the company or any subsidiary.

Where a director has agreed to waive future emoluments, details should be given of such waiver together with details relating to emoluments that were waived in the year.

Where an executive director is released to serve as non-executive director elsewhere, state whether remuneration is retained.

Continuation of the remuneration report for the year ended 31 December 2011

This part of the remuneration report is audited.

LR 9.8.8R(2)(a) **Directors' detailed emoluments**

(Amounts in table below are in C thousands.)

						2011	2010
SI 2008/410 8 Sch 7(1), (2), (4)	*Executive*	Salary and fees	Benefits in kinds	Expense allowance	Annual bonus	Compensation for loss of office	Total	Total

Executive	Salary and fees	Benefits in kinds	Expense allowance	Annual bonus	Compensation for loss of office	Total	Total
C D Suede	132	29	–	41	–	**202**	140
G Wallace	107	24	–	33	–	**164**	118
F Leather[1]	161	13	5	34	–	**213**	174
E F Logan	63	13	–	18	–	**94**	24
D Scott	31	3	–	8	103	**145**	73
J Rush	–	–	–	–	–	**–**	92
Non-executive							
R Graham (chairman)	12	–	–	–	–	**12**	10
Lord Callender	10	–	–	–	–	**10**	10
N Chamois	10	–	–	–	–	**10**	10
A Cartwright	10	–	–	–	–	**10**	10
	536	82	5	134	103	**860**	661

SI 2008/410 8 Sch 7(3)

Benefits in kind include the provision of a company car, fuel, financial counselling and medical and life insurance for every executive director. In addition, Mr C D Suede and Mr G Wallace have the use of a driver.

UKCGC Sch A

Half of each executive director's annual bonus comprises shares in IFRS GAAP plc. Shares awarded in this way are required to be held for three years.

SI 2008/410 8 Sch 7(1)(d), 7(3)

The compensation for loss of office payment to Mr D Scott, who resigned on 29 March 2011, includes the monetary value of a car retained by the director, a contribution to his personal money purchase pension plan and a cash bonus. The discretionary elements of this compensation were approved by the remuneration committee and were paid in respect of his past service to the company.

SI 2008/410 8 Sch 6 (2) LR 9.8.8R2(c)

In addition to the payments included in the table above, C100,000 (2010: C nil) was paid to Mr K W Grommitt, who resigned as a director in 2005. This sum was in respect of a claim by Mr K W Grommitt for unfair dismissal and represents the contractual entitlement under his then service contract, plus interest thereon, which was withheld by the company pending the outcome of the litigation.

LR 9.8.4R(5), (6)

No director waived emoluments in respect of the years ended 31 December 2011 or 31 December 2010.

SI 2008/410 8 Sch 14(1) LR 9.8.8R(2)(a)

In addition to the amounts included in the table above, an additional pension of C11,376 (2010: C nil) was paid to Mr J Rush in the year in connection with his retirement in 2010. The payment is in excess of Mr J Rush's normal entitlement under the group's defined benefit pension scheme arrangements.

DV

In the year ended 31 December 2010, C87,000 was paid in respect of compensation for loss of office to Mr J Rush, former director. This amount is included in the amount disclosed for Mr J Rush in the table above.

---

[1] Salary and fees include an amount of C54,000 (2010: C63,000) paid to third parties in respect of making available the services of Mr F Leather to the company. [SI 2008/410].
8 Sch 16(1); LR 9.8.8R(2)(a)].

Share schemes

Date of grant	Earliest exercise date	Expiry date	Exercise price (C)	Number at 1 January 2010 (C1 shares)	Granted in year	Exercised in year	Lapsed in year	Number at 31 December 2011 (C1 shares)[1]
CD Suede								
01 Jul 03	01 Jul 06	30 Jun 11	1.10	500	–	500	–	–
01 Jul 04	01 Jul 07	30 Jun 12	1.20	55,000	–	55,000	–	–
01 Jul 07	01 Jul 10	30 Jun 15	1.35	300,000	–	55,000	–	245,000
01 Jul 09	01 Jul 12	30 Jun 17	2.00	100,000	–	–	–	100,000
01 Jul 10	01 Jul 13	30 Jun 18	2.38	500,000	–	–	–	500,000
01 Jul 11	01 Jul 14	30 Jun 19	2.95		300,000	–	–	300,000
				955,500	300,000	110,500	–	1,145,000
G Wallace								
01 Jul 09	01 Jul 12	30 Jun 17	2.00	75,000	–	–	–	75,000
01 Jul 10	01 Jul 13	30 Jun 18	2.38	120,000	–	–	–	120,000
01 Jul 11	01 Jul 14	30 Jun 19	2.95	–	80,000	–	–	80,000
				195,000	80,000	–	–	275,000
D Scott								
01 Jul 09	01 Jul 12	30 Jun 17	2.00	25,000	–	–	25,000	–
01 Jul 10	01 Jul 13	30 Jun 18	2.38	100,000	–	–	100,000	–
				125,000	–	–	125,000	–
F Leather								
01 Jul 04	01 Jul 07	30 Jun 12	1.20	50,000	–	50,000	–	–
01 Jul 07	01 Jul 10	30 Jun 15	1.35	50,000	–	50,000	–	–
01 Jul 09	01 Jul 12	30 Jun 17	2.00	300,000	–	–	–	300,000
01 Jul 10	01 Jul 13	30 Jun 18	2.38	400,000	–	–	–	400,000
01 Jul 11	01 Jul 14	30 Jun 19	2.95	–	250,000	–	–	250,000
				800,000	250,000	100,000	–	950,000
E F Logan								
01 Jul 10	01 Jul 13	30 Jun 18	2.38	200,000	–	–	–	200,000
01 Jul 11	01 Jul 14	30 Jun 19	2.95	–	95,000	–	–	95,000
				200,000	95,000	–	–	295,000

SI 2008/410 8 Sch 9(d)

No other directors have been granted share options in the shares in the company or other group entities. None of the terms and conditions of the share options was varied during the year. All options were granted in respect of qualifying services.

SI 2008/410 8 Sch 9(c)(i), 9(e)

The options were granted at nil cost to the directors and were in respect of past performance. The performance criteria for all the above share options were consistent with the remuneration policy. Once the award has vested, the exercise of the share options is unconditional.

SI 2008/410 8 Sch 9(g)

The market price of the company's shares at the end of the financial year was 290p. The range of market prices during the year was between 210p and 293p.

SI 2008/410 8 Sch 9(f)

The market price when Mr C D Suede and Mr F Leather exercised their share options was 275p.

Long-term incentive scheme

LR 9.8.8R(3), (4), (5), (6)

Directors' interests in the long-term incentive plan

SI 2008/410 8 Sch 11, 12

Shares awarded to executive directors and former directors under the long-term incentive plan are as follows:

[1] Or date of resignation, if earlier.

	Cycle ending	Award date	At 1 January 2011 Number	Shares awarded Number	Shares vested Number	Shares lapsed	At 31 Dec 2011[1] Number	Value vested C'000	Vesting date
C D Suede	2010	01 Jul 07	30,000	–	(15,000)	(15,000)	0	40	01 Jul 09
	2011	01 Jul 08	25,000	–	–	–	25,000	–	01 Jul 10
	2012	01 Jul 09	33,000	–	–	–	33,000	–	01 Jul 11
	2013	01 Jul 10	–	20,000	–	–	20,000	–	01 Jul 12
G Wallace	2011	01 Jul 08	10,000	–	–	–	10,000	–	01 Jul 10
	2012	01 Jul 09	8,000	–	–	–	8,000	–	01 Jul 11
	2013	01 Jul 10	–	7,000	–	–	7,000	–	01 Jul 12
D Scott	2010	01 Jul 07	22,000	–	–	(22,000)	–	–	01 Jul 09
	2011	01 Jul 08	15,000	–	–	(15,000)	–	–	01 Jul 10
	2012	01 Jul 09	17,000	–	–	(17,000)	–	–	01 Jul 11
	2013	01 Jul 10	–	7,000	–	(7,000)	–	–	01 Jul 12
F Leather	2010	01 Jul 07	27,500	–	(13,750)	(13,750)	–	36	01 Jul 09
	2011	01 Jul 08	25,000	–	–	–	25,000	–	01 Jul 10
	2012	01 Jul 09	33,000	–	–	–	33,000	–	01 Jul 11
	2013	01 Jul 10	–	28,750	–	–	20,000	–	01 Jul 12
Totals of awards vested in 2011					**28,750**			**76**	

SI 2008/410 8 Sch 12(3)(c) The market price on 1 July 2008 was 155p; on 1 July 2009, 230p; on 1 July 2010, 274p; and on 1 July 2011, 339p.

SI 2008/410 8 Sch 12(3)(e) The performance criteria attached to the awards that vested on 1 July 2011 and those awarded on the same date was TSR versus companies in the FTSE 100. If the company's cumulative TSR over the three-year period is in the upper quartile of the comparator group, the options will vest in full. If the company's TSR over that period is in the second quartile, 50% of the options will vest. If the company is in the third or fourth quartiles, the options will lapse. For the options that vested on 1 July 2011, the TSR was in the second quartile; 50% of the award therefore vested.

SI 2008/410 8 Sch 12(1)(d) There have been no variations in the terms and conditions of scheme interests during the year.

SI 2008/410 8 Sch 12(1)(e) The shares awarded in July 2008 vested on 1 July 2011; based on the performance of the company over the three-year period ended on that date, the shares vested at 50 per cent.

DV Any shares issued arising from meeting the requisite performance criteria on the conditional shares awarded in July 2009, July 2010 and July 2011 will vest in July 2012, July 2013 and July 2014 respectively. At 31 December 2011 the performance percentage reflecting performance to date was 50% for the shares awarded in July 2009 and July 2010, and 100% for the shares awarded in July 2011.

Pensions

Directors' pension entitlement

(Amounts in the three following tables are in C thousands.)

SI 2008/410 8 Sch 13(2) Set out below are details of the pension benefits to which each of the executive directors is entitled.

	Additional accrued benefits earned in the year	Accrued entitlement	Transfer value at 31 December 2011	Transfer value at 31 December 2010	Increase in transfer value less directors' contributions
C D Suede	28	181	1,719	1,472	236
G Wallace	31	98	962	684	269
F Leather	18	103	984	820	153
E F Logan	26	94	907	687	215
D Scott[2]	7	27	243	194	41

[1] Or if earlier on date of retirement. Mr D Scott retired on 29 March 2011 and all his share options under the long-term incentive scheme lapsed on this date.
[2] Mr D Scott retired on 29 March 2011.

	Additional accrued benefits earned in the year (excluding inflation)	Transfer value of increase in accrued benefits less directors' contributions
C D Suede	26	173
G Wallace	28	184
F James	16	113
F Leather	25	164
D Scott[1]	7	36

SI 2008/410 8 Sch 13(2)(a)(ii) LR 9.8.8R(12)(a)

The accrued pension entitlement is the amount that the director would receive if he retired at the end of the year.

The increase in the accrued entitlement is the difference between the accrued benefit at the year end and that at the previous year end. The Listing Rules require this to be disclosed excluding inflation.

SI 2008/410 8 Sch 13(2)(b) LR 9.8.8R(12)(b)

All transfer values have been calculated on the basis of actuarial advice in accordance with Actuarial Guidance Note GN 11. The transfer values of the accrued entitlement represent the value of assets that the pension scheme would need to transfer to another pension provider on transferring the scheme's liability in respect of the directors' pension benefits. They do not represent sums payable to individual directors. They cannot therefore be added meaningfully to annual remuneration.

SI 2008/410 8 Sch 13(2)(d)

The increase in the transfer value less directors' contributions is the increase in the transfer value of the accrued benefits during the year after deducting the director's personal contributions to the scheme.

The transfer value of the increase in accrued benefits required by the Listing Rules discloses the current value of the increase in accrued benefits that the director has earned in the period; the change in his transfer value required by the Companies Act discloses the absolute increase or decrease in his/her transfer value and includes the change in value of the accrued benefits that results from market volatility affecting the transfer value at the beginning of the period, as well as the additional value earned in the year.

SI 2008/410 8 Sch 13(3)

Mr C D Suede and Mr G Wallace also participate in a US defined contribution pension arrangement. During the year, the group contributed C54,000 (2010: C nil) and C18,000 (2010: C nil) respectively.

Gains made by directors on share options[2]

The table below shows gains made by individual directors from the exercise of share options during 2011. The gains are calculated as at the exercise date, although the shares may have been retained.

	2011	2010
C D Suede	163	99
F Leather	148	58
Total gains on share options	311	157

[1] Mr D Scott retired on 29 March 2011.
[2] It is no longer necessary to disclose this separately. It is treated as disclosed if readily ascertainable from other disclosures.

This part of the remuneration report is unaudited.

Interests in shares (and derivatives or any other financial instrument relating to those shares)[1]

LR 9.8.6R(1) The interests of the directors and their connected persons in the shares of the company and other group members were:

	1 January 2011	31 December 2011
The company – ordinary shares 1p		
Executive directors		
C D Suede	1,000,000	1,110,500
G Wallace	110,000	110,000
F Leather	–	27,500
EF Logan	–	1,500
Non-executive directors		
R Graham	80,000	80,000
Lord Callender	25,000	25,000
Executive directors		
A Limited – ordinary shares C1		
F Leather	10,000	10,000
Non-executive directors		
T Limited – preference shares 50c		
A Cartwright	5,000	5,000

LR 9.8.6R(1) There has been no change in the interests set out above between 31 December 2011 and 25 March 2012.

On behalf of the board

R Graham
Chairman of the remuneration committee[2]
24 February 2012

[1] This disclosure is only required by the Listing Rules.
[2] The remuneration report should be approved by the board and signed on its behalf by a director or the company secretary. The remuneration report includes the requirements of Schedule 8 to SI 2008/410. In addition, Schedule 5 to SI 2008/410 requires certain aggregate information on emoluments to be included by quoted companies in the notes to the financial statements.

Corporate governance

Introduction

This chapter sets out the disclosure requirements that a UK premium listed company needs to take into consideration when presenting its corporate governance statement. Premium listed companies are those companies with equity listings which are subject to the more stringent, super-equivalent UK listing requirements as set out in the FSA's Listing Rules (see Issue 2 of the FSA Listing Regime FAQs published in June 2010). The relevant corporate governance disclosure requirements are set out in three places:

- FSA Listing Rule 9.8.6 (which includes the 'comply or explain' requirement);
- FSA Disclosure and Transparency Rules (DTR) Section 7.2 (which sets out certain mandatory disclosures); and
- The UK Corporate Governance Code (issued in June 2010) and associated guidance from the Financial Reporting Council (FRC).

The UK Corporate Governance Code (UKCGC) applies for accounting periods beginning on or after 29 June 2010.

The provisions of the UKCGC are also set out under each section below. Those provisions and other rules that require specific disclosures in the corporate governance statement are given immediately after the relevant principles, in normal font. The remaining provisions relating to each principle are given in *italics* for information purposes.

The UKCGC has promoted a number of Supporting Principles to Main Principles (A.3, A.4 and B.3) to reflect the additional emphasis given to these areas in the new Code. The structure of the UKCGC has been changed by creating separate sections for 'Leadership' and 'Effectiveness'. Blue text identifies new provisions (B.6.2, B.7.1 and C.1.2) and the provision where the concept was previously included as a supporting principle in the Combined Code (2008) (B.4.2). There are also other minor wording amendments throughout the UKCGC.

Commentary

The corporate governance disclosures included in these illustrative financial statements are based on the requirements for a UK premium listed company. Overseas premium listed companies (ie companies incorporated overseas but with an equity listing in the UK) are now also required to comply with the UKCGC. The FSA has not, however, applied Listing Rule 9.8.6(3), which requires "a statement made by the directors that the business is a going concern" to overseas premium listed companies. Notwithstanding this, provision C.1.3 of the UKCGC states that "the directors should report in annual and half yearly financial statements that the business is a going concern..." so any failure of an overseas premium listed company to do this would need to be explained under Listing Rule 9.8.6(6).

Overseas companies (whether standard or premium listed) are required to comply with DTR 7.2 (Corporate Governance statements) but not DTR 7.1 (Audit Committees). All UK companies with a premium listing are required to comply with both DTR 7.1 and DTR 7.2. The requirements are summarised in the table below.

	UK premium	UK standard	Overseas premium	Overseas standard
Listing Rule 9.8.6(5) and (6) (Compliance statement)	✓	✗	✓	✗
The UKCGC ('comply or explain')	✓	✗	✓ (for financial years beginning after 31/12/09)	✗
Listing Rule 9.8.6(3) (Going concern statement)	✓	✗	✗ (though UKCGC provision C.1.3 requires similar going concern disclosures)	✗
FSA Corporate Governance Rules				
DTR 7.1 (Audit Committees)	✓	✓	✗	✗
DTR 7.2 (Corporate Governance Statement)	✓	✓	✓	✓
Auditors' Report (LR 9.8.10) – 9 code provisions	✓	✗	✓ (though APB guidance relates only to UK companies)	✗

Reference publications

'Best practice compendium'

PricewaterhouseCoopers published its 'Best practice corporate governance reporting' compendium in January 2010. It provides good practice examples of corporate governance reporting, featuring extracts from the annual reports of FTSE 350 companies which meet current regulatory requirements. The compendium aims to:

- illustrate good practice reporting including explanations of departure from the Combined Code (2008); and
- show how reporting has evolved.

Helpful hints accompanying the extracts highlight new trends and good practice suggestions. Many of the examples given in the January 2010 publication remain appropriate where Code provisions remain unchanged in the UKCGC. Good practice examples for new provisions under the UKCGC will be made available when companies have reported publicly under the UKCGC in their June 2011 annual reports onwards.

'Corporate governance and AIM'

PricewaterhouseCoopers has also published a report on best practice reporting for companies on the Alternative Investment market ('AIM'). There is, however, no requirement for an AIM company to provide corporate governance disclosures.

DTR reporting requirements – all companies

DTR 7.2.1R The issuer must include a corporate governance statement in its directors' report. This statement must be included as a specific section of the directors' report and must contain at least the information set out in DTR 7.2.2R to 7.2.7R and, where consolidated accounts are prepared, DTR 7.2.10R.

DTR 7.2.2R The corporate governance statement must contain a reference to: (1) the corporate governance code to which the issuer is subject, (2) the governance code which the issuer may have voluntarily decided to apply; and/or (3) all relevant information about the corporate governance practices applied beyond the requirements under national law.

DTR 7.2.3R (1) An issuer which is complying with DTR 7.2.2R (1) or (2) must:

(a) state in its directors' report where the relevant corporate governance code is publicly available; and

(b) to the extent that it departs from that corporate governance code, explain which parts of the corporate governance code it departs from and the reasons for doing so.

(2) Where DTR 7.2.2R(3) applies, the issuer must make its corporate governance practices publicly available and state in its directors' report where they can be found.

(3) If an issuer has decided not to apply any provision of a corporate governance code referred to under DTR 7.2.2R(1) and (2), it must explain its reasons for that decision.

DTR 7.2.5R The corporate governance statement must contain a description of the main features of the issuer's internal control and risk management systems in relation to the financial reporting process.

DTR 7.2.6R The corporate governance statement must contain the information required by paragraph 13(2)(c), (d), (f), (h) and (i) of Schedule 7 to the Large and Medium-sized Companies and Groups (accounts and Reports) Regulations 2008 (SI 2008/410) (information about share capital required under Directive 2004/25/EC (the Takeover Directive)) where the issuer is subject to the requirements of that paragraph. (For disclosure requirements refer to the Directors' Report).

DTR 7.2.7R The corporate governance statement must contain a description of the composition and operation of the issuer's administrative, management and supervisory bodies and their committees.

DTR 7.2.9R An issuer may elect that instead of including its corporate governance statement in its directors' report, the information required by DTR 7.2.1R to DTR 7.2.7R may be set out:

(1) in a separate report published together with and in the same manner as its annual report. In the event of a separate report, the corporate governance statement must contain either the information required by DTR 7.2.6R or a reference to the directors' report where that information is made available; or

(2) by means of a reference in its directors' report to where such document is publicly available on the issuer's website.

Commentary

Although DTR 7.2.9R is relevant to all listed companies, a premium listed company is subject to Listing Rule requirements and will therefore have to include the corporate governance information within its annual report rather than only on its website.

DTR 7.2.10R Subject to DTR 7.2.11R, an issuer which is required to prepare a group directors' report within the meaning of section 415(2) of the Companies Act 2006 must include in that report a description of the main features of the group's internal control and risk management systems in relation to the process for preparing consolidated accounts. In the event that the issuer presents its own annual report and its consolidated annual report as a single report, this information must be included in the corporate governance statement required by DTR 7.2.1R.

DTR 7.2.11R   An issuer that elects to include its corporate governance statement in a separate report as permitted by DTR 7.2.9(1) must provide the information required by DTR 7.2.10R in that report.

Commentary

DTR 7.2.4G
DTR 7.2.8G   The DTR requirements above apply to both premium and standard listed companies. There are a number of overlaps between the provisions in the UKCGC and the DTR requirements. These are explained in the guidance provisions from the DTR set out below. Where there are additional disclosure requirements in the DTR, these are included under the relevant area of governance in this chapter.

A listed company which complies with LR 9.8.6R(6) (the comply or explain rule in relation to the UKCGC) will satisfy the requirements of DTR 7.2.2R and 7.2.3R.

In the FSA's view, the information specified in provisions A.1.1, A.1.2, B.2.4, C.3.3 and D.2.1 of the UKCGC will satisfy the requirements of DTR 7.2.7R.

Compliance

LR 9.8.6(5)   A statement must be made of how the company has applied the **main principles** of the UKCGC in a manner that enables shareholders to evaluate how the principles have been applied. The form and content of this part of the statement are not prescribed. The intention is for companies to explain their governance policies in light of the UKCGC principles, although the 'Comply or explain' section in the 'preamble' to the Combined Code 2008 contains some guidance in this area.

LR 9.8.6(6)
DTR 7.2.3R
(1)(b), (2), (3)   A statement must be made as to whether the company has complied throughout the accounting period with all relevant UKCGC provisions. Where the company has not complied with all of the provisions, or has complied for only part of the accounting period, a statement to that effect must be made specifying the provisions that have not been complied with and where details of the company's corporate governance practices can be found. Reasons must also be given for any non-compliance, and where relevant, the period of non-compliance must be stated. It is considered best practice for the company to set out the steps it is taking, or will be taking, towards full compliance in the future, if indeed the board judges full compliance to be best for the business.

Commentary

A listed company that complies with LR 9.8.6R(6) (the comply-or-explain rule in relation to the UKCGC) will satisfy the requirements of DTR 7.2.2R and 7.2.3R.

The board

Main principle A.1   Every company should be headed by an effective board, which is collectively responsible for the long-term success of the company.

Main principle A.2   There should be a clear division of responsibilities at the head of the company between the running of the board and the executive responsibility for the running of the company's business. No one individual should have unfettered powers of decision.

Main principle A.3   The chairman is responsible for leadership of the board and ensuring its effectiveness on all aspects of the role.

Main principle A.4   As part of their role as members of a unitary board, non-executive directors should constructively challenge and help develop proposals on strategy.

UKCGC A.1.1   A statement should be made about how the board operates, including a high-level statement of which types of decisions are taken by the board and which are delegated to management.

DTR 7.2.7R   The corporate governance statement must contain a description of the composition and operation of the company's administrative, management and supervisory bodies and their committees.

Commentary

The above provisions overlap; the DTR confirms that, if a company provides the information specified by UKCGC A.1.1 above, it will satisfy the relevant requirements of DTR 7.2.7R.

UKCGC A.1.2   The annual report should identify:

- The chairman.
- The deputy chairman (where applicable).
- The chief executive.
- The senior independent director.
- The chairmen and members of each of the nomination, audit and remuneration committees.

UKCGC A.1.2   It should also set out the number of meetings of the board and each committee and individual attendance by directors.

DTR 7.1.5R   The company must make a statement available on how the audit committee (or equivalent body) carries out its responsibilities and how it is composed.

Commentary

The above provisions overlap; the DTR confirms that, if a company provides the information specified by UKCGC A.1.2 above and UKCGC C.3.3, it will satisfy the relevant requirements of DTR 7.1.5 and DTR 7.2.7.

Other related provisions

UKCGC A.1.1   *(a)   The board should meet sufficiently regularly to discharge its duties effectively. There should be a formal schedule of matters specifically reserved for its decision.*

UKCGC A.2.1   *(b)   The roles of chairman and chief executive should not be exercised by the same individual. The division of responsibilities between the chairman and chief executive should be clearly established, set out in writing and agreed by the board.*

UKCGC A.1.3   *(c)   The company should arrange appropriate insurance cover in respect of legal action against its directors.*

UKCGC A.4.3   *(d)   Where directors have concerns which cannot be resolved about the running of the company or a proposed action, they should ensure that their concerns are recorded in the board minutes. On resignation, non-executive directors should provide a written statement to the chairman, for circulation to the board, if they have any such concerns.*

UKCGC B.2.1, C.3.3, D.2.1   *(e)   The terms of reference of the nomination, audit and remuneration committees, including each committee's role and authority delegated to it by the board, should be made available. The recommendation can be met by making the information available on the company's web site.*

Board balance and independence

Main principle B.1   The board and its committees should have the appropriate balance of skills, experience, independence and knowledge of the company to enable them to discharge their respective duties and responsibilities effectively.

UKCGC B.1   The annual report should identify each non-executive director that the board considers to be independent. If the board considers a director to be independent, but circumstances or relationships exist that may appear relevant to that decision, disclosure should be made of the reasons for determining that director to be independent.

Other related provisions

UKCGC B.1.1   *(a)   The board should determine whether each non-executive director is independent in character and judgement and whether there are relationships or circumstances which are likely to affect a director's independence. These include:*
- *Employment with the company or group within the last five years.*
- *A material business relationship within the last three years between the company and the director, or a body of which he/she is a partner, shareholder, director or senior employee.*
- *Any entitlement to remuneration from the company other than a director's fee or participation in the share option or performance-related pay scheme or membership of the company's pension scheme.*
- *Close family ties between the director and any of the company's advisers, directors or senior employees.*
- *A cross-directorship or significant links with other directors through involvement in other companies or bodies.*
- *Representing a significant shareholder.*
- *More than nine years' service on the board.*

UKCGC B.1.2   *(b)   At least half the board, excluding the chairman, should comprise independent non- executive directors. A smaller company (that is, a company below the FTSE 350 throughout the year immediately prior to the reporting year) should have at least two independent non-executive directors.*

UKCGC A.4.1   *(c)   An independent non-executive director should be appointed by the board as the senior independent director. The director should provide a sounding board for the chairman and serve as an intermediary for other directors. This director should also be available to shareholders if they have concerns which contact through the normal channels of chairman, chief executive or finance director has failed to resolve or for which such contact is inappropriate.*

UKCGC A.3.1   *(d)   A chief executive should not go on to be chairman of the same company. If, exceptionally, the board decides that a chief executive should become chairman, the board should consult major shareholders in advance and set out its reasons for that appointment in the next annual report.*

UKCGC A.3.1   *(e)   On appointment, the chairman should meet the independence criteria set out in B.1.1.*

Appointments to the board

Main principle B.2   There should be a formal, rigorous and transparent procedure for the appointment of new directors to the board.

Main principle B.3   All directors should be able to allocate sufficient time to the company to discharge their responsibilities effectively.

Main principle B.4	All directors should receive induction on joining the board and should regularly update and refresh their skills and knowledge.
Main principle B.5	The board should be supplied in a timely manner with information in a form and of a quality appropriate to enable it to discharge its duties.
UKCGC B.3.1	Disclosure should be made of the chairman's other significant commitments before his/her appointment. Any changes to these should be reported to the board as they arise and their impact explained in the next annual report.

Other related provisions

UKCGC B.3.1	(a)	The nomination committee should prepare a job specification for the appointment of a chairman, including an assessment of the time commitment expected, recognising the need for availability in the event of crises.
UKCGC B.3.2	(b)	The terms and conditions of appointment of non-executive directors should be made available for inspection (at the company's registered office during business hours and at the AGM (for 15 minutes before the meeting and during the meeting).
UKCGC B.3.2	(c)	Letters of appointment should set out the expected time commitment. Non-executive directors should undertake that they will have sufficient time to meet what is expected of them. Their other significant commitments should be disclosed to the board before appointment, along with and indication of the time involved, and upon subsequent changes.
UKCGC B.3.3	(d)	The board should not agree to a full time executive director taking on more than one non- executive directorship in a FTSE 100 company nor the chairmanship of such a company.
UKCGC D.1.2	(e)	Where a company releases an executive director to serve as a non-executive director elsewhere, the remuneration report should include a statement as to whether or not the director will retain such earnings and, if so, what the remuneration is.
UKCGC B.5.1	(f)	All directors, especially non-executive directors, should have access to independent professional advice, at the expense of the company, where they judge it necessary to discharge their responsibilities as directors. Committees should be provided with sufficient resources to undertake their duties.
UKCGC B.5.2	(g)	All directors should have access to the advice and services of the company secretary who is responsible to the board for ensuring that board procedures are complied with. The appointment and removal of the company secretary should be a matter for the board as a whole.
UKCGC B.4.1	(h)	The chairman should ensure that new directors receive a full, formal and tailored induction on joining the board. The directors should avail themselves of opportunities to meet major shareholders.
UKCGC B.4.2	(i)	The chairman should regularly review and agree with each director their training and development needs.

Commentary

Directors' conflicts of interest

The Companies Act 2006 (S.171–177) introduced new statutory duties for directors. It includes a duty to avoid a conflict of interest: a director must avoid any situation where he/she has a conflict, although such conflicts may be authorised by non-interested directors as long as there is authority in the company's Articles for this to happen. It is recommended that companies include a transparent disclosure in their corporate governance statement in confirming to shareholders that the conflicts authorisation procedures have been followed.

Re-election of directors

Main principle B.7	All directors should be submitted for re-election at regular intervals, subject to continued satisfactory performance.
UKCGC B.7.1	The names of directors submitted for election or re-election should be accompanied by sufficient biographical details to enable shareholders to make an informed decision on their election.

Other related provisions

UKCGC B.2.1	(a)	There should be a nomination committee which should lead the process for board appointment and make recommendations to the board.
UKCGC B.7.2	(b)	The board should set out to shareholders in its papers why they believe an individual should be elected as a non-executive director. When proposing re- election, the chairman should confirm that, following formal performance evaluation, the individual's performance continues to be effective and to demonstrate commitment to the role.
UKCGC B.2.3	(c)	Non-executive directors should be appointed for specified terms subject to re-election and to statutory provisions relating to the removal of a director. Any term beyond six years for a non-executive director should be subject to particularly rigorous review and should take into account progressive refreshing of the board.

UKCGC B.7.1	(d)	*All directors of FTSE 350 companies should be subject to annual re-election by shareholders. All other directors should be subject to election by shareholders at the first AGM after their appointment and to re-election thereafter at intervals of no more than three years. Non-executive directors who have served longer than nine years should be subject to annual re-election.*
UKCGC C.3.1, UKCGC D.2.1	(e)	*The board should establish both an audit committee and a remuneration committee of at least three, or in the case of smaller companies (that is, those below the FTSE 350 throughout the year immediately prior to the reporting year) two independent non- executive directors.*
UKCGC D.2.1	(f)	*The company chairman may also be a member of, but not chair, the remuneration committee if he or she was considered independent on appointment.*
UKCGC C.3.1	(g)	*For smaller companies, the company chairman may also be a member of, but not chair, the audit committee if he or she was considered independent on appointment. This is in addition to the two independent non-executive directors.*
UKCGC B.2.1	(h)	*The nomination committee should have a majority of independent non-executive directors. The chairman or an independent non-executive director should be chair of the committee. The chairman should not chair the nomination committee when it is dealing with the appointment of a successor to the chairmanship.*

Performance evaluation

Main principle B.6	The board should undertake a formal and rigorous annual evaluation of its own performance and that of its committees and individual directors.
UKCGC B.6.1	The report should state how performance evaluations of the board, its committees and its individual directors have been conducted.
UKCGC B.6.2	Where an external facilitator is used to evaluate the board, a statement should be made as to whether the facilitator has any other connection with the company.

Other related provisions:

UKCGC B.6.2	(a)	*All FTSE 350 companies should engage an external party to evaluate the performance of the board at least every three years.*
UKCGC A.4.2, UKCGC B.6.3	(b)	*The chairman should hold meetings with the non-executive directors without the executive directors present. The non-executive directors, led by the senior independent director, should be responsible for performance evaluation of the chairman, taking into account the views of the executive directors.*

Report of the nomination committee

UKCGC B.2.4	A separate section describing the work of the nomination committee should be given in the annual report. This should include the process used in relation to board appointments. An explanation should be given if neither an external search consultancy nor open advertising has been used in the appointment of a chairman or a non-executive director.

Commentary

The above provision overlaps and, the DTR confirms that, if a company provides the information specified by UKCGC B.2.4 above, it will satisfy the relevant requirements of DTR 7.2.7.

Other related provisions

UKCGC	(a)	*The nomination committee should lead the process for board appointments and make recommendations to the board. The majority of the committee should be independent non-executive directors. The chairman should chair the committee, but the chairman should not chair the nomination committee when it is dealing with the appointment of a successor to the chairmanship.*
UKCGC B.2.2	(b)	*The nomination committee should evaluate the balance of skills, experience, independence and knowledge of the board and, in the light of this evaluation, prepare a description of the role and responsibilities required for a particular appointment.*

Commentary

In February 2011, Lord Davies published his report *Women on Boards*. This is in line with the new supporting principle (B.2), which states that 'the search for board candidates should be conducted, and appointments made, on merit, against objective criteria and with due regard for the benefits of diversity on the board, including gender'. Lord Davies recommended that FTSE 350 companies should announce by September 2011 their targets for female board representation by 2013 and 2015; a number of companies are making these disclosures in their annual reports.

As a result of the Davies Report, the FRC published a consultation paper proposing that the following changes be made to the Code:

- The nomination committee report should disclose the policy concerning boardroom diversity together with progress against it (Code provision); and
- The annual board effectiveness evaluation should also consider that policy (Code supporting principle).

It is likely that there will be a change to the UKCGC
arising from this consultation, but the date of any change is still to be determined.

Audit committee and auditors

Main principle C.3 The board should establish formal and transparent arrangements for considering how they should apply the corporate reporting and risk management and internal control principles and for maintaining an appropriate relationship with the company's auditors.

Report of the audit committee

Commentary

The FRC Guidance on Audit Committees (ACG) (formerly known as the Smith Guidance) was updated in 2008. A further update, focusing on non-audit services, was made in 2010. It is designed to assist company boards in making suitable arrangements for their audit committees in carrying out their role. The disclosure requirements have been included below. Boards are not required to follow this guidance, but it is intended to assist them when implementing the relevant provisions of the UKCGC.

Best practice suggests that every board should consider in detail what arrangements for its audit committee are best suited for its particular circumstances. Audit committee arrangements need to be proportionate to the task, and will vary according to the size, complexity and risk profile of the company. The recent FRC consultation, *Effective Company Stewardship: Enhancing corporate reporting and audit,* may see an expansion in audit committee reporting in the future.

UKCGC C.3.3, ACG 5.1 The terms of reference of the audit committee, including its role and the authority delegated to it by the board, should be made available. A separate section in the annual report should describe the work of the committee in discharging its responsibilities.

ACG 5.2 The audit committee section should include, inter alia:

- a summary of the role of the audit committee;
- the names and qualifications of all members of the audit committee during the period;
- the number of audit committee meetings;
- a report on the way the audit committee has discharged its responsibilities; and
- the explanations provided for in paragraphs 4.23 and 4.37. (See below)

UKCGC C.3.5, ACG 4.10 Where there is no internal audit function, the reasons for its absence should be explained.

UKCGC C.3.6, ACG 4.18 The audit committee should have primary responsibility for making a recommendation to the board on the appointment, reappointment and removal of the external auditors. If the board does not accept the audit committee's recommendation, the annual report should include a statement from the audit committee explaining its recommendation and the reasons why the board has taken a different position.

ACG 4.23 The audit committee section of the annual report should explain to shareholders how it reached its recommendation to the board on the appointment, reappointment or removal of the external auditors. This explanation should normally include supporting information on tendering frequency, the tenure of the incumbent auditor, and any contractual obligations that acted to restrict the audit committee's choice of external auditors.

UKCGC C.3.7, ACG 4.37 If the auditor provides non-audit services, it should be explained how auditor objectivity and independence is safeguarded.

ACG 4.38 The explanation of how auditor objectivity and independence is safeguarded should:

- describe the work of the committee in discharging its responsibilities;
- set out the audit committee's policy on the engagement of the external auditor to supply non-audit services in sufficient detail to describe each of the elements in paragraph 4.30 (see below), or cross-refer to where this information can be found on the company's website;
- set out or cross-refer to the fees paid to the auditor for audit services, audit related services and other non-audit services; and
- if the auditor provides non-audit services other than audit related services, explain for each significant engagement, or category of engagement, what the services are, why the audit committee concluded it was in the interests of the company to purchase them from the external auditor (rather than another supplier) and how auditor objectivity and independence has been safeguarded.

Other related provisions

ACG 4.30   The audit committee should set and apply a formal policy specifying the types of non-audit service (if any):

- for which the use of the external auditor is pre-approved (that is, approval has been given in advance as a matter of policy, rather than the specific approval of an engagement being sought before it is contracted);
- for which specific approval from the audit committee is required before they are contracted; and
- from which the external auditor is excluded.

UKCGC C.3.1, ACG 2.1 and 2.3   (a) The audit committee should consist of at least three, or in the case of smaller companies, (that is, those below the FTSE 350 throughout the year immediately prior to the reporting year), two independent non-executive directors. In smaller companies the chairman may be a member of, but not chair, the committee in addition to the independent non-executive directors, provided he or she was considered independent on appointment as chairman. The board should satisfy itself that at least one member of the audit committee has recent and relevant financial experience.

DTR 7.1.1R, 7.1.2G   (b) The audit committee should have at least one member who is independent; at least one member should have competence in accounting and/or auditing. These requirements may be satisfied by the same member or by different members of the committee.

Commentary

This is a relaxation for smaller companies that were below the FTSE 350 throughout the year immediately prior to the reporting year and was introduced to help smaller companies comply with this Code provision, as it is usually the chairman of a smaller company who has recent and relevant financial experience.

There is a slight difference between the Code recommendation and the DTR requirement as to the composition of the audit committee; however, if a company complies with the Code provision, it will fulfil the DTR requirement.

DTR 7.1.4R   (c) A company must base any proposal to appoint the auditor on a recommendation by the audit committee (or equivalent body).

UKCGC C.3.2, ACG 2.2   (d) The audit committee should have written terms of reference setting out its responsibilities that should include:

- Monitoring the integrity of the company's financial statements and announcements relating to financial performance and reviewing significant financial reporting judgements contained in them.
- Reviewing the company's financial and non-financial internal controls and risk management systems (to the extent that these are not delegated to another committee made up of independent non-executive directors).
- Monitoring and reviewing the effectiveness of the group's internal audit function.
- Making recommendations to the board relating to the appointment, reappointment and removal of the external auditor and approving the remuneration and terms of engagement of the external auditor.
- Reviewing and monitoring the external auditor's independence and objectivity and the effectiveness of the audit processes.
- Developing and implementing a policy on the engagement of the external auditor to supply non-audit services and reporting to the board, identifying matters where action or improvement is needed.

DTR 7.1.3R   (e) As a minimum, the audit committee must:

- monitor the financial reporting process;
- monitor the effectiveness of the company's internal control, internal audit where applicable, and risk management systems;
- monitor the statutory audit of the annual and consolidated accounts;
- review and monitor the external auditor's independence and the provision of additional services

Commentary

The above provisions overlap, and the DTR confirms, that if a company provides the information specified by C.3.2 above, it will satisfy the requirements of DTR 7.1.3.

UKCGC C.3.5, ACG 4.10   (f) The audit committee should monitor and review the effectiveness of the internal audit activities. Where there is no internal audit function, the audit committee should consider annually whether there is a need for one and make a recommendation to the board.

UKCGC C.3.4   (g) The audit committee should review arrangements by which staff of the company may, in confidence, raise concerns about possible improprieties in matters of financial reporting or other matters. It should ensure the proportionate and independent investigation of such matters and follow up actions.

Remuneration committee

UKCGC D.1.2   The remuneration report should include a description of the work of the remuneration committee, including, where an executive director serves as a non-executive director elsewhere, whether or not the director will retain such earnings and, if so, what the remuneration is.

| UKCGC D.2.1 | Where remuneration consultants are appointed, a statement should be made available of whether they have any other connection with the company. This statement may be made on the company's website. |

Risk and internal control

| Main principle C.2 | The board is responsible for determining the nature and extent of the significant risks it is willing to take in achieving its strategic objectives. The board should maintain sound risk management and internal control systems. |

| UKCGC C.2.1 | The board should at least annually conduct a review of the effectiveness of the company's risk management and internal control systems and should report to shareholders that they have done so. The review should cover all material controls, including financial, operational and compliance controls and risk management systems. |

| DTR 7.2.5R | The corporate governance statement must include a description of the main features of the company's internal control and risk management systems in relation to the financial reporting process. |

| DTR 7.2.10R | Where the issuer is required to prepare a group directors' report, they should include a description of the main features of the group's internal control and risk management systems in relation to the process for preparing consolidated accounts. |

Commentary

The DTR requirement differs from the recommendation in the UKCGC; however, the FRC envisage that both could be met by a single internal control statement.

Reporting under the Turnbull guidance (2005)

| TG 34 | ■ The board should, as a minimum, disclose that there is an ongoing process for identifying, evaluating and managing the significant risks faced by the company, that it has been in place for the year under review and up to the date of approval of the annual report, that it is regularly reviewed by the board and accords with the Turnbull guidance (2005). |

| TG 33 | ■ The annual report should include such meaningful, high-level information as the board considers necessary to assist shareholders' understanding of the main features of the company's risk management processes and system of internal control, and should not give a misleading impression. |

| TG 35 | ■ The board should acknowledge that it is responsible for the company's system of internal control and for reviewing its effectiveness. It should also explain that such a system is designed to manage rather than eliminate the risk of failure to achieve business objectives and can only provide reasonable, but not absolute assurance against material misstatement or loss. |

| TG 36 | ■ The board should summarise the process it (where applicable, through its committees) has applied in reviewing the effectiveness of the system of internal control and confirm that necessary actions have been or are being taken to remedy any significant failings or weaknesses identified from that review. It should also disclose the process it has applied to deal with material internal control aspects of any significant problems disclosed in the annual report. |

| TG 37 | ■ Where a board cannot make one or more of the disclosures in paragraphs 34 and 36 described above, it should state this fact and provide an explanation. The Listing Rules require the board to disclose if it has failed to conduct a review of the effectiveness of the company's system of internal control. |

| TG 38 | ■ Where material joint ventures and associates have not been dealt with as part of the group for the purposes of applying this guidance, this should be disclosed. |

Other aspects of the Turnbull guidance

| TG 30 | *For the purpose of making its public statement on internal control the board should undertake an annual assessment. The assessment should consider issues dealt with in reports reviewed by it during the year together with any additional information necessary to ensure that the board has taken account of all significant aspects of internal control for the company for the year under review and up to the date of approval of the annual report.* |

| TG 31 | *The board's annual assessment should, in particular, consider:* |

■ *The changes since the last annual assessment in the nature and extent of significant risks and the company's ability to respond to changes in its business and the external environment.*

■ *The scope and quality of management's ongoing monitoring of risks and of the system of internal control and, where applicable, the work of its internal audit function and other providers of assurance.*

■ *The extent and frequency of the communication of the results of the monitoring to the board (or board committee(s)) that enables it to build up a cumulative assessment of the state of control in the company and the effectiveness with which risk is being managed.*

■ *The incidence of significant control failings or weaknesses that have been identified at any time during the period and the extent to which they have resulted in unforeseen outcomes or contingencies that have had, could have had, or may in the future have, a material impact on the company's financial performance or condition.*

■ *The effectiveness of the company's public reporting processes.*

Requirements from the Takeover Directive

DTR 7.2.9R(1) Where the corporate governance statement is excluded from the directors' report but included elsewhere in the annual report, a cross-reference to the directors' report, where this information is disclosed as required by company law, must be given.

DTR 7.2.6R The corporate governance statement must contain the information required by paragraph 13(2)(c), (d), (f), (h) and (i) of Schedule 7 to the Large and Medium-sized Companies and Groups (Accounts and Reports) Regulations 2008 (SI 2008/410) (information about share capital required under Directive 2004/25/EC (the Takeover Directive) where the issuer is subject to the requirements of that paragraph.

Commentary

These disclosures are similar to the Takeover Directive requirements usually given in the Directors' Report. These disclosures must either be repeated in the corporate governance statement or cross-referred to the relevant part of the Directors' Report. Refer to page XX of the illustrative financial statements.

Financial reporting

Main principle C.1 The board should present a balanced and understandable assessment of the company's position and prospects.

UKCGC C.1.1 There should be a statement from the directors explaining their responsibility for preparing the annual report and accounts.

UKCGC C.1.2 The directors should include in the annual report an explanation of the basis on which the company generates or preserves value over the longer term (the business model) and the strategy for delivering the objectives of the company.

LR 9.8.6(3), UKCGC C.1.3 There must be a statement by the directors in both the annual and half-yearly statements, that the business is a going concern, with supporting assumptions or qualifications as necessary. This statement should cover both the parent company and the group as a whole.

Commentary

The wording of provision C.1.3 has been changed in the UKCGC
to specify that a going concern statement is required in both the annual and half-yearly financial statements.
The FRC Guidance 'Going concern and liquidity risk: Guidance for Directors of UK Companies 2009'' ('GC') applies to accounting periods ending on or after 31 December 2009. It replaces the guidance issued in 1994 for directors of listed companies and extends the application of the guidance to all sizes of company for annual and half-yearly financial statements. The guidance provides a framework to assist directors, audit committees and finance teams, of all sizes of company, in determining whether it is appropriate to adopt the going concern basis for preparing financial statements (both annual and half yearly) and in making balanced, proportionate and clear disclosures.

GC principle 3 Directors should make balanced, proportionate and clear disclosures about going concern for the financial statements to give a true and fair view. Directors should disclose if the period that they have reviewed is less than twelve months from the date of approval of annual and half- yearly financial statements and explain their justification for limiting their review period.

GC para 80 It is helpful to investors and other stakeholders if all of these disclosures are brought together in a single place in the company's financial statements. It may be necessary to provide a cross reference to that single place from other parts of the annual report. If it is not practicable to provide all of the information in a single place, it is still helpful if the key disclosures are brought together by way of a note that includes appropriate cross-references to information in the financial statements and from the financial statements to information included elsewhere in the annual report. Refer to Note 2 of the IFRS GAAP Plc financial statements for illustrative going concern disclosures.

GC para 81 Balanced, proportionate and clear disclosures would include the following components:

- the key disclosures or references thereto;
- the particular factors which the directors have considered in reaching a conclusion on going concern; and
- a concluding statement as to whether the use of the going concern basis of accounting is appropriate, explaining the basis of that conclusion.

GC para 83 Examples illustrating such disclosures and how they can be brought together are included in Appendix I for small companies and in Appendix II for other companies of the FRC guidance 'Going concern and liquidity risk: Guidance for Directors of UK Companies 2009'.

Dialogue with shareholders

Main principle E.1 There should be a dialogue with shareholders based on the mutual understanding of objectives. The board as a whole has responsibility for ensuring that a satisfactory dialogue with shareholders takes place.

UKCGC E.1.2   Disclosure should be made of the steps that the board has taken to ensure that the members of the board, and in particular the non-executive directors, develop an understanding of the views of the major shareholders (for example through direct face-to-face contact, analysts' or brokers' briefings and surveys of shareholder opinion) about their company.

Other related provisions

UKCGC E.1.1   (a)   *The chairman should ensure that the views of shareholders are communicated to the board as a whole.*

UKCGC E.1.1   (b)   *The chairman should discuss governance and strategy with major shareholders. Non-executive directors should be offered the opportunity to attend scheduled meetings with major shareholders and should expect to attend if requested by major shareholders. The senior independent director should also attend sufficient meetings with a range of major shareholders to listen to their views in order to help develop a balance of understanding of their concerns.*

Constructive use of the AGM

Main principle E.2   The board should use the AGM to communicate with investors and to encourage their participation.

Other related provisions

UKCGC E.2.3   (a)   *The chairman should arrange for the chairmen of the audit, remuneration and nomination committees to attend the AGM to answer questions and for all directors to attend.*

UKCGC E.2.1   (b)   *The company should propose a separate resolution on each substantially separate issue and should in particular propose a resolution at the AGM relating to the report and accounts. For each resolution, proxy appointment forms should provide shareholders with the option to direct their proxy to vote either for or against the resolution or to withhold their vote. The proxy form and any announcement of the results of a vote should make clear that a 'vote withheld' is not a vote in law and will not be counted in the calculation of the proportion of votes for and against the resolution.*

UKCGC E.2.2   (c)   *The company should ensure that all valid proxy appointments received for general meetings are properly recorded and counted. For each resolution, after a vote has been taken, except where taken on a poll, the company should ensure that the following information is given at the general meeting and made available as soon as reasonably practicable on the company's web site:*
- *the number of shares in respect of which proxy appointments have been validly made; and*
- *the number of votes (i) for, and (ii) against the resolution, and (iii) the number of shares in respect of which the vote was directed to be withheld.*

UKCGC E.2.4   (d)   *The company should arrange for the Notice of the AGM and related papers to be sent to shareholders at least 20 working days before the meeting.*

Statement of directors' responsibilities

CC C.1.1
APB2007/01
ISA (UK and
Ireland) 700
p9-1

The directors are responsible for preparing the Annual Report, the Remuneration Report and the financial statements in accordance with applicable law and regulations.

Company law requires the directors to prepare financial statements for each financial year. Under that law the directors have prepared the group and parent company financial statements in accordance with International Financial Reporting Standards (IFRSs) as adopted by the European Union. Under company law the directors must not approve the financial statements unless they are satisfied that they give a true and fair view of the state of affairs of the group and the company and of the profit or loss of the group for that period. In preparing these financial statements, the directors are required to:

■ select suitable accounting policies and then apply them consistently[1];
■ make judgements and accounting estimates that are reasonable and prudent[2];
■ state whether applicable IFRSs as adopted by the European Union have been followed, subject to any material departures disclosed and explained in the financial statements[3]; and
■ prepare the financial statements on the going concern basis unless it is inappropriate to presume that the company will continue in business[4].

The directors are responsible for keeping adequate accounting records that are sufficient to show and explain the company's transactions and disclose with reasonable accuracy at any time the financial position of the company and the group and enable them to ensure that the financial statements and the directors' remuneration report comply with the Companies Act 2006 and, as regards the group financial statements, Article 4 of the IAS Regulation. They are also responsible for safeguarding the assets of the company and the group and hence for taking reasonable steps for the prevention and detection of fraud and other irregularities

The directors are responsible for the maintenance and integrity of the company's website and legislation in the United Kingdom governing the preparation and dissemination of financial statements may differ from legislation in other jurisdictions.

Directors' statement pursuant to the Disclosure and Transparency Rules

Each of the directors, whose names and functions are listed in [refer to section of annual report containing details of directors] confirm that, to the best of each person's knowledge and belief:

■ the financial statements, prepared in accordance with IFRSs as adopted by the EU, give a true and fair view of the assets, liabilities, financial position and profit [loss] of the group and company; and
■ the directors' report contained in the annual report includes a fair review of the development and performance of the business and the position of the company and group, together with a description of the principal risks and uncertainties that they face.

The directors are responsible for the maintenance and integrity of the group web site, www.IFRSGAAPplc.com. Legislation in the UK governing the preparation and dissemination of financial statements may differ from legislation in other jurisdictions.

By order of the board
AB Smith
Company Secretary
24 February 2011

Notes:

(a) *There is no requirement for the corporate governance report to be signed. However, it is good practice for the company secretary or the senior non-executive director to sign it.*
(b) *The statement by the directors should be made in accordance with what is known to them at the date on which they approve the financial statements; in practice directors will need to perform their work to a date before the approval of the financial statements and update their work as appropriate.*

LR 9.8.10R *The Listing Rules require that the auditors should review the following aspects of the company's 'statement of compliance' with the Combined Code of corporate governance:*

CC C.1.1 ■ *Directors' responsibility statement for preparing the financial statements and auditors' reporting responsibilities.*

CC C.2.1 ■ *Directors' report to shareholders on the company's system of internal controls.*

CC C.3.1-7 ■ *Disclosure relating to the audit committee and auditors.*

[1] Reference to the company has been deleted as the parent company takes the section 408 of the Companies Act 2006 and does not present the parent company income statement.
[2] Paragraph 29 of Part 2 of Schedule 1 to SI 2008/410 requires that the amount of any item 'shall be determined on a prudent basis'.
[3] This bullet does not apply to small and medium-sized companies as defined by CA06.
[4] This bullet can be omitted if the directors have voluntarily given a separate statement about going concern.

LR 9.8.8R ■ *Detailed disclosure in the directors' remuneration report relating to total remuneration, share options, long-term incentive schemes and pension entitlements.*

LR 9.8.6R(3) *In addition, the Listing Rules require that the auditors should review the directors' statement on going concern.*

Independent auditors' report to the members of IFRS GAAP plc

APB 2010/02   *Warning – this audit report was current at the date of going to press. However, it may not be the most up-to-date version. It should not be used without checking that it is the appropriate version.*

We have audited the financial statements of IFRS GAAP plc for the year ended 31 December 2011 which comprise the consolidated income statement, the group and company balance sheets, the group and company statement of cash flows, the consolidated statement of other comprehensive income, the consolidated statement of changes in equity and the related notes. The financial reporting framework that has been applied in their preparation is applicable law and International Financial Reporting Standards (IFRSs) as adopted by the European Union and, as regards the parent company financial statements, as applied in accordance with the provisions of the Companies Act 2006.

Respective responsibilities of directors and auditors

As explained more fully in the directors' responsibilities statement set out on page 33, the directors are responsible for the preparation of the financial statements and for being satisfied that they give a true and fair view. Our responsibility is to audit the financial statements in accordance with applicable law and International Standards on Auditing (UK and Ireland). Those standards require us to comply with the Auditing Practices Board's Ethical Standards for Auditors.

This report, including the opinions, has been prepared for and only for the company's members as a body in accordance with Chapter 3 of Part 16 of the Companies Act 2006 and for no other purpose. We do not, in giving these opinions, accept or assume responsibility for any other purpose or to any other person to whom this report is shown or into whose hands it may come save where expressly agreed by our prior consent in writing.

Scope of the audit of the financial statements

An audit involves obtaining evidence about the amounts and disclosures in the financial statements sufficient to give reasonable assurance that the financial statements are free from material misstatement, whether caused by fraud or error. This includes an assessment of: whether the accounting policies are appropriate to the group's and the parent company's circumstances and have been consistently applied and adequately disclosed; the reasonableness of significant accounting estimates made by the directors; and the overall presentation of the financial statements.

Opinion on financial statements

In our opinion:

- the financial statements give a true and fair view of the state of the group's and of the parent company's affairs as at 31 December 2011 and of the group's profit and group's and parent company's cash flows for the year then ended;
- the group financial statements have been properly prepared in accordance with IFRSs as adopted by the European Union;
- the parent company financial statements have been properly prepared in accordance with IFRSs as adopted by the European Union and as applied in accordance with the provisions of the Companies Act 2006; and
- the financial statements have been prepared in accordance with the requirements of the Companies Act 2006 and, as regards the group financial statements, Article 4 of the IAS Regulation.

Opinion on other matters prescribed by the Companies Act 2006

In our opinion:

- the part of the Remuneration report to be audited has been properly prepared in accordance with the Companies Act 2006; and
- the information given in the Directors' report for the financial year for which the financial statements are prepared is consistent with the financial statements.

Matters on which we are required to report by exception

We have nothing to report in respect of the following:

Under the Companies Act 2006 we are required to report to you if, in our opinion:

- adequate accounting records have not been kept by the parent company, or returns adequate for our audit have not been received from branches not visited by us; or
- the parent company financial statements and the part of the Remuneration report to be audited are not in agreement with the accounting records and returns; or
- certain disclosures of directors' remuneration specified by law are not made; or
- we have not received all the information and explanations we require for our audit.

Under the Listing Rules we are required to review:

- the directors' statement, set out on page 33, in relation to going concern; and
- the parts of the corporate governance statement relating to the company's compliance with the nine provisions of the UK Corporate Governance Code specified for our review.

John Smith (Senior Statutory Auditor)
For and on behalf of PricewaterhouseCoopers LLP
Chartered Accountants and Statutory Auditors
London
28 February 2012

Notes:

Where the report is included on the client's web site, include notes (a) and (b) below (on the web site version of the audit report, but not on the hard copy version) unless the statement of directors' responsibilities clearly:

- *states the directors' responsibility for the maintenance and integrity of the web site; and*
- *refers to the fact that uncertainty regarding legal requirements is compounded as information published on the internet is accessible in many countries with different legal requirements relating to the preparation and dissemination of financial statements.*
  - *(a) The maintenance and integrity of the IFRS GAAP plc web site is the responsibility of the directors; the work carried out by the auditors does not involve consideration of these matters and, accordingly, the auditors accept no responsibility for any changes that may have occurred to the financial statements since they were initially presented on the web site.*
  - *(b) Legislation in the United Kingdom governing the preparation and dissemination of financial statements may differ from legislation in other jurisdictions.*

(All amounts in C thousands unless otherwise stated)

Consolidated income statement[1]

1p10(b),81(a)

1p113, 1p38

		Note	Group Year ended 31 December 2011	2010
	Continuing operations			
1p82(a)	Revenue	5	**211,034**	112,360
1p99, 103	Cost of sales	6	**(77,366)**	(46,682)
1p103	**Gross profit**		**133,668**	65,678
1p99, 103	Distribution costs		**(52,529)**	(21,213)
1p99, 103	Administrative expenses		**(29,895)**	(10,426)
1p99,103	Other income	7	**2,750**	1,259
1p85	Other (losses)/gains – net	8	**(90)**	63
1p85	**Operating profit[2]**		**53,904**	35,361
1p85	Finance income	11	**1,730**	1,609
1p82(b)	Finance costs	11	**(8,173)**	(12,197)
1p85	Finance costs – net	11	**(6,443)**	(10,588)
1p82(c)	Share of (loss)/profit of associates	12b	**215**	145
1p85	**Profit before income tax**		**47,676**	24,918
1p82(d), 12p77	Income tax expense	13	**(14,611)**	(8,670)
1p85	**Profit for the year from continuing operations**		**33,065**	16,248
IFRS5p33(a)	**Discontinued operations**			
	Profit for the year from discontinued operations (attributable to equity holders of the company)	25	**100**	120
1p82(f)	**Profit for the year**		**33,165**	16,368
	Profit attributable to:			
1p83(a)(ii), 1p83(a)(i)	Owners of the parent		**30,617**	15,512
27p27	Non-controlling interests		**2,548**	856
			33,165	16,368
	Earnings per share from continuing and discontinued operations attributable to the equity holders of the company during the year (expressed in C per share)			
	Basic earnings per share			
33p66	From continuing operations	14	**1.31**	0.75
33p68	From discontinued operations[3]		**0.01**	0.01
33p66	From profit for the year		**1.32**	0.76
	Diluted earnings per share			
33p66	From continuing operations	14	**1.19**	0.71
33p68	From discontinued operations		**0.01**	0.01
33p66	From profit for the year		**1.20**	0.72

The notes on pages 15 to 74 are an integral part of these consolidated financial statements.

CA06 s408 The company has elected to take the exemption under section 408 of the Companies Act 2006 not to present the parent company profit and loss account.

The profit for the parent company for the year was C9,098 (2010: C10,491).

---

[1] This income statement presents expenses by function. See Commentary, paras 12 and 13.
[2] IAS 1 does not prescribe the disclosure of operating profit on the face of the income statement. However, entities are not prohibited from disclosing this or a similar line item.
[3] EPS for discontinued operations may be given in the notes to the accounts instead of in the income statement.

(All amounts in C thousands unless otherwise stated)

Consolidated statement of comprehensive income

			Group Year ended 31 December	
		Note	2011	2010
	Profit for the year		**33,165**	16,368
	Other comprehensive income:			
1p82(g)	Gains on revaluation of land and buildings	29	**755**	759
IFRS7p20(a)(ii)	Change in value of available-for-sale financial assets	29	**362**	62
1p82(h)	Share of other comprehensive income of associates	29	**(86)**	91
19p93B, 1p82(g)	Actuarial loss on post employment benefit obligations	28, 33	**–**	(494)
1p82(g)	Impact of change in Euravian tax rate on deferred tax[1]	28, 32	**(10)**	–
IFRS7p23(c)	Cash flow hedges	29	**64**	(3)
1p82(g)	Net investment hedge	29	**(45)**	40
1p82(g), 21p52(b)	Currency translation differences	29	**2,413**	(1,111)
IFRS3p59, 1p82(g)	Recycling of revaluation of previously held interest in ABC Group	29, 39	**(850)**	850
	Other comprehensive income for the year, net of tax		**2,603**	194
1p82(i)	**Total comprehensive income for the year**		**35,768**	16,562
	Attributable to:			
1p83(b)(ii)	– Owners of the parent		**32,968**	15,746
1p83(b)(i)	– Non-controlling interests		**2,800**	816
	Total comprehensive income for the year		**35,768**	16,562
	Total comprehensive income attributable to equity shareholders arises from:			
	– Continuing operations		**32,868**	15,626
IFRS5p33(d)	– Discontinued operations	25	**100**	120
			32,968	15,746

Items in the statement above are disclosed net of tax. The income tax relating to each component of other comprehensive income is disclosed in note 13.

The notes on pages 15 to 74 are an integral part of these consolidated financial statements.

Commentary – income statement and statement of comprehensive income

The commentary that follows explains some of the key requirements in IAS 1, 'Presentation of financial statements', and other requirements that impact the income statement/statement of comprehensive income.

1p81   1. Entities have a choice of presenting all items of income and expense recognised in a period either:
(a) in a single statement of comprehensive income; or
(b) in two statements (as adopted by IFRS GAAP plc) comprising:
  (i) a separate income statement, which displays components of profit or loss; and
  (ii) a statement of comprehensive income, which begins with profit or loss and displays components of other comprehensive income.
The main difference between these two options is that in option (a), profit for the year is shown as a sub-total rather than the 'bottom line', and the statement continues down to total comprehensive income for the year.

1p82   2. A single statement of comprehensive income includes, as a minimum, the following line items:
(a) Revenue.
(b) Finance costs.
(c) Share of the profit or loss of associates and joint ventures accounted for using the equity method.
(d) Tax expense.
(e) A single amount comprising the total of:
  (i) the post-tax profit or loss of discontinued operations; and
  (ii) the post-tax gain or loss recognised on the measurement to fair value less costs to sell or on the disposal of the assets or disposal group(s) constituting the discontinued operation.
(f) Profit or loss.
(g) Each component of other comprehensive income classified by nature.
(h) Share of the other comprehensive income of associates and joint ventures accounted for using the equity method.
(i) Total comprehensive income.

[1] The impact of change in Euravian tax rate is shown for illustrative purposes. UK Companies with 31 December 2011 year ends will need to consider the impact of the reduction in tax rates in the Finance (No.2) Act 2010.

(All amounts in C thousands unless otherwise stated)

1p83   3. The following items are disclosed as allocations for the period:
(a) Profit or loss attributable to:
    (i) non-controlling interests; and
    (ii) owners.
(b) Total comprehensive income for the period attributable to:
    (i) non-controlling interests; and
    (ii) owners.

IFRS5 p33(d)   (c) The amount of income attributable to equity holders of the company from:
    (i) continuing operations; and
    (ii) discontinued operations.

1p84   4. If the entity prepares a separate income statement, this includes:
(a) Items (a)-(f) in paragraph 2 above.
(b) Item (a) in paragraph 3 above.

1p12   5. If the two-statement presentation is used, the statement of comprehensive income follows immediately after the income statement.

1p85   6. Additional line items, headings and subtotals are presented in the statement of comprehensive income and the income statement (where presented) when such presentation is relevant to an understanding of the entity's financial performance. For example, a sub-total of gross profit (revenue less cost of sales) may be included where expenses have been classified by function.

7. Additional sub-headings should be used with care. The apparent flexibility in IAS 1 can only be used to enhance users' understanding of the GAAP-compliant numbers. It cannot be used to detract from the GAAP numbers. Set out below are overall principles that entities should apply when presenting additional line items, headings, sub-totals and alternative performance measures:
(a) GAAP numbers should be given at least equal prominence to non-GAAP numbers.
(b) Additional line items, sub-totals and columns may be used, but only if they do not detract from the GAAP numbers by introducing bias or by overcrowding the income statement.
(c) Each additional line item or column should contain all the revenue or expenses that relate to the particular line item or column inserted.
(d) Each additional line item or column should contain only revenue or expense that is revenue or expense of the entity itself.
(e) Items may be segregated (for example, by use of columns or sub-totals) where they are different in nature or function from other items in the income statement.
(f) It is generally not permissible to mix natural and functional classifications of expenses where these categories of expenses overlap.
(g) Terms used for additional line items and sub-totals should be defined if they are not terms recognised in IFRS.
(h) Additional line items, columns and sub-totals should only be presented when they are used internally to manage the business.
(i) Various presentations will be acceptable individually, but consideration should be given to the aggregate effect of these presentations, so that the overall message of the income statement is not distorted or confused.
(j) The presentation method should generally be consistent from year to year.
(k) The presentation method should comply with any local regulatory rules.

8. EBIT (earnings before interest and tax) may be an appropriate sub-heading to show in the income statement. This line item usually distinguishes between the pre-tax profits arising from operating activities and those arising from financing activities.

9. In contrast, a sub-total for EBITDA (earnings before interest, tax, depreciation and amortisation) can only be included as a sub-total where the entity presents its expenses by nature and provided the sub-total does not detract from the GAAP numbers either by implying that EBITDA is the 'real' profit or by overcrowding the income statement so that the reader cannot determine easily the entity's GAAP performance. Where an entity presents its expenses by function, it will not be possible to show depreciation and amortisation as separate line items in arriving at operating profit, because depreciation and amortisation are types of expense, not functions of the business. In this case, EBITDA can only be disclosed by way of supplemental information in a box, in a footnote, in the notes or in the review of operations.

Material items of income and expense

1p97   10. When items of income and expense are material, their nature and amount is disclosed separately either in the income statement or in the notes. In the case of IFRS GAAP plc these disclosures are made in note 6. Some entities provide this information on the face of the income statement in the form of additional analyses, boxes or columns. Further discussion is available in the Manual of Accounting.

1p85, 97   11. IAS 1 does not provide a specific name for the types of items that should be separately disclosed. Where an entity discloses a separate category of 'exceptional', 'significant' or 'unusual' items either in the income statement or in the

(All amounts in C thousands unless otherwise stated)

notes, the accounting policy note should include a definition of the chosen term. The presentation and definition of these items should be applied consistently from year to year.

Analysis of expenses by nature or function

12. Where an entity classifies its expenses by nature, it must take care to ensure that each class of expense includes all items related to that class. Material restructuring cost may, for example, include redundancy payments (employee benefit cost), inventory write-downs (changes in inventory) and impairments in property, plant and equipment. It is not normally acceptable to show restructuring costs as a separate line item in an analysis of expenses by nature where there is an overlap with other line items.

13. Entities that classify their expenses by function include the material items within the function to which they relate. In this case, material items can be disclosed as footnotes or in the notes to the financial statements.

Operating profit

1BC56

14. An entity may elect to include a sub-total for its result from operating activities. This is permitted, but care should be taken that the amount disclosed is representative of activities that would normally be considered to be 'operating'. Items that are clearly of an operating nature (for example, inventory write-downs, restructuring and relocation expenses) are not excluded simply because they occur infrequently or are unusual in amount. Nor can expenses be excluded on the grounds that they do not involve cash flows (for example, depreciation or amortisation). As a general rule, operating profit is the subtotal after 'other expenses' – that is, excluding finance costs and the share of profits of equity-accounted investments – although in some circumstances it may be appropriate for the share of profits of equity-accounted investments to be included in operating profit (see paragraph 16 below).

Re-ordering of line items

1p86

15. The line items and descriptions of those items are re-ordered where this is necessary to explain the elements of performance. However, entities are required to make a 'fair presentation' and should not make any changes unless there is a good reason to do so.

16. Normally, the share of profit of associates is shown after finance costs; this recognises that the share of profits from associates arises from what is essentially an investing activity, rather than part of the group's operating activities. However, were associates (and joint ventures) an integral vehicle for the conduct of the group's operations and its strategy, it may be more appropriate to show finance costs after the share of profit of associates and joint ventures. In such cases, it may be appropriate either to insert a sub-total 'profit before finance costs' or to include the share of profits from associates and joint ventures in arriving at operating profit (if disclosed). It would not, however, be appropriate to include the share of associates and joint ventures within 'revenue' (and, therefore, within 'gross profit').

17. Finance revenue cannot be netted against finance costs; it is included in 'other revenue/other income' or shown separately in the income statement. Where finance income is an incidental benefit, it is acceptable to present finance revenue immediately before finance costs and include a sub-total of 'net finance costs' in the income statement. Where earning interest income is one of the entity's main line of business, it is presented as 'revenue'.

Discontinued operations

1p82(e)
IFRS5
p33(a)(b)

18. As stated in paragraph 2(e) above, entities disclose a single amount in the statement of comprehensive income (or separate income statement), comprising the total of (i) the post-tax profit or loss of discontinued operations, and (ii) the post-tax gain or loss recognised on the measurement to fair value less costs to sell or on the disposal of the assets or disposal group(s) constituting the discontinued operation. Paragraph 33 of IFRS 5, 'Non-current assets held for sale and discontinued operations', also requires an analysis of this single amount. This analysis may be presented in the notes or in the statement of comprehensive income (separate income statement). If it is presented in the income statement, it should be presented in a section identified as relating to discontinued operations – that is, separate from continuing operations. The analysis is not required for disposal groups that are newly acquired subsidiaries that meet the criteria to be classified as held for sale on acquisition (see IFRS 5 para 11).

Earnings per share

33p66

19. IAS 33, 'Earnings per share', requires an entity to present in the statement of comprehensive income basic and diluted earnings per share (EPS) for profit or loss from continuing operations attributable to the ordinary equity holders of the parent entity and for total profit or loss attributable to the ordinary equity holders of the parent entity for each class of ordinary shares. Basic and diluted EPS are disclosed with equal prominence for all periods presented.

33p67A

20. If an entity presents a separate income statement, basic and diluted earnings per share are presented at the end of that statement.

33p73

21. Earnings per share based on alternative measures of earnings may also be given if considered necessary but should be presented in the notes to the financial statements only.

(All amounts in C thousands unless otherwise stated)

33p67	22. If diluted EPS is reported for at least one period, it should be reported for all periods presented, even if it equals basic EPS. If basic and diluted EPS are equal, dual presentation can be accomplished in one line in the statement of comprehensive income.
33p68	23. An entity that reports a discontinued operation discloses the basic and diluted amounts per share for the discontinued operation either in the statement of comprehensive income or in the notes to the financial statements.
33p69, 41, 43	24. Basic and diluted EPS are disclosed even if the amounts are negative (that is, a loss per share). However, potential ordinary shares are only dilutive if their conversion would increase the loss per share. If the loss decreases, the shares are anti-dilutive.
33p4	25. When an entity presents both consolidated financial statements and separate financial statements prepared in accordance with IAS 27, 'Consolidated and separate financial statements', the disclosures required by IAS 33 are presented only on the basis of the consolidated information. An entity that chooses to disclose EPS based on its separate financial statements presents such EPS information only in its separate statement of comprehensive income.

Components of other comprehensive income

1p7	26. Components of other comprehensive income (OCI) are items of income and expense (including reclassification adjustments) that are not recognised in profit or loss as required or permitted by other IFRSs. They include: changes in the revaluation surplus relating to property, plant and equipment or intangible assets; actuarial gains and losses on defined benefit plans; gains and losses arising from translating the financial statements of a foreign operation; gains and losses on re-measuring available-for-sale financial assets; and the effective portion of gains and losses on hedging instruments in a cash flow hedge.
1p91 1p90	27. Entities may present components of other comprehensive income either net of related tax effect or before related tax effects. IFRS GAAP plc has chosen to present the items net of tax. In this case the amount of income tax relating to each component of OCI, including reclassification adjustments, is disclosed in the notes.
1p92, 94	28. An entity discloses separately any reclassification adjustments relating to components of other comprehensive income either in the statement of comprehensive income or in the notes. IFRS GAAP plc provides this information in note 29, 'Other reserves'.
1p7, 95	29. Reclassification adjustments are amounts reclassified to profit or loss in the current period that were recognised in other comprehensive income in the current or previous periods. They arise, for example, on disposal of a foreign operation, on derecognition of an available-for-sale financial asset and when a hedged forecast transaction affects profit or loss.
	30.1 IAS 1 has been amended, effective for annual periods beginning on or after 1 July 2012. The amendment requires items of other comprehensive income, classified by nature, to be grouped into those that will be reclassified subsequently to profit or loss when specific conditions are met and those that will not be reclassified to profit or loss. The amendment also requires that if an entity presents items of other comprehensive income before related tax effects with the aggregate tax shown separately, it should allocate the tax between the items that might be reclassified subsequently to the profit or loss section and those that will not be reclassified.
1p107	31. The amount of dividends recognised as distributions to owners during the period and the related amount per share are presented either in the statement of changes in equity or in the notes. Dividends cannot be displayed in the statement of comprehensive income or income statement.

Consistency

1p45	32. The presentation and classification of items in the financial statements is retained from one period to the next unless: (a) it is apparent, following a significant change in the nature of the entity's operations or a review of its financial statements that another presentation or classification would be more appropriate, addressing the criteria for the selection and application of accounting policies in IAS 8, 'Accounting policies, changes in accounting estimates and errors'; or (b) IFRS requires a change in presentation.

Materiality and aggregation

1p29	33. Each material class of similar items is presented separately in the financial statements. Items of a dissimilar nature or function are presented separately unless they are immaterial.

(All amounts in C thousands unless otherwise stated)

Offsetting

1p32 34. Assets and liabilities, and income and expenses, are not offset unless required or permitted by an IFRS. Examples of income and expenses that are required or permitted to be offset are as follows:

1p34(a) (a) Gains and losses on the disposal of non-current assets, including investments and operating assets, are reported by deducting from the proceeds on disposal the carrying amount of the asset and related selling expenses.

1p34(b) (b) Expenditure related to a provision that is recognised in accordance with IAS 37, 'Provisions, contingent liabilities and contingent assets', and reimbursed under a contractual arrangement with a third party (for example, a supplier's warranty agreement) may be netted against the related reimbursement.

1p35 (c) Gains and losses arising from a group of similar transactions are reported on a net basis (for example, foreign exchange gains and losses or gains and losses arising on financial instruments held for trading). However, such gains and losses are reported separately if they are material.

Summary

35. The requirements surrounding components of OCI can be summarised as follows:

Item	Reference	Requirement in standard	Presentation in IFRS GAAP plc
Each component of other comprehensive income recognised during the period, classified by nature	IAS 1 p82(g)	Statement of comprehensive income	Statement of comprehensive income
Reclassification adjustments during the period relating to components of other comprehensive income	IAS 1 p92	Statement of comprehensive income or notes	Note 29
Tax relating to each component of other comprehensive income, including reclassification adjustments	IAS 1 p90	Statement of comprehensive income or notes	Note 13
Reconciliation for each component of equity, showing separately: – Profit/loss – Other comprehensive income – Transactions with owners	IAS 1 p106(d)	Statement of changes in equity	Statement of changes in equity
For each component of equity, an analysis of other comprehensive income by item	IAS 1p106A	Statement of changes in equity or notes	Note 29

(All amounts in C thousands unless otherwise stated)

Consolidated balance sheet

		Note	Group As at 31 December 2011	Group As at 31 December 2010	Company As at 31 December 2011	Company As at 31 December 2010
1p10(a), 113	**Assets**					
1p60, 66	**Non-current assets**					
1p54(a)	Property, plant and equipment	16	**155,341**	100,233	–	–
1p54(c)	Intangible assets	17	**26,272**	20,700	–	–
	Investments in subsidiaries	12a	**–**	–	**38,592**	22,170
1p54(e),28p38	Investments in associates	12b	**13,373**	13,244	–	–
1p54(o),56	Deferred income tax assets	32	**3,520**	3,321	–	–
1p54(d), IFRS7p8(d)	Available-for-sale financial assets	19	**17,420**	14,910	–	–
1p54(d), IFRS7p8(a)	Derivative financial instruments	20	**395**	245	–	–
1p54(h), IFRS7p8(c)	Trade and other receivables	21	**2,322**	1,352	–	–
			218,643	154,005	**38,592**	22,170
1p60, 1p66	**Current assets**					
1p54(g)	Inventories	22	**24,700**	18,182	–	–
1p54(h), IFRS7p8(c)	Trade and other receivables	21	**19,765**	18,330	**41,147**	31,296
1p54(d), IFRS7p8(d)	Available-for-sale financial assets	19	**1,950**	–	–	–
1p54(d), IFRS7p8(a)	Derivative financial instruments	20	**1,069**	951	–	–
1p54(d), IFRS7p8(a)	Financial assets at fair value through profit or loss	23	**11,820**	7,972	–	–
1p54(i), IFRS7p8	Cash and cash equivalents (excluding bank overdrafts)	24	**17,928**	34,062	**3,261**	6,234
			77,232	79,497	**44,408**	37,530
IFRS5p38,40	Assets of disposal group classified as held for sale	25	**3,333**	–	–	–
			80,565	79,497	**44,408**	37,530
	Total assets		**299,208**	233,502	**83,000**	59,700
	Equity and liabilities					
1p54(r)	**Equity attributable to owners of the parent**					
1p78(e) 1p54(r)	Ordinary shares	26	**25,300**	21,000	**25,300**	21,000
1p78(e),1p55	Share premium	26	**17,144**	10,494	**17,144**	10,494
1p78(e)	Other reserves	29	**11,435**	7,005	–	–
1p78(e), 1p55	Retained earnings	28	**70,006**	48,681	**8,735**	11,613
			123,885	87,180	**51,179**	43,107
1p54(q)	**Non-controlling interests**		**7,888**	1,766	–	–
	Total equity		**131,773**	88,946	**51,179**	43,107
	Liabilities					
1p60,69	**Non-current liabilities**					
1p54(m), IFRS7p8(f)	Borrowings	31	**115,121**	96,346	–	–
1p54(m), IFRS7p8(e)	Derivative financial instruments	20	**135**	129	–	–
1p54(o), 1p56	Deferred income tax liabilities	32	**12,370**	9,053	–	–
1p55, 1p78(d)	Retirement benefit obligations	33	**4,635**	2,233	–	–
1p54(l), 1p78(d)	Provisions for other liabilities and charges	34	**1,320**	274	–	–
			133,581	108,035	–	–

(All amounts in C thousands unless otherwise stated)

		Group		Company	
		As at 31 December		**As at 31 December**	
	Note	**2011**	2010	**2011**	2010
Current liabilities					
Trade and other payables	30	**16,670**	12,478	**31,821**	16,593
Current income tax liabilities		**2,566**	2,771	–	–
Borrowings	31	**11,716**	18,258	–	–
Derivative financial instruments	20	**460**	618	–	–
Provisions for other liabilities and charges	34	**2,222**	2,396	–	–
		33,634	36,521	**31,821**	16,593
Liabilities of disposal group classified as held-for-sale	25	**220**	–	–	–
		33,854	36,521	**31,821**	16,593
Total liabilities		**167,435**	144,556	**31,821**	16,593
Total equity and liabilities		**299,208**	233,502	**83,000**	59,700

1p60, 1p69 / 1p54(k), IFRS7p8(f) / 1p54(n) / 1p54(m), IFRS7p8(f) / 1p54(m), IFRS7p8(e) / 1p54(l) / IFRS5p38, 1p54(p)

10p17 The notes on pages 15 to 74 are an integral part of these consolidated financial statements.

The financial statements on pages 15 to 74 were authorised for issue by the board of directors on 24 February 2012 and were signed on its behalf.

CD Suede
Chief Executive

G Wallace
Finance Director
IFRS GAAP PLC
Registered no. xxyyzz

Commentary – balance sheet

The commentary that follows explains some of the key requirements in IAS 1, 'Presentation of financial statements', that impact the balance sheet/statement of financial position.

1p10 1. IAS 1 refers to the balance sheet as the 'statement of financial position'. This title is not mandatory, so IFRS GAAP plc has elected to retain the better-known title of 'balance sheet'.

1p54, 55 2. Paragraph 54 of IAS 1 sets out the line items that are, as a minimum, required to be presented in the balance sheet. Additional line items, headings and subtotals are presented in the balance sheet when such presentation is relevant to an understanding of the entity's financial position.

1p77, 78 3. An entity discloses, either in the balance sheet or in the notes, further sub- classifications of the line items presented, classified in a manner appropriate to the entity's operations. The detail provided in sub-classifications depends on the IFRS requirements and on the size, nature and function of the amounts involved.

Current/non-current distinction

1p60 4. An entity presents current and non-current assets, and current and non-current liabilities, as separate classifications in its balance sheet except when a presentation based on liquidity provides information that is reliable and is more relevant. When that exception applies, all assets and liabilities are presented broadly in order of liquidity.

1p61 5. Whichever method of presentation is adopted, an entity discloses for each asset and liability line item that combines amounts expected to be recovered or settled (a) no more than 12 months after the reporting period; and (b) more than 12 months after the reporting period, the amount expected to be recovered or settled after more than 12 months.

1p66-70 6. Current assets include assets (such as inventories and trade receivables) that are sold, consumed or realised as part of the normal operating cycle even when they are not expected to be realised within 12 months after the reporting period. Some current liabilities, such as trade payables and some accruals for employee and other operating costs, are part of the working capital used in the entity's normal operating cycle. Such operating items are classified as current liabilities even if they are due to be settled more than 12 months after the reporting period.

(All amounts in C thousands unless otherwise stated)

| 1p68 | 7. The operating cycle of an entity is the time between the acquisition of assets for processing and their realisation in the form of cash or cash equivalents. When the entity's normal operating cycle is not clearly identifiable, its duration is assumed to be 12 months. |

Consistency

| 1p45 | 8. The presentation and classification of items in the financial statements is retained from one period to the next unless:
| | (a) it is apparent, following a significant change in the nature of the entity's operations or a review of its financial statements, that another presentation or classification would be more appropriate according to the criteria for selecting and applying accounting policies in IAS 8, 'Accounting policies, changes in accounting estimates and errors'; or
| | (b) an IFRS requires a change in presentation. |

Materiality and aggregation

| 1p29 | 9. Each material class of similar items is presented separately in the financial statements. Items of a dissimilar nature or function are presented separately unless they are immaterial.
| | *Current and deferred tax assets and liabilities* |

| 1p54, 56 | 10. Current and deferred tax assets and liabilities are presented separately from each other and from other assets and liabilities. When a distinction is made between current and non-current assets and liabilities in the balance sheet, deferred tax assets and liabilities are presented as non-current. |

Offsetting

| 1p32 | 11. An entity does not offset assets and liabilities unless required or permitted to by an IFRS. Measuring assets net of valuation allowances – for example, obsolescence allowances on inventories and doubtful debt allowances on receivables – is not offsetting. |

Three balance sheets required in certain circumstances

| 1p39 | 12. If an entity has applied an accounting policy retrospectively, restated items retrospectively or reclassified items in its financial statements, it provides a third balance sheet as at the beginning of the earliest comparative period presented. However, where the retrospective change in policy or the restatement has no effect on this earliest statement of financial position, we believe that it would be sufficient for the entity merely to disclose that fact. |

(All amounts in C thousands unless otherwise stated)

Consolidated statement of changes in equity[1]

1p108,109		Notes	Share capital	Share premium	Other reserves[2]	Retained earnings	Total	Non-controlling interest	Total equity
			Attributable to equity holders of the company						
	Balance at 1 January 2010		20,000	10,424	6,364	48,470	85,258	1,500	86,758
1p106(d)(i)	Profit for the year		–	–	–	15,512	15,512	856	16,368
	Other comprehensive income for the year[3]				641	(407)	234	(40)	194
1p106(a)	**Total comprehensive income for the year**		**–**	**–**	**641**	**15,105**	**15,746**	**816**	**16,562**
IFRS2p50	Value of employee services	28	–	–	–	822	822	–	822
	Tax credit relating to share option scheme	28	–	–	–	20	20	–	20
	Proceeds from shares issued	26	1,000	70	–	–	1,070	–	1,070
1p106(d)(iii)	Dividends to equity holders of the company	35	–	–	–	(15,736)	(15,736)	(550)	(16,286)
1p106(d)(iii)	**Total contributions by and distributions to owners of the company, recognised directly in equity**		**1,000**	**70**	**–**	**(14,894)**	**(13,824)**	**(550)**	**(14,374)**
	Balance at 31 December 2010		**21,000**	**10,494**	**7,005**	**48,681**	**87,180**	**1,766**	**88,946**
	Balance at 1 January 2011		21,000	10,494	7,005	48,681	87,180	1,766	88,946
1p106(d)(i)	Profit for the year		–	–	–	30,617	30,617	2,548	33,165
	Other comprehensive income for the year[3]		–	–	2,261	90	2,351	252	2,603
1p106(a)	**Total comprehensive income for the year**		**–**	**–**	**2,261**	**30,707**	**32,968**	**2,800**	**35,768**
IFRS2p50	Value of employee services	28	–	–	–	690	690	–	690
	Tax credit relating to share option scheme	28	–	–	–	30	30	–	30
	Proceeds from shares issued	26	750	200	–	–	950	–	950
	Purchase of treasury shares	29	–	–	(2,564)	–	(2,564)	–	(2,564)
	Issue of ordinary shares related to business combination	26	3,550	6,450	–	–	10,000	–	10,000
	Convertible bond – equity component	29	–	–	5,433	–	5,433	–	5,433
1p106(d)(iii)	Dividends to equity holders of the company	35	–	–	–	(10,102)	(10,102)	(1,920)	(12,022)
1p106(d)(iii)	**Total contributions by and distributions to owners of the Company**		**4,300**	**6,650**	**2,869**	**(9,382)**	**4,437**	**(1,920)**	**2,517**

[1] A statement of changes in equity for the company is required by IAS 1. It has not been included in this set of illustrative financial statements.
[2] Individual reserves can be grouped into 'other reserves' in the statement of changes in equity if these are similar in nature and can be regarded as a component of equity. If the individual reserves are not shown in the statement of changes in equity, an analysis should be given in the notes.
[3] The single-line presentation for other comprehensive income illustrated above reflects the group's application of the amendment to IAS 1 arising from 'Improvements to IFRSs' issued in 2010. Management can implement this by either (a) showing each line item of other comprehensive income separately in the above statement; or (b) by having a single-line presentation of other comprehensive income (as shown above) plus a separate note showing an analysis of each item of other comprehensive income for each component of equity. This has not been illustrated in these financial statements.

(All amounts in C thousands unless otherwise stated)

	Notes	Share capital	Share premium	Other reserves	Retained earnings	Total	Non-controlling interest	Total equity
						Attributable to equity holders of the company		
1p106(d)(iii) Non-controlling interest arising on business combination	39	–	–	–	–	–	4,542	4,542
1p106(d)(iii) Acquisition of non-controlling interest in XYZ Group	40	–	–	(400)	–	(400)	(300)	(700)
1p106(d)(iii) Decrease in ownership	40	–	–	(300)	–	(300)	1000	700
1p106(d)(iii) **Total transactions with owners of the company, recognised directly in equity**		**4,300**	**6,650**	**2,869**	**(9,382)**	**4,437**	**2,622**	**7,059**
Balance at 31 December 2011		**25,300**	**17,144**	**11,435**	**70,006**	**123,885**	**7,888**	**131,773**

The notes to pages 15 to 74 are an integral part of these consolidated financial statements.

Commentary – statement of changes in equity

The commentary that follows explains some of the key requirements in IAS 1, 'Presentation of financial statements', and other aspects that impact the statement of changes in equity.

Non-controlling interest

1p106

1. Information to be included in the statement of changes in equity includes:
   (a) Total comprehensive income for the period, showing separately the total amounts attributable to equity holders of the company and to non-controlling interest.
   (b) For each component of equity, the effects of retrospective application or retrospective restatement recognised in accordance with IAS 8.
   (c) For each component of equity, a reconciliation between the carrying amount at the beginning and the end of the period, separately disclosing changes resulting from:
      (i) profit or loss;
      (ii) other comprehensive income; and
      (iii) transactions with owners in their capacity as owners, showing separately contributions by and distributions to owners and changes in ownership interests in subsidiaries that do not result in loss of control.
2. IAS 1 was amended in the 2010 'Improvements to IFRSs' issued in May 2010. The amendment clarifies that for each component of equity, the analysis of other comprehensive income by item may be presented either in the statement of changes in equity or disclosed within the notes. The amendment is applicable for annual periods beginning on or after 1 January 2011.

(All amounts in C thousands unless otherwise stated)

Consolidated statement of cash flows

			Group Year ended 31 December		Company Year ended 31 December	
7p10, 18(b), 1p38 1p113		Note	2011	2010	2011	2010
	Cash flows from operating activities					
	Cash generated from operations	36	**56,234**	41,776	**(4,693)**	(4,315)
7p31	Interest paid		**(7,835)**	(14,773)	–	–
7p35	Income tax paid		**(14,317)**	(10,526)	–	–
	Net cash generated from operating activities		**34,082**	16,477	**(4,693)**	(4,315)
7p21, 7p10	**Cash flows from investing activities**					
7p39	Acquisition of subsidiary, net of cash acquired	39	**(3,950)**	–	**(4,250)**	–
7p16(a)	Purchases of property, plant and equipment (PPE)	16	**(9,505)**	(6,042)	–	–
7p16(b)	Proceeds from sale of PPE	36	**6,354**	2,979	–	–
7p16(a)	Purchases of intangible assets	17	**(3,050)**	(700)	–	–
7p16(c)	Purchases of available-for-sale financial assets	19	**(2,781)**	(1,126)	–	–
7p16(e)	Loans granted to associates	41	**(1,000)**	(50)	–	–
7p16(f)	Loan repayments received from associates	41	**14**	64	–	–
7p16(e)	Loans granted to subsidiary undertakings		–	–	**(9,851)**	–
7p16(f)	Loan repayments received from subsidiary undertakings		–	–	–	1,126
7p31	Interest received		**1,054**	1,193	–	–
7p31	Dividends received		**1,130**	1,120	**13,809**	14,806
	Net cash used in investing activities		**(11,734)**	(2,562)	**(292)**	15,932
7p21, 7p10	**Cash flows from financing activities**					
7p17(a)	Proceeds from issuance of ordinary shares	26	**950**	1,070	**950**	1,070
7p17(b)	Purchase of treasury shares	28	**(2,564)**	–	**(2,564)**	–
7p17(c)	Proceeds from issuance of convertible bonds	31	**50,000**	–	–	–
7p17(c)	Proceeds from issuance of redeemable preference shares	31	–	30,000	–	–
7p17(c)	Proceeds from borrowings		**8,500**	18,000	–	–
7p17(d)	Repayments of borrowings		**(78,117)**	(34,674)	–	–
7p17(c)	Proceeds from loan from subsidiary undertaking		–	–	**13,210**	7,209
7p31	Dividends paid to company's shareholders	35	**(10,102)**	(15,736)	**(10,102)**	(15,736)
7p31	Dividends paid to holders of redeemable preferences shares		**(1,950)**	(1,950)	–	–
7p31	Dividends paid to non-controlling interests		**(1,920)**	(550)	–	–
	Net cash used in financing activities		**(35,203)**	(3,840)	**1,494**	(7,457)
	Net (decrease)/increase in cash and cash equivalents		**(12,855)**	10,075	**(3,491)**	4,160
	Cash, cash equivalents and bank overdrafts at beginning of year	24	**27,598**	17,587	**6,234**	2,074
	Exchange gains/(losses) on cash and cash equivalents		**535**	(64)	–	–
	Cash and cash equivalents at end of year	24	**15,278**	27,598	**2,743**	6,234

The notes on pages 15 to 74 are an integral part of these consolidated financial statements.

(All amounts in C thousands unless otherwise stated)

Commentary – statement of cash flows

The commentary that follows explains some of the key requirements in IAS 7, 'Statements of cash flows'.

Reporting cash flows

Cash flows from operating activities

7p18
1. Cash flows from operating activities are reported using either:
(a) the direct method, whereby major classes of gross cash receipts and gross cash payments are disclosed; or
(b) the indirect method, whereby profit or loss is adjusted for the effects of transactions of a non-cash nature, any deferrals or accruals of past or future operating cash receipts or payments, and items of income or expense associated with investing or financing cash flows.

7p20
2. IFRS GAAP plc continues to use the indirect method. For an illustration of a statement of cash flows presented using the direct method, refer to appendix I.

Cash flows from investing and financing activities

7p21
3. Major classes of gross cash receipts and gross cash payments arising from investing and financing activities are reported separately, except to the extent that cash flows described in paragraphs 22 and 24 of IAS 7 are reported on a net basis.

Sale of property, plant and equipment held for rental to others

7p14
4. Cash flows from the sale of property, plant and equipment are normally presented as cash flows from investing activities. However, cash payments to manufacture or acquire assets that will be held for rental to others and subsequently for sale are cash flows from operating activities. The cash receipts from rents and subsequent sales of such assets are also therefore cash flows from operating activities.

Reporting on a net basis

7p22, 23
5. Cash flows arising from the following operating, investing or financing activities may be reported on a net basis:
(a) cash receipts and payments on behalf of customers when the cash flows reflect the activities of the customer rather than those of the entity (for example, rents collected on behalf of, and paid over to, the owners of properties); and
(b) cash receipts and payments for items in which the turnover is quick, the amounts are large, and the maturities are short (for example, advances made for, and repayment of, principal amounts relating to credit card customers).

7p24
6. Cash flows arising from each of the following activities of a financial institution may be reported on a net basis:
(a) Cash receipts and payments for the acceptance and repayment of deposits with a fixed maturity date.
(b) The placement of deposits with, and withdrawal of deposits from, other financial institutions.
(c) Cash advances and loans made to customers and the repayment of those advances and loans.

Interest and dividends

7p31
7. Cash flows from interest and dividends received and paid are each disclosed separately. Each is classified in a consistent manner from period to period as either operating, investing or financing activities.

7p33
8. Interest paid and interest and dividends received are usually classified as operating cash flows for a financial institution. However, there is no consensus on the classification of these cash flows for other entities. Interest paid and interest and dividends received may be classified as operating cash flows because they enter into the determination of net profit or loss. Alternatively, interest paid and interest and dividends received may be classified as financing cash flows and investing cash flows respectively, because they are costs of obtaining financial resources or returns on investments.

7p34
9. Dividends paid may be classified as 'financing cash flows' because they are a cost of obtaining financial resources. Alternatively, they may be classified as operating cash flows to assist users to determine the ability of an entity to pay dividends out of operating cash flows.

Income taxes

7p35
10. Cash flows arising from income taxes are separately disclosed and classified as cash flows from operating activities unless they can be specifically identified with financing and investing activities.

(All amounts in C thousands unless otherwise stated)

Effects of exchange rate changes

7p28   11. Unrealised gains and losses arising from changes in foreign currency exchange rates are not cash flows. However, the effect of exchange rate changes on cash and cash equivalents held or due in a foreign currency are reported in the statement of cash flows in order to reconcile cash and cash equivalents at the beginning and the end of the period. This amount is presented separately from cash flows from operating, investing and financing activities. It also includes the differences, if any, had those cash flows been reported at period-end exchange rates.

Additional recommended disclosures

7p50   12. Additional information may be relevant to users in understanding the financial position and liquidity of an entity. Disclosure of this information, together with a commentary by management, is encouraged and may include:

7p50(a)   (a)   The amount of undrawn borrowing facilities that may be available for future operating activities and to settle capital commitments, indicating any restrictions on the use of these facilities.

7p50(c)   (b)   The aggregate amount of cash flows that represent increases in operating capacity separately from those cash flows that are required to maintain operating capacity.

7p50(d)   (c)   The amount of the cash flows arising from the operating, investing and financing activities of each reportable segment (see IFRS 8, 'Operating segments').

(All amounts in C thousands unless otherwise stated)

Notes to the consolidated financial statements

1 General information

1p138(b)-(c)

1p51(a)(b)

IFRS GAAP plc ('the company') and its subsidiaries (together, 'the group') manufacture distribute and sell shoes through a network of independent retailers. The group has manufacturing plants around the world and sells mainly in countries within the UK, the US, Europe and Russia. During the year, the group acquired control of 'ABC Group', a shoe and leather goods retailer operating in the US and most western European countries.

1p138(a)

The company is a public limited company, which is listed on the London Stock Exchange and incorporated and domiciled in the UK. The address of its registered office is Nice Walk Way, London, UK.

2 Summary of significant accounting policies

1p112(a)
1p117(b)
1p119

The principal accounting policies applied in the preparation of these consolidated financial statements are set out below. These policies have been consistently applied to all the years presented, unless otherwise stated.

2.1 Basis of preparation

1p116
1p117(a)

The consolidated financial statements of IFRS GAAP plc have been prepared in accordance with International Financial Reporting Standards as adopted by the European Union (IFRSs as adopted by the EU), and the Companies Act 2006 applicable to companies reporting under IFRS. The consolidated financial statements have been prepared under the historical cost convention, as modified by the revaluation of land and buildings, available-for-sale financial assets, and financial assets and financial liabilities (including derivative instruments) at fair value through profit or loss.

The preparation of financial statements in conformity with IFRS requires the use of certain critical accounting estimates. It also requires management to exercise its judgement in the process of applying the group's accounting policies. The areas involving a higher degree of judgement or complexity, or areas where assumptions and estimates are significant to the consolidated financial statements are disclosed in note 4.

2.1.1 Going concern

C.1.3

The group meets its day-to-day working capital requirements through its bank facilities. The current economic conditions continue to create uncertainty particularly over (a) the level of demand for the group's products; and (b) the availability of bank finance for the foreseeable future. The group's forecasts and projections, taking account of reasonably possible changes in trading performance, show that the group should be able to operate within the level of its current facilities. After making enquiries, the directors have a reasonable expectation that the group has adequate resources to continue in operational existence for the foreseeable future. The group therefore continues to adopt the going concern basis in preparing its consolidated financial statements. Further information on the group's borrowings is given in note 31.

2.1.2 Changes in accounting policy and disclosures

(a) New and amended standards adopted by the group

8p28

There are no IFRSs or IFRIC interpretations that are effective for the first time for the financial year beginning on or after 1 January 2011 that would be expected to have a material impact on the group[1].

8p30

(b) New standards, amendments and interpretations issued but not effective for the financial year beginning 1 January 2011 and not early adopted

IAS 19, 'Employee benefits' was amended in June 2011. The impact on the group will be as follows: to eliminate the corridor approach and recognise all actuarial gains and losses in OCI as they occur; to immediately recognise all past service costs; and to replace interest cost and expected return on plan assets with a net interest amount that is calculated by applying the discount rate to the net defined benefit liability (asset). The group is yet to assess the full impact of the amendments.

IFRS 9, 'Financial instruments', addresses the classification, measurement and recognition of financial assets and financial liabilities. IFRS 9 was issued in November 2009 and October 2010. It replaces the parts of IAS 39 that relate to the classification and measurement of financial instruments. IFRS 9 requires financial assets to be classified into two measurement categories: those measured as at fair value and those measured at amortised cost. The determination is made at initial recognition. The classification depends on the entity's business model for managing its financial instruments and the contractual cash flow characteristics of the instrument. For financial liabilities, the standard retains most of the IAS 39 requirements. The main change is that, in cases where the fair value option is taken for financial liabilities, the part of a fair value change due to an entity's own credit risk is recorded in other comprehensive income rather than the income statement, unless this creates an accounting mismatch. The group is yet to assess IFRS 9's full impact and intends to adopt IFRS 9 no later than the accounting period beginning on or after 1 January 2013, subject to endorsement by the EU.

---

[1] A detailed list of IFRSs and IFRIC interpretations effective on or after 1 January 2011 is included as appendix III.

(All amounts in C thousands unless otherwise stated)

IFRS 10, Consolidated financial statements' builds on existing principles by identifying the concept of control as the determining factor in whether an entity should be included within the consolidated financial statements of the parent company. The standard provides additional guidance to assist in the determination of control where this is difficult to assess. The group is yet to assess IFRS 10's full impact and intends to adopt IFRS 10 no later than the accounting period beginning on or after 1 January 2013, subject to endorsement by the EU.

IFRS 12, 'Disclosures of interests in other entities' includes the disclosure requirements for all forms of interests in other entities, including joint arrangements, associates, special purpose vehicles and other off balance sheet vehicles. The group is yet to assess IFRS 12's full impact and intends to adopt IFRS 12 no later than the accounting period beginning on or after 1 January 2013, subject to endorsement by the EU.

IFRS 13, 'Fair value measurement', aims to improve consistency and reduce complexity by providing a precise definition of fair value and a single source of fair value measurement and disclosure requirements for use across IFRSs. The requirements, which are largely aligned between IFRSs and US GAAP, do not extend the use of fair value accounting but provide guidance on how it should be applied where its use is already required or permitted by other standards within IFRSs or US GAAP. The group is yet to assess IFRS13's full impact and intends to adopt IFRS 13 no later than the accounting period beginning on or after 1 January 2012, subject to endorsement by the EU.

There are no other IFRSs or IFRIC interpretations that are not yet effective that would be expected to have a material impact on the group.

1p119	**2.2 Consolidation**
27p12	*(a) Subsidiaries*
27p14 27p30	Subsidiaries are all entities (including special purpose entities) over which the group has the power to govern the financial and operating policies generally accompanying a shareholding of more than one half of the voting rights. The existence and effect of potential voting rights that are currently exercisable or convertible are considered when assessing whether the group controls another entity. The group also assesses existence of control where it does not have more than 50% of the voting power but is able to govern the financial and operating policies by virtue of de-facto control. De-facto control may arise in circumstances where the size of the group's voting rights relative to the size and dispersion of holdings of other shareholders give the group the power to govern the financial and operating policies, etc.
	Subsidiaries are fully consolidated from the date on which control is transferred to the group. They are de-consolidated from the date that control ceases.
IFRS3p5 IFRS3p37 IFRS3p39 IFRS3p18 IFRS3p19	The group applies the acquisition method to account for business combinations. The consideration transferred for the acquisition of a subsidiary is the fair values of the assets transferred, the liabilities incurred to the former owners of the acquiree and the equity interests issued by the group. The consideration transferred includes the fair value of any asset or liability resulting from a contingent consideration arrangement. Identifiable assets acquired and liabilities and contingent liabilities assumed in a business combination are measured initially at their fair values at the acquisition date. The group recognises any non-controlling interest in the acquiree on an acquisition- by-acquisition basis, either at fair value or at the non-controlling interest's proportionate share of the recognised amounts of acquiree's identifiable net assets.
IFRS3p53	Acquisition-related costs are expensed as incurred.
IFRS3p42	If the business combination is achieved in stages, the acquisition date fair value of the acquirer's previously held equity interest in the acquiree is remeasured to fair value at the acquisition date through profit or loss.
IFRS3p58	Any contingent consideration to be transferred by the group is recognised at fair value at the acquisition date. Subsequent changes to the fair value of the contingent consideration that is deemed to be an asset or liability is recognised in accordance with IAS 39 either in profit or loss or as a change to other comprehensive income. Contingent consideration that is classified as equity is not remeasured, and its subsequent settlement is accounted for within equity.
IFRS3p32 IFRS3B63(a), 36p80	Goodwill is initially measured as the excess of the aggregate of the consideration transferred and the fair value of non-controlling interest over the net identifiable assets acquired and liabilities assumed. If this consideration is lower than the fair value of the net assets of the subsidiary acquired, the difference is recognised in profit or loss.
27p20 27p24	Inter-company transactions, balances, income and expenses on transactions between group companies are eliminated. Profits and losses resulting from inter-company transactions that are recognised in assets are also eliminated. Accounting policies of subsidiaries have been changed where necessary to ensure consistency with the policies adopted by the group.
	(b) Changes in ownership interests in subsidiaries without change of control
27p30, 31	Transactions with non-controlling interests that do not result in loss of control are accounted for as equity transactions – that is, as transactions with the owners in their capacity as owners. The difference between fair value of any consideration paid and the relevant share acquired of the carrying value of net assets of the subsidiary is recorded in equity. Gains or losses on disposals to non-controlling interests are also recorded in equity.

(All amounts in C thousands unless otherwise stated)

(c) Disposal of subsidiaries

27p34
27p35
28p18

When the group ceases to have control any retained interest in the entity is re-measured to its fair value at the date when control is lost, with the change in carrying amount recognised in profit or loss. The fair value is the initial carrying amount for the purposes of subsequently accounting for the retained interest as an associate, joint venture or financial asset. In addition, any amounts previously recognised in other comprehensive income in respect of that entity are accounted for as if the group had directly disposed of the related assets or liabilities. This may mean that amounts previously recognised in other comprehensive income are reclassified to profit or loss.

1p119

(d) Associates

28p13
28p11

Associates are all entities over which the group has significant influence but not control, generally accompanying a shareholding of between 20% and 50% of the voting rights. Investments in associates are accounted for using the equity method of accounting. Under the equity method, the investment is initially recognised at cost, and the carrying amount is increased or decreased to recognise the investor's share of the profit or loss of the investee after the date of acquisition. The group's investment in associates includes goodwill identified on acquisition.

28p19A

If the ownership interest in an associate is reduced but significant influence is retained, only a proportionate share of the amounts previously recognised in other comprehensive income is reclassified to profit or loss where appropriate.

28p29
28p30

The group's share of post-acquisition profit or loss is recognised in the income statement, and its share of post-acquisition movements in other comprehensive income is recognised in other comprehensive income with a corresponding adjustment to the carrying amount of the investment. When the group's share of losses in an associate equals or exceeds its interest in the associate, including any other unsecured receivables, the group does not recognise further losses, unless it has incurred legal or constructive obligations or made payments on behalf of the associate.

28p31
28p33

The group determines at each reporting date whether there is any objective evidence that the investment in the associate is impaired. If this is the case, the group calculates the amount of impairment as the difference between the recoverable amount of the associate and its carrying value and recognises the amount adjacent to 'share of profit/ (loss) of an associate' in the income statement.

28p22
28p26

Profits and losses resulting from upstream and downstream transactions between the group and its associate are recognised in the group's financial statements only to the extent of unrelated investor's interests in the associates. Unrealised losses are eliminated unless the transaction provides evidence of an impairment of the asset transferred. Accounting policies of associates have been changed where necessary to ensure consistency with the policies adopted by the group.

Dilution gains and losses arising in investments in associates are recognised in the income statement.

1p119

2.3 Segment reporting

IFRS8p5(b)

Operating segments are reported in a manner consistent with the internal reporting provided to the chief operating decision-maker. The chief operating decision-maker, who is responsible for allocating resources and assessing performance of the operating segments, has been identified as the steering committee that makes strategic decisions.

1p119

2.4 Foreign currency translation

1p119

(a) Functional and presentation currency

21p17
21p9, 18
1p51(d)

Items included in the financial statements of each of the group's entities are measured using the currency of the primary economic environment in which the entity operates ('the functional currency'). The consolidated financial statements are presented in 'currency' (C), which is the group's presentation currency.

1p119

(b) Transactions and balances

21p21, 28
21p32
39p95(a)
39p102(a)

Foreign currency transactions are translated into the functional currency using the exchange rates prevailing at the dates of the transactions or valuation where items are re-measured. Foreign exchange gains and losses resulting from the settlement of such transactions and from the translation at year-end exchange rates of monetary assets and liabilities denominated in foreign currencies are recognised in the income statement, except when deferred in other comprehensive income as qualifying cash flow hedges and qualifying net investment hedges.

Foreign exchange gains and losses that relate to borrowings and cash and cash equivalents are presented in the income statement within 'finance income or cost'. All other foreign exchange gains and losses are presented in the income statement within 'other (losses)/gains – net'.

39AG83

Changes in the fair value of monetary securities denominated in foreign currency classified as available for sale are analysed between translation differences resulting from changes in the amortised cost of the security and other changes in the carrying amount of the security. Translation differences related to changes in amortised cost are recognised in profit or loss, and other changes in carrying amount are recognised in other comprehensive income.

21p30

Translation differences on non-monetary financial assets and liabilities such as equities held at fair value through profit or loss are recognised in profit or loss as part of the fair value gain or loss. Translation differences on non-monetary financial assets, such as equities classified as available for sale, are included in other comprehensive income.

(All amounts in C thousands unless otherwise stated)

1p119	*(c) Group companies*
21p39	The results and financial position of all the group entities (none of which has the currency of a hyper-inflationary economy) that have a functional currency different from the presentation currency are translated into the presentation currency as follows:
21p39(a)	(a) assets and liabilities for each balance sheet presented are translated at the closing rate at the date of that balance sheet;
21p39(b) 21p39	(b) income and expenses for each income statement are translated at average exchange rates (unless this average is not a reasonable approximation of the cumulative effect of the rates prevailing on the transaction dates, in which case income and expenses are translated at the rate on the dates of the transactions); and
1p79(b)	(c) all resulting exchange differences are recognised in other comprehensive income.
21p47	Goodwill and fair value adjustments arising on the acquisition of a foreign entity are treated as assets and liabilities of the foreign entity and translated at the closing rate. Exchange differences arising are recognised in equity.

2.5 Property, plant and equipment

1p119

16p73(a)
16p35(b)
16p15
16p17
39p98(b)

Land and buildings comprise mainly factories, retail outlets and offices. Land and buildings are shown at fair value, based on valuations by external independent valuers, less subsequent depreciation for buildings. Valuations are performed with sufficient regularity to ensure that the fair value of a revalued asset does not differ materially from its carrying amount. Any accumulated depreciation at the date of revaluation is eliminated against the gross carrying amount of the asset, and the net amount is restated to the revalued amount of the asset. All other property, plant and equipment is stated at historical cost less depreciation. Historical cost includes expenditure that is directly attributable to the acquisition of the items. Cost may also include transfers from equity of any gains/losses on qualifying cash flow hedges of foreign currency purchases of property, plant and equipment.

16p12

Subsequent costs are included in the asset's carrying amount or recognised as a separate asset, as appropriate, only when it is probable that future economic benefits associated with the item will flow to the group and the cost of the item can be measured reliably. The carrying amount of the replaced part is derecognised. All other repairs and maintenance are charged to the income statement during the financial period in which they are incurred.

16p39, 1p79(b)
1p79(b)
16p40
16p41

Increases in the carrying amount arising on revaluation of land and buildings are credited to other comprehensive income and shown as other reserves in shareholders' equity. Decreases that offset previous increases of the same asset are charged in other comprehensive income and debited against other reserves directly in equity; all other decreases are charged to the income statement. Each year the difference between depreciation based on the revalued carrying amount of the asset charged to the income statement, and depreciation based on the asset's original cost is transferred from 'other reserves' to 'retained earnings'.

16p73(b), 50
16p73(c)

Land is not depreciated. Depreciation on other assets is calculated using the straight-line method to allocate their cost or revalued amounts to their residual values over their estimated useful lives, as follows:

- Buildings — 25-40 years
- Machinery — 10-15 years
- Vehicles — 3-5 years
- Furniture, fittings and equipment — 3-8 years

16p51

The assets' residual values and useful lives are reviewed, and adjusted if appropriate, at the end of each reporting period.

36p59

An asset's carrying amount is written down immediately to its recoverable amount if the asset's carrying amount is greater than its estimated recoverable amount (note 2.7).

16p68, 71

Gains and losses on disposals are determined by comparing the proceeds with the carrying amount and are recognised within 'Other (losses)/gains – net' in the income statement.

16p41, 1p79(b)

When revalued assets are sold, the amounts included in other reserves are transferred to retained earnings.

2.6 Intangible assets

1p119

(a) Goodwill

IFRS3p51
38p108(a)
IFRS3p54
36p124

Goodwill arises on the acquisition of subsidiaries, associates and joint ventures and represents the excess of the consideration transferred over IFRS GAAP Plc's interest in net fair value of the net identifiable assets, liabilities and contingent liabilities of the acquiree and the fair value of the non-controlling interest in the acquiree.

For the purpose of impairment testing, goodwill acquired in a business combination is allocated to each of the CGUs, or groups of CGUs, that is expected to benefit from the synergies of the combination. Each unit or group of units to which the goodwill is allocated represents the lowest level within the entity at which the goodwill is monitored for internal management purposes. Goodwill is monitored at the operating segment level.

Goodwill impairment reviews are undertaken annually or more frequently if events or changes in circumstances indicate a potential impairment. The carrying value of goodwill is compared to the recoverable amount, which is the

(All amounts in C thousands unless otherwise stated)

higher of value in use and the fair value less costs to sell. Any impairment is recognised immediately as an expense and is not subsequently reversed.

1p119 *(b) Trademarks and licences*

38p74
38p97
38p118(a),(b)
Separately acquired trademarks and licences are shown at historical cost. Trademarks and licences acquired in a business combination are recognised at fair value at the acquisition date. Trademarks and licences have a finite useful life and are carried at cost less accumulated amortisation. Amortisation is calculated using the straight-line method to allocate the cost of trademarks and licences over their estimated useful lives of 15 to 20 years.

38p4
38p118(a),(b)
Acquired computer software licences are capitalised on the basis of the costs incurred to acquire and bring to use the specific software. These costs are amortised over their estimated useful lives of three to five years.

1p119 *(c) Computer software*

38p57
Costs associated with maintaining computer software programmes are recognised as an expense as incurred. Development costs that are directly attributable to the design and testing of identifiable and unique software products controlled by the group are recognised as intangible assets when the following criteria are met:

- it is technically feasible to complete the software product so that it will be available for use;
- management intends to complete the software product and use or sell it;
- there is an ability to use or sell the software product;
- it can be demonstrated how the software product will generate probable future economic benefits;
- adequate technical, financial and other resources to complete the development and to use or sell the software product are available; and
- the expenditure attributable to the software product during its development can be reliably measured.

38p66
Directly attributable costs that are capitalised as part of the software product include the software development employee costs and an appropriate portion of relevant overheads.

38p68,71
Other development expenditures that do not meet these criteria are recognised as an expense as incurred. Development costs previously recognised as an expense are not recognised as an asset in a subsequent period.

38p97
38p118(a),(b)
Computer software development costs recognised as assets are amortised over their estimated useful lives, which does not exceed three years.

1p119 **2.7 Impairment of non-financial assets**

36p9
36p10
Assets that have an indefinite useful life – for example, goodwill or intangible assets not ready to use – are not subject to amortisation and are tested annually for impairment. Assets that are subject to amortisation are reviewed for impairment whenever events or changes in circumstances indicate that the carrying amount may not be recoverable. An impairment loss is recognised for the amount by which the asset's carrying amount exceeds its recoverable amount. The recoverable amount is the higher of an asset's fair value less costs to sell and value in use. For the purposes of assessing impairment, assets are grouped at the lowest levels for which there are separately identifiable cash flows (cash-generating units). Non-financial assets other than goodwill that suffered an impairment are reviewed for possible reversal of the impairment at each reporting date.

1p119 **2.8 Non-current assets (or disposal groups) held for sale**

IFRS5p6, 15
Non-current assets (or disposal groups) are classified as assets held for sale when their carrying amount is to be recovered principally through a sale transaction and a sale is considered highly probable. They are stated at the lower of carrying amount and fair value less costs to sell.

1p119 **2.9 Financial assets**

2.9.1 Classification

IFRS7p21
39p9
The group classifies its financial assets in the following categories: at fair value through profit or loss, loans and receivables, and available for sale. The classification depends on the purpose for which the financial assets were acquired. Management determines the classification of its financial assets at initial recognition.

(a) Financial assets at fair value through profit or loss

39p9
Financial assets at fair value through profit or loss are financial assets held for trading. A financial asset is classified in this category if acquired principally for the purpose of selling in the short term. Derivatives are also categorised as held for trading unless they are designated as hedges. Assets in this category are classified as current assets if expected to be settled within 12 months; otherwise, they are classified as non-current.

(b) Loans and receivables

39p9
1p66, 68
Loans and receivables are non-derivative financial assets with fixed or determinable payments that are not quoted in an active market. They are included in current assets, except for maturities greater than 12 months after the end of the reporting period. These are classified as non-current assets. The group's loans and receivables comprise 'trade and other receivables' and 'cash and cash equivalents' in the balance sheet (notes 2.14 and 2.15).

(All amounts in C thousands unless otherwise stated)

(c) Available-for-sale financial assets

39p9
1p66, 68
IFRS7
AppxB5(b)

Available-for-sale financial assets are non-derivatives that are either designated in this category or not classified in any of the other categories. They are included in non-current assets unless the investment matures or management intends to dispose of it within 12 months of the end of the reporting period.

2.9.2 Recognition and measurement

39p38
IFRS7
AppxBp5
39p43
39p16
39p46

Regular purchases and sales of financial assets are recognised on the trade-date – the date on which the group commits to purchase or sell the asset. Investments are initially recognised at fair value plus transaction costs for all financial assets not carried at fair value through profit or loss. Financial assets carried at fair value through profit or loss are initially recognised at fair value, and transaction costs are expensed in the income statement. Financial assets are derecognised when the rights to receive cash flows from the investments have expired or have been transferred and the group has transferred substantially all risks and rewards of ownership. Available-for- sale financial assets and financial assets at fair value through profit or loss are subsequently carried at fair value. Loans and receivables are subsequently carried at amortised cost using the effective interest method.

39p55(a)
IFRS7Appx
Bp5(e)

Gains or losses arising from changes in the fair value of the 'financial assets at fair value through profit or loss' category are presented in the income statement within 'other (losses)/gains – net' in the period in which they arise. Dividend income from financial assets at fair value through profit or loss is recognised in the income statement as part of other income when the group's right to receive payments is established.

39p55(b)
IFRS7
AppxBp5(e)
39AG83
1p79(b)

Changes in the fair value of monetary and non-monetary securities classified as available for sale are recognised in other comprehensive income.

39p67

When securities classified as available for sale are sold or impaired, the accumulated fair value adjustments recognised in equity are included in the income statement as 'gains and losses from investment securities'.

Interest on available-for-sale securities calculated using the effective interest method is recognised in the income statement as part of other income. Dividends on available-for-sale equity instruments are recognised in the income statement as part of other income when the group's right to receive payments is established.

2.10 Offsetting financial instruments

32p42

Financial assets and liabilities are offset and the net amount reported in the balance sheet when there is a legally enforceable right to offset the recognised amounts and there is an intention to settle on a net basis or realise the asset and settle the liability simultaneously.

2.11 Impairment of financial assets

(a) Assets carried at amortised cost

39p58
39p59

The group assesses at the end of each reporting period whether there is objective evidence that a financial asset or group of financial assets is impaired. A financial asset or a group of financial assets is impaired and impairment losses are incurred only if there is objective evidence of impairment as a result of one or more events that occurred after the initial recognition of the asset (a 'loss event') and that loss event (or events) has an impact on the estimated future cash flows of the financial asset or group of financial assets that can be reliably estimated.

IFRS7B5(f)

Evidence of impairment may include indications that the debtors or a group of debtors is experiencing significant financial difficulty, default or delinquency in interest or principal payments, the probability that they will enter bankruptcy or other financial reorganisation, and where observable data indicate that there is a measurable decrease in the estimated future cash flows, such as changes in arrears or economic conditions that correlate with defaults.

IFRS7p16
39AG84

For loans and receivables category, the amount of the loss is measured as the difference between the asset's carrying amount and the present value of estimated future cash flows (excluding future credit losses that have not been incurred) discounted at the financial asset's original effective interest rate. The carrying amount of the asset is reduced and the amount of the loss is recognised in the consolidated income statement. If a loan or held-to-maturity investment has a variable interest rate, the discount rate for measuring any impairment loss is the current effective interest rate determined under the contract. As a practical expedient, the group may measure impairment on the basis of an instrument's fair value using an observable market price.

IFRS7
AppxB5(d)
39p65

If, in a subsequent period, the amount of the impairment loss decreases and the decrease can be related objectively to an event occurring after the impairment was recognised (such as an improvement in the debtor's credit rating), the reversal of the previously recognised impairment loss is recognised in the consolidated income statement.

(b) Assets classified as available for sale

39p67-70

The group assesses at the end of each reporting period whether there is objective evidence that a financial asset or a group of financial assets is impaired. For debt securities, the group uses the criteria referred to in (a) above. In the

(All amounts in C thousands unless otherwise stated)

case of equity investments classified as available for sale, a significant or prolonged decline in the fair value of the security below its cost is also evidence that the assets are impaired. If any such evidence exists for available-for-sale financial assets, the cumulative loss – measured as the difference between the acquisition cost and the current fair value, less any impairment loss on that financial asset previously recognised in profit or loss – is removed from equity and recognised in profit or loss. Impairment losses recognised in the consolidated income statement on equity instruments are not reversed through the consolidated income statement. If, in a subsequent period, the fair value of a debt instrument classified as available for sale increases and the increase can be objectively related to an event occurring after the impairment loss was recognised in profit or loss, the impairment loss is reversed through the consolidated income statement.

1p119	**2.12 Derivative financial instruments and hedging activities**
IFRS7p21 IFRS7p22	Derivatives are initially recognised at fair value on the date a derivative contract is entered into and are subsequently re-measured at their fair value. The method of recognising the resulting gain or loss depends on whether the derivative is designated as a hedging instrument, and if so, the nature of the item being hedged. The group designates certain derivatives as either:
	(a) hedges of the fair value of recognised assets or liabilities or a firm commitment (fair value hedge);
	(b) hedges of a particular risk associated with a recognised asset or liability or a highly probable forecast transaction (cash flow hedge); or
	(c) hedges of a net investment in a foreign operation (net investment hedge).
39p88	The group documents at the inception of the transaction the relationship between hedging instruments and hedged items, as well as its risk management objectives and strategy for undertaking various hedging transactions. The group also documents its assessment, both at hedge inception and on an ongoing basis, of whether the derivatives that are used in hedging transactions are highly effective in offsetting changes in fair values or cash flows of hedged items.
IFRS7p23, 24	The fair values of various derivative instruments used for hedging purposes are disclosed in note 11. Movements on the hedging reserve in other comprehensive income are shown in note 20. The full fair value of a hedging derivative is classified as a non-current asset or liability when the remaining hedged item is more than 12 months, and as a current asset or liability when the remaining maturity of the hedged item is less than 12 months. Trading derivatives are classified as a current asset or liability.
39p89	*(a) Fair value hedge*
	Changes in the fair value of derivatives that are designated and qualify as fair value hedges are recorded in the income statement, together with any changes in the fair value of the hedged asset or liability that are attributable to the hedged risk. The group only applies fair value hedge accounting for hedging fixed interest risk on borrowings. The gain or loss relating to the effective portion of interest rate swaps hedging fixed rate borrowings is recognised in the income statement within 'finance costs'. The gain or loss relating to the ineffective portion is recognised in the income statement within 'other gains/(losses) – net'. Changes in the fair value of the hedge fixed rate borrowings attributable to interest rate risk are recognised in the income statement within 'finance costs'.
39p92	If the hedge no longer meets the criteria for hedge accounting, the adjustment to the carrying amount of a hedged item for which the effective interest method is used is amortised to profit or loss over the period to maturity.
39p95	*(b) Cash flow hedge*
1p79(b)	The effective portion of changes in the fair value of derivatives that are designated and qualify as cash flow hedges is recognised in other comprehensive income. The gain or loss relating to the ineffective portion is recognised immediately in the income statement within 'other gains/(losses) – net'.
39p99, 100 39p98(b)	Amounts accumulated in equity are reclassified to profit or loss in the periods when the hedged item affects profit or loss (for example, when the forecast sale that is hedged takes place). The gain or loss relating to the effective portion of interest rate swaps hedging variable rate borrowings is recognised in the income statement within 'revenue'. However, when the forecast transaction that is hedged results in the recognition of a non-financial asset (for example, inventory or fixed assets), the gains and losses previously deferred in equity are transferred from equity and included in the initial measurement of the cost of the asset. The deferred amounts are ultimately recognised in cost of goods sold in the case of inventory or in depreciation in the case of fixed assets.
39p101	When a hedging instrument expires or is sold, or when a hedge no longer meets the criteria for hedge accounting, any cumulative gain or loss existing in equity at that time remains in equity and is recognised when the forecast transaction is ultimately recognised in the income statement. When a forecast transaction is no longer expected to occur, the cumulative gain or loss that was reported in equity is immediately transferred to the income statement within 'other gains/(losses) – net'.
39p102 (a)(b)	*(c) Net investment hedge*
	Hedges of net investments in foreign operations are accounted for similarly to cash flow hedges.
1p79(b)	Any gain or loss on the hedging instrument relating to the effective portion of the hedge is recognised in other comprehensive income. The gain or loss relating to the ineffective portion is recognised in the income statement.

(All amounts in C thousands unless otherwise stated)

Gains and losses accumulated in equity are included in the income statement when the foreign operation is partially disposed of or sold.

1p119	**2.13 Inventories**
2p36(a), 9 2p10, 25 23p6, 7 2p28, 30 39p98(b)	Inventories are stated at the lower of cost and net realisable value. Cost is determined using the first-in, first-out (FIFO) method. The cost of finished goods and work in progress comprises design costs, raw materials, direct labour, other direct costs and related production overheads (based on normal operating capacity). It excludes borrowing costs. Net realisable value is the estimated selling price in the ordinary course of business, less applicable variable selling expenses. Costs of inventories include the transfer from equity of any gains/losses on qualifying cash flow hedges purchases of raw materials[1].
1p119	**2.14 Trade receivables**
IFRS7p21	Trade receivables are amounts due from customers for merchandise sold or services performed in the ordinary course of business. If collection is expected in one year or less (or in the normal operating cycle of the business if longer), they are classified as current assets. If not, they are presented as non-current assets.
39p43 39p46(a) 39p59 IFRS7 AppxBp5(f) IFRS7 AppxB p5(d)	Trade receivables are recognised initially at fair value and subsequently measured at amortised cost using the effective interest method, less provision for impairment.
1p119	**2.15 Cash and cash equivalents**
IFRS7p21 7p45	In the consolidated statement of cash flows, cash and cash equivalents includes cash in hand, deposits held at call with banks, other short-term highly liquid investments with original maturities of three months or less and bank overdrafts. In the consolidated balance sheet, bank overdrafts are shown within borrowings in current liabilities.
1p119	**2.16 Share capital**
IFRS7p21 32p18(a)	Ordinary shares are classified as equity. Mandatorily redeemable preference shares are classified as liabilities (note 2.18).
32p37	Incremental costs directly attributable to the issue of new ordinary shares or options are shown in equity as a deduction, net of tax, from the proceeds.
32p33	Where any group company purchases the company's equity share capital (treasury shares), the consideration paid, including any directly attributable incremental costs (net of income taxes) is deducted from equity attributable to the company's equity holders until the shares are cancelled or reissued. Where such ordinary shares are subsequently reissued, any consideration received, net of any directly attributable incremental transaction costs and the related income tax effects, is included in equity attributable to the company's equity holders.
1p119	**2.17 Trade payables**
	Trade payables are obligations to pay for goods or services that have been acquired in the ordinary course of business from suppliers. Accounts payable are classified as current liabilities if payment is due within one year or less (or in the normal operating cycle of the business if longer). If not, they are presented as non-current liabilities.
IFRS7p21 39p43	Trade payables are recognised initially at fair value and subsequently measured at amortised cost using the effective interest method.
1p119	**2.18 Borrowings**
IFRS7p21 39p43 39p47	Borrowings are recognised initially at fair value, net of transaction costs incurred. Borrowings are subsequently carried at amortised cost; any difference between the proceeds (net of transaction costs) and the redemption value is recognised in the income statement over the period of the borrowings using the effective interest method.
	Fees paid on the establishment of loan facilities are recognised as transaction costs of the loan to the extent that it is probable that some or all of the facility will be drawn down. In this case, the fee is deferred until the draw-down occurs. To the extent there is no evidence that it is probable that some or all of the facility will be drawn down, the fee is capitalised as a pre-payment for liquidity services and amortised over the period of the facility to which it relates.
32p18(a) 32p35	Preference shares, which are mandatorily redeemable on a specific date, are classified as liabilities. The dividends on these preference shares are recognised in the income statement as interest expense.

---

[1] Management may choose to keep these gains in equity until the acquired asset affects profit or loss. At this time, management should re-classify the gains to profit or loss.

(All amounts in C thousands unless otherwise stated)

1p119   **2.19 Borrowing costs**

23p8   General and specific borrowing costs directly attributable to the acquisition, construction or production of qualifying assets, which are assets that necessarily take a substantial period of time to get ready for their intended use or sale, are added to the cost of those assets, until such time as the assets are substantially ready for their intended use or sale.

23p12   Investment income earned on the temporary investment of specific borrowings pending their expenditure on qualifying assets is deducted from the borrowing costs eligible for capitalisation.

All other borrowing costs are recognised in profit or loss in the period in which they are incurred.

1p119   **2.20 Compound financial instruments**

32p28   Compound financial instruments issued by the group comprise convertible notes that can be converted to share capital at the option of the holder, and the number of shares to be issued does not vary with changes in their fair value.

32AG31 The liability component of a compound financial instrument is recognised initially at the fair value of a similar liability that does not have an equity conversion option. The equity component is recognised initially at the difference between the fair value of the compound financial instrument as a whole and the fair value of the liability component. Any directly attributable transaction costs are allocated to the liability and equity components in proportion to their initial carrying amounts.

32p36   Subsequent to initial recognition, the liability component of a compound financial instrument is measured at amortised cost using the effective interest method. The equity component of a compound financial instrument is not re-measured subsequent to initial recognition except on conversion or expiry.

1p69, 71 Borrowings are classified as current liabilities unless the group has an unconditional right to defer settlement of the liability for at least 12 months after the end of the reporting period.

1p119   **2.21 Current and deferred income tax**

12p58   The tax expense for the period comprises current and deferred tax. Tax is recognised in the income statement, except
12p61A   to the extent that it relates to items recognised in other comprehensive income or directly in equity. In this case, the tax is also recognised in other comprehensive income or directly in equity, respectively.

12p12   The current income tax charge is calculated on the basis of the tax laws enacted or substantively enacted at the
12p46   balance sheet date in the countries where the company and its subsidiaries operate and generate taxable income. Management periodically evaluates positions taken in tax returns with respect to situations in which applicable tax regulation is subject to interpretation. It establishes provisions where appropriate on the basis of amounts expected to be paid to the tax authorities.

12p24   Deferred income tax is recognised, using the liability method, on temporary differences arising between the tax bases
12p15   of assets and liabilities and their carrying amounts in the consolidated financial statements. However, deferred tax
12p47   liabilities are not recognised if they arise from the initial recognition of goodwill; deferred income tax is not accounted for if it arises from initial recognition of an asset or liability in a transaction other than a business combination that at the time of the transaction affects neither accounting nor taxable profit or loss. Deferred income tax is determined using tax rates (and laws) that have been enacted or substantially enacted by the balance sheet date and are expected to apply when the related deferred income tax asset is realised or the deferred income tax liability is settled.

12p24   Deferred income tax assets are recognised only to the extent that it is probable that future taxable profit will be
12p34   available against which the temporary differences can be utilised.

12p39   Deferred income tax is provided on temporary differences arising on investments in subsidiaries and associates,
12p44   except for deferred income tax liability where the timing of the reversal of the temporary difference is controlled by the group and it is probable that the temporary difference will not reverse in the foreseeable future.

12p74   Deferred income tax assets and liabilities are offset when there is a legally enforceable right to offset current tax assets against current tax liabilities and when the deferred income taxes assets and liabilities relate to income taxes levied by the same taxation authority on either the same taxable entity or different taxable entities where there is an intention to settle the balances on a net basis.

1p119   **2.22 Employee benefits**

(a) Pension obligations

19p27   Group companies operate various pension schemes. The schemes are generally funded through payments to
19p25   insurance companies or trustee-administered funds, determined by periodic actuarial calculations. The group has
19p7   both defined benefit and defined contribution plans. A defined contribution plan is a pension plan under which the
19p120A(b) group pays fixed contributions into a separate entity. The group has no legal or constructive obligations to pay further contributions if the fund does not hold sufficient assets to pay all employees the benefits relating to employee service in the current and prior periods. A defined benefit plan is a pension plan that is not a defined contribution plan.

(All amounts in C thousands unless otherwise stated)

Typically defined benefit plans define an amount of pension benefit that an employee will receive on retirement, usually dependent on one or more factors such as age, years of service and compensation.

19p79
19p80
19p64

The liability recognised in the balance sheet in respect of defined benefit pension plans is the present value of the defined benefit obligation at the end of the reporting period less the fair value of plan assets, together with adjustments for unrecognised past-service costs. The defined benefit obligation is calculated annually by independent actuaries using the projected unit credit method. The present value of the defined benefit obligation is determined by discounting the estimated future cash outflows using interest rates of high-quality corporate bonds that are denominated in the currency in which the benefits will be paid, and that have terms to maturity approximating to the terms of the related pension obligation. In countries where there is no deep market in such bonds, the market rates on government bonds are used.

19p93-93D
19p120A(a)

Actuarial gains and losses arising from experience adjustments and changes in actuarial assumptions are charged or credited to equity in other comprehensive income in the period in which they arise.

19p96

Past-service costs are recognised immediately in income, unless the changes to the pension plan are conditional on the employees remaining in service for a specified period of time (the vesting period). In this case, the past-service costs are amortised on a straight-line basis over the vesting period.

19p44

For defined contribution plans, the group pays contributions to publicly or privately administered pension insurance plans on a mandatory, contractual or voluntary basis. The group has no further payment obligations once the contributions have been paid. The contributions are recognised as employee benefit expense when they are due. Prepaid contributions are recognised as an asset to the extent that a cash refund or a reduction in the future payments is available.

(b) Other post-employment obligations

19p120A
(a-b)

Some group companies provide post-retirement healthcare benefits to their retirees. The entitlement to these benefits is usually conditional on the employee remaining in service up to retirement age and the completion of a minimum service period. The expected costs of these benefits are accrued over the period of employment using the same accounting methodology as used for defined benefit pension plans. Actuarial gains and losses arising from experience adjustments and changes in actuarial assumptions are charged or credited to equity in other comprehensive income in the period in which they arise. These obligations are valued annually by independent qualified actuaries.

(c) Termination benefits

19p133
19p134
19p139
19p140

Termination benefits are payable when employment is terminated by the group before the normal retirement date, or whenever an employee accepts voluntary redundancy in exchange for these benefits. The group recognises termination benefits when it is demonstrably committed to a termination when the entity has a detailed formal plan to terminate the employment of current employees without possibility of withdrawal. In the case of an offer made to encourage voluntary redundancy, the termination benefits are measured based on the number of employees expected to accept the offer. Benefits falling due more than 12 months after the end of the reporting period are discounted to their present value.

(d) Profit-sharing and bonus plans

19p17

The group recognises a liability and an expense for bonuses and profit-sharing, based on a formula that takes into consideration the profit attributable to the company's shareholders after certain adjustments. The group recognises a provision where contractually obliged or where there is a past practice that has created a constructive obligation.

1p119

2.23 Share-based payments

IFRS2 p15(b)
IFRS2p19

The group operates a number of equity-settled, share-based compensation plans, under which the entity receives services from employees as consideration for equity instruments (options) of the group. The fair value of the employee services received in exchange for the grant of the options is recognised as an expense. The total amount to be expensed is determined by reference to the fair value of the options granted:

IFRS2p21 ■ including any market performance conditions (for example, an entity's share price);

IFRS2p20 ■ excluding the impact of any service and non-market performance vesting conditions (for example, profitability, sales growth targets and remaining an employee of the entity over a specified time period); and

IFRS2p21A ■ including the impact of any non-vesting conditions (for example, the requirement for employees to save).

IFRS2p15
IFRS2p20

Non-market performance and service conditions are included in assumptions about the number of options that are expected to vest. The total expense is recognised over the vesting period, which is the period over which all of the specified vesting conditions are to be satisfied.

In addition, in some circumstances employees may provide services in advance of the grant date and therefore the grant date fair value is estimated for the purposes of recognising the expense during the period between service commencement period and grant date.

(All amounts in C thousands unless otherwise stated)

At the end of each reporting period, the group revises its estimates of the number of options that are expected to vest based on the non-market vesting conditions. It recognises the impact of the revision to original estimates, if any, in the income statement, with a corresponding adjustment to equity.

When the options are exercised, the company issues new shares. The proceeds received net of any directly attributable transaction costs are credited to share capital (nominal value) and share premium.

The grant by the company of options over its equity instruments to the employees of subsidiary undertakings in the group is treated as a capital contribution. The fair value of employee services received, measured by reference to the grant date fair value, is recognised over the vesting period as an increase to investment in subsidiary undertakings, with a corresponding credit to equity in the parent entity accounts.

The social security contributions payable in connection with the grant of the share options is considered an integral part of the grant itself, and the charge will be treated as a cash-settled transaction.

1p119   2.24 Provisions

37p14
37p72
37p63
Provisions for environmental restoration, restructuring costs and legal claims are recognised when: the group has a present legal or constructive obligation as a result of past events; it is probable that an outflow of resources will be required to settle the obligation; and the amount has been reliably estimated. Restructuring provisions comprise lease termination penalties and employee termination payments. Provisions are not recognised for future operating losses.

37p24
Where there are a number of similar obligations, the likelihood that an outflow will be required in settlement is determined by considering the class of obligations as a whole. A provision is recognised even if the likelihood of an outflow with respect to any one item included in the same class of obligations may be small.

37p45
Provisions are measured at the present value of the expenditures expected to be required to settle the obligation using a pre-tax rate that reflects current market assessments of the time value of money and the risks specific to the obligation. The increase in the provision due to passage of time is recognised as interest expense.

1p119   2.25 Revenue recognition

18p35(a)
Revenue is measured at the fair value of the consideration received or receivable, and represents amounts receivable for goods supplied, stated net of discounts, returns and value added taxes. The group recognises revenue when the amount of revenue can be reliably measured; when it is probable that future economic benefits will flow to the entity; and when specific criteria have been met for each of the group's activities, as described below. The group bases its estimate of return on historical results, taking into consideration the type of customer, the type of transaction and the specifics of each arrangement.

18p14
(a) Sales of goods – wholesale

The group manufactures and sells a range of footwear products in the wholesale market. Sales of goods are recognised when a group entity has delivered products to the wholesaler, the wholesaler has full discretion over the channel and price to sell the products, and there is no unfulfilled obligation that could affect the wholesaler's acceptance of the products. Delivery does not occur until the products have been shipped to the specified location, the risks of obsolescence and loss have been transferred to the wholesaler, and either the wholesaler has accepted the products in accordance with the sales contract, the acceptance provisions have lapsed or the group has objective evidence that all criteria for acceptance have been satisfied.

The footwear products are often sold with volume discounts; customers have a right to return faulty products in the wholesale market. Sales are recorded based on the price specified in the sales contracts, net of the estimated volume discounts and returns at the time of sale. Accumulated experience is used to estimate and provide for the discounts and returns. The volume discounts are assessed based on anticipated annual purchases. No element of financing is deemed present as the sales are made with a credit term of 60 days, which is consistent with the market practice.

18p14
(b) Sales of goods – retail

The group operates a chain of retail outlets for selling shoes and other leather products. Sales of goods are recognised when a group entity sells a product to the customer. Retail sales are usually in cash or by credit card.

It is the group's policy to sell its products to the retail customer with a right to return within 28 days. Accumulated experience is used to estimate and provide for such returns at the time of sale. The group does not operate any loyalty programmes.

18p14
(c) Internet revenue

Revenue from the provision of the sale of goods on the internet is recognised at the point that the risks and rewards of the inventory have passed to the customer, which is the point of dispatch. Transactions are settled by credit or payment card.

Provisions are made for internet credit notes based on the expected level of returns, which in turn is based upon the historical rate of returns.

(All amounts in C thousands unless otherwise stated)

18p20   *(d) Sales of services*

The group sells design services and transportation services to other shoe manufacturers. For sales of services, revenue is recognised in the accounting period in which the services are rendered, by reference to stage of completion of the specific transaction and assessed on the basis of the actual service provided as a proportion of the total services to be provided.

18p30(b)   *(e) Royalty income*

Royalty income is recognised on an accruals basis in accordance with the substance of the relevant agreements.

18p30(a)   **2.26 Interest income**

39p63   Interest income is recognised using the effective interest method. When a loan and receivable is impaired, the group reduces the carrying amount to its recoverable amount, being the estimated future cash flow discounted at the original effective interest rate of the instrument, and continues unwinding the discount as interest income. Interest income on impaired loan and receivables is recognised using the original effective interest rate.

2.27 Dividend income

Dividend income is recognised when the right to receive payment is established.

1p119   **2.28 Leases**

17p33
SIC-15p5   Leases in which a significant portion of the risks and rewards of ownership are retained by the lessor are classified as operating leases. Payments made under operating leases (net of any incentives received from the lessor) are charged to the income statement on a straight-line basis over the period of the lease.

17p71   The group leases certain property, plant and equipment. Leases of property, plant and equipment where the group has substantially all the risks and rewards of ownership are classified as finance leases. Finance leases are capitalised at the lease's commencement at the lower of the fair value of the leased property and the present value of the minimum lease payments.

17p20
17p27   Each lease payment is allocated between the liability and finance charges. The corresponding rental obligations, net of finance charges, are included in other long-term payables. The interest element of the finance cost is charged to the income statement over the lease period so as to produce a constant periodic rate of interest on the remaining balance of the liability for each period. The property, plant and equipment acquired under finance leases is depreciated over the shorter of the useful life of the asset and the lease term.

1p119   **2.29 Dividend distribution**

10p12   Dividend distribution to the company's shareholders is recognised as a liability in the group's financial statements in the period in which the dividends are approved by the company's shareholders.

1p119   **2.30 Exceptional items**

Exceptional items are disclosed separately in the financial statements where it is necessary to do so to provide further understanding of the financial performance of the group. They are material items of income or expense that have been shown separately due to the significance of their nature or amount.

Commentary – summary of significant accounting policies

Statement of compliance with IFRS

1p16   1. An entity whose financial statements and notes comply with IFRS makes an explicit and unreserved statement of such compliance in the notes. The financial statements and notes are not described as complying with IFRS unless they comply with all the requirements of IFRS.

2. Where an entity can make the explicit and unreserved statement of compliance in respect of only:
(a)   the parent financial statements and notes, or
(b)   the consolidated financial statements and notes,
it clearly identifies to which financial statements and notes the statement of compliance relates.

Summary of accounting policies

3. A summary of significant accounting policies includes:
1p117(a)   (a)   the measurement basis (or bases) used in preparing the financial statements; and
1p117(b)   (b)   the other accounting policies used that are relevant to an understanding of the financial statements.

1p116   4. The summary may be presented as a separate component of the financial statements.

(All amounts in C thousands unless otherwise stated)

1p119	5. In deciding whether a particular accounting policy should be disclosed, management considers whether disclosure would assist users in understanding how transactions, other events and conditions are reflected in the reported financial performance and financial position. Some IFRSs specifically require disclosure of particular accounting policies, including choices made by management between different policies they allow. For example, IAS 16, 'Property, plant and equipment', requires disclosure of the measurement bases used for classes of property, plant and equipment.

Changes in accounting policies

Initial application of IFRS

8p28	6. When initial application of an IFRS:

(a) has an effect on the current period or any prior period;
(b) would have such an effect except that it is impracticable to determine the amount of the adjustment; or
(c) might have an effect on future periods, an entity discloses:
  (i) the title of the IFRS;
  (ii) when applicable, that the change in accounting policy is made in accordance with its transitional provisions;
  (iii) the nature of the change in accounting policy;
  (iv) when applicable, a description of the transitional provisions;
  (v) when applicable, the transitional provisions that might have an effect on future periods;
  (vi) for the current period and each prior period presented, to the extent practicable, the amount of the adjustment:
    ▪ for each financial statement line item affected;
    ▪ if IAS 33, 'Earnings per share', applies to the entity, for basic and diluted earnings per share;
  (vii) the amount of the adjustment relating to periods before those presented, to the extent practicable; and
  (viii) if retrospective application required by paragraph 19(a) or (b) of IAS 8, 'Accounting policies, changes in accounting estimates and errors', is impracticable for a particular prior period, or for periods before those presented, the circumstances that led to the existence of that condition and a description of how and from when the change in accounting policy has been applied.

Financial statements of subsequent periods need not repeat these disclosures.

Voluntary change in accounting policy

8p29	7. When a voluntary change in accounting policy:

(a) has an effect on the current period or any prior period,
(b) would have an effect on that period except that it is impracticable to determine the amount of the adjustment, or
(c) might have an effect on future periods,
  an entity discloses:
  (i) the nature of the change in accounting policy;
  (ii) the reasons why applying the new accounting policy provides reliable and more relevant information;
  (iii) for the current period and each prior period presented, to the extent practicable, the amount of the adjustment:
    ▪ for each financial statement line item affected, and
    ▪ if IAS 33 applies to the entity, for basic and diluted earnings per share;
  (iv) the amount of the adjustment relating to periods before those presented, to the extent practicable; and
  (v) if retrospective application is impracticable for a particular prior period, or for periods before those presented, the circumstances that led to the existence of that condition and a description of how and from when the change in accounting policy has been applied.

Financial statements of subsequent periods need not repeat these disclosures.

Change during interim periods

1p112(c)	8. There is no longer an explicit requirement to disclose the financial effect of a change in accounting policy that was made during the final interim period on prior interim financial reports of the current annual reporting period. However, where the impact on prior interim reporting periods is significant, an entity should consider explaining this fact and the financial effect.

IFRSs issued but not yet effective

8p30	9. When an entity has not applied a new IFRS that has been issued but is not yet effective, it discloses:

(a) this fact; and
(b) known or reasonably estimable information relevant to assessing the possible impact that application of the new IFRS will have on the entity's financial statements in the period of initial application.

8p31	10. An entity considers disclosing:

(a) the title of the new IFRS;
(b) the nature of the impending change or changes in accounting policy;
(c) the date by which application of the IFRS is required;

(All amounts in C thousands unless otherwise stated)

> (d) the date as at which it plans to apply it initially; and
> (e) either:
>   (i) a discussion of the impact that initial application of the IFRS is expected to have on the entity's financial statements, or
>   (ii) if that impact is not known or reasonably estimable, a statement to that effect.
>
> 11. Our view is that disclosures in the paragraph above are not necessary in respect of standards and interpretations that are clearly not applicable to the entity (for example industry-specific standards) or that are not expected to have a material effect on the entity. Instead, disclosure should be given in respect of the developments that are, or could be, significant to the entity. Management will need to apply judgement in determining whether a standard is expected to have a material effect. The assessment of materiality should consider the impact both on previous transactions and financial position and on reasonably foreseeable future transactions. For pronouncements where there is an option that could have an impact on the entity, the management expectation on whether the entity will use the option should be disclosed.
>
> **Disclosures not illustrated in IFRS GAAP plc financial statements**
>
> For disclosures relating to IAS 29, 'Financial reporting in hyperinflationary economies', and IFRS 6, 'Exploration for and evaluation of mineral resources', please refer to PwC's *IFRS disclosure checklist 2011*.

3 Financial risk management

Group

3.1 Financial risk factors

IFRS7p31

The group's activities expose it to a variety of financial risks: market risk (including currency risk, fair value interest rate risk, cash flow interest rate risk and price risk), credit risk and liquidity risk. The group's overall risk management programme focuses on the unpredictability of financial markets and seeks to minimise potential adverse effects on the group's financial performance. The group uses derivative financial instruments to hedge certain risk exposures.

Risk management is carried out by a central treasury department (group treasury) under policies approved by the board of directors. Group treasury identifies, evaluates and hedges financial risks in close co-operation with the group's operating units. The board provides written principles for overall risk management, as well as written policies covering specific areas, such as foreign exchange risk, interest rate risk, credit risk, use of derivative financial instruments and non-derivative financial instruments, and investment of excess liquidity.

(a) Market risk

(i) Foreign exchange risk

IFRS7 p33(a)

The group operates internationally and is exposed to foreign exchange risk arising from various currency exposures, primarily with respect to the US dollar and the UK pound. Foreign exchange risk arises from future commercial transactions, recognised assets and liabilities and net investments in foreign operations.

IFRS7 p33(b), 22(c)

Management has set up a policy to require group companies to manage their foreign exchange risk against their functional currency. The group companies are required to hedge their entire foreign exchange risk exposure with the group treasury. To manage their foreign exchange risk arising from future commercial transactions and recognised assets and liabilities, entities in the group use forward contracts, transacted with group treasury. Foreign exchange risk arises when future commercial transactions or recognised assets or liabilities are denominated in a currency that is not the entity's functional currency.

IFRS7 p22(c)

The group treasury's risk management policy is to hedge between 75% and 100% of anticipated cash flows (mainly export sales and purchase of inventory) in each major foreign currency for the subsequent 12 months. Approximately 90% (2010: 95%) of projected sales in each major currency qualify as 'highly probable' forecast transactions for hedge accounting purposes.

IFRS7 p33(a)(b) IFRS7 p22(c)

The group has certain investments in foreign operations, whose net assets are exposed to foreign currency translation risk. Currency exposure arising from the net assets of the group's foreign operations is managed primarily through borrowings denominated in the relevant foreign currencies.

IFRS7p40 IFRS7IG36

At 31 December 2011, if the currency had weakened/strengthened by 11% against the US dollar with all other variables held constant, post-tax profit for the year would have been C362 (2010: C51) higher/lower, mainly as a result of foreign exchange gains/losses on translation of US dollar-denominated trade receivables, financial assets at fair value through profit or loss, debt securities classified as available-for-sale and foreign exchange losses/gains on translation of US dollar-denominated borrowings. Profit is more sensitive to movement in currency/US dollar exchange rates in 2011 than 2010 because of the increased amount of US dollar-denominated borrowings. Similarly, the impact on equity would have been C6,850 (2010: C6,650) higher/ lower due to an increase in the volume of cash flow hedging in US dollars.

(All amounts in C thousands unless otherwise stated)

At 31 December 2011, if the currency had weakened/strengthened by 4% against the UK pound with all other variables held constant, post-tax profit for the year would have been C135 (2010: C172) lower/higher, mainly as a result of foreign exchange gains/losses on translation of UK pound-denominated trade receivables, financial assets at fair value through profit or loss, debt securities classified as available-for-sale and foreign exchange losses/gains on translation of UK pound-denominated borrowings.

(ii) Price risk

IFRS7 p33(a)(b) The group is exposed to equity securities price risk because of investments held by the group and classified on the consolidated balance sheet either as available-for-sale or at fair value through profit or loss. The group is not exposed to commodity price risk. To manage its price risk arising from investments in equity securities, the group diversifies its portfolio. Diversification of the portfolio is done in accordance with the limits set by the group.

The group's investments in equity of other entities that are publicly traded are included in one of the following three equity indexes: DAX equity index, Dow Jones equity index and FTSE 100 UK equity index.

IFRS7p40 IFRS7IG36 The table below summarises the impact of increases/decreases of the three equity indexes on the group's post-tax profit for the year and on equity. The analysis is based on the assumption that the equity indexes had increased/decreased by 5% with all other variables held constant and all the group's equity instruments moved according to the historical correlation with the index:

	Impact on post-tax profit in C		Impact on other components of equity in C	
	2011	2010	**2011**	2010
Index				
DAX	**200**	120	**290**	290
Dow Jones	**150**	120	**200**	70
FTSE 100 UK	**60**	30	**160**	150

Post-tax profit for the year would increase/decrease as a result of gains/losses on equity securities classified as at fair value through profit or loss. Other components of equity would increase/ decrease as a result of gains/losses on equity securities classified as available for sale.

(iii) Cash flow and fair value interest rate risk

IFRS7p33 (a)(b), IFRSp22(c) The group's interest rate risk arises from long-term borrowings. Borrowings issued at variable rates expose the group to cash flow interest rate risk which is partially offset by cash held at variable rates. Borrowings issued at fixed rates expose the group to fair value interest rate risk. Group policy is to maintain approximately 60% of its borrowings in fixed rate instruments. During 2011 and 2010, the group's borrowings at variable rate were denominated in the Currency and the UK pound.

IFRS7p22(b)(c) The group analyses its interest rate exposure on a dynamic basis. Various scenarios are simulated taking into consideration refinancing, renewal of existing positions, alternative financing and hedging. Based on these scenarios, the group calculates the impact on profit and loss of a defined interest rate shift. For each simulation, the same interest rate shift is used for all currencies. The scenarios are run only for liabilities that represent the major interest-bearing positions.

Based on the simulations performed, the impact on post tax profit of a 0.1% shift would be a maximum increase of C41 (2010: C37) or decrease of C34 (2010: C29), respectively. The simulation is done on a quarterly basis to verify that the maximum loss potential is within the limit given by the management.

IFRS7p22(b)(c) Based on the various scenarios, the group manages its cash flow interest rate risk by using floating-to-fixed interest rate swaps. Such interest rate swaps have the economic effect of converting borrowings from floating rates to fixed rates. Generally, the group raises long-term borrowings at floating rates and swaps them into fixed rates that are lower than those available if the group borrowed at fixed rates directly. Under the interest rate swaps, the group agrees with other parties to exchange, at specified intervals (primarily quarterly), the difference between fixed contract rates and floating-rate interest amounts calculated by reference to the agreed notional amounts.

IFRS7p22(b)(c) Occasionally the group also enters into fixed-to-floating interest rate swaps to hedge the fair value interest rate risk arising where it has borrowed at fixed rates in excess of the 60% target.

IFRS7p40 IFRS7IG36 At 31 December 2011, if interest rates on Currency-denominated borrowings had been 10 basis points higher/lower with all other variables held constant, post-tax profit for the year would have been C22 (2010: C21) lower/higher, mainly as a result of higher/lower interest expense on floating rate borrowings; other components of equity would have been C5 (2010: C3) lower/ higher mainly as a result of a decrease/increase in the fair value of fixed rate financial assets classified as available for sale. At 31 December 2011, if interest rates on UK pound-denominated borrowings at that date had been 0.5% higher/lower with all other variables held constant, post- tax profit for the year would have been C57 (2010: C38) lower/higher, mainly as a result of higher/lower interest expense on floating rate borrowings; other components of equity would have been C6 (2010: C4) lower/higher mainly as a result of a decrease/increase in the fair value of fixed rate financial assets classified as available for sale.

(All amounts in C thousands unless otherwise stated)

(b) Credit risk

IFRS7p33(a)(b)
IFRS7p34(a)

Credit risk is managed on group basis, except for credit risk relating to accounts receivable balances. Each local entity is responsible for managing and analysing the credit risk for each of their new clients before standard payment and delivery terms and conditions are offered. Credit risk arises from cash and cash equivalents, derivative financial instruments and deposits with banks and financial institutions, as well as credit exposures to wholesale and retail customers, including outstanding receivables and committed transactions. For banks and financial institutions, only independently rated parties with a minimum rating of 'A' are accepted. If wholesale customers are independently rated, these ratings are used. If there is no independent rating, risk control assesses the credit quality of the customer, taking into account its financial position, past experience and other factors. Individual risk limits are set based on internal or external ratings in accordance with limits set by the board. The utilisation of credit limits is regularly monitored. Sales to retail customers are settled in cash or using major credit cards. See note 9(b) for further disclosure on credit risk.

No credit limits were exceeded during the reporting period, and management does not expect any losses from non-performance by these counterparties.

(c) Liquidity risk

IFRS7
p33(a),(b)
34(a)

Cash flow forecasting is performed in the operating entities of the group in and aggregated by group finance. Group finance monitors rolling forecasts of the group's liquidity requirements to ensure it has sufficient cash to meet operational needs while maintaining sufficient headroom on its undrawn committed borrowing facilities (note 22) at all times so that the group does not breach borrowing limits or covenants (where applicable) on any of its borrowing facilities. Such forecasting takes into consideration the group's debt financing plans, covenant compliance, compliance with internal balance sheet ratio targets and, if applicable external regulatory or legal requirements – for example, currency restrictions.

IFRS7
p33(a),(b)
39(c)
IFRS7B11E

Surplus cash held by the operating entities over and above balance required for working capital management are transferred to the group treasury. Group treasury invests surplus cash in interest bearing current accounts, time deposits, money market deposits and marketable securities, choosing instruments with appropriate maturities or sufficient liquidity to provide sufficient head-room as determined by the above-mentioned forecasts. At the reporting date, the group held money market funds of C6, 312 (2010: C934) and other liquid assets of C321 (2010: C1, 400) that are expected to readily generate cash inflows for managing liquidity risk.

IFRS7p39(a)(b)

The table below analyses the group's non-derivative financial liabilities and net-settled derivative financial liabilities into relevant maturity groupings based on the remaining period at the balance sheet date to the contractual maturity date. Derivative financial liabilities are included in the analysis if their contractual maturities are essential for an understanding of the timing of the cash flows. The amounts disclosed in the table are the contractual undiscounted cash flows[1].

At 31 December 2011	Less than 3 months	Between 3 months and 1 year[2]	Between 1 and 2 years[2]	Between 2 and 5 years[2]	Over 5 years[2]
Borrowings (ex finance lease liabilities)	5,112	15,384	22,002	67,457	38,050
Finance lease liabilities	639	2,110	1,573	4,719	2,063
Trading and net settled derivative financial instruments (interest rate swaps)	280	–	10	116	41
Trade and other payables	12,543	3,125[2]	–	–	–
Financial guarantee contracts	21	–	–		
At 31 December 2010					
Borrowings (ex finance lease liability)	4,061	12,197	11,575	58,679	38,103
Finance lease liabilities	697	2,506	1,790	5,370	2,891
Trading and net settled derivative financial instruments (interest rate swaps)	317	–	15	81	50
Trade and other payables	9,214	2,304[3]	–	–	–
Financial guarantee contracts	10	–	–		

IFRS7
B10A(a)

Of the C67,457 disclosed in the 2011 borrowings time band 'Between 2 and 5 years' the company intends to repay C40,000 in the first quarter of 2011 (2010: nil).

IFRS7p39(b)

The group's trading portfolio derivative instruments with a negative fair value have been included at their fair value of C268 (2010: C298) within the less than three month time bucket. This is because the contractual maturities are not

[1] IFRS7 p39(a)(b) The amounts included in the table are the contractual undiscounted cash flows, except for trading derivatives, which are included at their fair value (see below). As a result, these amounts will not reconcile to the amounts disclosed on the balance sheet except for short-term payables where discounting is not applied. Entities can choose to add a reconciling column and a final total that ties into the balance sheet, if they wish.

[2] The specific time-buckets presented are not mandated by the standard but are based on a choice by management based on how the business is managed. Sufficient time buckets should be provided to give sufficient granularity to provide the reader with an understanding of the entity's liquidity.

[3] The maturity analysis applies to financial instruments only; non-financial liabilities are not therefore included.

(All amounts in C thousands unless otherwise stated)

essential for an understanding of the timing of the cash flows These contracts are managed on a net-fair value basis rather than by maturity date. Net settled derivatives comprise interest rate swaps used by the group to manage the group's interest rate profile.

IFRS7p39(b) All of the non-trading group's gross settled derivative financial instruments are in hedge relationships and are due to settle within 12 months of the balance sheet date. These contracts require undiscounted contractual cash inflows of C78,756 (2010: C83,077) and undiscounted contractual cash outflows of C78,241 (2010: C83,366).

1p134,135,
IG10

3.2 Capital management

The group's objectives when managing capital are to safeguard the group's ability to continue as a going concern in order to provide returns for shareholders and benefits for other stakeholders and to maintain an optimal capital structure to reduce the cost of capital.

In order to maintain or adjust the capital structure, the group may adjust the amount of dividends paid to shareholders, return capital to shareholders, issue new shares or sell assets to reduce debt.

Consistent with others in the industry, the group monitors capital on the basis of the gearing ratio. This ratio is calculated as net debt divided by total capital. Net debt is calculated as total borrowings (including 'current and non-current borrowings' as shown in the consolidated balance sheet) less cash and cash equivalents. Total capital is calculated as 'equity' as shown in the consolidated balance sheet plus net debt.

During 2011, the group's strategy, which was unchanged from 2010, was to maintain the gearing ratio within 45% to 50% and a BB credit rating. The BB credit rating has been maintained throughout the period. The gearing ratios at 31 December 2011 and 2010 were as follows:

	2011	2010
Total borrowings (note 22)	126,837	114,604
Less: cash and cash equivalents (note 15)	(17,928)	(34,062)
Net debt	108,909	80,542
Total equity	131,773	88,946
Total capital	240,682	169,488
Gearing ratio	45%	48%

The decrease in the gearing ratio during 2011 resulted primarily from the issue of share capital as part of the consideration for the acquisition of a subsidiary (notes 17 and 39).

3.3 Fair value estimation

The table below analyses financial instruments carried at fair value, by valuation method. The different levels have been defined as follows:

- Quoted prices (unadjusted) in active markets for identical assets or liabilities (Level 1).
- Inputs other than quoted prices included within Level 1 that are observable for the asset or liability, either directly (that is, as prices) or indirectly (that is, derived from prices) (Level 2).
- Inputs for the asset or liability that are not based on observable market data (that is, unobservable inputs) (Level 3).

IFRS7
p27B(a)

The following table presents the group's assets and liabilities that are measured at fair value at 31 December 2011.

	Level 1	Level 2	Level 3	Total
Assets				
Financial assets at fair value through profit or loss				
– Trading derivatives	–	250	111	361
– Trading securities	11,820	–	–	11,820
Derivatives used for hedging	–	1,103	–	1,103
Available-for-sale financial assets				
– Equity securities	18,735	–	–	18,735
– Debt investments	288	347	–	635
Total assets	30,843	1,700	111	32,654
Liabilities				
Financial liabilities at fair value through profit or loss				
– Trading derivatives	–	268	–	268
Derivatives used for hedging	–	327	–	327
Total liabilities	–	595	–	595

(All amounts in C thousands unless otherwise stated)

The following table presents the group's assets and liabilities that are measured at fair value at 31 December 2010.

	Level 1	Level 2	Level 3	Total
Assets				
Financial assets at fair value through profit or loss:				
– Trading derivatives	–	321	–	321
– Trading securities	7,972	–	–	7,972
Derivatives used for hedging	–	875	–	875
Available-for-sale financial assets:				
– Equity securities	14,646	–	–	14,646
– Debt investments	–	264	–	264
Total assets	22,618	1,460		24,078
Liabilities				
Financial liabilities at fair value through profit or loss:				
– Trading derivatives	–	298	–	298
Derivatives used for hedging	–	449	–	449
Total liabilities	–	747	–	747

IFRS7p27   The fair value of financial instruments traded in active markets is based on quoted market prices at the balance sheet date. A market is regarded as active if quoted prices are readily and regularly available from an exchange, dealer, broker, industry group, pricing service, or regulatory agency, and those prices represent actual and regularly occurring market transactions on an arm's length basis. The quoted market price used for financial assets held by the group is the current bid price. These instruments are included in Level 1. Instruments included in Level 1 comprise primarily DAX, FTSE 100 and Dow Jones equity investments classified as trading securities or available for sale.

The fair value of financial instruments that are not traded in an active market (for example, over-the-counter derivatives) is determined by using valuation techniques. These valuation techniques maximise the use of observable market data where it is available and rely as little as possible on entity specific estimates. If all significant inputs required to fair value an instrument are observable, the instrument is included in Level 2.

If one or more of the significant inputs is not based on observable market data, the instrument is included in Level 3.

Specific valuation techniques used to value financial instruments include:

- Quoted market prices or dealer quotes for similar instruments.
- The fair value of interest rate swaps is calculated as the present value of the estimated future cash flows based on observable yield curves.
- The fair value of forward foreign exchange contracts is determined using forward exchange rates at the balance sheet date, with the resulting value discounted back to present value.
- Other techniques, such as discounted cash flow analysis, are used to determine fair value for the remaining financial instruments.

Note that all of the resulting fair value estimates are included in Level 2 except for certain forward foreign exchange contracts explained below.

IFRS7p27B(c)   The following table presents the changes in Level 3 instruments for the year ended 31 December 2011.

	Trading derivative's at fair value through profit or loss	Total
Opening balance	–	–
Transfers into Level 3	115	115
Gains and losses recognised in profit or loss	(4)	(4)
Closing balance	111	111
Total gains or losses for the period included in profit or loss for assets held at the end of the reporting period	(4)	(4)

(All amounts in C thousands unless otherwise stated)

The following table presents the changes in Level 3 instruments for the year ended 31 December 2010.

	Trading derivative's at fair value through profit or loss	Total
Opening balance	62	62
Settlements	(51)	(51)
Gains and losses recognised in profit or loss	(11)	(11)
Closing balance	–	–
Total gains or losses for the period included in profit or loss for assets held at the end of the reporting period	–	–

In 2011, the group transferred a held-for-trading forward foreign exchange contract from Level 2 into Level 3. This is because the counterparty for the derivative encountered significant financial difficulties, which resulted in a significant increase to the discount rate due to increased counterparty credit risk, which is not based on observable inputs.

IFRS7 p27B(e)

If the change in the credit default rate would be shifted +/- 5% the impact on profit or loss would be C20.

Commentary – financial risk management

Accounting standard for presentation and disclosure of financial instruments

IFRS7p3

1. IFRS 7, 'Financial instruments: Disclosures', applies to all reporting entities and to all types of financial instruments except:
   - Those interests in subsidiaries, associates and joint ventures that are accounted for under IAS 27, 'Consolidated and separate financial statements', IAS 28, 'Investments in associates', or IAS 31, 'Interests in joint ventures'. However, entities should apply IFRS 7 to an interest in a subsidiary, associate or joint venture that according to IAS 27, IAS 28 or IAS 31 is accounted for under IAS 39, 'Financial instruments: Recognition and measurement'. Entities should also apply IFRS 7 to all derivatives on interests in subsidiaries, associates or joint ventures unless the derivative meets the definition of an equity instrument in IAS 32, 'Financial instruments: Presentation'. .
   - Employers' rights and obligations under employee benefit plans, to which IAS 19, 'Employee benefits', applies.
   - Insurance contracts as defined in IFRS 4, 'Insurance contracts'. However, IFRS 7 applies to derivatives that are embedded in insurance contracts if IAS 39 requires the entity to account for them separately. It also applies to financial guarantee contracts if the issuer applies IAS 39 in recognising and measuring the contracts.
   - Financial instruments, contracts and obligations under share-based payment transactions to which IFRS 2, 'Share-based payment', applies, except for contracts within the scope of paragraphs 5-7 of IAS 39, which are disclosed under IFRS 7.
   - Puttable financial instruments that are required to be classified as equity instruments in accordance with paragraphs 16A and 16B or 16C and 16D of IAS 32 .

Parent entity disclosures

IFRS7

2. Where applicable, all disclosure requirements outlined in IFRS 7 should be made for both the parent and consolidated entity. The relief from making parent entity disclosures, which was previously available under IAS 30, 'Disclosures in the financial statements of banks and similar financial institutions', and IAS 32, has not been retained in IFRS 7.

Classes of financial instrument

IFRS7p6, B1-B3

3. Where IFRS 7 requires disclosures by class of financial instrument, the entity groups its financial instruments into classes that are appropriate to the nature of the information disclosed and that take into account the characteristics of those financial instruments. The entity should provide sufficient information to permit reconciliation to the line items presented in the balance sheet. Guidance on classes of financial instruments and the level of required disclosures is provided in appendix B of IFRS 7.

Level of detail and selection of assumptions – information through the eyes of management

IFRS7p34(a)

4. The disclosures in relation to an entity's financial risk management should reflect the information provided internally to key management personnel. As such, the disclosures that will be provided by an entity, their level of detail and the underlying assumptions used will vary greatly from entity to entity. The disclosures in this illustrative financial statement are only one example of the kind of information that may be disclosed; the entity should consider carefully what may be appropriate in its individual circumstances.

(All amounts in C thousands unless otherwise stated)

Nature and extent of risks arising from financial instruments

IFRS7p31
IFRS8p32
5. The financial statement should include qualitative and quantitative disclosures that enable users to evaluate the nature and extent of risks arising from financial instruments to which the entity is exposed at the end of the reporting period. These risks typically include, but are not limited to, credit risk, liquidity risk and market risk.

Qualitative disclosures

IFRS7p33
6. An entity should disclose for each type of risk:
(a) the exposures to the risk and how they arise;
(b) the entity's objectives, policies and processes for managing the risk and the methods used to measure the risk; and
(c) any changes in (a) or (b) from the previous period.

Quantitative disclosures

IFRS7p34(a)(c)
7. An entity should provide for each type of risk, summary quantitative data on risk exposure at the end of the reporting period, based on information provided internally to key management personnel and any concentrations of risk. This information can be presented in narrative form as is done on pages x to x of this publication. Alternatively, entities could provide the data in a table that sets out the impact of each major risk on each type of financial instruments. This table could also be a useful tool for compiling the information that should be disclosed under paragraph 34 of IFRS 7.

IFRS7p34(b)
8. If not already provided as part of the summary quantitative data, the entity should also provide the information in paragraphs 9-15 below, unless the risk is not material.

Credit risk

IFRS7p36
IFRS7p37
9. For each class of financial instrument, the entity should disclose:
(a) the maximum exposure to credit risk and any related collateral held;
(b) information about the credit quality of financial assets that are neither past due nor impaired;
(c) an analysis of the age of financial assets that are past due but not impaired; and
(d) an analysis of financial assets that are individually determined to be impaired including the factors in determining that they are impaired.

Liquidity risk

IFRS7p34(a)
IFRS7p39
10 Information about liquidity risk shall be provided by way of:
(a) a maturity analysis for non-derivative financial liabilities (including issued financial guarantee contracts) that shows the remaining contractual maturities;
(b) a maturity analysis for derivative financial liabilities (see paragraph 12 below for details); and
(c) a description of how the entity manages the liquidity risk inherent in (a) and (b).

IFRS7B11F
11 In describing how liquidity risk is being managed, an entity should consider discussing whether it:
(a) has committed borrowing facilities or other lines of credit that it can access to meet liquidity needs;
(b) holds deposits at central banks to meet liquidity needs;
(c) has very diverse funding sources;
(d) has significant concentrations of liquidity risk in either its assets or its funding sources;
(e) has internal control processes and contingency plans for managing liquidity risk;
(f) has instruments that include accelerated repayment terms (for example, on the downgrade of the entity's credit rating);
(g) has instruments that could require the posting of collateral (for example, margin calls for derivatives);
(h) has instruments that allow the entity to choose whether it settles its financial liabilities by delivering cash (or another financial asset) or by delivering its own shares; and
(i) has instruments that are subject to master netting agreements.

Maturity analysis

IFRS7B11B
12. The maturity analysis for derivative financial liabilities should disclose the remaining contractual maturities if these maturities are essential for an understanding of the timing of the cash flows. For example, this will be the case for interest rate swaps in a cash flow hedge of a variable rate financial asset or liability and for all loan commitments. Where the remaining contractual maturities are not essential for an understanding of the timing of the cash flows, the expected maturities may be disclosed instead.

IFRS7p39,
IFRS7B11D
13. For derivative financial instruments where gross cash flows are exchanged and contractual maturities are essential to understanding, the maturity analysis should disclose the contractual amounts that are to be exchanged on a gross basis. The amount disclosed should be the amount expected to be paid in future periods, determined by reference to the conditions existing at the end of the reporting period. However, IFRS 7 does not specify whether current or forward rates should be used. We therefore recommend that entities explain which approach has been chosen. This approach should be applied consistently.

(All amounts in C thousands unless otherwise stated)

IFRS7B11	14. The specific time buckets presented are not mandated by the standard but are based on what is reported internally to the key management personnel. The entity uses judgement to determine the appropriate number of time bands.
IFRS7B11D	15. If the amounts included in the maturity tables are the contractual undiscounted cash flows, these amounts will not reconcile to the amounts disclosed on the balance sheet for borrowings, derivative financial instruments and trade and other payables. Entities can choose to add a column with the carrying amounts that ties into the balance sheet and a reconciling column if they so wish, but this is not mandatory.
IFRS7B10A	16. If an outflow of cash could occur either significantly earlier than indicated or be for significantly different amounts from those indicated in the entity's disclosures about its exposure to liquidity risk, the entity should state that fact and provide quantitative information that enables users of its financial statements to evaluate the extent of this risk. This disclosure is not necessary if that information is included in the contractual maturity analysis.

Financing arrangements

IFRS7p39(c)	17. Committed borrowing facilities are a major element of liquidity management. Entities should therefore consider providing information about their undrawn facilities. IAS 7, 'Statements of cash flows', also recommends disclosure of undrawn borrowing facilities that may be available for future operating activities and to settle capital commitments, indicating any restrictions on the use of these facilities.

Market risk

IFRS7p40(a)(b)	18. Entities should disclose a sensitivity analysis for each type of market risk (currency, interest rate and other price risk) to which an entity is exposed at the end of the reporting period, showing how profit or loss and equity would have been affected by 'reasonably possible' changes in the relevant risk variable, as well as the methods and assumptions used in preparing such an analysis.
IFRS7p40(c)	19. If there have been any changes in methods and assumptions from the previous period, this should be disclosed, together with the reasons for the change.

Foreign currency risk

IFRS7B23	20. Foreign currency risk can only arise on financial instruments that are denominated in a currency other than the functional currency in which they are measured. Translation related risks are therefore not included in the assessment of the entity's exposure to currency risks. Translation exposures arise from financial and non-financial items held by an entity (for example, a subsidiary) with a functional currency different from the group's presentation currency. However, foreign currency denominated inter- company receivables and payables that do not form part of a net investment in a foreign operation are included in the sensitivity analysis for foreign currency risks, because even though the balances eliminate in the consolidated balance sheet, the effect on profit or loss of their revaluation under IAS 21 is not fully eliminated.

Interest rate risk

21. Sensitivity to changes in interest rates is relevant to financial assets or financial liabilities bearing floating interest rates due to the risk that future cash flows will fluctuate. However, sensitivity will also be relevant to fixed rate financial assets and financial liabilities that are re-measured to fair value.

Fair value disclosures

Financial instruments carried at other than fair value

IFRS7p25 IFRS7p29	22. An entity should disclose the fair value for each class of financial assets and financial liabilities (see paragraph 3 above) in a way that permits it to be compared with its carrying amount. Fair values do not need to be disclosed for the following: (a) when the carrying amount is a reasonable approximation of fair value; (b) investments in equity instruments (and derivatives linked to such equity instruments) that do not have a quoted market price in an active market and that are measured at cost in accordance with IAS 39 because their fair value cannot be measured reliably; or (c) A contract containing a discretionary participation feature (as described in IFRS 4, 'Insurance contracts') where the fair value of that feature cannot be measured reliably.

23. The information about the fair values can be provided either in a combined financial instruments note or in the individual notes. However, fair values should be separately disclosed for each class of financial instrument (see paragraph 3 above), which means that each line item in the table would have to be broken down into individual classes. For that reason, IFRS GAAP plc has chosen to provide the information in the relevant notes.

Methods and assumptions in determining fair value

IFRS7p27	24. An entity should disclose for each class of financial instruments (see paragraph 3 above) the methods and, when a valuation technique is used, the assumptions applied in determining fair values. Examples of assumptions that

(All amounts in C thousands unless otherwise stated)

should be disclosed are assumptions relating to prepayment rates, rates of estimated credit losses, interest rates or discount rates. If the entity has changed a valuation technique, that fact and the reason for the change should also be disclosed.

Financial instruments measured at cost where fair value cannot be determined reliably

IFRS7p30 25. If the fair value of investments in unquoted equity instruments, derivatives linked to such equity instruments or a contract containing a discretionary participation feature (as described in IFRS 4, 'Insurance contracts') cannot be measured reliably, the entity should disclose:

(a) the fact that fair value information has not been disclosed because it cannot be measured reliably;

(b) a description of the financial instruments, their carrying amount and an explanation of why fair value cannot be measured reliably;

(c) information about the market for the instruments;

(d) information about whether and how the entity intends to dispose of the financial instruments; and

(e) if the instruments are subsequently derecognised, that fact, their carrying amount at the time of derecognition and the amount of gain or loss recognised.

Fair value measurements recognised in the balance sheet

IFRS7p27B 26. For fair value measurements recognised in the balance sheet, the entity should also disclose for each class of financial instruments:

(a) the level in the fair value hierarchy into which the fair value measurements are categorised;

(b) any significant transfers between Level 1 and Level 2 of the fair value hierarchy and the reasons for those transfers;

(c) for fair value measurements in Level 3 of the hierarchy, a reconciliation from the beginning balances to the ending balances, showing separately changes during the period attributable to the following:

  (i) total gains or losses for the period recognised in profit or loss, together with a description of where they are presented in the statement of comprehensive income or the income statement (as applicable);

  (ii) total gains or losses recognised in other comprehensive income;

  (iii) purchases, sales issues and settlements (each type disclosed separately); and

  (iv) transfers into or out of Level 3 and the reasons for those transfers;

(d) the amount of total gains or losses for the period included in profit or loss that are attributable to gains or losses relating to assets and liabilities held at the end of the reporting period, together with a description of where the gains and losses are presented in the statement of comprehensive income or the income statement (as applicable); and

(e) for fair value measurements in Level 3, if changing one or more of the inputs to reasonably possible alternative assumptions would change fair value significantly, that fact, the effect of those changes and how the effect was calculated.

IFRS7p27A 27. Entities should classify fair value measurements using a fair value hierarchy that reflects the significance of the inputs used in making the measurements. The fair value hierarchy should have the following levels:

(a) Level 1: quoted prices (unadjusted) in active markets for identical assets or liabilities.

(b) Level 2: inputs other than quoted prices that are observable for the asset or liability, either directly (for example, as prices) or indirectly (for example, derived from prices).

(c) Level 3: inputs for the asset or liability that are not based on observable market data.

The appropriate level is determined on the basis of the lowest level input that is significant to the fair value measurement.

Additional information where quantitative data about risk exposure is unrepresentative

IFRS7p35 28. If the quantitative data disclosed under paragraphs 7, 9, 10 and 14 above is unrepresentative of the entity's
IFRS7p42 exposure to risk during the period, the entity should provide further information that is representative. If the sensitivity analyses are unrepresentative of a risk inherent in a financial instrument (for example, where the year end exposure does not reflect the exposure during the year), the entity should disclose that fact and the reason why the sensitivity analyses are unrepresentative.

4 Critical accounting estimates and judgements

Estimates and judgements are continually evaluated and are based on historical experience and other factors, including expectations of future events that are believed to be reasonable under the circumstances.

1p125 ### 4.1 Critical accounting estimates and assumptions

The group makes estimates and assumptions concerning the future. The resulting accounting estimates will, by definition, seldom equal the related actual results. The estimates and assumptions that have a significant risk of causing a material adjustment to the carrying amounts of assets and liabilities within the next financial year are addressed below.

(All amounts in C thousands unless otherwise stated)

(a) Estimated impairment of goodwill

The group tests annually whether goodwill has suffered any impairment, in accordance with the accounting policy stated in note 2.6. The recoverable amounts of cash-generating units have been determined based on value-in-use calculations. These calculations require the use of estimates (note 17).

1p129, 36p134 (f)(i)-(iii) An impairment charge of C4,650 arose in the wholesale CGU in Step-land (included in the Russian operating segment) during the course of the 2011 year, resulting in the carrying amount of the CGU being written down to its recoverable amount. If the budgeted gross margin used in the value-in-use calculation for the wholesale CGU in Step-land had been 10% lower than management's estimates at 31 December 2011 (for example, 46% instead of 56%), the group would have recognised a further impairment of goodwill by C100 and would need to reduce the carrying value of property, plant and equipment by C300.

If the estimated cost of capital used in determining the pre-tax discount rate for the wholesale CGU in Step-land had been 1% higher than management's estimates (for example, 13.8% instead of 12.8%), the group would have recognised a further impairment against goodwill of C300.

(b) Income taxes

The group is subject to income taxes in numerous jurisdictions. Significant judgement is required in determining the worldwide provision for income taxes. There are many transactions and calculations for which the ultimate tax determination is uncertain. The group recognises liabilities for anticipated tax audit issues based on estimates of whether additional taxes will be due. Where the final tax outcome of these matters is different from the amounts that were initially recorded, such differences will impact the current and deferred income tax assets and liabilities in the period in which such determination is made.

Were the actual final outcome (on the judgement areas) of expected cash flows to differ by 10% from management's estimates, the group would need to:

- increase the income tax liability by C120 and the deferred tax liability by C230, if unfavourable; or
- decrease the income tax liability by C110 and the deferred tax liability by C215, if favourable.

(c) Fair value of derivatives and other financial instruments

IFRS7p27 The fair value of financial instruments that are not traded in an active market (for example, over-the-counter derivatives) is determined by using valuation techniques. The group uses its judgement to select a variety of methods and make assumptions that are mainly based on market conditions existing at the end of each reporting period. The group has used discounted cash flow analysis for various available-for-sale financial assets that are not traded in active markets.

The carrying amount of available-for-sale financial assets would be an estimated C12 lower or C15 higher were the discount rate used in the discount cash flow analysis to differ by 10% from management's estimates.

(d) Revenue recognition

The group uses the percentage-of-completion method in accounting for its fixed-price contracts to deliver design services. Use of the percentage-of-completion method requires the group to estimate the services performed to date as a proportion of the total services to be performed. Were the proportion of services performed to total services to be performed to differ by 10% from management's estimates, the amount of revenue recognised in the year would be increased by C1175 if the proportion performed were increased, or would be decreased by C1160 if the proportion performed were decreased.

(e) Pension benefits

The present value of the pension obligations depends on a number of factors that are determined on an actuarial basis using a number of assumptions. The assumptions used in determining the net cost (income) for pensions include the discount rate. Any changes in these assumptions will impact the carrying amount of pension obligations.

The group determines the appropriate discount rate at the end of each year. This is the interest rate that should be used to determine the present value of estimated future cash outflows expected to be required to settle the pension obligations. In determining the appropriate discount rate, the group considers the interest rates of high-quality corporate bonds that are denominated in the currency in which the benefits will be paid and that have terms to maturity approximating the terms of the related pension obligation.

Other key assumptions for pension obligations are based in part on current market conditions. Additional information is disclosed in note 33.

Were the discount rate used to differ by 10% from management's estimates, the carrying amount of pension obligations would be an estimated C425 lower or C450 higher.

(All amounts in C thousands unless otherwise stated)

1p122   **4.2 Critical judgements in applying the entity's accounting policies**

(a) Revenue recognition

The group has recognised revenue amounting to C950 for sales of goods to L&Co in the UK during 2011. The buyer has the right to return the goods if their customers are dissatisfied. The group believes that, based on past experience with similar sales, the dissatisfaction rate will not exceed 3%. The group has, therefore, recognised revenue on this transaction with a corresponding provision against revenue for estimated returns. If the estimate changes by 1%, revenue will be reduced/increased by C10.

(b) Impairment of available-for-sale equity investments

The group follows the guidance of IAS 39 to determine when an available-for-sale equity investment is impaired. This determination requires significant judgement. In making this judgement, the group evaluates, among other factors, the duration and extent to which the fair value of an investment is less than its cost; and the financial health of and short-term business outlook for the investee, including factors such as industry and sector performance, changes in technology and operational and financing cash flow.

If all of the declines in fair value below cost were considered significant or prolonged, the group would suffer an additional loss of C1,300 in its 2011 financial statements, being the transfer of the accumulated fair value adjustments recognised in equity on the impaired available-for-sale financial assets to the income statement.

(c) Investment in Alpha Limited

Management has assessed the level of influence that the Group has on Alpha Limited and determined that it has significant influence even though the share holding is below 20% because of the board representation and contractual terms. Consequently, this investment has been classified as an associate.

5 Segment information

IFRS8p22(a)   The strategic steering committee is the group's chief operating decision-maker. Management has determined the operating segments based on the information reviewed by the strategic steering committee for the purposes of allocating resources and assessing performance.

IFRS8p22(a)(b) The strategic steering committee considers the business from both a geographic and product perspective. Geographically, management considers the performance in the UK, US, China, Russia and Europe. From a product perspective, management separately considers the wholesale and retail activities in these geographies. The group only has retail activities in the UK and US. The wholesale segments derive their revenue primarily from the manufacture and wholesale sale of the group's own brand of shoes, Footsy Tootsy. The UK and US retail segments derive their revenue from retail sales of shoe and leather goods including the group's own brand and other major retail shoe brands.

IFRS8 p22(a)   Although the China segment does not meet the quantitative thresholds required by IFRS 8 for reportable segments, management has concluded that this segment should be reported, as it is closely monitored by the strategic steering committee as a potential growth region and is expected to materially contribute to group revenue in the future.

IFRS8p29   During 2010, US retail did not qualify as a reportable operating segment. However, with the acquisition in 2011 of ABC Group (see note 39), retail qualifies as a reportable operating segment; the comparatives have been restated.

IFRS8p16   All other segments primarily relate to the sale of design services and goods transportation services to other shoe manufacturers in the UK and Europe and wholesale shoe revenue from the Central American region. These activities are excluded from the reportable operating segments, as these activities are not reviewed by the strategic steering committee.

IFRS8p27(b), 28   The strategic steering committee assesses the performance of the operating segments based on a measure of adjusted EBITDA. This measurement basis excludes discontinued operations and the effects of non-recurring expenditure from the operating segments such as restructuring costs, legal expenses and goodwill impairments when the impairment is the result of an isolated, non-recurring event. The measure also excludes the effects of equity-settled share-based payments and unrealised gains/losses on financial instruments. Interest income and expenditure are not allocated to segments, as this type of activity is driven by the central treasury function, which manages the cash position of the group.

(All amounts in C thousands unless otherwise stated)

Revenue

	Year ended 31 December 2011			Year ended 31 December 2010		
	Total segment revenue	Inter-segment revenue	Revenue from external customers	Total segment revenue	Inter-segment revenue	Revenue from external customers
UK wholesale	46,638	(11,403)	**35,235**	57,284	(11,457)	**45,827**
UK retail	43,257	–	**43,257**	1,682	–	**1,682**
US wholesale	28,820	(7,364)	**21,456**	33,990	(6,798)	**27,192**
US retail	42,672	–	**42,672**	2,390	–	**2,390**
Russia	26,273	(5,255)	**21,018**	8,778	(1,756)	**7,022**
China	5,818	(1,164)	**4,654**	3,209	(642)	**2,567**
Europe	40,273	(8,055)	**32,218**	26,223	(5,245)	**20,978**
All other segments	13,155	(2,631)	**10,524**	5,724	(1,022)	**4,702**
Total	246,906	(35,872)	**211,034**	139,280	(26,920)	**112,360**

IFRS8p27(a) Sales between segments are carried out at arm's length. The revenue from external parties reported to the strategic steering committee is measured in a manner consistent with that in the income statement.

IFRS8p28(b)

EBITDA

	Year ended 31 December 2011	Year ended 31 December 2010
	Adjusted EBITDA	Adjusted EBITDA
UK Wholesale	**17,298**	17,183
UK Retail	**9,550**	800
US Wholesale	**9,146**	10,369
US Retail	**9,686**	1,298
Russia	**12,322**	3,471
China	**2,323**	1,506
Europe	**16,003**	10,755
All other segments	**3,504**	1,682
Total	**79,832**	**47,064**
Depreciation	(17,754)	(9,662)
Amortisation	(800)	(565)
Restructuring costs	(1,986)	–
Legal expenses	(737)	(855)
Goodwill impairment	(4,650)	–
Unrealised financial instrument gains	102	101
Share options granted to directors and employees	(690	(820)
Finance costs – net	(6,443)	(10,588)
Other	802	243
Profit before tax and discontinued operations	**47,676**	**24,918**

IFRS8p23

Other profit and loss disclosures[1]

	Year ended 31 December 2011					Year ended 31 December 2010			
	Depreciation and amortisation	Goodwill impairment	Restructuring costs	Income tax expense	Share of profit/ (loss) from associates	Depreciation and amortisation	Income tax expense	Share of profit/ (loss) from associates
UK wholesale	(3,226)	–	–	(2,550)	200	(3,801)	(2,772)	155
UK retail	(3,830)	–	–	(2,780)	–	(201)	(650)	–
US wholesale	(1,894)	–	–	(1,395)	–	(2,448)	–1,407	–
US retail	(3,789)	–	–	(3,040)	–	(199)	(489)	–
Russia	(2,454)	(4,650)	(1,986)	(1,591)	–	(453)	(509)	–
China	(386)	–	–	(365)	–	(286)	(150)	–
Europe	(2,706)	–	–	(2,490)		(2,701)	(2,201)	–
All other segments	(269)	–	–	(400)	15	(138)	(492)	(10)
Total	**(18,554)**	**(4,650)**	**(1,986)**	**(14,611)**	**215**	**(10,227)**	**(8,670)**	**145**

IFRS 8p23(i) See note 7 for details of the impairment of goodwill of C4,650 in the Russian operating segment in 2011 relating to the decision to reduce manufacturing output. There has been no further impact on the measurement of the group's assets and liabilities. There was no impairment charge or restructuring costs recognised in 2010.

[1] Paragraph 23 of IFRS 8 requires disclosures of interest revenue and expense even if not included in the measure of segment profit and loss. This disclosure has not been included in the illustrative because these balances are not allocated to the segments.

(All amounts in C thousands unless otherwise stated)

IFRS8p27(f) Due to the European operations utilising excess capacity in certain Russian assets that are geographically close to the European region, a portion of the depreciation charge of C197 (2010: C50) relating to the Russian assets has been allocated to the European segment to take account of this.

IFRS8p23,24, 28(c) Assets[1]

	Year ended 31 December 2011			Year ended 31 December 2010		
	Total assets	Investments in associates	Additions to non-current assets[2]	Total assets	Investments in associates	Additions to non-current assets[2]
UK wholesale	46,957	7,207	–	43,320	7,050	–
UK retail	46,197	–	35,543	9580	–	47
US wholesale	27,313	–	–	32,967	–	–
US retail	45,529	–	39,817	8,550	–	46
Russia	22,659	–	–	5,067	–	–
China	6,226	–	11,380	20,899	–	2,971
Europe	42,636	–	–	36,450	–	–
All other segments	22,184	6,166	1,500	49,270	6,194	3,678
Total	**259,701**	**13,373**	**88,240**	**206,103**	**13,244**	**6,742**
Unallocated						
Deferred tax	3,520			3,321		
Available-for-sale financial assets	19,370			14,910		
Financial assets at fair value through the profit and loss	11,820			7,972		
Derivative financial instruments	1,464			1,196		
Assets of disposal group classified as held for sale	3,333			–		
Total assets per the balance sheet	**299,208**			**233,502**		

IFRS8p27(c) The amounts provided to the strategic steering committee with respect to total assets are measured in a manner consistent with that of the financial statements. These assets are allocated based on the operations of the segment and the physical location of the asset.

Investment in shares (classified as available-for-sale financial assets or financial assets at fair value through profit or loss) held by the group are not considered to be segment assets but rather are managed by the treasury function. The group's interest-bearing liabilities are not considered to be segment liabilities but rather are managed by the treasury function.

Entity-wide information

IFRS8p32 Breakdown of the revenue from all services is as follows:

	2011	2010
Analysis of revenue by category:		
– Sales of goods	202,884	104,495
– Revenue from services	8,000	7,800
– Royalty income	150	65
Total	**211,034**	**112,360**

IFRS8 p33(a) The group is domiciled in the UK. The result of its revenue from external customers in the UK is C50,697 (2010: C48,951), and the total of revenue from external customers from other countries is C160,337 (2010: C63,409). The breakdown of the major component of the total of revenue from external customers from other countries is disclosed above.

IFRS8 p33(b) The total of non-current assets other than financial instruments and deferred tax assets (there are no employment benefit assets and rights arising under insurance contracts) located in the UK is C49,696 (2010: C39,567), and the total of such non-current assets located in other countries is C146,762 (2010: C93,299).

IFRS8p34 Revenues of approximately C32,023 (2010: C28,034) are derived from a single external customer. These revenues are attributable to the US retail and UK wholesale segments.

[1] The measure of assets has been disclosed for each reportable segment as is regularly provided to the chief operating decision-maker. If the chief operating decision-maker reviews a measure of liabilities, This should also be disclosed.
[2] Additions to non-current assets exclude other than financial instruments and deferred tax assets.

(All amounts in C thousands unless otherwise stated)

6 Exceptional items

Items that are material either because of their size or their nature, are presented within their relevant consolidated income statement category and disclosed separately in the notes to the financial statements. The separate reporting of exceptional items helps provide an understanding of the group's underlying performance.

An analysis of the amount presented as exceptional item in these financial statements is given below.

	2011	2010
Operating items:		
– Inventory write-down	3,117	–

The inventory write-down of C3,117 relates to leather accessories that have been destroyed by fire In an accident. This amount is included within cost of sales in the income statement.

7 Other income

	Group	2011	2010
	Gain on re-measuring existing interest in ABC Group on acquisition (note 39)	850	–
18p35(b)(v)	Dividend income on available-for-sale financial assets	1,100	883
18p35(b)(v)	Dividend income on financial assets at fair value through profit or loss	800	310
	Investment income	2,750	1,193
	Insurance reimbursement	–	66
	Total	2,750	1,259

The insurance reimbursement relates to the excess of insurance proceeds over the carrying values of goods damaged.

8 Other (losses)/gains – net

	Group	2011	2010
IFRS7 p20(a)(i)	Financial assets at fair value through profit or loss (note 23):		
	– Fair value losses	(508)	(238)
	– Fair value gains	593	–
IFRS7 p20(a)(i)	Foreign exchange forward contracts:		
	– Held for trading	86	88
21p52(a)	– Net foreign exchange gains/(losses) (note 15)	(277)	200
IFRS7 p24(a)	Ineffectiveness on fair value hedges (note 20)	(1)	(1)
IFRS7 p24(b)	Ineffectiveness on cash flow hedges (note 20)	17	14
	Total	(90)	63

9(a) Expenses by nature

		Group		Company	
		2011	2010	**2011**	2010
1p104	Changes in inventories of finished goods and work in progress	6,950	(2,300)	–	–
1p104	Raw materials and consumables used	53,302	31,845	–	–
1p104	Employee benefit expense (note 10a)	40,082	15,492	4,574	4,190
1p104	Depreciation, amortisation and impairment charges (notes 16 and 17)	23,204	10,227	–	–
1p104	Transportation expenses	8,584	6,236	–	–
1p104	Advertising costs	14,265	6,662	–	–
1p104	Operating lease payments (note 16)	10,604	8,500	–	–
1p104	Other expenses	2,799	1,659	–	–
	Total cost of sales, distribution costs and administrative expenses[1]	158,284	78,321	4,574	4,190

[1] This disclosure does not need to be totalled or reconciled to the income statement.

(All amounts in C thousands unless otherwise stated)

9(b) Auditor remuneration

Tech 06/06   **Services provided by the company's auditor and its associates[1]**

SI 2008/489   During the year the group (including its overseas subsidiaries) obtained the following services from the company's auditor and its associates:

Group	2011	2010
Fees payable to company's auditor for the audit of parent company and consolidated financial statements	**738**	625
Fees payable to the company's auditor and its associates for other services:		
– The audit of company's subsidiaries pursuant to legislation	**901**	543
– Other services pursuant to legislations	**312**	154
– Tax services	**107**	143
	2,058	1,465

	2011	2010
Fees in respect of the IFRS GAAP plc pension scheme:		
– Audit	**1,204**	931
– Other services pursuant to legislation	**123**	–
	1,327	931

10(a) Employee benefit expense

	Group		Company	
	2011	2010	**2011**	2010
19p142 Wages and salaries, including restructuring costs C799 (2010: nil) and other termination benefits C1,600 (2010: nil) (note 34)	**28,363**	10,041	**2,824**	2,486
Social security costs	**9,369**	3,802	**1,160**	1,087
IFRS2p51(a) Share options granted to directors and employees (notes 27 and 28)	**690**	822	**518**	617
19p46 Pension costs – defined contribution plans	**756**	232	**72**	–
19p120A(g) Pension costs – defined benefit plans (note 33)	**755**	488	–	–
19p120A(g) Other post-employment benefits (note 33)	**149**	107	–	–
	40,082	15,492	**4,574**	4,190

10(b) Average number of people employed

		2011	2010
DV	Number of employees	**535**	210

		2011	2010
S411(1)	Average number of people (including executive directors) employed:		
	Wholesale	**257**	95
	Retail	**178**	75
	Administration	**100**	40
	Total average headcount	**535**	210

Company

The average number of administration staff employed by the company during the year, including executive directors was C50 (2010: C48).

---

[1] The annual report should outline how the directors ensure that the independence of the group's auditors has not been compromised by the provision of non-audit services. For listed companies, guidance on independence is included in the Combined Code. This disclosure may be given as part of the corporate governance statement or disclosure in the annual report. [C.C.D3].

(All amounts in C thousands unless otherwise stated)

11 Finance income and costs

		2011	2010
IFRS7p20(b)	Interest expense:		
	– Bank borrowings	(5,317)	(10,646)
	– Dividend on redeemable preference shares (note 31)	(1,950)	(1,950)
	– Convertible bond (note 31)	(3,083)	–
	– Finance lease liabilities	(550)	(648)
37p84(e)	– Provisions: unwinding of discount (note 34)	(44)	(37)
21p52(a)	Net foreign exchange gains on financing activities (note 15)	2,594	996
	Fair value gains on financial instruments:		
IFRS7p23(d)	– Interest rate swaps: cash flow hedges, transfer from equity	102	88
IFRS7p24(a)(i)	– Interest rate swaps: fair value hedges	16	31
IFRS7p24(a)(ii)	Fair value adjustment of bank borrowings attributable to interest rate risk	(16)	(31)
	Finance costs	**(8,248)**	**(12,197)**
	Less: amounts capitalised on qualifying assets	75	–
	Total finance cost	(8,173)	(12,197)
	Finance income:		
	– Interest income on short-term bank deposits	550	489
IFRS7p20(b)	– Interest income on available-for-sale financial assets	963	984
IFRS7p20(b)	– Interest income on loans to related parties (note 41)	217	136
	Finance income	**1,730**	**1,609**
	Net finance costs	**(6,443)**	**(10,588)**

12(a) Investments in subsidiaries

		2011	2010
27p42	**Company**	2011	2010
	Shares in group undertakings		
	Beginning of year	22,786	21,964
	Additions in year (Note 39)	16,250	–
	Capital contribution relating to share based payment	173	206
	End of year	38,592	22,170

27p42(c) Investments in group undertakings are recorded at cost, which is the fair value of the consideration paid.

DV The capital contribution relating to share based payment relates to 1,210 share options granted by the company to employees of subsidiary undertakings in the group. Refer to note 27 for further details on the group's share option schemes.

12(b) Investments in associates

		2011	2010
	At 1 January	13,244	13,008
28p38	Share of profit[1]	215	145
	Exchange differences (note 20)	(74)	105
	Other equity movements: available-for-sale investments reserve (note 29)	(12)	(14)
28p38	**At 31 December**	13,373	13,244

28p37(b) The group's share of the results of its principal associates, and its aggregated assets (including goodwill) and liabilities, are as follows[2]:

Name	Country of incorporation	Assets	Liabilities	Revenues	Profit/ (Loss)	% interest held
31 December 2010:						
– Alfa Limited	Cyprus	27,345	20,295	35,012	155	18
– Beta SA	Greece	9,573	3,379	10,001	(10)	30
		36,918	23,674	45,013	145	
31 December 2011:						
– Alfa Limited	Cyprus	32,381	25,174	31,123	200	18
– Beta SA	Greece	12,115	5,949	9,001	15	30
		44,496	31,123	40,124	215	

[1] Share of profit/(loss) is after tax (IG14).
[2] An alternative method of presentation is to give the gross amounts of assets and liabilities (excluding goodwill) of associates and not of the group's share.

(All amounts in C thousands unless otherwise stated)

28p37(a) As at 31 December 2011, the fair value of the groups interest in Beta SA, which is listed on the Euro Money Stock Exchange, was C5,500 (2010: C5,000) and the carrying amount of the groups interest was C5,000 (2010: 4,500).

28p37(c) Although the group holds less than 20% of the equity shares of Alfa Limited, the group exercises significant influence by virtue of its contractual right to appoint two directors to the board of directors of that company and has the power to participate in the financial and operating policy decisions of Alfa Limited.

13 Income tax expense

Group	2011	2010
Current tax:		
Current tax on profits for the year	14,082	6,035
Adjustments in respect of prior years	150	–
Total current tax	**14,232**	6,035
Deferred tax (note 32):		
Origination and reversal of temporary differences	476	2,635
Impact of change in the Euravian tax rate[1]	(97)	–
Total deferred tax	**379**	2,635
Income tax expense	**14,611**	8,670

The labels in the left margin are: 12p80(a), 12p80(b) (for current tax lines); 12p80(c), 12p80(d) (for deferred tax lines).

12p81(c) The tax on the group's profit before tax differs from the theoretical amount that would arise using the weighted average tax rate applicable to profits of the consolidated entities as follows:

	2011	2010
Profit before tax	**47,676**	24,918
Tax calculated at domestic tax rates applicable to profits in the respective countries	15,453	7,475
Tax effects of:		
– Associates' results reported net of tax	57	(44)
– Income not subject to tax	(1,072)	(212)
– Expenses not deductible for tax purposes	1,540	1,104
– Utilisation of previously unrecognised tax losses	(1,450)	–
– Tax losses for which no deferred income tax asset was recognised	30	347
Re-measurement of deferred tax – change in the Euravian tax rate	(97)	–
Adjustment in respect of prior years	150	–
Tax charge	**14,611**	8,670

12p81(d) The weighted average applicable tax rate was 33% (2010: 30%). The increase is caused by a change in the profitability of the group's subsidiaries in the respective countries partially offset by the impact of the reduction in the Euravian tax rate (see below).

12p81(d) During the year, as a result of the change in the Euravian corporation tax rate from 30% to 28% that was substantively enacted on 26 June 2011 and that will be effective from 1 April 2012, the relevant deferred tax balances have been re-measured. Deferred tax expected to reverse in the year to 31 December 2011 has been measured using the effective rate that will apply in Euravia for the period (28.5%).[2]

1p125
10p21 Further reductions to the Euravian tax rate have been announced. The changes, which are expected to be enacted separately each year, propose to reduce the rate by 1% per annum to 24% by 1 April 2016. The changes had not been substantively enacted at the balance sheet date and, therefore, are not recognised in these financial statements.[3]

[1] The impact of change in Euravian tax rate is shown for illustrative purposes. UK companies with 31 December 2011 year ends will need to consider the impact of the reduction in tax rates in the Finance Act 2011.

[2] If the effect of the proposed changes is material, disclosure should be given of the effect of the changes, either as disclosure of events after the reporting period or as future material adjustment to the carrying amounts of assets and liabilities. This disclosure does not need to be totalled or reconciled to the income statement.

[3] Disclosure in respect of the impact of change in Euravian tax rate is shown for illustrative purposes. UK companies with 31 December 2011 year ends will need to consider the impact of the reduction in tax rates from 28% to 27% in the Finance Act 2011 and the announcement in the June 2011 Budget of future reductions in tax rates to 24%.

(All amounts in C thousands unless otherwise stated)

12p81(ab)   The tax (charge)/credit relating to components of other comprehensive income is as follows:

		2011			2010	
	Before tax	Tax (charge) credit	After tax	Before tax	Tax (charge) credit	After tax
Fair value gains:						
1p90 – Land and buildings	1,005	(250)	–755	1,133	(374)	759
1p90 – Available-for-sale financial assets	560	(198)	362	123	(61)	62
1p90 Share of other comprehensive income of associates	(86)	–	(86)	91	–	91
1p90 Actuarial loss on retirement benefit obligations	–	–	–	(705)	211	(494)
1p90 Impact of change in the Euravian tax rate on deferred tax[1]	–	(10)	(10)	–	–	–
1p90 Cash flow hedges	97	(33)	64	(3)	–	(3)
1p90 Net investment hedge	(45)	–	(45)	40	–	40
1p90 Currency translation differences	2,413	–	2,413	(1,111)	–	(1,111)
IFRS3p59 Recycling of revaluation of previously held interest in ABC Group	(850)	–	(850)	850	–	850
Other comprehensive income	**3,094**	**(491)**	**2,603**	**418**	**(224)**	**194**
Current tax[2]		–			–	
Deferred tax (note 32)		(491)			(224)	
		(491)			(224)	

12p81(a)   The income tax (charged)/credited directly to equity during the year is as follows:

	2011	2010
Current tax[3]		
Share option scheme	–	–
Deferred tax[4]		
Share option scheme	30	20
Convertible bond – equity component[5] (note 20)	(2,328)	–
	(2,298)	20

In addition, deferred income tax of C49 (2010: C43) was transferred from other reserves (note 29) to retained earnings (note 28). This represents deferred tax on the difference between the actual depreciation on buildings and the equivalent depreciation based on the historical cost of buildings.

14 Earnings per share

(a) Basic

Basic earnings per share is calculated by dividing the profit attributable to equity holders of the company by the weighted average number of ordinary shares in issue during the year excluding ordinary shares purchased by the company and held as treasury shares (note 26).

Group	2011	2010
33p70(a) Profit attributable to equity holders of the company	30,517	15,392
Profit from discontinued operation attributable to equity holders of the company	100	120
Total	**30,617**	**15,512**
33p70(b) Weighted average number of ordinary shares in issue (thousands)	23,454	20,500

(b) Diluted

Diluted earnings per share is calculated by adjusting the weighted average number of ordinary shares outstanding to assume conversion of all dilutive potential ordinary shares. The company has two categories of dilutive potential ordinary shares: convertible debt and share options. The convertible debt is assumed to have been converted into ordinary shares, and the net profit is adjusted to eliminate the interest expense less the tax effect. For the share options, a calculation is done to determine the number of shares that could have been acquired at fair value (determined as the average annual market share price of the company's shares) based on the monetary value of the

---

[1] The impact of change in Euravian tax rate is shown for illustrative purposes. UK companies with 31 December 2011 year ends will need to consider the impact of the reduction in tax rates from 28% to 27% in the Finance Act 2011.
[2] There are no current tax items relating to other comprehensive income in these financial statements, but the line item is shown for illustrative purposes.
[3] IAS 12 requires disclosure of current tax charged/credited directly to equity, in addition to deferred tax. There are no current tax items shown directly in equity in these financial statements, but the line item is shown for illustrative purposes.
[4] UK companies with 31 December 2011 year ends will need to consider the impact of the reduction in tax rates from 28% to 27% in the Finance Act 2011.
[5] It is assumed that the tax base on the convertible bond is not split between the debt and equity elements. If the tax base were split, this would impact the deferred tax position.

(All amounts in C thousands unless otherwise stated)

subscription rights attached to outstanding share options. The number of shares calculated as above is compared with the number of shares that would have been issued assuming the exercise of the share options.

		2011	2010
	Earnings		
	Profit attributable to equity holders of the company	**30,517**	15,392
	Interest expense on convertible debt (net of tax)	**2,158**	–
33p70(a)	Profit used to determine diluted earnings per share	**32,675**	15,392
	Profit from discontinued operations attributable to equity holders of the company	**100**	120
		32,775	15,512
	Weighted average number of ordinary shares in issue (thousands)	**23,454**	20,500
	Adjustments for:		
	– Assumed conversion of convertible debt (thousands)	**3,030**	–
	– Share options (thousands)	**1,213**	1,329
33p70(b)	Weighted average number of ordinary shares for diluted earnings per share (thousands)	**27,697**	21,829

15 Net foreign exchange gains/(losses)

21p52(a) The exchange differences (charged)/credited to the income statement are included as follows:

Group	2011	2010
Other (losses)/gains – net (note 26)	**(277)**	200
Net finance costs (note 31)	**2,594**	996
Total	**2,317**	1,196

16 Property, plant and equipment

1p78(a)		Land and buildings	Vehicles and machinery	Furniture, fittings and equipment	Construction in progress	Total
16p73(d)	**At 1 January 2010**					
	Cost or valuation	39,664	71,072	20,025	–	130,761
	Accumulated depreciation	(2,333)	(17,524)	(3,690)	–	(23,547)
	Net book amount	**37,331**	**53,548**	**16,335**	**–**	**107,214**
16p73(e)	**Year ended 31 December 2010**					
	Opening net book amount	37,331	53,548	16,335	–	107,214
16p73(e)(viii)	Exchange differences	(381)	(703)	(423)	–	(1,507)
16p73(e)(iv)	Revaluation surplus (note 29)	1,133	–	–	–	1,133
16p73(e)(i)	Additions	1,588	2,970	1,484	–	6,042
16p73(e)(ix)	Disposals (note 36)	–	(2,607)	(380)	–	(2,987)
16p73(e)(vii)	Depreciation charge (note 9a)	(636)	(4,186)	(4,840)	–	(9,662)
	Closing net book amount	**39,035**	**49,022**	**12,176**	**–**	**100,233**
16p73(d)	**At 31 December 2010**				–	
	Cost or valuation	40,232	68,125	20,026	–	128,383
	Accumulated depreciation	(1,197)	(19,103)	(7,850)	–	(28,150)
	Net book amount	**39,035**	**49,022**	**12,176**	**–**	**100,233**
	Year ended 31 December 2011					
16p73(e)	Opening net book amount	39,035	49,022	12,176	–	100,233
16p73(e)(viii)	Exchange differences	846	1,280	342	–	2,468
16p73(e)(iv)	Revaluation surplus (note 29)	1,005	–	–	–	1,005
16p73(e)(iii)	Acquisition of subsidiary (note 39)	49,072	5,513	13,199	–	67,784
16p73(e)(i)	Additions	4,421	427	2,202	2,455	9,505
16p73(e)(ix)	Disposals (note 36)	(2,000)	(3,729)	(608)		(6,337)
	Transfers	1,245	–	–	(1,245)	–
16p73(e)(vii)	Depreciation charge (note 9(a))	(3,545)	(4,768)	(9,441)	–	(17,754)
IFRS5p38	Transferred to disposal group classified as held for sale	(341)	(1,222)	–	–	(1,563)
	Closing net book amount	**89,738**	**46,523**	**17,870**	**1,210**	**155,341**
16p73(d)	**At 31 December 2011**					
	Cost or valuation	93,919	58,268	26,927	1,210	180,324
	Accumulated depreciation	(4,181)	(11,745)	(9,057)	–	(24,983)
	Net book amount	**89,738**	**46,523**	**17,870**	**1,210**	**155,341**

(All amounts in C thousands unless otherwise stated)

DV   Property, plant and equipment transferred to the disposal group classified as held-for-sale amounts to C1,563 and relates to assets that are used by Shoes Limited (part of the UK wholesale segment). See note 16 for further details regarding the disposal group held for sale.

16p77(a-d)
1p79(b)   An independent valuation of the group's land and buildings was performed by valuers to determine the fair value of the land and buildings as at 31 December 2011 and 2010. The valuation, which conforms to International Valuation Standards, was determined by reference to recent market transactions on arm's length terms. The revaluation surplus net of applicable deferred income taxes was credited to other comprehensive income and is shown in 'other reserves in shareholders' equity (note 29).

DV, 1p104   Depreciation expense of C8,054 (2010: C5,252) has been charged in 'cost of goods sold', C5,568 (2010: C2,410) in 'selling and marketing costs' and C4,132 (2010: C2,000) in 'administrative expenses'.

17p35(c)   Lease rentals amounting to C1,172 (2010: C895) and C9,432 (2010: C7,605) relating to the lease of machinery and property, respectively, are included in the income statement (note 9).

Construction work in progress as at 31 December 2011 mainly comprises new shoe manufacturing equipment being constructed in the UK.

23p26   During the year, the group has capitalised borrowing costs amounting to 75 (2010: nil) on qualifying assets. Borrowing costs were capitalised at the weighted average rate of its general borrowings of 7.5%.

16p77(e)   If land and buildings were stated on the historical cost basis, the amounts would be as follows:

	2011	2010
Cost	93,079	37,684
Accumulated depreciation	(6,131)	(2,197)
Net book amount	**86,948**	35,487

16p74(a)   Bank borrowings are secured on land and buildings for the value of C37,680 (2010: C51,306) (note 31).

Vehicles and machinery includes the following amounts where the group is a lessee under a finance lease:

	2011	2010
Cost – capitalised finance leases	13,996	14,074
Accumulated depreciation	(5,150)	(3,926)
Net book amount	**8,846**	10,148

17p35(d)   The group leases various vehicles and machinery under non-cancellable finance lease agreements. The lease terms are between three and 15 years, and ownership of the assets lie within the group.

(All amounts in C thousands unless otherwise stated)

17 Intangible assets

IFRS3B67(d)(i) Cost		Goodwill	Trademarks and licences	Internally generated software development costs	Total
38p118(c)	At 1 January 2010	12,546	8,301	1,455	22,302
IFRS3 B67(d)(viii)	Exchange differences	(546)	(306)	(45)	(897)
38p118(e)(i)	Additions	–	700	–	700
	As at 31 December 2010	**12,000**	**8,695**	**1,410**	**22,105**
IFRS3 B67(d)(viii)	Exchange differences	341	96	134	571
38p118(e)(i)	Additions	–	684	2,366	3,050
IFRS3B67(d)(ii)	Acquisition of subsidiary (note 39)	4,501	4,000	–	8,501
IFRS5p38	Transferred to disposal group classified as held for sale	(100)	(1,000)		(1,100)
	As at 31 December 2011	**16,742**	**12,475**	**3,910**	**33,127**
	Accumulated amortisation and impairment				
	At 1 January 2010	–	(330)	(510)	(840)
IFRS3B67(d)(i)	Amortisation charge	–	(365)	(200)	(565)
	At 31 December 2010	**–**	**(695)**	**(710)**	**(1,405)**
IFRS3B67(d)(v)	Impairment charge	(4,650)	–	–	(4,650)
IFRS3B67(d)(i)	Amortisation charge	–	(680)	(120)	(800)
	At 31 December 2011	**(4,650)**	**(1,375)**	**(830)**	**(6,855)**
	Net book value				
	Cost	12,000	8,695	1,410	22,105
IFRS3B67 (d)(v)	Accumulated amortisation and impairment	–	(695)	(710)	(1,405)
	At 31 December 2010	**12,000**	**8,000**	**700**	**20,700**
	Cost	16,742	12,475	3,910	33,127
IFRS 3B67 (d)(v)	Accumulated amortisation and impairment	(4,650)	(1,375)	(830)	(6,855)
	At 31 December 2011	**12,092**	**11,100**	**3,080**	**26,272**

36p126(a) The carrying amount of the segment (Russia – wholesale) has been reduced to its recoverable amount through recognition of an impairment loss against goodwill. This loss has been included in 'cost of goods sold' in the income statement.

38p118(d) Amortisation of C40 (2010: C100) is included in the 'cost of goods sold' the income statement; C680 (2010: C365) in 'distribution costs; and C80 (2010: C100) in 'administrative expenses'.

DV The trademark transferred to the disposal group classified as held for sale relates to the Shoes Limited trademark (part of the wholesale segment), which was previously recognised by the group on the acquisition of the entity in 2006. A further net book amount of C100 transferred to the disposal group relates to goodwill. See note 25 for further details regarding the disposal group held for sale.

Impairment tests for goodwill

36p134(d) Management reviews the business performance based on geography and type of business. It has identified UK, US, China, Russia and Europe as the main geographies. There are both retail and wholesale segments in the UK and the US. In all other geographies, the group has only wholesale business. Goodwill is monitored by the management at the operating segment level. The following is a summary of goodwill allocation for each operating segment:

(All amounts in C thousands unless otherwise stated)

36p134(a)

2011	Opening	Addition	Disposal	Impairment	Other adjustments	Closing
UK wholesale	6,070	–	(100)	–	285	6,255
UK retail	20	–	–	–	–	120
US wholesale	125	–	–	–	–	125
US retail	30	3,597	–	–	–	3,627
Europe wholesale	705	904	–	–	–	1,609
Russia wholesale	4,750	–	–	(4,650)	–	100
China wholesale	100	-	–	–	46	146
All other segments	200	–	–	–	10	210
Total	**12,000**	**4,501**	**(100)**	**(4,650)**	**341**	**12,092**

2010	Opening	Addition	Disposal	Impairment	Other adjustments	Closing
UK wholesale	6,370	–	–	–	(300)	6,070
UK retail	20	–	–	–	–	20
US wholesale	125	–	–	–	–	125
US retail	131	–	–	–	(101)	30
Europe wholesale	705	–	–	–	–	705
Russia wholesale	4,750	–	–	–	–	4,750
China wholesale	175	–	–	–	(75)	100
All other segments	270	–	–	–	(70)	200
Total	**12,546**	**–**	**–**	**–**	**(546)**	**12,000**

During 2010, US retail did not qualify as a reportable operating segment. However, with the acquisition in 2011 of ABC Group (note 39), US retail qualifies as a separate reportable operating segment; the comparatives have therefore been restated to be consistent.

36p130(e)
36p134(c)
36p134
(d)(iii)

The recoverable amount of all CGUs has been determined based on value-in-use calculations. These calculations use pre-tax cash flow projections based on financial budgets approved by management covering a five-year period. Cash flows beyond the five-year period are extrapolated using the estimated growth rates stated below. The growth rate does not exceed the long-term average growth rate for the shoe business in which the CGU operates.

36p134
(d)(i)

The key assumptions used for value-in-use calculations in 2011 are as follows[1]:

	UK wholesale	US wholesale	Europe– wholesale	Russia wholesale	China wholesale	UK retail	US retail	All other segments
36p134(d) — Gross margin[2]	60.0%	59.0%	60.0%	55.5%	47.0%	48.0%	46.0%	46.00%
36p134(d)(iv) — Growth rate[3]	1.8%	1.8%	1.8%	2.0%	3.0%	2.1%	2.3%	3.90%
36p134(d)(v) 36p130(g) — Discount rate[4]	12.5%	12.0%	12.7%	13.8%	14.0%	14.5%	14.0%	14.80%

36p134(d)(i)

The key assumptions used for value-in-use calculations in 2010 are as follows:

	UK wholesale	US wholesale	Europe wholesale	Russia wholesale	China wholesale	UK retail	US retail	All other segments
36p134(d) — Gross margin[2]	62.5%	61.0%	62.5%	58.0%	49.0%	50.0%	50.8%	48.0%
36p134(d)(iv) — Growth rate[3]	2.0%	2.0%	2.0%	2.5%	3.5%	2.3%	2.5%	3.3%
36p134(d)(v) 36p130g — Discount rate[4]	12.0%	11.5%	12.1%	13.5%	14.5%	13.0%	14.4%	13.0%

36p134
(d)(ii)

These assumptions have been used for the analysis of each CGU within the operating segment.

36p134
(d)(ii)

Management determined budgeted gross margin based on past performance and its expectations of market development. The weighted average growth rates used are consistent with the forecasts included in industry reports. The discount rates used are pre-tax and reflect specific risks relating to the relevant operating segments.

36p130(a)

The impairment charge arose in a wholesale CGU in Step-land (included in the Russian operating segment) following a decision in early 2011 to reduce the manufacturing output allocated to these operations (note 34). This was a result of a redefinition of the group's allocation of manufacturing volumes across all CGUs in order to benefit from advantageous market conditions. Following this decision, the group reassessed the depreciation policies of its property, plant and equipment in this country and estimated that their useful lives would not be affected. No class of

---

[1] Disclosure of long-term growth rates and discount rates is required. Other key assumptions are required to be disclosed and quantified where a reasonably possible change in the key assumption would remove any remaining headroom in the impairment calculation. Otherwise the additional disclosures are encouraged but not required.
[2] Budgeted gross margin.
[3] Weighted average growth rate used to extrapolate cash flows beyond the budget period.
[4] Pre-tax discount rate applied to the cash flow projections.

(All amounts in C thousands unless otherwise stated)

asset other than goodwill was impaired. The pre-tax discount rate used in the previous years for the wholesale CGU in Step-land was 13.5%.

36p134(f) In European Wholesale, the recoverable amount calculated based on value in use exceeded carrying value by C205. A reduction in gross margin of 1.5%, a fall in growth rate to 1.6% or a rise in discount rate to 10.9% would remove the remaining headroom.

18(a) Financial instruments by category

31 December 2011

IFRS7p6

Group	Loans and receivables	Assets at fair value through the profit and loss	Derivatives used for hedging	Available for sale	Total
Assets as per balance sheet					
Available-for-sale financial assets	–	–	–	19,370	19,370
Derivative financial instruments	–	361	1,103	–	1,464
Trade and other receivables excluding pre-payments[1]	20,787	–	–	–	20,787
Financial assets at fair value through profit or loss	–	11,820	–	–	11,820
Cash and cash equivalents	17,928	–	–	–	17,928
Total	**38,715**	**12,181**	**1,103**	**19,370**	**71,369**

	Liabilities at fair value through the profit and loss	Derivatives used for hedging	Other financial liabilities at amortised cost	Total
Liabilities as per balance sheet				
Borrowings (excluding finance lease liabilities)	–	–	117,839	117,839
Finance lease liabilities	–	–	8,998	8,998
Derivative financial instruments	268	327	–	595
Trade and other payables excluding non-financial liabilities[2]	–	–	15,668	15,668
Total	**268**	**327**	**142,505**	**143,100**

31 December 2010

	Loans and receivables	Assets at fair value through the profit and loss	Derivatives used for hedging	Available for sale	Total
Assets as per balance sheet					
Available-for-sale financial assets	–	–	–	14,910	14,910
Derivative financial instruments	–	321	875	–	1,196
Trade and other receivables excluding prepayments[1]	18,536	–	–	–	18,536
Financial assets at fair value through profit or loss	–	7,972	–	–	7,972
Cash and cash equivalents	34,062	–	–	–	34,062
Total	**52,598**	**8,293**	**875**	**14,910**	**76,676**

[1] Pre-payments are excluded from the trade and other receivables balance, as this analysis is required only for financial instruments.
[2] Non-financial liabilities are excluded from the trade payables balance, as this analysis is required only for financial instruments.

(All amounts in C thousands unless otherwise stated)

	Liabilities at fair value through the profit and loss	Derivatives used for hedging	Other financial liabilities	Total
Liabilities as per balance sheet				
Borrowings excluding finance lease liabilities[1]	–	–	104,006	104,006
Finance lease liabilities[1]	–	–	10,598	10,598
Derivative financial instruments	298	449	–	747
Trade and other payables excluding non-financial liabilities[2]	–	–	11,518	11,518
Total	**298**	**449**	**126,122**	**126,869**

Company	Loans and receivables	Assets at fair value through the profit and loss	Derivatives used for hedging	Available for sale	Total
31 December 2011					
Assets as per balance sheet					
Trade and other receivables	41,147	–	–	–	41,147
Cash and cash equivalents	3,261	–	–	–	3,261
Total	**44,408**	**–**	**–**	**–**	**44,408**

	Loans and receivables	Assets at fair value through the profit and loss	Derivatives used for hedging	Available for sale	Total
31 December 2010					
Assets as per balance sheet					
Trade and other receivables	31,296	–	–	–	31,296
Cash and cash equivalents	6,234	–	–	–	6,234
Total	**37,530**	**–**	**–**	**–**	**37,530**

[1] The categories in this disclosure are determined by IAS 39. Finance leases are mostly outside the scope of IAS 39, but they remain within the scope of IFRS 7. Therefore finance leases have been shown separately.

[2] Non-financial liabilities are excluded from the trade payables balance, as this analysis is required only for financial instruments.

(All amounts in C thousands unless otherwise stated)

18(b) Credit quality of financial assets

IFRS7
p36(c)

The credit quality of financial assets that are neither past due nor impaired can be assessed by reference to external credit ratings (if available) or to historical information about counterparty default rates:

Group	2011	2010
Trade receivables		
Counterparties with external credit rating (Moody's)		
A	5,895	5,757
BB	3,200	3,980
BBB	1,500	1,830
	10,595	11,567
Counterparties without external credit rating		
Group 1	750	555
Group 2	4,832	3,596
Group 3	1,770	1,312
	7,352	5,463
Total unimpaired trade receivables	17,947	17,030
Cash at bank and short-term bank deposits[1]		
AAA	8,790	15,890
AA	5,300	7,840
A	3,038	9,832
	17,128	33,562

DV

Available-for-sale debt securities		
AA	347	264
	347	264

DV

Derivative financial assets		
AAA	1,046	826
AA	418	370
	1,464	1,196

Loans to related parties		
Group 2	2,501	1,301
Group 3	167	87
	2,668	1,388

- Group 1 – new customers/related parties (less than 6 months).
- Group 2 – existing customers/related parties (more than 6 months) with no defaults in the past.
- Group 3 – existing customers/related parties (more than 6 months) with some defaults in the past. All defaults were fully recovered.

Note: None of the loans to related parties is past due but not impaired.

19 Available-for-sale financial assets

Group	2011	2010
At 1 January	14,910	14,096
Exchange differences	646	(435)
Acquisition of subsidiary (note 39)	473	–
Additions	4,037	1,126
Disposals	(1,256)	–
Net gains/(losses) transfer from equity (note 29)	(130)	(152)
Net gains/(losses) transfer to equity (note 29)	690	275
At 31 December	19,370	14,910
Less: non-current portion	(17,420)	(14,910)
Current portion	1,950	–

1p79(b) (row: Net gains/(losses) transfer to equity (note 29))

1p66 (row: Less: non-current portion)

1p66 (row: Current portion)

IFRS7
p20(a)(ii)

The group removed profits of C217 (2010: C187) and losses C87 (2010: C35) from equity into the income statement. Losses in the amount of C55 (2010: C20) were due to impairments.

---

[1] The rest of the balance sheet item 'cash and cash equivalents' is cash in hand.

(All amounts in C thousands unless otherwise stated)

IFRS7p,31, 34 Available-for-sale financial assets include the following:

	2011	2010
Listed securities:		
–Equity securities – UK	**8,335**	8,300
–Equity securities – Europe	**5,850**	2,086
–Equity securities – US	**4,550**	4,260
–Debentures with fixed interest of 6.5% and maturity date of 27 August 2013	**210**	–
–Non-cumulative 9.0% non-redeemable preference shares	**78**	–
Unlisted securities:		
–Debt securities with fixed interest ranging from 6.3% to 6.5% and maturity dates between July 2012 and May 2014	**347**	264
Total	**19,370**	14,910

IFRS7 p34(c) Available-for-sale financial assets are denominated in the following currencies:

	2011	2010
UK pound	**7,897**	8,121
Euro	**5,850**	2,086
US dollar	**4,550**	4,260
Other currencies	**1,073**	443
Total	**19,370**	14,910

IFRS7p27 The fair values of unlisted securities are based on cash flows discounted using a rate based on the market interest rate and the risk premium specific to the unlisted securities (2011: 6%; 2010: 5.8%).

IFRS7 p36(a) The maximum exposure to credit risk at the reporting date is the carrying value of the debt securities classified as available for sale.

IFRS7 p36(c) None of these financial assets is either past due or impaired.

20 Derivative financial instruments

	2011		2010	
Group	**Assets**	**Liabilities**	**Assets**	**Liabilities**
Interest rate swaps – cash flow hedges	351	110	220	121
Interest rate swaps – fair value hedges	57	37	49	11
Forward foreign exchange contracts – cash flow hedges	695	180	606	317
Forward foreign exchange contracts – held-for- trading	361	268	321	298
Total	**1,464**	**595**	**1,196**	**747**
Less non-current portion:				
Interest rate swaps – cash flow hedges	345	100	200	120
Interest rate swaps – fair value hedges	50	35	45	9
	395	135	245	129
Current portion	**1,069**	**460**	951	618

Left margin references: **IFRS7 p22(a)(b)** (Interest rate swaps – cash flow hedges), **IFRS7 p22(a)(b)** (Interest rate swaps – fair value hedges), **IFRS7 p22(a)(b)** (Forward foreign exchange contracts), **1p66,69** (Less non-current portion), **1p66,69** (Current portion)

Trading derivatives are classified as a current asset or liability. The full fair value of a hedging derivative is classified as a non-current asset or liability if the remaining maturity of the hedged item is more than 12 months and, as a current asset or liability, if the maturity of the hedged item is less than 12 months.

IFRS7p24 The ineffective portion recognised in the profit or loss that arises from fair value hedges amounts to a loss of C1 (2010: loss of C1) (note 8). The ineffective portion recognised in the profit or loss that arises from cash flow hedges amounts to a gain of C17 (2010: a gain of C14) (note 8). There was no ineffectiveness to be recorded from net investment in foreign entity hedges.

(a) Forward foreign exchange contracts

IFRS7p31 The notional principal amounts of the outstanding forward foreign exchange contracts at 31 December 2011 were C92,370 (2010: C89,689).

IFRS7 p23(a) 39p100, 1p79(b) The hedged highly probable forecast transactions denominated in foreign currency are expected to occur at various dates during the next 12 months. Gains and losses recognised in the hedging reserve in equity (note 29) on forward foreign exchange contracts as of 31 December 2011 are recognised in the income statement in the period or periods

(All amounts in C thousands unless otherwise stated)

during which the hedged forecast transaction affects the income statement. This is generally within 12 months of the end of the reporting period unless the gain or loss is included in the initial amount recognised for the purchase of fixed assets, in which case recognition is over the lifetime of the asset (five to 10 years).

(b) Interest rate swaps

IFRS7p31

The notional principal amounts of the outstanding interest rate swap contracts at 31 December 2011 were C4,314 (2010: C3,839).

IFRS7 p23(a)

At 31 December 2011, the fixed interest rates vary from 6.9% to 7.4% (2010: 6.7% to 7.2%), and the main floating rates are EURIBOR and LIBOR. Gains and losses recognised in the hedging reserve in equity (note 29) on interest rate swap contracts as of 31 December 2011 will be continuously released to the income statement within finance cost until the repayment of the bank borrowings (note 31).

(c) Hedge of net investment in foreign entity

IFRS7p22, 1p79(b)

A proportion of the group's US dollar-denominated borrowing amounting to C321 (2010: C321) is designated as a hedge of the net investment in the group's US subsidiary. The fair value of the borrowing at 31 December 2011 was C370 (2010: C279). The foreign exchange loss of C45 (2010: gain of C40) on translation of the borrowing to currency at the end of the reporting period is recognised in other comprehensive income.

IFRS7 p36(a)

The maximum exposure to credit risk at the reporting date is the fair value of the derivative assets in the balance sheet.

21 Trade and other receivables

		Group		Company	
		2011	2010	**2011**	2010
IFRS7p36, 1p77	Trade receivables	**18,174**	17,172	**–**	–
	Less: provision for impairment of trade receivables	**(109)**	(70)	**–**	–
1p78(b)	Trade receivables – net	**18,065**	17,102	**–**	–
1p78(b)	Prepayments	**1,300**	1,146	**–**	–
1p78(b), 24Rp18(b)	Receivables from related parties (note 41)	**54**	46	**41,147**	31,296
1p78(b), 24Rp18(b)	Loans to related parties (note 41)	**2,668**	1,388	**–**	–
		22,087	19,682	**41,147**	31,296
1p78(b), 1p66	Less non-current portion: loans to related parties	**(2,322)**	(1,352)	**–**	–
1p66	**Current portion**	**19,765**	18,330	**41,147**	31,296

All non-current receivables are due within five years from the end of the reporting period.

IFRS7p25

The fair values of trade and other receivables are as follows:

	Group		Company	
	2011	2010	**2011**	2010
Trade receivables	**18,065**	17,102	**–**	–
Receivables from related parties	**54**	46	**41,147**	31,296
Loans to related parties	**2,722**	1,398	**–**	–
	20,841	18,546	**41,147**	31,296

IFRS7p27

The fair values of loans to related parties are based on cash flows discounted using a rate based on the borrowings rate of 7.5% (2010: 7.2%). The discount rate equals to LIBOR plus appropriate credit rating.

24Rp18(b)(i)

The effective interest rates on non-current receivables were as follows:

	2011	2010
Loans to related parties (note 41)	**6.5-7.0%**	6.5-7.0%

IFRS7p14

Certain European subsidiaries of the group transferred receivable balances amounting to C1,014 to a bank in exchange for cash during the year ended 31 December 2011. The transaction has been accounted for as a collateralised borrowing (note 31). In case the entities default under the loan agreement, the bank has the right to receive the cash flows from the receivables transferred. Without default, the entities will collect the receivables and allocate new receivables as collateral.

DV

As of 31 December 2011, trade receivables of C17,670 (2010: C16,823) were fully performing.

(All amounts in C thousands unless otherwise stated)

IFRS7 p37(a)
As of 31 December 2011, trade receivables of C277 (2010: C207) were past due but not impaired. These relate to a number of independent customers for whom there is no recent history of default. The ageing analysis of these trade receivables is as follows:

	2011	2010
Up to 3 months	177	108
3 to 6 months	100	99
	277	207

IFRS7 p37(b)
As of 31 December 2011, trade receivables of C227 (2010: C142) were impaired. The amount of the provision was C109 as of 31 December 2011 (2010: C70). The individually impaired receivables mainly relate to wholesalers, which are in unexpectedly difficult economic situations. It was assessed that a portion of the receivables is expected to be recovered. The ageing of these receivables is as follows:

	2011	2010
3 to 6 months	177	108
Over 6 months	50	34
	227	142

The carrying amounts of the group's trade and other receivables are denominated in the following currencies:

	2011	2010
UK pound	9,846	8,669
Euros	5,987	6,365
US dollar	6,098	4,500
Other currencies	156	148
	22,087	19,682

IFRS7p16
Movements on the group provision for impairment of trade receivables are as follows:

	2011	2010
At 1 January	70	38
Provision for receivables impairment	74	61
Receivables written off during the year as uncollectible	(28)	(23)
Unused amounts reversed	(10)	(8)
Unwind of discount	3	2
At 31 December	109	70

IFRS7 p20(e)

The creation and release of provision for impaired receivables have been included in 'other expenses' in the income statement (note 9). Unwind of discount is included in 'finance costs' in the income statement (note 11). Amounts charged to the allowance account are generally written off, when there is no expectation of recovering additional cash.

IFRS7p16
The other classes within trade and other receivables do not contain impaired assets.

IFRS7 p36(a)
The maximum exposure to credit risk at the reporting date is the carrying value of each class of receivable mentioned above. The group does not hold any collateral as security.

Company

IFRS7p25
The fair values of trade and other receivables are as follows:

Company	2011	2010
Receivables from related parties	41,147	31,296
	41,147	31,296

DV
As of 31 December 2011, company receivables from related parties of C14,120 (2010: 16,279) were fully performing.

(All amounts in C thousands unless otherwise stated)

IFRS7p37(a)
IFRS7p36(c)
As of 31 December 2011, receivables of C27,027 (2010: C15, 017) were past due but not impaired. These relate to subsidiary undertakings for which there is no history of default. The ageing analysis of these trade receivables is as follows:

	2011	2010
3 to 6 months	27,027	15,017
	27,027	15,017

IFRS7p31,
34(c)
The carrying amounts of the company's receivables are denominated in the following currencies:

	2011	2010
UK pound	41,147	31,296

22 Inventories

Group	2011	2010
2p36(b),		
1p78(c) Raw materials	7,622	7,612
Work in progress	1,810	1,796
Finished goods[1]	15,268	8,774
	24,700	18,182

2p36(d), 38 The cost of inventories recognised as expense and included in 'cost of sales' amounted to C60,252 (2010: C29,545).

2p36 (f)(g) The group reversed C603 of a previous inventory write-down in July 2011. The group has sold all the goods that were written down to an independent retailer in Australia at original cost. The amount reversed has been included in 'cost of sales' in the income statement.

23 Financial assets at fair value through profit or loss

Group	2011	2010
IFRS7p8(a),		
31, 34(c) Listed securities – held for trading		
– Equity securities – UK	5,850	3,560
– Equity securities – Europe	4,250	3,540
—Equity securities – US	1,720	872
	11,820	7,972

7p15 Financial assets at fair value through profit or loss are presented within 'operating activities' as part of changes in working capital in the statement of cash flows (note 36).

Changes in fair values of financial assets at fair value through profit or loss are recorded in 'other (losses)/gains – net' in the income statement (note 8).

IFRS7p27 The fair value of all equity securities is based on their current bid prices in an active market.

24 Cash and cash equivalents

	Group		Company	
	2011	2010	**2011**	2010
Cash at bank and on hand	8,398	28,648	3,261	6,234
Short-term bank deposits	9,530	5,414	–	–
Cash and cash equivalents (excluding bank overdrafts)	17,928	34,062	3,261	6,234

7p45 Cash and cash equivalents include the following for the purposes of the statement of cash flows:

	Group		Company	
	2011	2010	**2011**	2010
Cash and cash equivalents	17,928	34,062	3,261	6,234
7p8 Bank overdrafts (note 31)	(2,650)	(6,464)	–	–
Cash and cash equivalents	15,278	27,598	3,261	6,234

[1] Separate disclosure of finished goods at fair value less cost to sell is required, where applicable.

(All amounts in C thousands unless otherwise stated)

25 Non-current assets held for sale and discontinued operations

Group

IFRS5p41
(a)(b)(d)

The assets and liabilities related to company Shoes Limited (part of the UK wholesale segment) have been presented as held for sale following the approval of the group's management and shareholders on 23 September 2011 to sell company Shoes Limited in the UK. The completion date for the transaction is expected by May 2012.

Group and company	2011	2010
Operating cash flows[1]	300	190
Investing cash flows[1]	(103)	(20)
Financing cash flows[1]	(295)	(66)
Total cash flows	**(98)**	104

IFRS5p33(c)
IFRS5p33(c)
IFRS5p33(c)

IFRS5p38

(a) Assets of disposal group classified as held for sale

	2011	2010
Property, plant and equipment	1,563	–
Goodwill	100	–
Other intangible assets	1,000	–
Inventory	442	–
Other current assets	228	–
Total	**3,333**	**–**

IFRS5p38

(b) Liabilities of disposal group classified as held for sale

	2011	2010
Trade and other payables	104	–
Other current liabilities	20	–
Provisions	96	–
Total	**220**	**–**

IFRS5p38

(c) Cumulative income or expense recognised in other comprehensive income relating to disposal group classified as held for sale

	2011	2010
Foreign exchange translation adjustments[2]	–	–
Total	**–**	**–**

IFRS5p33(b)

Analysis of the result of discontinued operations, and the result recognised on the re- measurement of assets or disposal group, is as follows[3]:

	2011	2010
Revenue	1,200	1,150
Expenses	(960)	(950)
Profit before tax of discontinued operations	240	200
Tax	(96)	(80)
Profit after tax of discontinued operations	**144**	**120**
Pre-tax gain/(loss) recognised on the re-measurement of assets of disposal group	(73)	–
Tax	29	–
After tax gain/(loss) recognised on the re-measurement of assets of disposal group	(44)	–
Profit for the year from discontinued operations	**100**	**120**

12p81(h)(ii)

12p81(h)(ii)

[1] Under this approach, the entity presents the statement of cash flows as if no discontinued operation has occurred and makes the required IFRS 5 para 33 disclosures in the notes. It would also be acceptable to present the three categories separately on the face of the statement of cash flows and present the line-by-line breakdown of the categories, either in the notes or on the face of the statement of cash flows. It would not be acceptable to present all cash flows from discontinued operations in one line either as investing or operating activity.

[2] IFRS 5 requires the separate presentation of any cumulative income or expense recognised in other comprehensive income relating to a non-current asset (or disposal group) classified as held for sale. There are no items recognised in equity relating to the disposal group classified as held-for-sale, but the line items are shown for illustrative purposes.

[3] These disclosures can also be given on the face of the primary financial statements.

(All amounts in C thousands unless otherwise stated)

26 Share capital and premium

1p79

Group and company	Number of shares (thousands)	Ordinary shares	Share premium	Total
At 1 January 2010	20,000	20,000	10,424	30,424
Employee share option scheme:				
– Proceeds from shares issued	1,000	1,000	70	1,070
At 31 December 2010	21,000	21,000	10,494	31,494
Employee share option scheme:				
– Proceeds from shares issued	750	750	200	950
Acquisition of subsidiary (note 39)	3,550	3,550	6,450	10,000
At 31 December 2011	**25,300**	**25,300**	**17,144**	**42,444**

1p106
(d)(iii)

1p106
(d)(iii)

IFRS3
p67(d)(ii)

1p79(a)

From 1 October 2010, the Companies Act 2006 abolished the requirement for a company to have an authorised share capital. Shareholders wishing to restrict the number of shares that can be issued by a company need to address this issue in the company's articles.

1p79(a) The company acquired 875,000 of its own shares through purchases on the EuroMoney stock exchange on 18 April 2011. The total amount paid to acquire the shares, net of income tax, was C2,564. The shares are held as 'treasury shares'[1]. The company has the right to re-issue these shares at a later date. All shares issued by the company were fully paid.

The group issued 3,550,000 shares on 1 March 2011 (14.0% of the total ordinary share capital issued) to the shareholders of ABC group as part of the purchase consideration for 70% of its ordinary share capital. The ordinary shares issued have the same rights as the other shares in issue. The fair value of the shares issued amounted to C10,050 (C2.83 per share). The related transaction costs amounting to C50 have been netted off with the deemed proceeds.

27 Share-based payment

IFRS2
p45(a)

Share options are granted to directors and to selected employees. The exercise price of the granted options is equal to the market price of the shares less 15% on the date of the grant. Options are conditional on the employee completing three years' service (the vesting period). The options are exercisable starting three years from the grant date, subject to the group achieving its target growth in earnings per share over the period of inflation plus 4%; the options have a contractual option term of five years. The group has no legal or constructive obligation to repurchase or settle the options in cash.

Movements in the number of share options outstanding and their related weighted average exercise prices are as follows:

	2011		2010	
	Average exercise price in C per share option	Options (thousands)	Average exercise price in C per share option	Options (thousands)
At 1 January	1.73	4,744	1.29	4,150
Granted	2.95	964	2.38	1,827
Forfeited	2.30	(125)	0.80	(33)
Exercised	1.28	(750)	1.08	(1,000)
Expired	–	–	2.00	(200)
At 31 December	**2.03**	**4,833**	1.73	4,744

IFRS2p45(b)(i)
IFRS2p45(b)(ii)
IFRS2p45(b)(iii)
IFRS2p45(b)(iv)
IFRS2p45(b)(v)
IFRS2p45(b)(vi)

IFRS2p45
(b)(vii), IFRS2
p45(c)

Out of the 4,833,000 outstanding options (2010: 4,744,000 options), 1,875,000 options (2010: 1,400,000) were exercisable. Options exercised in 2011 resulted in 750,000 shares (2010: 1,000,000 shares) being issued at a weighted average price of C1.28 each (2010: C1.08 each). The related weighted average share price at the time of exercise was C2.85 (2010: C2.65) per share. The related transaction costs amounting to C10 (2010: C10) have been netted off with the proceeds received.

---

[1] The accounting treatment of treasury shares should be recorded in accordance with local company law and practice. Treasury shares may be disclosed separately on the balance sheet or deducted from retained earnings or a specific reserve. Depending on local company law, the company could have the right to resell the treasury shares.

(All amounts in C thousands unless otherwise stated)

IFRS2
p45(d)

Share options outstanding at the end of the year have the following expiry date and exercise prices:

Grant-vest	Expiry date – 1 July	Exercise price in C per share	Shares	
			2011	2010
2006-9	2011	1.10	–	500
2007-10	2012	1.20	**800**	900
2008-11	2013	1.35	**1,075**	1,250
2009-12	2014	2.00	**217**	267
2010-13	2015	2.38	**1,777**	1,827
2011-14	2016	2.95	**964**	–
			4,833	4,744

IFRS2p46
IFRS2
p47(a)

The weighted average fair value of options granted during the period determined using the Black-Scholes valuation model was C0.86 per option (2010: C0.66). The significant inputs into the model were weighted average share price of C3.47 (2010: C2.80) at the grant date, exercise price shown above, volatility of 30% (2010: 27%), dividend yield of 4.3% (2010: 3.5%), an expected option life of three years (2010: 3 years) and an annual risk-free interest rate of 5% (2010: 4%). The volatility measured at the standard deviation of continuously compounded share returns is based on statistical analysis of daily share prices over the last three years. See note 30a for the total expense recognised in the income statement for share options granted to directors and employees.

28 Retained earnings

		Group	Company
1p106(d)	At 1 January 2010	48,470	16,036
	Profit for the year	15,512	10,491
1p106(d)	Dividends paid relating to 2009	(15,736)	(15,736)
IFRS2p50	Value of employee services[1]	822	822
16p41	Depreciation transfer on land and buildings net of tax	87	–
12p68C	Tax credit relating to share option scheme	20	–
19p93A	Actuarial loss on post employment benefit obligations net of tax	(494)	–
	At 31 December 2010	**48,681**	**11,613**
1p106(d)	At 1 January 2011	48,681	11,613
	Profit for the year	30,617	9,098
1p106(d)	Dividends relating to 2010	(10,102)	(10,102)
IFRS2p50	Value of employee services[1]	690	690
16p41	Depreciation transfer on land and buildings net of tax	100	–
12p68C	Tax credit relating to share option scheme	30	–
19p93A	Actuarial loss on post employment benefit obligations net of tax	–	–
12p81(a),(b)	Impact of change in Euravian tax rate on deferred tax	(10)	–
	At 31 December 2011	**70,006**	**11,299**

[1] The credit entry to equity in respect of the IFRS 2 charge should be recorded in accordance with local company law and practice. This may be a specific reserve, retained earnings or share capital.

(All amounts in C thousands unless otherwise stated)

29 Other reserves

	Group	Convertible bond	Land and buildings revaluation[1]	Hedging	Treasury shares	Available-for-sale investments	Translation	Transactions with NCI	Total
	At 1 January 2010	–	1,152	65	–	1,320	2,977	–	5,514
16p39, IFRS7 p20(a)(ii)	Revaluation – gross (notes 16 and 19)	–	1,133	–		275	–	–	1,408
	Revaluation transfer – gross (note 19)	–		–	–	(152)	–	–	(152)
12p61A, 81(ab)	Revaluation – tax (note 13)	–	(374)	–	–	(61)	–	–	(435)
28p39	Revaluation – associates (note 12)	–	–	–	–	(14)	–	–	(14)
16p41	Depreciation transfer – gross	–	(130)	–	–	–	–	–	(130)
16p41	Depreciation transfer – tax	–	43	–	–	–	–	–	43
1p106(d)	Cash flow hedges:								
IFRS7p23(c)	– Fair value gains in year	–	–	300	–	–	–	–	300
12p61, 81(a)	– Tax on fair value gains (note 13)	–	–	(101)	–	–	–	–	(101)
IFRS7p23(d)	– Transfers to sales	–	–	(236)	–	–	–	–	(236)
12p61A, 81(ab)	– Tax on transfers to sales (note 13)	–	–	79	–	–	–	–	79
IFRS7p23(e)	– Transfers to inventory	–	–	(67)	–	–	–	–	(67)
12p61, 81(a)	– Tax on transfers to inventory (note 13)	–	–	22	–	–	–	–	22
39p102(a)	Net investment hedge (note 20)	–	–	–	–	–	40	–	40
1p106(d)	Currency translation differences:								
21p52(b)	– Group	–	(50)	–	–	–	(171)	–	(221)
28p39	– Associates	–	–	–	–	–	105	–	105
IFRS3p59	Recycling of revaluation of previously held interest in ABC Group	–	–	–	–	850	–	–	850
	At 31 December 2010	**–**	**1,774**	**62**	**–**	**2,218**	**2,951**	**–**	**7,005**
16p39, IFRS7 p20(a)(ii)	Revaluation – gross (note 16 and note 30)	–	1,005	–	–	690	–	–	1,695
	Revaluation transfer – gross (note 19)	–	–	–	–	(130)	–	–	(130)
12p61A, 81(a),(b)	Revaluation – tax (note 13)	–	(250)	–	–	(198)	–	–	(448)
28p39	Revaluation – associates (note 12)	–	–	–	–	(12)	–	–	(12)
16p41	Depreciation transfer - gross	–	(149)	–	–	–	–	–	(149)
16p41	Depreciation transfer – tax	–	49	–	–	–	–	–	49
1p96(b)	Cash flow hedges:								
IFRS7p23(c)	– Fair value gains in year	–	–	368	–	–	–	–	368
12p61A, 81(a)(b)	– Tax on fair value gains (note 13)	–	–	(123)	–	–	–	–	(123)
IFRS7p23(d)	– Transfers sales	–	–	(120)	–	–	–	–	(120)
12p61A, 81(a)(b)	– Tax on transfers to sales (note 13)	–	–	40	–	–	–	–	40
IFRS7p23(e)	– Transfers to inventory	–	–	(151)	–	–	–	–	(151)
12p61A, 81(a)(b)	– Tax on transfers to inventory (note 13)	–	–	50	–	–	–	–	50
39p102(a)	Net investment hedge (note 20)	–	–	–	–	–	(45)	–	(45)
1p106(d)	Currency translation differences:								
21p52(b)	– Group	–	15	–	–	–	2,146	–	2,161
28p39	– Associates	–	–	–	–	–	(74)	–	(74)
	Convertible bond – equity component (note 31)	7,761	–	–	–	–	–	–	7,761
12p61A, 81(a)	Tax on convertible bond (note 13)[2]	(2,328)	–	–	–	–	–	–	(2,328)

[1] An entity should disclose in its financial statements whether there are any restrictions on the distribution of the 'land and buildings' fair value reserve to the equity holders of the company (IAS16p77(f)).
[2] Temporary taxable difference for the liability component of the convertible bond in accordance with paragraph 23 of IAS 12.

(All amounts in C thousands unless otherwise stated)

	Convertible bond	Land and buildings revalu ation	Hedging	Treasury shares	Available-for-sale invest ments	Trans-lation	Trans-actions with NCI	Total
1p106(d)(iii) Purchase of treasury shares	–	–	–	(2,564)	–	–	–	(2,564)
Acquisition of non-controlling interest in XYZ Group	–	–	–	–	–	–	(400)	(400)
1p106(d)(iii) Decrease in ownership interest in Red Limited	–	–	–	–	–	–	(300)	(300)
IFRS3p59 Recycling of revaluation of previously held interest in ABC Group	–	–	–	–	(850)	–	–	(850)
At 31 December 2011	**5,433**	**2,444**	**126**	**(2,564)**	**1,718**	**4,978**	**(700)**	**11,435**

Note: It is assumed that the tax base on the convertible bond is not split between the debt and equity elements. If the tax base were split, this would impact the deferred tax position.

30 Trade and other payables

		Group		Company	
		2011	2010	**2011**	2010
1p77	Trade payables	**8,983**	9,495	**–**	–
24p17	Amounts due to related parties (note 41)	**3,202**	1,195	**30,162**	16,452
	Social security and other taxes	**1,502**	960	**21**	16
	Other liabilities – contingent consideration (note 39)	**1,500**	–	**1,500**	–
	Accrued expenses	**1,483**	828	**138**	125
		16,670	12,478	**31,821**	16,593

31 Borrowings

Group	**2011**	2010
Non-current		
Bank borrowings	**32,193**	40,244
Convertible bond	**42,822**	–
Debentures and other loans	**3,300**	18,092
Redeemable preference shares	**30,000**	30,000
Finance lease liabilities	**6,806**	8,010
	115,121	96,346
Current		
Bank overdrafts (note 24)	**2,650**	6,464
Collateralised borrowings	**1,014**	–
Bank borrowings	**3,368**	4,598
Debentures and other loans	**2,492**	4,608
Finance lease liabilities	**2,192**	2,588
	11,716	18,258
Total borrowings	**126,837**	114,604

(a) Bank borrowings

IFRS7p31 Bank borrowings mature until 2015 and bear average coupons of 7.5% annually (2010: 7.4% annually).

IFRS7p14 Total borrowings include secured liabilities (bank and collateralised borrowings) of C37,680 (2010: C51,306). Bank borrowings are secured by the land and buildings of the group (note 16). Collateralised borrowings are secured by trade receivables (note 21).

IFRS7p31 The exposure of the group's borrowings to interest rate changes and the contractual repricing dates at the end of the reporting period are as follows:

	2011	2010
6 months or less	**10,496**	16,748
6-12 months	**36,713**	29,100
1-5 years	**47,722**	38,555
Over 5 years	**31,906**	30,201
	126,837	114,604

(All amounts in C thousands unless otherwise stated)

IFRS7p25 The carrying amounts and fair value of the non-current borrowings are as follows:

	Carrying amount		Fair value	
	2011	2010	**2011**	2010
Bank borrowings	**32,193**	40,244	**32,590**	39,960
Redeemable preference shares	**30,000**	30,000	**28,450**	28,850
Debentures and other loans	**3,300**	18,092	**3,240**	17,730
Convertible bond	**42,822**	–	**42,752**	–
Finance lease liabilities	**6,806**	8,010	**6,205**	7,990
Total	**115,121**	96,346	**113,237**	94,530

IFRS7
p29(a)
IFRS7p25

The fair value of current borrowings equals their carrying amount, as the impact of discounting is not significant. The fair values are based on cash flows discounted using a rate based on the borrowing rate of 7.5% (2010: 7.2%).

IFRS7p31,
34(c)

The carrying amounts of the group's borrowings are denominated in the following currencies:

	2011	2010
UK pound	**80,100**	80,200
Euro	**28,353**	16,142
US dollar	**17,998**	17,898
Other currencies	**386**	364
Total	**126,837**	114,604

DV7p50(a) The group has the following undrawn borrowing facilities:

	2011	2010
Floating rate:		
– Expiring within one year	**6,150**	4,100
– Expiring beyond one year	**14,000**	8,400
Fixed rate:		
– Expiring within one year	**18,750**	12,500
Total	**38,900**	25,000

The facilities expiring within one year are annual facilities subject to review at various dates during 2012. The other facilities have been arranged to help finance the proposed expansion of the group's activities in Europe.

(b) Convertible bonds

IFRS7p17
1p79(b)

The company issued 500,000 5.0% convertible bonds at a par value of C50 million[1] on 2 January 2011. The bonds mature five years from the issue date at their nominal value of C50 million or can be converted into shares at the holder's option at the maturity date at the rate of 33 shares per C5,000. The values of the liability component and the equity conversion component were determined at issuance of the bond.

32p28
32p31
1p79(b)

The fair value of the liability component, included in non-current borrowings, was calculated using a market interest rate for an equivalent non-convertible bond. The residual amount, representing the value of the equity conversion option, is included in shareholders' equity in other reserves (note 29), net of income taxes.

The convertible bond recognised in the balance sheet is calculated as follows:

	2011	2010
Face value of convertible bond issued on 2 January 2011	**50,000**	–
Equity component (note 29)	**(7,761)**	–
Liability component on initial recognition at 2 January 2011	**42,239**	–
Interest expense (note 11)	**3,083**	–
Interest paid	**(2,500)**	–
Liability component at 31 December 2011	**42,822**	–

12Appx
BEx4

IFRS7p27 The fair value of the liability component of the convertible bond at 31 December 2011 amounted to C42,617. The fair value is calculated using cash flows discounted at a rate based on the borrowings rate of 7.5%.

[1] These amounts are not in C thousands.

(All amounts in C thousands unless otherwise stated)

(c) Redeemable preference shares

32p15,
32p18(a)

The group issued 30 million cumulative redeemable preference shares with a par value of C1 per share on 4 January 2010. The shares are mandatorily redeemable at their par value on 4 January 2014, and pay dividends at 6.5% annually.

10p21

On 1 February 2012, the group issued C6,777 6.5% US dollar bonds to finance its expansion programme and working capital requirements in the US. The bonds are repayable on 31 December 2015.

(d) Finance lease liabilities

Lease liabilities are effectively secured as the rights to the leased asset revert to the lessor in the event of default.

	2011	2010
17p31(b) Gross finance lease liabilities – minimum lease payments:		
– No later than 1 year	2,749	3,203
– Later than 1 year and no later than 5 years	6,292	7,160
– Later than 5 years	2,063	2,891
	11,104	13,254
Future finance charges on finance leases	(2,106)	(2,656)
Present value of finance lease liabilities	8,998	10,598

17p31(b) The present value of finance lease liabilities is as follows:

	2011	2010
No later than 1 year	2,192	2,588
Later than 1 year and no later than 5 years	4,900	5,287
Later than 5 years	1,906	2,723
	8,998	10,598

32 Deferred income tax

The analysis of deferred tax assets and deferred tax liabilities is as follows:

Group	2011	2010
1p61 Deferred tax assets:		
– Deferred tax asset to be recovered after more than 12 months	(2,873)	(3,257)
– Deferred tax asset to be recovered within 12 months	(647)	(64)
	(3,520)	(3,321)
Deferred tax liabilities:		
– Deferred tax liability to be recovered after more than 12 months	10,743	8,016
– Deferred tax liability to be recovered within 12 months	1,627	1,037
	12,370	9,053
Deferred tax liabilities (net)	8,850	5,732

The gross movement on the deferred income tax account is as follows:

	2011	2010
At 1 January	5,732	3,047
Exchange differences	(2,003)	(154)
Acquisition of subsidiary (note 39)	1,953	–
Income statement charge (note 13)	379	2,635
Tax charge/(credit) relating to components of other comprehensive income (note 32)	491	224
Tax charged/(credited) directly to equity	2,298	(20)
At 31 December	8,850	5,732

(All amounts in C thousands unless otherwise stated)

12p81(g)(i)(ii) The movement in deferred income tax assets and liabilities during the year, without taking into consideration the offsetting of balances within the same tax jurisdiction, is as follows:

Deferred tax liabilities	Accelerated tax depreciation	Fair value gains	Convertible bond	Other	Total
At 1 January 2010	6,058	272	–	284	6,614
Charged/(credited) to the income statement	1,786	–	–	799	2,585
Charged/(credited) to other comprehensive income	241	535	–	–	776
At 31 December 2010	8,085	807	–	1,083	9,975
Charged/(credited) to the income statement	425	–	(193)	138	370
Charged/(credited) to other comprehensive income	(571)	(32)	–	(123)	(726)
Charged directly to equity	–	–	2,328	–	2,328
Acquisition of subsidiary	553	1,375	–	275	2,203
At 31 December 2011	**8,492**	**2,150**	**2,135**	**1,373**	**14,150**

Row labels (left margin):
- At 1 January 2010
- 12p81(g)(ii) Charged/(credited) to the income statement
- 12p81(ab) Charged/(credited) to other comprehensive income
- 12p81(g)(i) At 31 December 2010
- 12p81(g)(ii) Charged/(credited) to the income statement
- 12p81(ab) Charged/(credited) to other comprehensive income
- 12p81(a) Charged directly to equity
- Acquisition of subsidiary
- 12p81(g)(i) At 31 December 2011

Deferred tax assets	Retirement benefit obligation	Provisions	Impairment losses	Tax losses	Other	Total
At 1 January 2010	(428)	(962)	(732)	(1,072)	(373)	(3,567)
Charged/(credited) to the income statement	–	181	–	–	(131)	50
Charged/(credited) to other comprehensive income	(211)	(35)	–	(460)	–	(706)
Charged/(credited) directly to equity	–	–	–	–	(20)	(20)
At 31 December 2010	(639)	(816)	(732)	(1,532)	(524)	(4,243)
(Credited)/charged to the income statement	–	(538)	(322)	1,000	(131)	9
Charged/(credited) to other comprehensive income	10	(125)	(85)	(350)	(236)	(786)
Charged/(credited) directly to equity	–	–	–	–	(30)	(30)
Acquisition of subsidiary (note 39)	(250)	–	–	–	–	(250)
At 31 December 2011	**(879)**	**(1,479)**	**(1,139)**	**(882)**	**(921)**	**(5,300)**

Row labels (left margin):
- At 1 January 2010
- 12p81(g)(ii) Charged/(credited) to the income statement
- 12p81(ab) Charged/(credited) to other comprehensive income
- 12p81(a) Charged/(credited) directly to equity
- 12p81(g)(i) At 31 December 2010
- (Credited)/charged to the income statement
- 12p81(ab) Charged/(credited) to other comprehensive income
- 12p81(a) Charged/(credited) directly to equity
- Acquisition of subsidiary (note 39)
- 12p81(g)(i) At 31 December 2011

12p81(e) Deferred income tax assets are recognised for tax loss carry-forwards to the extent that the realisation of the related tax benefit through future taxable profits is probable. The group did not recognise deferred income tax assets of C333 (2010: C1,588) in respect of losses amounting to C1,000 (2010: C5,294) that can be carried forward against future taxable income. Losses amounting to C900 (2010: C5,294) and C100 (2010: nil) expire in 2013 and 2014 respectively.

12p81(f) Deferred income tax liabilities of C3,141 (2010: C2,016) have not been recognised for the withholding tax and other taxes that would be payable on the unremitted earnings of certain subsidiaries. Such amounts are permanently reinvested. Unremitted earnings totalled C30,671 at 31 December 2011 (2010: C23,294).

33 Retirement benefit obligations

Group	2011	2010
Balance sheet obligations for:		
– Pension benefits	3,225	1,532
– Post-employment medical benefits	1,410	701
Liability in the balance sheet	4,635	2,233
Income statement charge for (note 10a):		
– Pension benefits	755	488
– Post-employment medical benefits	149	107
	904	595
19p120A(h) Actuarial losses recognised in the statement of other comprehensive income in the period	–	705
19p120A(i) Cumulative actuarial losses recognised in the statement of other comprehensive income	908	203

(a) Pension benefits

DV The group operates defined benefit pension plans in the UK and the US based on employee pensionable remuneration and length of service. The majority of plans are externally funded. Plan assets are held in trusts, foundations or similar entities, governed by local regulations and practice in each country, as is the nature of the relationship between the group and the trustees (or equivalent) and their composition.

(All amounts in C thousands unless otherwise stated)

19p120A (d)(f)	The amounts recognised in the balance sheet are determined as follows:	2011	2010
	Present value of funded obligations	**6,155**	2,943
	Fair value of plan assets	**(5,991)**	(2,797)
	Deficit of funded plans	**164**	146
	Present value of unfunded obligations	**3,206**	1,549
	Unrecognised past service cost	**(145)**	(163)
	Liability in the balance sheet	**3,225**	1,532

19p120A(c)	The movement in the defined benefit obligation over the year is as follows:	2011	2010
	At 1 January	**4,492**	3,479
	Current service cost	**751**	498
	Interest cost	**431**	214
	Employee contributions	**55**	30
	Actuarial losses/(gains)	**(15)**	706
	Exchange differences	**(61)**	(330)
	Past service cost	**18**	16
	Benefits paid	**(66)**	(121)
	Liabilities acquired in a business combination (note 39)	**3,691**	–
	Curtailments	**65**	–
	Settlements [37]	**–**	–
	At 31 December	**9,361**	4,492

19p120A(e)	The movement in the fair value of plan assets of the year is as follows:	2011	2010
	At 1 January	**2,797**	2,264
	Expected return on plan assets	**510**	240
	Actuarial (losses)/gains	**(15)**	1
	Exchange differences	**25**	(22)
	Employer contributions	**908**	411
	Employee contributions	**55**	30
	Benefits paid	**(66)**	(127)
	Assets acquired in a business combination (note 39)	**1,777**	–
	Settlements	**–**	–
	At 31 December	**5,991**	2,797

19p120A(g)	The amounts recognised in the income statement are as follows:	2011	2010
	Current service cost	**751**	498
	Interest cost	**431**	214
	Expected return on plan assets	**(510)**	(240)
	Past service cost	**18**	16
	Losses on curtailment[1]	**65**	–
	Total, included in staff costs (note 10a[1])	**755**	488

19p120A(g) Of the total charge, C516 (2010: C319) and C239 (2010: C169) were included in 'cost of goods sold' and 'administrative expenses' respectively.

19p120A(m) The actual return on plan assets was C495 (2010: C419).

19p120A(n) The principal actuarial assumptions were as follows:

	2011		2010	
	UK	US	UK	US
Discount rate	**6.0%**	**6.1%**	5.5%	5.6%
Inflation rate	**3.6%**	**3.0%**	3.3%	2.7%
Expected return on plan assets	**8.5%**	**8.3%**	8.7%	8.7%
Future salary increases	**5.0%**	**4.5%**	4.5%	4.0%
Future pension increases	**3.6%**	**2.8%**	3.1%	2.7%

[1] The gain or loss on curtailment is in principle the resulting change in surplus (or deficit) plus unrecognised past service cost attributable to the affected employees.

(All amounts in C thousands unless otherwise stated)

Assumptions regarding future mortality experience are set based on actuarial advice in accordance with published statistics and experience in each territory. Mortality assumptions for the most important countries are based on the following post-retirement mortality tables: (i) UK: PNMA 00 and PNFA 00 with medium cohort adjustment subject to a minimum annual improvement of 1% and scaling factors of 110% for current male pensioners, 125% for current female pensioners and 105% for future male and female pensioners; and (ii) US: RP2000 with a projection period of 10-15 years.

These tables translate into an average life expectancy in years for a pensioner retiring at age 65:

	2011		2010	
	UK	US	UK	US
Retiring at the end of the reporting period:				
– Male	22	20	22	20
– Female	25	24	25	24
– Retiring 20 years after the end of the reporting period:				
– Male	24	23	24	23
– Female	27	26	27	26

DV The sensitivity of the overall pension liability to changes in the weighted principal assumptions is:

	Change in assumption	Impact on overall liability
Discount rate	Increase/decrease by 0.5%	Increase/decrease by 7.2%
Inflation rate	Increase/decrease by 0.5%	Increase/decrease by 5.1%
Salary growth rate	Increase/decrease by 0.5%	Increase/decrease by 3.3%
Life expectancy	Increase by 1 year	Increase by 5.2%

19p122(b) *(b) Post-employment medical benefits*

The group operates a number of post-employment medical benefit schemes, principally in the US. The method of accounting, assumptions and the frequency of valuations are similar to those used for defined benefit pension schemes. The majority of these plans are unfunded.

19p120A(n) In addition to the assumptions set out above, the main actuarial assumption is a long-term increase in health costs of 8.0% a year (2010: 7.6%).

19p120A (d)(f) The amounts recognised in the balance sheet were determined as follows:

	2011	2010
Present value of funded obligations	705	340
Fair value of plan assets	(620)	(302)
Deficit of the funded plans	85	38
Present value of unfunded obligations	1,325	663
Liability in the balance sheet	1,410	701

19p120A(c) Movement in the defined benefit obligation is as follows:

	2011	2010
At 1 January	1,003	708
Current service cost	153	107
Interest cost	49	25
Employee contributions by plan participants[1]	–	–
Actuarial losses/(gains)	(2)	204
Exchange differences	25	(41)
Benefits paid[2]	–	–
Past service costs[1]	–	–
Liabilities acquired in a business combination (note 39)	802	–
Curtailments[1]	–	–
Settlements[1]	–	–
At 31 December	2,030	1,003

[1] IAS 19 requires the disclosure of employee contributions, benefits paid and settlements as part of the reconciliation of the opening and closing balances of plan assets. There is no such movement on the plan assets relating to post-employment medical benefits in these financial statements, but the line items have been shown for illustrative purposes.

[2] IAS 19 requires the disclosure of employee contributions, benefits paid, past service costs, settlements and curtailments as part of the reconciliation of the opening and closing balances of the present value of the defined benefit obligation. There is no such movement on the defined benefit obligation relating to pension plans in these financial statements, but the line item has been shown for illustrative purposes.

(All amounts in C thousands unless otherwise stated)

19p120A(e) The movement in the fair value of plan assets of the year is as follows:

	2011	2010
At 1 January	302	207
Expected return on plan assets	53	25
Actuarial gains/(losses)	(2)	(1)
Exchange differences	5	(2)
Employer contributions	185	73
Employee contributions[1]	–	–
Benefits paid[2]	–	–
Assets acquired in a business combination (note 39)	77	–
Settlements[2]	–	–
At 31 December	**620**	**302**

19p120A(g) The amounts recognised in the income statement were as follows:

	2011	2010
Current service cost	153	107
Interest cost	49	25
Expected return on plan assets	(53)	(25)
Total, included in staff costs (note 30a)	**149**	**107**

19p120A(g) Of the total charge, C102 (2010: C71) and C47 (2010: C36) respectively were included in cost of goods sold and administrative expenses.

19p120A(m) The actual return on plan assets was C51 (2010: C24).

19p120A(o) The effect of a 1% movement in the assumed medical cost trend rate is as follows:

	Increase	Decrease
Effect on the aggregate of the current service cost and interest cost	24	(20)
Effect on the defined benefit obligation	366	(313)

(c) Post-employment benefits (pension and medical)

19p120A(j) Plan assets are comprised as follows:

	2011		2010	
Equity instruments	3,256	49%	1,224	40%
Debt instruments	1,524	23%	571	18%
Property	1,047	16%	943	30%
Other	784	12%	361	12%
Total	**6,611**	**100%**	**3,099**	**100%**

DV Investments are well diversified, such that the failure of any single investment would not have a material impact on the overall level of assets. The largest proportion of assets is invested in equities, although the group also invests in property, bonds, hedge funds and cash. The group believes that equities offer the best returns over the long term with an acceptable level of risk. The majority of equities are in a globally diversified portfolio of international blue chip entities, with a target of 60% of equities held in the UK and Europe, 30% in the US and the remainder in emerging markets.

19p120A(k) Pension plan assets include the company's ordinary shares with a fair value of C136 (2010: C126) and a building occupied by the group with a fair value of C612 (2010: C609).

19p120A(l) The expected return on plan assets is determined by considering the expected returns available on the assets underlying the current investment policy. Expected yields on fixed interest investments are based on gross redemption yields as at the end of the reporting period. Expected returns on equity and property investments reflect long-term real rates of return experienced in the respective markets.

19p120(q) Expected contributions to post-employment benefit plans for the year ending 31 December 2012 are C1,150.

---

[1] IAS 19 requires the disclosure of employee contributions, benefits paid and settlements as part of the reconciliation of the opening and closing balances of plan assets. There is no such movement on the plan assets relating to post-employment medical benefits in these financial statements, but the line items have been shown for illustrative purposes.

[2] IAS 19 requires the disclosure of employee contributions, benefits paid, past service costs, settlements and curtailments as part of the reconciliation of the opening and closing balances of the present value of the defined benefit obligation. There is no such movement on the defined benefit obligation relating to pension plans in these financial statements, but the line item has been shown for illustrative purposes.

(All amounts in C thousands unless otherwise stated)

DV The group has agreed that it will aim to eliminate the deficit over the next nine years. Funding levels are monitored on an annual basis and the current agreed regular contribution rate is 14% of pensionable salaries in the UK and 12% in the US. The next triennial valuation is due to be completed as at 31 December 2012. The group considers that the contribution rates set at the last valuation date are sufficient to eliminate the deficit over the agreed period and that regular contributions, which are based on service costs, will not increase significantly.

DV An alternative method of valuation to the projected unit credit method is a buy-out valuation. This assumes that the entire post-employment benefit obligation will be settled by transferring all obligations to a suitable insurer. The group estimates the amount required to settle the post- employment benefit obligation at the end of the reporting period would be C15,500.

19p120A(p)

	2011	2010	2009	2008	2007
At 31 December					
Present value of defined benefit obligation	**11,391**	5,495	4,187	3,937	3,823
Fair value of plan assets	**(6,611)**	(3,099)	(2,471)	(2,222)	(2,102)
Deficit in the plan	**4,780**	2,396	1,716	1,715	1,721
Experience adjustments on plan liabilities	**(17)**	910	55	18	(32)
Experience adjustments on plan assets	**17**	–	(197)	(50)	(16)

34 Provisions for other liabilities and charges

		Environmental restoration	Restructuring	Legal claims	Profit-sharing and bonuses	Contingent liability arising on a business combination	Total
1p78(d)							
37p84(a)	At 1 January 2011	842	–	828	1,000	–	2,670
	Charged/(credited) to the income statement:						
37p84(b)	– Additional provisions/fair value adjustment on acquisition of ABC Group	316	1,986	2,405	500	1,000	6,207
37p84(d)	– Unused amounts reversed	(15)	–	(15)	(10)	–	(40)
37p84(e)	– Unwinding of discount	40	–	–	–	4	44
37p84(c)	Used during year	(233)	(886)	(3,059)	(990)	–	(5,168)
	Exchange differences	(7)	–	(68)	–	–	(75)
IFRS5p38	Transferred to disposal group/ classified as held for sale	(96)	–	–	–	–	(96)
37p84(a)	**At 31 December 2011**	**847**	**1,100**	**91**	**500**	**1,004**	**3,542**

Analysis of total provisions:

		2011	2010
1p69	Non-current	**1,320**	274
1p69	Current	**2,222**	2,396
	Total	**3,542**	2,670

(a) Environmental restoration

37p85 (a)-(c) The group uses various chemicals in working with leather. A provision is recognised for the present value of costs to be incurred for the restoration of the manufacturing sites. It is expected that C531 will be used during 2012 and C320 during 2013. Total expected costs to be incurred are C880 (2010: C760).

DV The provision transferred to the disposal group classified as held for sale amounts to C96 and relates to an environmental restoration provision for Shoes Limited (part of the UK wholesale segment). See note 25 for further details regarding the disposal group held for sale.

(b) Restructuring

37p85(a)-(c) The reduction of the volumes assigned to manufacturing operations in Step-land (a subsidiary) will result in the reduction of a total of 155 jobs at two factories. An agreement was reached with the local union representatives, which specifies the number of staff involved and the voluntary redundancy compensation package offered by the group, as well as amounts payable to those made redundant, before the financial year-end. The estimated staff restructuring costs to be incurred are C799 at 31 December 2011 (note 10a). Other direct costs attributable to the restructuring, including lease termination, are C1,187. These costs were fully provided for in 2011. The provision of C1,100 at 31 December 2011 is expected to be fully utilised during the first half of 2012.

(All amounts in C thousands unless otherwise stated)

| 36p130 | A goodwill impairment charge of C4,650 was recognised in the cash-generating unit relating to Step-land as a result of this restructuring (note 17). |

(c) Legal claims

| 37p85(a)-(c) | The amounts represent a provision for certain legal claims brought against the group by customers of the US wholesale segment. The provision charge is recognised in profit or loss within 'administrative expenses'. The balance at 31 December 2011 is expected to be utilised in the first half of 2011. In the directors' opinion, after taking appropriate legal advice, the outcome of these legal claims will not give rise to any significant loss beyond the amounts provided at 31 December 2011. |

(d) Profit-sharing and bonuses

| 19p8(c),10, DV, 37p85(a) | The provision for profit-sharing and bonuses is payable within three month of finalisation of the audited financial statements. |

(e) Recognised contingent liability

A contingent liability of C1,000 has been recognised on the acquisition of ABC Group for a pending lawsuit in which the entity is a defendant. The claim has arisen from a customer alleging defects on products supplied to them. It is expected that the courts will have reached a decision on this case by the end of 2012. The potential undiscounted amount of all future payments that the group could be required to make if there was an adverse decision related to the lawsuit is estimated to be between C500 and C1,500. As of 31 December 2011, there has been no change in the amount recognised (except for the unwinding of the discount of C4) for the liability at 31 March 2011, as there has been no change in the probability of the outcome of the lawsuit.

| IFRS3B64(g), p57 | The selling shareholders of ABC Group have contractually agreed to indemnify IFRS GAAP plc for the claim that may become payable in respect of the above-mentioned lawsuit. An indemnification asset of C1,000, equivalent to the fair value of the indemnified liability, has been recognised by the group. The indemnification asset is deducted from consideration transferred for the business combination. As is the case with the indemnified liability, there has been no change in the amount recognised for the indemnification asset as at 31 December 2011, as there has been no change in the range of outcomes or assumptions used to develop the estimate of the liability. |

35 Dividends per share

Group

| 1p107, 1p137(a) 10p12 | The dividends paid in 2011 and 2010 were C10,102 (C0.48 per share) and C15,736 (C0.78 per share) respectively. A dividend in respect of the year ended 31 December 2011 of C0.51 per share, amounting to a total dividend of C12,945, is to be proposed at the annual general meeting on 30 April 2012. These financial statements do not reflect this dividend payable. |

36 Cash generated from operations

		Group		Company	
		2011	2010	**2011**	2010
7p18(b), 20	Profit before income tax including discontinued operations	**47,916**	25,118	**9,098**	10,491
	Adjustments for:				
	– Depreciation (note 16)	**17,754**	9,662	–	–
	– Amortisation (note 17)	**800**	565	–	–
	– Goodwill impairment charge (note 17)	**4,650**	–	–	–
	– (Profit)/loss on disposal of property, plant and equipment (see below)	**(17)**	8	–	–
	– Share-based payment and increase in retirement benefit obligations	**509**	1,470	–	–
	– Fair value gains on derivative financial instruments (note 8)	**(86)**	(88)	–	–
	– Fair value (gains)/losses on financial assets at fair value through profit or loss (note 8)	**(85)**	238	–	–
	– Dividend income on available-for-sale financial assets (note 7)	**(1,100)**	(883)	**(13,809)**	(14,806)
	– Dividend income on financial assets at fair value through profit or loss (note 7)	**(800)**	(310)	–	–
	– Finance costs – net (note 11)	**6,443**	10,588	–	–
	– Share of loss/(profit) from associates (note 12)	**(215)**	(145)	–	–
	– Foreign exchange losses/(gains) in operating activities (note 8)	277	(200)		
	Gains on revaluation of existing investments (Note 39)	(850)			
	Changes in working capital (excluding the effects of acquisition and exchange differences on consolidation):				
	– Inventories	**(6,077)**	(966)	–	–
	– Trade and other receivables	**(1,893)**	(2,966)	–	–
	– Financial assets at fair value through profit or loss	**(3,747)**	(858)	–	–
	– Trade and other payables	**(7,245)**	543	**18**	–
	Cash generated from operations	**56,234**	41,776	**(4,693)**	(4,315)

(All amounts in C thousands unless otherwise stated)

In the statement of cash flows, proceeds from sale of property, plant and equipment comprise:

Group	2011	2010
Net book amount (note 16)	6,337	2,987
Profit/(loss) on disposal of property, plant and equipment	17	(8)
Proceeds from disposal of property, plant and equipment	6,354	2,979

Non-cash transactions

7p43   The principal non-cash transaction is the issue of shares as consideration for the acquisition discussed in note 39.

37 Contingencies

Group

37p86   The group has contingent liabilities in respect of legal claims arising in the ordinary course of business.

It is not anticipated that any material liabilities will arise from the contingent liabilities other than those provided for (note 34).

38 Commitments

(a) Capital commitments

Capital expenditure contracted for at the end of the reporting period but not yet incurred is as follows:

Group	2011	2010
Property, plant and equipment	3,593	3,667
Intangible assets	460	474
Total	4,053	4,141

16p74(c)
38p122(e)

(b) Operating lease commitments – group company as lessee

17p35(d)   The group leases various retail outlets, offices and warehouses under non-cancellable operating lease agreements. The lease terms are between five and 10 years, and the majority of lease agreements are renewable at the end of the lease period at market rate.

17p35(d)   The group also leases various plant and machinery under cancellable operating lease agreements. The group is required to give a six-month notice for the termination of these agreements. The lease expenditure charged to the income statement during the year is disclosed in note 9(a).

17p35(a)   The future aggregate minimum lease payments under non-cancellable operating leases are as follows:

Group	2011	2010
No later than 1 year	11,664	10,604
Later than 1 year and no later than 5 years	45,651	45,651
Later than 5 years	15,710	27,374
Total	73,025	83,629

39 Business combinations

IFRS3B64(a-d)   On 30 June 2010, the group acquired 15% of the share capital of ABC Group for C1,150. On 1 March 2011, the group acquired a further 55% of the share capital and obtained control of ABC Group, a shoe and leather goods retailer operating in the US and most western European countries.

IFRS3B64(e)   As a result of the acquisition, the group is expected to increase its presence in these markets. It also expects to reduce costs through economies of scale. The goodwill of C 4,501 arising from the acquisition is attributable to acquired customer base and economies of scale expected from combining the operations of the group and ABC Group. None of the goodwill recognised is expected to be deductible for income tax purposes.

IFRS3B64(k)   The following table summarises the consideration paid for ABC group, the fair value of assets acquired, liabilities assumed and the non-controlling interest at the acquisition date.

(All amounts in C thousands unless otherwise stated)

Consideration at 1 March 2011

IFRS3B64(f)(i), B64(f)(iv)	Cash	4,050
IFRS3B64(f)(iii)	Equity instruments (3,55m ordinary shares)	10,000
IFRS3B64(g)(i)	Contingent consideration	1,000
IFRS3B64(f)	**Total consideration transferred**	**15,050**
	Indemnification asset	(1,000)
IFRS3B64(p)(i)	Fair value of equity interest in ABC Group held before the business combination	2,000
	Total consideration	**16,050**

IFRS3B64(i)	**Recognised amounts of identifiable assets acquired and liabilities assumed**	
	Cash and cash equivalents	300
	Property, plant and equipment (note 16)	67,784
	Trademarks (included in intangibles) (note 17)	2,500
	Licences (included in intangibles) (note 17)	1,500
	Available-for-sale financial assets (note 19)	473
	Inventories	2,313
	Trade and other receivables	585
	Trade and other payables	(11,409)
	Retirement benefit obligations:	
	– Pensions (note 33)	(3,691)
	– Other post-retirement obligations (note 33)	(802)
	Borrowings	(40,509)
	Contingent liability	(1,000)
	Deferred tax liabilities (note 32)	(1,953)
	Total identifiable net assets	**16,091**
IFRS3B64(o)(i)	**Non-controlling interest**	(4,542)
	Goodwill	4,501
	Total	**16,050**

IFRS3B64(m) Acquisition-related costs of C 200 have been charged to administrative expenses in the consolidated income statement for the year ended 31 December 2011.

IFRS3B64(f)(iv)
IFRS3B64(m) The fair value of the 3,550 thousand ordinary shares issued as part of the consideration paid for ABC Group (C10, 050) was based on the published share price on 1 March 2011. Issuance costs totalling C50 have been netted against the deemed proceeds.

IFRS3B64(f)(iii)
IFRS3B64(g)
IFRS3B67(b) The contingent consideration arrangement requires the group to pay in cash the former owners of ABC Group 10% of the average profit of ABC Group for three years from 2011 - 2013, in excess of C 7,500, up to a maximum undiscounted amount of C2,500.

The potential undiscounted amount of all future payments that the group could be required to make under this arrangement is between C0 and C2,500.

The fair value of the contingent consideration arrangement of C1,000 was estimated by applying the income approach. The fair value estimates are based on a discount rate of 8% and assumed probability-adjusted profit in ABC Group of C10,000 to C20,000.

As of 31 December 2011, there was an increase of C500 recognised in the income statement for the contingent consideration arrangement, as the assumed probability-adjusted profit in ABC Group was recalculated to be approximately C20,000-30,000.

IFRS3B64(h) The fair value of trade and other receivables is C585 and includes trade receivables with a fair value of C510. The gross contractual amount for trade receivables due is C960, of which C450 is expected to be uncollectible.

IFRS3B67(a) The fair value of the acquired identifiable intangible assets of C4,000 (including trademarks and licences) is provisional pending receipt of the final valuations for those assets.

IFRS3B64(j),
B67(c),
37p84, 85 A contingent liability of C1,000 has been recognised for a pending lawsuit in which ABC Group is a defendant. The claim has arisen from a customer alleging defects on products supplied to them. It is expected that the courts will have reached a decision on this case by the end of 2012. The potential undiscounted amount of all future payments that the group could be required to make if there was an adverse decision related to the lawsuit is estimated to be between C500 and C1,500. As of 31 December 2011, there has been no change in the amount recognised (except for unwinding of the discount C4) for the liability at 1 March 2011, as there has been no change in the range of outcomes or assumptions used to develop the estimates.

(All amounts in C thousands unless otherwise stated)

IFRS3B64(g), p57 The selling shareholders of ABC Group have contractually agreed to indemnify IFRS GAAP plc for the claim that may become payable in respect of the above-mentioned lawsuit. An indemnification asset of C1,000, equivalent to the fair value of the indemnified liability, has been recognised by the group. The indemnification asset is deducted from consideration transferred for the business combination. As is the case with the indemnified liability, there has been no change in the amount recognised for the indemnification asset as at 31 December 2011, as there has been no change in the range of outcomes or assumptions used to develop the estimate of the liability.

IFRS3B64(o) The fair value of the non-controlling interest in ABC Group, an unlisted company, was estimated by using the purchase price paid for acquisition of 55% stake in ABC group. This purchase price was adjusted for the lack of control and lack of marketability that market participants would consider when estimating the fair value of the non-controlling interest in ABC Group.

IFRS3B64(p)(ii) The group recognised a gain of C850 as a result of measuring at fair value its 15% equity interest in ABC Group held before the business combination. The gain is included in other income in the group's statement of comprehensive income for the year ended 31 December 2011.

IFRS3B64(q)(i) The revenue included in the consolidated statement of comprehensive income since 1 March 2011 contributed by ABC Group was C44,709. ABC Group also contributed profit of C12,762 over the same period.

IFRS3B64(q)(ii) Had ABC Group been consolidated from 1 January 2011, the consolidated statement of income would show revenue of C220,345 and profit of C35,565.

40 Transactions with non-controlling interests

(a) Acquisition of additional interest in a subsidiary

On 21 April 2011, the Company acquired the remaining 5% of the issued shares of XYZ group for a purchase consideration of C800. The group now holds 100% of the equity share capital of XYZ group. The carrying amount of the non-controlling interests in ABC Group on the date of acquisition was C300. The group derecognised non-controlling interests of C300and recorded a decrease in equity attributable to owners of the parent of C 200. The effect of changes in the ownership interest of XYZ group on the equity attributable to owners of the Company during the year is summarised as follows:

	2011	2010
Carrying amount of non-controlling interests acquired	300	–
Consideration paid to non-controlling interests	(700)	–
Excess of consideration paid recognised in parent's equity	(400)	–

(b) Disposal of interest in a subsidiary without loss of control

On 5 September 2011, the Company disposed of a 10% interest out of the 80% interest held in Red Limited at a consideration of C700. The carrying amount of the non-controlling interests in Red Limited on the date of disposal was C2,000 (representing 20% interest). This resulted in an increase in non-controlling interests of C1,000 and a decrease in equity attributable to owners of the parent of C300. The effect of changes in the ownership interest of Red Limited on the equity attributable to owners of the Company during the year is summarised as follows:

	31 December 2011	31 December 2010
Carrying amount of non-controlling interests disposed of	(1,000)	–
Consideration received from non-controlling interests	700	–
Loss on disposal recorded within parent's equity	**(300)**	–

There were no transactions with non-controlling interests in 2010.

27p41(e) *(c) Effects of transactions with non-controlling interests on the equity attributable to owners of the parent for the year ended 31 December 2011*

	31 December 2011
Changes in equity attributable to shareholders of the Company arising from:	
– Acquisition of additional interests in subsidiary	(400)
– Disposal of interests in a subsidiary without loss of control	(300)
Net effect in equity	**(700)**

(All amounts in C thousands unless otherwise stated)

41 Related-parties

Group

1p138(c)
24Rp13
The group is controlled by M Limited (incorporated in the UK), which owns 57% of the company's shares. The remaining 43% of the shares are widely held. The group's ultimate parent is G Limited (incorporated in the UK). The group's ultimate controlling party is Mr Power.

24Rp18, 19, 24 The following transactions were carried out with related parties:

24Rp18(a) *(a) Sales of goods and services*

	2011	2010
Sales of goods:		
– Associates	1,002	204
– Associates of G Limited	121	87
Sales of services:		
– Ultimate parent (legal and administration services)	67	127
– Close family members of the ultimate controlling party (design services)	100	104
Total	**1,290**	522

Goods are sold based on the price lists in force and terms that would be available to third parties[1]. Sales of services are negotiated with related parties on a cost-plus basis, allowing a margin ranging from 15% to 30% (2010: 10% to 18%).

24Rp18(a) *(b) Purchases of goods and services*

	2011	2010
Purchases of goods:		
– Associates	3,054	3,058
Purchases of services:		
– Entity controlled by key management personnel	83	70
– Immediate parent (management services)	295	268
Total	**3,432**	3,396

24Rp23
Goods and services are bought from associates and an entity controlled by key management personnel on normal commercial terms and conditions. The entity controlled by key management personnel is a firm belonging to Mr Chamois, a non-executive director of the company. Management services are bought from the immediate parent on a cost-plus basis, allowing a margin ranging from 15% to 30% (2010: 10% to 24%).

24Rp17 *(c) Key management compensation*

Key management includes directors (executive and non-executive), members of the Executive Committee, the Company Secretary and the Head of Internal Audit. The compensation paid or payable to key management for employee services is shown below:

	2011	2010
24Rp17(a) Salaries and other short-term employee benefits	2,200	1,890
24Rp17(d) Termination benefits	1,600	–
24Rp17(b) Post-employment benefits	123	85
24Rp17(c) Other long-term benefits	26	22
24Rp17(e) Share-based payments	150	107
Total	**4,099**	2,104

CA06 s412 *(d) Directors*

	2011	2010
SI 2008/410 5 Sch 1(1)(a) Aggregate emoluments	860	661
SI 2008/410 5 Sch 1 (1)(b) Aggregate gains made on the exercise of share options	311	157
SI 2008/410 5 Sch 1 (1)(c) Aggregate amounts receivable under long-term incentive schemes	211	239
SI 2008/410 5 Sch 1 (1)(d) Company contributions to money purchase pension scheme	72	–
Total	**1,454**	1,057

[1] Management should disclose that related-party transactions were made on an arm's length basis only when such terms can be substantiated (24Rp23).

(All amounts in C thousands unless otherwise stated)

(e) Year-end balances arising from sales/purchases of goods/services

	2011	2010
Receivables from related parties (note 12):		
– Associates	26	32
– Associates of G Limited	24	8
– Ultimate parent	50	40
– Close family members of key management personnel	4	6
Payables to related parties (note 21):		
– Immediate parent	200	190
– Associates	2,902	1,005
– Entity controlled by key management personnel	100	–

The receivables from related parties arise mainly from sale transactions and are due two months after the date of sales. The receivables are unsecured in nature and bear no interest. No provisions are held against receivables from related parties (2010: nil).

The payables to related parties arise mainly from purchase transactions and are due two months after the date of purchase. The payables bear no interest.

24Rp18, 1p77 *(f) Loans to related parties*

	2011	2010
Loans to key management of the company (and their families)[1]:		
At 1 January	196	168
Loans advanced during year	343	62
Loan repayments received	(49)	(34)
Interest charged	30	16
Interest received	(30)	(16)
At 31 December	**490**	196
Loans to associates:		
At 1 January	1,192	1,206
Loans advanced during year	1,000	50
Loan repayments received	(14)	(64)
Interest charged	187	120
Interest received	(187)	(120)
At 31 December	**2,178**	1,192
Total loans to related parties:		
At 1 January	1,388	1,374
Loans advanced during year	1,343	112
Loan repayments received	(63)	(98)
Interest charged	217	136
Interest received (note 11)	(217)	(136)
At 31 December (note 21)	**2,668**	1,388

24Rp18(b)(i) The loans advanced to key management have the following terms and conditions:

Name of key management	Amount of loan	Term	Interest rate
2011			
Mr Brown	173	Repayable monthly over 2 years	6.3%
Mr White	170	Repayable monthly over 2 years	6.3%
2010			
Mr Black	20	Repayable monthly over 2 years	6.5%
Mr White	42	Repayable monthly over 1 year	6.5%

IFRS7p15 Certain loans advanced to associates during the year amounting to C1,500 (2010: C500) are collateralised by shares in listed companies. The fair value of these shares was C65 at the end of the reporting period (2010: C590).

The loans to associates are due on 1 January 2012 and carry interest at 7.0% (2010:8%). The fair values and the effective interest rates of loans to associates are disclosed in note 21.

24Rp18(c) No provision was required in 2011 (2010: nil) for the loans made to key management personnel and associates.

[1] None of the loans made to members of key management has been made to directors.

(All amounts in C thousands unless otherwise stated)

24Rp19(a)   **Company**

The following transactions with subsidiaries occurred in the year.

	2011	2010
24Rp18(a) Dividends received	**13,809**	14,806

24Rp18(a)
24Rp18(b)   Treasury Limited, an indirect subsidiary of the company provided the company with additional cash funding of C13,210 on 1 March 2011. The funding was used to partially finance the acquisition of 'ABC Group', which resulted in a C4,250 cash outflow and the acquisition of 875,000 of the company's own shares on 18 April 2011 which resulted in cash outflow of C2,564. No interest is repayable on the outstanding loan of C29,662 as at 31 December 2011 (2010:C16,452) from Treasury Limited, which is repayable on demand. See note 30.

24Rp18(a), (b)   Short-term cash financing is provided to subsidiary undertakings in the group. The monies advanced are generally repayable within 3 months. The outstanding receivable balance is C41, 147 as at 31 December 2011 (2010:C31,296) (note 30).

No purchase or sales transactions were entered into between the company and subsidiary undertakings.

42 Events after the reporting period

(a) Business combinations

10p21,
IFRS3
B64(a)-(d)   The group acquired 100% of the share capital of K&Co, a group of companies specialising in the manufacture of shoes for extreme sports, for a cash consideration of C5, 950 on 1 February 2012.

Details of net assets acquired and goodwill are as follows:

	2011
IFRS3B64 Purchase consideration:	
(f),(i) – Cash paid	**5,950**
IFRS3B64(m) – Direct cost relating to the acquisition – charged in the income statement	**150**
7p40(a) Total purchase consideration	**5,950**
Fair value of assets acquired (see below)	**(5,145)**
Goodwill	**805**

IFRS3B64(e)   The above goodwill is attributable to K&Co's strong position and profitability in trading in the niche market for extreme-sports equipment.

IFRS3B64(i)   The assets and liabilities arising from the acquisition, provisionally determined, are as follows:

	Fair value
Cash and cash equivalents	195
Property, plant and equipment	29,056
Trademarks	1,000
Licences	700
Customer relationships	1,850
Favourable lease agreements	800
Inventories	995
Trade and other receivables	855
Trade and other payables	(9,646)
Retirement benefit obligations	(1,425)
Borrowings	(19,259)
Deferred tax assets	24
Net assets acquired	**5,145**

(All amounts in C thousands unless otherwise stated)

(b) Associates

10p21   The group acquired 40% of the share capital of L&Co, a group of companies specialising in the manufacture of leisure shoes, for a cash consideration of C2,050 on 25 January 2012.

Details of net assets acquired and goodwill are as follows:

	2011
Purchase consideration:	
– Cash paid	2,050
– Direct cost relating to the acquisition	70
Total purchase consideration	2,120
Share of fair value of net assets acquired (see below)	(2,000)
Goodwill	**120**

DV   The goodwill is attributable to L&Co's strong position and profitability in trading in the market of leisure shoes and to its workforce, which cannot be separately recognised as an intangible asset.

DV   The assets and liabilities arising from the acquisition, provisionally determined, are as follows:

	Fair value
Contractual customer relationships	380
Property, plant and equipment	3,200
Inventory	500
Cash	220
Trade creditors	(420)
Borrowings	(1,880)
Net assets acquired	**2,000**

(c) Equity transactions

10p21
33p71(e)
10p21, 22(f)

On 1 January 2012, 1,200 thousand share options were granted to directors and employees with an exercise price set at the market share prices less 15% on that date of C3.13 per share (share price: C3.68) (expiry date: 31 December 2016).

The company re-issued 500,000 treasury shares for a total consideration of C1, 500 on 15 January 2012.

(d) Borrowings

10p21   On 1 February 2012, the group issued C6,777 6.5% US dollar bonds to finance its expansion programme and working capital requirements in the US. The bonds are repayable on 31 December 2016.

(All amounts in C thousands unless otherwise stated)

43 Principal subsidiaries and associates

Group and Company

27p42(b) SI 2008/4104 Sch 1(1)-(3), 16(1)-(3) SI 2008/4104 Sch17 Name	Country of incorporation	Nature of business	Proportion of ordinary shares held by parent	Proportion of ordinary shares held by the group	Proportion of preference shares held by the group
Treasury Limited	UK	Head office financing company	100%	0%	0%
A Limited	UK	Intermediate holding company	0%	100%	100%
O Limited	UK	Shoe manufacturer and wholesaler	0%	100%	0%
S Limited	UK	Shoe and leather goods retailer	0%	100%	0%
L Limited	UK	Logistics company	100%	0%	0%
D Limited	UK	Design services	100%	0%	0%
ABC Group	US	Shoe and leather goods retailer	70%	0%	0%
M GbmH	Europe	Shoe manufacturer and wholesaler	0%	100%	0%
L SARL	Europe	Logistics company	0%	100%	0%
E GbmH	Europe	Design services	0%	100%	0%
C Group	China	Shoe manufacturer and wholesaler	0%	100%	0%
R Group	Russia	Shoe manufacturer and wholesaler	0%	100%	0%

All subsidiary undertakings are included in the consolidation. The proportion of the voting rights in the subsidiary undertakings held directly by the parent company do not differ from the proportion of ordinary shares held. The parent company further does not have any shareholdings in the preference shares of subsidiary undertakings included in the group.

Refer to note 12(b) for details of group holdings in associates.

(All amounts in C thousands unless otherwise stated)

Appendix I – Alternative presentation of primary statements

Consolidated statement of cash flows – direct method

IAS 7 encourages the use of the 'direct method' for the presentation of cash flows from operating activities. The presentation of cash flows from operating activities using the direct method in accordance with IAS 7p18 is as follows:

Consolidated statement of cash flows

1p113, 7p10

		Note	Year ended 31 December 2011	2010
7p18(a)	**Cash flows from operating activities**			
	Cash receipts from customers		212,847	114,451
	Cash paid to suppliers and employees		(156,613)	(72,675)
	Cash generated from operations		56,234	41,776
	Interest paid		(7,835)	14,773
	Income taxes paid		(14,317)	(10,526)
	Net cash flows from operating activities		34,082	16,477
7p21	**Cash flows from investing activities**			
7p39	Acquisition of subsidiary, net of cash acquired	39	(3,950)	–
7p16(a)	Purchases of property, plant and equipment (PPE)	6	(9,755)	(6,042)
7p16(b)	Proceeds from sale of PPE	36	6,354	2,979
7p16(a)	Purchases of intangible assets	7	(3,050)	(700)
7p16(c)	Purchases of available-for-sale financial assets	10	(2,781)	(1,126)
7p16(e)	Loans granted to associates	40	(1,000)	(50)
7p16(f)	Loan repayments received from associates	40	14	64
7p31	Interest received		1,254	1,193
7p31	Dividends received		1,180	1,120
	Net cash used in investing activities		(11,734)	(2,562)
7p21	**Cash flows from financing activities**			
7p17(a)	Proceeds from issuance of ordinary shares	17	950	1,070
7p17(b)	Purchase of treasury shares	17	(2,564)	–
7p17(c)	Proceeds from issuance of convertible bond		50,000	
7p17(c)	Proceeds from issuance of redeemable preference shares		–	30,000
7p17(c)	Proceeds from borrowings		8,500	18,000
7p17(d)	Repayments of borrowings		(78,117)	(34,674)
7p31	Dividends paid to group shareholders		(10,102)	(15,736)
7p31	Dividends paid to holders of redeemable preference shares		(1,950)	(1,950)
7p31	Dividends paid to non-controlling interests		(1,920)	(550)
	Net cash used in financing activities		(35,203)	(3,840)
	Net (decrease)/increase in cash, cash equivalents and bank overdrafts		(12,855)	10,075
	Cash, cash equivalents and bank overdrafts at beginning of the year		27,598	17,587
	Exchange gains/(losses) on cash, cash equivalents and bank overdrafts		535	(64)
	Cash, cash equivalents and bank overdrafts at end of the year	15	15,278	27,598

The notes on pages 15 to 74 are an integral part of these consolidated financial statements.

(All amounts in C thousands unless otherwise stated)

Consolidated statement of comprehensive income – single statement, showing expenses by function

1p10(b),81(a)		Note	Year ended 31 December 2011	2010
	Continuing operations			
1p82(a), 103	Revenue	5	**211,034**	112,360
1p99,103	Cost of sales		**(77,366)**	(46,68)
1p103	**Gross profit**		**133,668**	65,678
1p99, 103	Distribution costs		**(52,140)**	(21,213)
1p99, 103	Administrative expenses		**(28,778)**	(10,426)
1p99, 103	Other income	27	**2,750**	1,259
1p85	Other (losses)/gains – net	26	**(90)**	63
1p85	Loss on expropriated land	28	**(1,117)**	–
1p85	**Operating profit**		**54,293**	35,361
1p85	Finance income	31	**1,730**	1,609
1p82(b)	Finance cost	31	**(8,173)**	(12,197)
1p85	Finance costs – net	31	**(6,443)**	(10,558)
1p82(c)	Share of (loss)/profit of associates	8	**(174)**	145
1p85	**Profit before income tax**		**47,676**	24,918
1p82(d), 12p77	Income tax expense	32	**(14,611)**	(8,670)
1p85	Profit for the year from continuing operations	16	**33,065**	16,248
IFRS5p34,	**Discontinued operations:**			
	Profit for the year from discontinued operations		**100**	120
1p82(f)	**Profit for the year**		**33,165**	16,368
1p82(g),	**Other comprehensive income:**			
1p82(g),	Gains on revaluation of land and buildings	20	**–**	1,133
IFRS7p20(a)(ii)	Available-for-sale financial assets	20	**560**	123
28p39, 1p82(h)	Share of other comprehensive income of associates	20	**(12)**	(14)
1p82(g), 19p93B	Actuarial loss on retirement benefit obligations		**–**	(70)
12p80(d)	Impact of change in the Euravian tax rate on deferred tax	23	**(10)**	
IFRS7p23(c)	Cash flow hedges	20	**97**	(3)
1p82(g)	Net investment hedge	20	**(45)**	40
1p82(g)	Currency translation differences	20	**2,244**	(156)
1p91(b)	Income tax relating to components of other comprehensive income		**(231)**	(224)
	Other comprehensive income for the year, net of tax		**2,603**	194
1p82(i)	**Total comprehensive income for the year**		**35,768**	16,562
1p83(a)	**Profit attributable to:**			
1p83(a)(ii)	Equity holders of the company		**30,617**	15,512
1p83(a)(i) 27p27	Non-controlling interest		**2,548**	856
			33,165	16,368
1p83(b)	**Total comprehensive income attributable to:**			
1p83(b)(ii)	Equity holders of the company		**32,968**	15,746
1p83(b)(i)	Non-controlling interest		**2,800**	816
			35,768	16,562
	Total comprehensive income attributable to equity shareholders arises from:			
	Continuing operations		**32,868**	15,626
IFRS5p33(d)	Discontinued operations	16	**100**	120
			32,968	15,746

(All amounts in C thousands unless otherwise stated)

Earnings per share from continuing and discontinued operations to the equity holders of the company during the year
(expressed in C per share)

			2011	2010
	Basic earnings per share			
33p66	From continuing operations	34	**1.26**	0.75
33p68	From discontinued operations		**0.01**	0.01
			1.27	0.76
	Diluted earnings per share[1]			
33p66	From continuing operations	34	**1.15**	0.71
33p68	From discontinued operations		**0.01**	0.01
			1.16	0.72

The notes on pages 15 to 74 are an integral part of these consolidated financial statements.

---

[1] EPS for discontinued operations may be given in the notes to the accounts instead of the face of the income statement. The income tax effect has been presented on an aggregate basis; therefore an additional note disclosure resents the income tax effect of each component. Alternatively, this information could be presented within the statement of comprehensive income.

(All amounts in C thousands unless otherwise stated)

Appendix II – Areas not illustrated in financial statements of IFRS GAAP plc

(All amounts in C thousands unless otherwise stated)

1 Biological assets

Note 1 – General information

1p138(b),
41p46(a)

The group is engaged in the business of farming sheep and poultry, primarily for sale to meat processors. The group earns ancillary income from various agricultural produce, such as wool.

Note 2 – Accounting policies

Basis of preparation

1p117(a)

The consolidated financial statements have been prepared under the historical cost convention, as modified by the revaluation of land and buildings, available-for-sale financial assets, financial assets and financial liabilities (including derivative financial instruments at fair value through profit or loss) and certain biological assets.

1p119
41p41,47

Biological assets

Biological assets comprise sheep, poultry and hatching eggs.

Sheep are measured at fair value less estimated cost to sell, based on market prices at auction of livestock of similar age, breed and genetic merit with adjustments, where necessary, to reflect the differences.

Broiler chickens older than 10 weeks are measured at fair value less costs to sell based on estimated pre-tax net cash flows. The calculation is based on estimated selling prices of fully grown broiler chickens reduced by estimated farming costs to be incurred until they reach slaughter size.

The fair value of broiler chickens younger than 10 weeks and hatching eggs cannot be reliably estimated due to the high mortality rates and are carried at cost less impairment. Costs include cost of purchase of eggs and all direct and indirect farming costs. These assets are not depreciable.

41p54(a),
(b)

Costs to sell include the incremental selling costs, including auctioneers' fees and commission paid to brokers and dealers.

Changes in fair value of livestock are recognised in the income statement.

Farming costs such as feeding, labour costs, pasture maintenance, veterinary services and shearing are expensed as incurred. The cost of purchase of sheep and eggs plus transportation charges are capitalised as part of biological assets.

Note 3 – Estimates and judgements – Biological assets

40p47

In measuring fair value of poultry and sheep livestock, management estimates and judgements are required for the determination of fair value. These estimates and judgements relate to the market prices, average weight and quality of animals and mortality rates.

(a) Sheep

Market price of sheep is obtained from the weekly auctions at the local market. The quality of livestock sold at the local market is considered to approximate the group's breeding and slaughter livestock.

The sheep grow at different rates and there can be a considerable spread in the quality and weight of animals and that affects the price achieved. An average weight is assumed for the slaughter sheep livestock that are not yet at marketable weight.

(b) Poultry

For broiler chickens more than 10 weeks old, the estimated farming costs are allocated on a time proportionate basis. The cash flows are not discounted as the time value of money is insignificant due to the short-term nature of the livestock.

(All amounts in C thousands unless otherwise stated)

Consolidated income statement (extracts)

	Note	2011	2010
Revenue	4	**26,240**	27,548
Change in fair value of biological assets	5	**23,000**	19,028
Livestock cost of sales	5	**(23,180)**	(24,348)

41p40

Consolidated balance sheet (extracts)

1p68

	Note	2011	2010
Assets			
Non-current assets			
Property, plant and equipment		**155,341**	98,670
Biological assets	5	**4,300**	5,760
Current assets			
Biological assets	5	**37,500**	25,940

1p51
1p68(a)
1p54(f)
1p51
1p54(f)

Note 4 – Revenue (extracts)

	Note	2011	2010
Sale of livestock	5	**23,740**	25,198
Sale of wool		**2,500**	2,350
Total revenue		**26,240**	27,548

Note 5 – Biological assets[1]

	2011	2010
At 1 January	**31,700**	32,420
Value changes caused by:		
– Birth and growth of animals	**21,950**	17,930
– Increase due to purchases	**10,280**	4,600
– Livestock losses	**(480)**	(350)
Change in fair value of livestock due to price changes	**1,530**	1,448
Decrease due to sales	**(23,180)**	(24,348)
At 31 December	**41,800**	31,700
Sheep – at fair value less cost to sell:		
– Mature	**4,300**	5,760
– Immature	**28,200**	20,690
	32,500	26,450
Poultry		
– Immature – at fair value less cost to sell	**5,650**	3,030
– Immature – at cost less impairment	**2,150**	1,230
	7,800	4,260
Hatching eggs – at cost less impairment	**1,500**	990
At 31 December	**41,800**	31,700

41p50
41p50(a)
41p50(b)
41p50(a)
41p50(a)
41p50(c)

41p43,45

41p55

41p55

41p46(b) As at 31 December the group had 6,500 sheep and 26,000 poultry (2010: 5,397 sheep and 14,700 poultry). In addition, the biological assets include 25,000 hatching eggs (2010: 16,500). During the year the group sold 3,123 sheep (2010: 4,098 sheep) and 25,000 chickens (2010:18,000).

41p43 Breeding sheep are classified as mature livestock and slaughter sheep are classified as immature livestock. All chickens are classified as immature livestock as the carrying amount of chickens at slaughter weight is insignificant.

41p54(f), 55(a) The total gross carrying amount of broiler chicken and hatching eggs carried at cost at end of the year amount to C3,870 (2010:C2,405 and 2009:C2,650). The impairment losses included in profit or loss and carried at end of the year amount to C220 (2010:C185 and 2009:192).

Selling expenses of C560 (2010:C850) were incurred during the year.

Livestock are classified as current assets if they are to be sold within one year. These include broiler chickens, hatching eggs and slaughter sheep.

[1] The reconciliation per IAS 41p55 is not presented because of the short life of chickens (about 26 weeks). The information would not provide meaningful information. However, for longer-life assets such as forests, it would be a required disclosure.

(All amounts in C thousands unless otherwise stated)

41p49(c)   **Note 6 – Financial risk management strategies**

The group is exposed to risks arising from environmental and climatic changes, commodity prices and financing risks.

The group's geographic spread of farms allows a high degree of mitigation against adverse climatic conditions such as droughts and floods and disease outbreaks. The group has strong environmental policies and procedures in place to comply with environmental and other laws.

The group is exposed to risks arising from fluctuations in the price and sales volume of sheep. Where possible, the group enters into supply contracts for sheep to ensure sales volumes can be met by meat processing companies. The group has long-term contracts in place for supply of poultry to its major customers.

The seasonal nature of the sheep farming business requires a high level of cash flow in the second half of the year. The group actively manages the working capital requirements and has secured sufficient credit facilities sufficient to meet the cash flow requirements.

41p49(b)   **Note 7 – Commitments**

The group has entered into a contract to acquire 250 breeding sheep at 31 December 2011 for C1,250 (2010: nil).

2 Construction contracts

Note – Accounting policies

11p3   A construction contract is defined by IAS 11, 'Construction contracts', as a contract specifically negotiated for the construction of an asset.

11p22   When the outcome of a construction contract can be estimated reliably and it is probable that the contract will be profitable, contract revenue is recognised over the period of the contract by reference to the stage of completion. Contract costs are recognised as expenses by reference to the stage of completion of the contract activity at the end of the reporting period. When it is probable that total contract costs will exceed total contract revenue, the expected loss is recognised as an expense immediately.

When the outcome of a construction contract cannot be estimated reliably, contract revenue is recognised only to the extent of contract costs incurred that are likely to be recoverable.

Variations in contract work, claims and incentive payments are included in contract revenue to the extent that may have been agreed with the customer and are capable of being reliably measured.

The group uses the 'percentage-of-completion method' to determine the appropriate amount to recognise in a given period. The stage of completion is measured by reference to the contract costs incurred up to the end of the reporting period as a percentage of total estimated costs for each contract. Costs incurred in the year in connection with future activity on a contract are excluded from contract costs in determining the stage of completion.

On the balance sheet, the group reports the net contract position for each contract as either an asset or a liability. A contract represents an asset where costs incurred plus recognised profits (less recognised losses) exceed progress billings; a contract represents a liability where the opposite is the case.

Consolidated balance sheet (extracts)

	Note	2011	2010
1p60 **Current assets**			
1p54(h) Trade and other receivables	12	**23,303**	20,374
1p60 **Current liabilities**			
1p54(k) Trade and other payables	21	**17,667**	13,733

Consolidated income statement (extracts)

	Note	2011	2010
11p39(a) Contract revenue		**58,115**	39,212
11p16 Contract costs		**(54,729)**	(37,084)
1p103 Gross profit		**3,386**	2,128
1p103 Selling and marketing costs		**(386)**	(128)
1p103 Administrative expenses		**(500)**	(400)

(All amounts in C thousands unless otherwise stated)

Note – Trade and other receivables (extracts)[1]

		2011	2010
IFRS7p36, 1p78(b)	Trade receivables	18,174	16,944
	Less: Provision for impairment of receivables	(109)	(70)
	Trade receivables – net	18,065	16,874
11p42(a)	Amounts due from customers for contract work	1,216	920
	Prepayments	1,300	1,146
1p77, 24p17	Receivables from related parties (note 40)	54	46
1p77, 24p17	Loans to related parties (note 40)	2,668	1,388
	Total	**23,303**	**20,374**

Note – Trade and other payables (extracts)[2]

		2011	2010
1p77	Trade payables	10,983	9,495
24p17	Amounts due to related parties (note 40)	2,202	1,195
11p42(b)	Amounts due to customers for contract work	997	1,255
	Social security and other taxes	2,002	960
	Accrued expenses	1,483	828
	Total	**17,667**	**13,733**

Note – Construction contracts

		2011	2010
11p40(a)	The aggregate costs incurred and recognised profits (less recognised losses) to date	69,804	56,028
	Less: Progress billings	(69,585)	(56,383)
	Net balance sheet position for ongoing contracts	**219**	**(355)**

3 Oil and gas exploration assets

Note – Accounting policies

IFRS6p24   Oil and natural gas exploration and evaluation expenditures are accounted for using the 'successful efforts' method of accounting. Costs are accumulated on a field-by-field basis. Geological and geophysical costs are expensed as incurred. Costs directly associated with an exploration well, and exploration and property leasehold acquisition costs are capitalised until the determination of reserves is evaluated. If it is determined that commercial discovery has not been achieved, these costs are charged to expense.

Capitalisation is made within property, plant and equipment or intangible assets according to the nature of the expenditure.

Once commercial reserves are found, exploration and evaluation assets are tested for impairment and transferred to development tangible and intangible assets. No depreciation and/or amortisation is charged during the exploration and evaluation phase.

(a) Development tangible and intangible assets

Expenditure on the construction, installation or completion of infrastructure facilities such as platforms, pipelines and the drilling of commercially proven development wells, is capitalised within property, plant and equipment and intangible assets according to nature. When development is completed on a specific field, it is transferred to production or intangible assets. No depreciation or amortisation is charged during the exploration and evaluation phase.

(b) Oil and gas production assets

Oil and gas production properties are aggregated exploration and evaluation tangible assets, and development expenditures associated with the production of proved reserves.

(c) Depreciation/amortisation

Oil and gas properties intangible assets are depreciated or amortised using the unit-of-production method. Unit-of-production rates are based on proved developed reserves, which are oil, gas and other mineral reserves estimated to

---

[1] For the purpose of this illustrative appendix, comparatives for the year ended 31 December 2010 are not disclosed, although they are required by IAS 1.
[2] At 31 December 2011, trade and other payables include customer advances of C142 (2010: C355) related to construction contracts in progress

(All amounts in C thousands unless otherwise stated)

be recovered from existing facilities using current operating methods. Oil and gas volumes are considered produced once they have been measured through meters at custody transfer or sales transaction points at the outlet valve on the field storage tank.

(d) Impairment – exploration and evaluation assets

Exploration and evaluation assets are tested for impairment when reclassified to development tangible or intangible assets, or whenever facts and circumstances indicate impairment. An impairment loss is recognised for the amount by which the exploration and evaluation assets' carrying amount exceeds their recoverable amount. The recoverable amount is the higher of the exploration and evaluation assets' fair value less costs to sell and their value in use. For the purposes of assessing impairment, the exploration and evaluation assets subject to testing are grouped with existing cash-generating units of production fields that are located in the same geographical region.

(e) Impairment – proved oil and gas production properties and intangible assets

Proven oil and gas properties and intangible assets are reviewed for impairment whenever events or changes in circumstances indicate that the carrying amount may not be recoverable. An impairment loss is recognised for the amount by which the asset's carrying amount exceeds its recoverable amount. The recoverable amount is the higher of an asset's fair value less costs to sell and value in use. For the purposes of assessing impairment, assets are grouped at the lowest levels for which there are separately identifiable cash flows.

Note – Property, plant and equipment[1]

	Capitalised exploration and evaluation expenditure	Capitalised development expenditure	Subtotal – assets under construction	Production assets	Other businesses and corporate assets	Total
At 1 January 2011						
Cost	218	12,450	12,668	58,720	3,951	75,339
Accumulated amortisation and impairment	(33)	–	(33)	(5,100)	(77)	(5,210)
Net book amount	185	12,450	12,635	53,620	3,874	70,129
Year ended 31 December 2011						
Opening net book amount	185	12,450	12,635	53,620	3,874	70,129
Exchange differences	17	346	363	1,182	325	1,870
Acquisitions	–	386	386	125	4	515
Additions	45	1,526	1,571	5,530	95	7,196
Transfers	(9)	(958)	(967)	1,712	–	745
Disposals	(12)	(1,687)	(1,699)	–	–	(1,699)
Depreciation charge	–	–	–	(725)	(42)	(767)
Impairment charge	(7)	(36)	(43)	(250)	(3)	(296)
Closing net book amount	**219**	**12,027**	**12,246**	**61,194**	**4,253**	**77,693**
At 31 December 2011						
Cost	264	12,027	12,291	67,019	4,330	83,640
Accumulated amortisation and impairment	(45)	–	(45)	(5,825)	(77)	(5,947)
Net book amount	**219**	**12,027**	**12,246**	**61,194**	**4,253**	**77,693**

[1] For the purpose of this illustrative appendix, comparatives for the year ended 31 December 2010 are not disclosed, although they are required by IAS 1.

(All amounts in C thousands unless otherwise stated)

Note – Intangible assets[1]

	Capitalised exploration and evaluation expenditure	Capitalised development expenditure	Subtotal – intangible assets in progress expenditure	Production assets	Goodwill	Other	Total
At 1 January 2011							
Cost	5,192	750	5,942	3,412	9,475	545	19,374
Accumulated amortisation and impairment	(924)	–	(924)	(852)	(75)	(19)	(1,870)
Net book amount	**4,268**	**750**	**5,018**	**2,560**	**9,400**	**526**	**17,504**
Year ended 31 December 2011							
Opening net book amount	4,268	750	5,018	2,560	9,400	526	17,504
Exchange differences	152	8	160	195	423	28	806
Acquisitions	26	32	58	5	–	5	68
Additions	381	8	389	15	–	86	490
Transfers	(548)	548	–	–	–	–	-
Transfers to production	–	(850)	(850)	105	–	–	(745)
Disposals	–	(28)	(28)	(15)	–	–	(43)
Amortisation charge	–	–	–	(98)	–	(42)	(140)
Impairment charge	(45)	–	(45)	–	(175)	(5)	(225)
Closing net book amount	**4,234**	**468**	**4,702**	**2,767**	**9,648**	**598**	**17,715**
At 31 December 2011							
Cost	5,203	468	5,671	3,717	9,898	659	19,945
Accumulated amortisation and impairment	(969)	–	(969)	(950)	(250)	(61)	(2,230)
Net book amount	**4,234**	**468**	**4,702**	**2,767**	**9,648**	**598**	**17,715**

Assets and liabilities related to the exploration and evaluation of mineral resources other than those presented above are as follows:

	2011	2010
Receivables from joint venture partners	**25**	22
Payable to subcontractors and operators	**32**	34

Exploration and evaluation activities have led to total expenses of C59,000 (2010: C57,000), of which C52,000 (2010: C43,000) are impairment charges.

In 2011, the disposal of a 16.67% interest in an offshore exploration stage 'Field X' resulted in post-tax profits on sale of C3000 (2010: nil).

Cash payments of C415,000 (2010: C395,000) have been incurred related to exploration and evaluation activities. The cash proceeds due to the disposal of the interest in Field X were C8,000 (2010: nil).

4 Financial guarantee contracts

39p9

Note – Accounting policies (under IAS 39)

Financial guarantee contracts are contracts that require the issuer to make specified payments to reimburse the holder for a loss it incurs because a specified debtor fails to make payments when due, in accordance with the terms of a debt instrument. Such financial guarantees are given to banks, financial institutions and other bodies on behalf of subsidiaries or associates to secure loans, overdrafts and other banking facilities.

39p43, 47
39AG4(a)
IFRS7p3(d)

Financial guarantees are initially recognised in the financial statements at fair value on the date the guarantee was given. The fair value of a financial guarantee at the time of signature is zero because all guarantees are agreed on arm's length terms, and the value of the premium agreed corresponds to the value of the guarantee obligation. No receivable for the future premiums is recognised. Subsequent to initial recognition, the company's liabilities under such guarantees are measured at the higher of the initial amount, less amortisation of fees recognised in accordance with IAS 18, 'Employee benefits', and the best estimate of the amount required to settle the guarantee. These estimates are determined based on experience of similar transactions and history of past losses, supplemented by management's judgement. The fee income earned is recognised on a straight-line basis over the life of the guarantee. Any increase in the liability relating to guarantees is reported in the consolidated income statement within other operating expenses.

---

[1] For the purpose of this illustrative appendix, comparatives for the year ended 31 December 2010 are not disclosed, although they are required by IAS 1.

(All amounts in C thousands unless otherwise stated)

Where guarantees in relation to loans or other payables of subsidiaries or associates are provided for no compensation, the fair values are accounted for as contributions and recognised as part of the cost of the investment in the financial statements of the company.

Note – Financial risk factors

IFRS7p34(a), 36(a)
IFRS 7 Appx B9,10
IFRS7 IG21

Maximum exposure to credit risk before collateral held or other credit enhancements

	Company Maximum exposure	
	2011	**2010**
Credit risk exposure relating to off-balance sheet items		
Financial guarantees	660	789
At 31 December	660	789

Liquidity risk (extracts)

	Company	
	Less than 1 year	**Between 1 and 2 years**
At 31 December 2011		
Financial guarantee contracts	21	–
At 31 December 2010		
Financial guarantee contracts	10	–

Note – Other financial liabilities (extracts)

	Company	
	2011	**2010**
Current		
Liabilities for financial guarantees	90	10
Total current other financial liabilities	90	10
Non-current		
Liabilities for financial guarantees	30	80
Total non-current other financial liabilities	30	80

Note – Financial guarantees

The company has guaranteed the bank overdrafts and drawn components of bank loans of a number of subsidiaries. Under the terms of the financial guarantee contracts, the company will make payments to reimburse the lenders upon failure of the guaranteed entity to make payments when due.

Terms and face values of the liabilities guaranteed were as follows:

	Year of maturity	31 December 2011 Face value	31 December 2010 Face value
Bank term loans of controlled entities	2011-2013	660	789

The method used in determining the fair value of these guarantees has been disclosed in the company's entity's accounting policy 'Financial guarantee contracts'. See note 3.3.

	Company	
	2011	**2010**
Amortisation of financial guarantee contracts	3	2

(All amounts in C thousands unless otherwise stated)

5 Leases: accounting by lessor

17p4 A lease is an agreement whereby the lessor conveys to the lessee in return for a payment, or series of payments, the right to use an asset for an agreed period of time.

Note – Accounting policies

1p119 When assets are leased out under a finance lease, the present value of the lease payments is recognised as a receivable. The difference between the gross receivable and the present value of the receivable is recognised as unearned finance income.

The method for allocating gross earnings to accounting periods is referred to a as the 'actuarial method'. The actuarial method allocates rentals between finance income and repayment of capital in each accounting period in such a way that finance income will emerge as a constant rate of return on the lessor's net investment in the lease.

17p49 When assets are leased out under an operating lease, the asset is included in the balance sheet based on the nature of the asset.

17p50 Lease income on operating leases is recognised over the term of the lease on a straight-line basis.

(All amounts in C thousands unless otherwise stated)

Note – Property, plant and equipment

The category of vehicles and equipment includes vehicles leased by the group to third parties under operating leases with the following carrying amounts:

17p57		2011	2010
	Cost	70,234	–
	Accumulated depreciation at 1 January	(14,818)	–
	Depreciation charge for the year	(5,058)	–
	Net book amount	**50,358**	**–**

Note – Trade and other receivables

		2011	2010
1p78(b)			
	Non-current receivables		
17p47(a)	Finance leases – gross receivables	1,810	630
17p47(b)	Unearned finance income	(222)	(98)
		1,588	532
1p78(b)	**Current receivables**		
17p47(a)	Finance leases – gross receivables	1,336	316
17p47(b)	Unearned finance income	(300)	(98)
		1,036	218
1p78(b)	Gross receivables from finance leases:		
17p47(a)	– No later than 1 year	1,336	316
	– Later than 1 year and no later than 5 years	1,810	630
	– Later than 5 years	–	–
		3,146	946
1p78(b), 17p47(b)	Unearned future finance income on finance leases	(522)	(196)
	Net investment in finance leases	**2,624**	**750**

1p78(b)	The net investment in finance leases may be analysed as follows:		
		2011	2010
17p47(a)	No later than 1 year	1,036	218
	Later than 1 year and no later than 5 years	1,588	532
	Later than 5 years	–	–
	Total	**2,624**	**750**

Note – Operating leases

17p56(a)   **Operating leases rental receivables – group company as lessor**

The future minimum lease payments receivable under non-cancellable operating leases are as follows:

	2011	2010
No later than 1 year	12,920	12,920
Later than 1 year and no later than 5 years	41,800	41,800
Later than 5 years	840	10,840
Total	**55,560**	**65,560**

17p56(b)   Contingent-based rents recognised in the income statement were C235 (2010: C40).

17p56(c)   The company leases vehicles under various agreements which terminate between 2011 and 2016. The agreements do not include an extension option.

6 Government grants

Note – Accounting policies

Government grants

20p39(a) 20p12   Grants from the government are recognised at their fair value where there is a reasonable assurance that the grant will be received and the group will comply with all attached conditions.

Government grants relating to costs are deferred and recognised in the income statement over the period necessary to match them with the costs that they are intended to compensate.

(All amounts in C thousands unless otherwise stated)

Government grants relating to property, plant and equipment are included in non-current liabilities as deferred government grants and are credited to the income statement on a straight-line basis over the expected lives of the related assets.

Note – Other (losses)/gains

20p39(b)
20p39(c)
The group obtained and recognised as income a government grant of C100 (2010: nil) to compensate for losses caused by flooding incurred in the previous year. The group is obliged not to reduce its average number of employees over the next three years under the terms of this government grant.

The group benefits from government assistance for promoting in international markets products made in the UK; such assistance includes marketing research and similar services provided by various UK government agencies free of charge.

7 Joint ventures

Note – Accounting policies

1p119   **Consolidation**

(c) Joint ventures

31p57
The group's interests in jointly controlled entities are accounted for by proportionate consolidation. The group combines its share of the joint ventures' individual income and expenses, assets and liabilities and cash flows on a line-by-line basis with similar items in the group's financial statements. The group recognises the portion of gains or losses on the sale of assets by the group to the joint venture that is attributable to the other venturers. The group does not recognise its share of profits or losses from the joint venture that result from the group's purchase of assets from the joint venture until it re-sells the assets to an independent party. However, a loss on the transaction is recognised immediately if the loss provides evidence of a reduction in the net realisable value of current assets, or an impairment loss.

Note – Interest in joint venture

31p56
The group has a 50% interest in a joint venture, JV&Co, which provides products and services to the automotive industry. The following amounts represent the group's 50% share of the assets and liabilities, and sales and results of the joint venture. They are included in the balance sheet and income statement:

	2011	2010
Assets:		
– Non-current assets	2,730	2,124
– Current assets	803	717
	3,533	2,841
Liabilities:		
– Non-current liabilities	1,114	1,104
– Current liabilities	355	375
	1,469	1,479
Net assets	2,064	1,362
– Income	5,276	5,618
– Expenses	(3,754)	(4,009)
Profit after income tax	1,522	1,609
31p55(b) **Proportionate interest in joint venture's commitments**	90	92

31p54
There are no contingent liabilities relating to the group's interest in the joint venture, and no contingent liabilities of the venture itself.

8 Revenue recognition: multiple-element arrangements

Note – Accounting policies

The group offers certain arrangements whereby a customer can purchase a personal computer together with a two-year servicing agreement. Where such multiple-element arrangements exist, the amount of revenue allocated to each element is based upon the relative fair values of the various elements. The fair values of each element are determined based on the current market price of each of the elements when sold separately. The revenue relating to the computer is recognised when risks and rewards of the computer are transferred to the customer, which occurs on delivery. Revenue relating to the service element is recognised on a straight-line basis over the service period.

(All amounts in C thousands unless otherwise stated)

9 Customer loyalty programme

Note – Accounting policy

The group operates a loyalty programme where customers accumulate points for purchases made, which entitle them to discounts on future purchases. The reward points are recognised as a separately identifiable component of the initial sale transaction by allocating the fair value of the consideration received between the award points and the other components of the sale such that the reward points are initially recognised as deferred income at their fair value. Revenue from the reward points is recognised when the points are redeemed. Breakage is recognised as reward points are redeemed based upon expected redemption rates. Reward points expire 12 months after the initial sale.

Note – Current liabilities – other liabilities

	Group		Company	
	2011	2010	**2011**	2010
Deferred revenue: customer loyalty programme	**395**	370	–	–

10 Put option arrangements

The potential cash payments related to put options issued by the group over the equity of subsidiary companies are accounted for as financial liabilities when such options may only be settled other than by exchange of a fixed amount of cash or another financial asset for a fixed number of shares in the subsidiary. The amount that may become payable under the option on exercise is initially recognised at fair value within borrowings with a corresponding charge directly to equity. The charge to equity is recognised separately as written put options over non-controlling interests, adjacent to non-controlling interests in the net assets of consolidated subsidiaries

The group recognises the cost of writing such put options, determined as the excess of the fair value of the option over any consideration received as a financing cost. Such options are subsequently measured at amortised cost, using the effective interest rate method, in order to accrete the liability up to the amount payable under the option at the date at which it first becomes exercisable. The charge arising is recorded as a financing cost. In the event that the option expires unexercised, the liability is derecognised with a corresponding adjustment to equity.

11 Foreign currency translations – disposal of foreign operation and partial disposal

21p48, 48A, 48B, 48C

On the disposal of a foreign operation (that is, a disposal of the group's entire interest in a foreign operation, or a disposal involving loss of control over a subsidiary that includes a foreign operation, a disposal involving loss of joint control over a jointly controlled entity that includes a foreign operation, or a disposal involving loss of significant influence over an associate that includes a foreign operation), all of the exchange differences accumulated in equity in respect of that operation attributable to the equity holders of the company are reclassified to profit or loss.

In the case of a partial disposal that does not result in the group losing control over a subsidiary that includes a foreign operation, the proportionate share of accumulated exchange differences are re-attributed to non-controlling interests and are not recognised in profit or loss. For all other partial disposals (that is, reductions in the group's ownership interest in associates or jointly controlled entities that do not result in the group losing significant influence or joint control) the proportionate share of the accumulated exchange difference is reclassified to profit or loss.

12 Share-based payments – modification and cancellation

If the terms of an equity-settled award are modified, at a minimum an expense is recognised as if the terms had not been modified. An additional expense is recognised for any modification that increases the total fair value of the share-based payment arrangement, or is otherwise beneficial to the employee, as measured at the date of modification.

If an equity-settled award is cancelled, it is treated as if it had vested on the date of cancellation, and any expense not yet recognised for the award is recognised immediately. However, if a new award is substituted for the cancelled award, and designated as a replacement award on the date that it is granted, the cancelled and new award are treated as if they were a modification of the original award, as described in the previous paragraph.

If an equity award is cancelled by forfeiture, when the vesting conditions (other than market conditions) have not been met, any expense not yet recognised for that award, as at the date of forfeiture, is treated as if it had never been recognised. At the same time, any expense previously recognised on such cancelled equity awards are reversed from the accounts effective as at the date of forfeiture.

The dilutive effect, if any, of outstanding options is reflected as additional share dilution in the computation of earnings per share.

(All amounts in C thousands unless otherwise stated)

Appendix III – New standards and amendments

This appendix details (a) new standards and amendments effective for the first time for periods on or after 1 January 2011; (b) improvements to IFRSs; and (c) forthcoming requirements that is, new standards and amendments issued and effective after 1 January 2011.

New standards and amendments

Below is a list of standards/interpretations that have been issued and are effective for periods starting on or after 1 January 2011.

Topic	Key requirements	Effective date
Amendment to IAS 32, 'Financial instruments: Presentation – Classification of rights issues'	Amended to allow rights, options or warrants to acquire a fixed number of the entity's own equity instruments for a fixed amount of any currency to be classified as equity instruments provided the entity offers the rights, options or warrants pro rata to all of its existing owners of the same class of its own non-derivative equity instruments.	1 February 2010. EU-endorsed 23 December 2009.
IFRIC 19, 'Extinguishing financial liabilities with equity instruments'	Clarifies the requirements of IFRSs when an entity renegotiates the terms of a financial liability with its creditor and the creditor agrees to accept the entity's shares or other equity instruments to settle the financial liability fully or partially.	1 July 2010. EU-endorsed 23 January 2010.
Amendment to IFRS 1, 'First-time adoption of IFRS – Limited exemption from comparative IFRS 7 disclosures for first-time adopters'	Provides the same relief to first-time adopters as was given to current users of IFRSs upon adoption of the amendments to IFRS 7. Also clarifies the transition provisions of the amendments to IFRS 7.	1 July 2010. EU-endorsed 30 June 2010.
IAS 24, 'Related party disclosures' (revised 2009)	Amends the definition of a related party and modifies certain related-party disclosure requirements for government-related entities.	1 January 2011. EU-endorsed 19 July 2010.
Amendment to IFRIC 14, 'IAS 19 – The limit on a defined benefit assets, minimum funding requirements and their interaction'	Removes unintended consequences arising from the treatment of pre-payments where there is a minimum funding requirement. Results in pre-payments of contributions in certain circumstances being recognised as an asset rather than an expense.	1 January 2011. EU-endorsed 19 July 2010.

Improvements to IFRSs 2010

The amendments are applicable for annual periods beginning after 1 January 2011 unless otherwise stated. They were all EU-endorsed on 18 February 2011.

Topic	Key requirements	Effective date
IFRS 1, 'First-time adoption of IFRS'	*(a) Accounting policy changes in the year of adoption* Clarifies that, if a first-time adopter changes its accounting policies or its use of the exemptions in IFRS 1 after it has published an interim financial report in accordance with IAS 34, 'Interim financial reporting', it should explain those changes and update the reconciliations between previous GAAP and IFRS.	Applied prospectively.
	(b) Revaluation basis as deemed cost Allows first-time adopters to use an event-driven fair value as deemed cost, even if the event occurs after the date of transition but before the first IFRS financial statements are issued. When such remeasurement occurs after the date of transition to IFRSs but during the period covered by its first IFRS financial statements, any subsequent adjustment to that event-driven fair value is recognised in equity.	Entities that adopted IFRSs in previous periods are permitted to apply the amendment retrospectively in the first annual period after the amendment is effective, provided the measurement date is within the period covered by the first IFRS financial statements.
	(c) Use of deemed cost for operations subject to rate regulation Entities subject to rate regulation are allowed to use previous GAAP carrying amounts of property, plant and equipment or intangible assets as deemed cost on an item-by-item basis. Entities that use this exemption are required to test each item for impairment under IAS 36 at the date of transition.	Applied prospectively.

(All amounts in C thousands unless otherwise stated)

Topic	Key requirements	Effective date
IFRS 3, 'Business combinations'	*(a) Transition requirements for contingent consideration from a business combination that occurred before the effective date of the revised IFRS* Clarifies that the amendments to IFRS 7, 'Financial instruments: Disclosures', IAS 32, 'Financial instruments: Presentation', and IAS 39, 'Financial instruments: Recognition and measurement', that eliminate the exemption for contingent consideration, do not apply to contingent consideration that arose from business combinations whose acquisition dates precede the application of IFRS 3 (as revised in 2008).	Applicable to annual periods beginning on or after 1 July 2010. Applied retrospectively.
	(b) Measurement of non- controlling interests The choice of measuring non-controlling interests at fair value or at the proportionate share of the acquiree's net assets applies only to instruments that represent present ownership interests and entitle their holders to a proportionate share of the net assets in the event of liquidation. All other components of non-controlling interest are measured at fair value unless another measurement basis is required by IFRS.	Applicable to annual periods beginning on or after 1 July 2010. Applied prospectively from the date the entity applies IFRS 3.
	(c) Un-replaced and voluntarily replaced share- based payment awards The application guidance in IFRS 3 applies to all share-based payment transactions that are part of a business combination, including un-replaced and voluntarily replaced share-based payment awards	Applicable to annual periods beginning on or after 1 July 2010. Applied prospectively.
IFRS 7, 'Financial instruments'	Emphasises the interaction between quantitative and qualitative disclosures about the nature and extent of risks associated with financial instruments.	1 January 2011. Applied retrospectively.
IAS 1, 'Presentation of financial statements'	Clarifies that an entity will present an analysis of other comprehensive income for each component of equity, either in the statement of changes in equity or in the notes to the financial statements.	1 January 2011. Applied retrospectively.
IAS 27, 'Consolidated and separate financial statements'	Clarifies that the consequential amendments from IAS 27 made to IAS 21, 'The effect of changes in foreign exchange rates', IAS 28, 'Investments in associates', and IAS 31, 'Interests in joint ventures', apply prospectively for annual periods beginning on or after 1 July 2009, or earlier when IAS 27 is applied earlier.	Applicable to annual periods beginning on or after 1 July 2010. Applied retrospectively.
IAS 34, 'Interim financial reporting'	Provide guidance to illustrate how to apply disclosure principles in IAS 34 and add disclosure requirements around: • The circumstances likely to affect fair values of financial instruments and their classification; • Transfers of financial instruments between different levels of the fair value hierarchy; • Changes in classification of financial assets; and • Changes in contingent liabilities and assets	1 January 2011. Applied retrospectively.
IFRIC 13, 'Customer loyalty programmes'	The meaning of 'fair value' is clarified in the context of measuring award credits under customer loyalty programmes.	1 January 2011

(All amounts in C thousands unless otherwise stated)

Forthcoming requirements

Below is a list of standards/interpretations that have been issued and are effective for periods after 1 January 2011. None of these had been EU-endorsed at time of going to print (October 2011).

Topic	Key requirements	Effective date
Amendments to IFRS 7, 'Financial instruments: Disclosures' on derecognition	This amendment will promote transparency in the reporting of transfer transactions and improve users' understanding of the risk exposures relating to transfers of financial assets and the effect of those risks on an entity's financial position, particularly those involving securitisation of financial assets. Earlier application subject to EU endorsement is permitted.	1 July 2011
Amendment to IFRS 1, 'First time adoption', on fixed dates and hyperinflation	These amendments include two changes to IFRS 1, 'First-time adoption of IFRS'. The first replaces references to a fixed date of 1 January 2004 with 'the date of transition to IFRSs', thus eliminating the need for entities adopting IFRSs for the first time to restate derecognition transactions that occurred before the date of transition to IFRSs. The second amendment provides guidance on how an entity should resume presenting financial statements in accordance with IFRSs after a period when the entity was unable to comply with IFRSs because its functional currency was subject to severe hyperinflation.	1 July 2011
Amendment to IAS 12, 'Income taxes' on deferred tax	IAS 12, 'Income taxes', currently requires an entity to measure the deferred tax relating to an asset depending on whether the entity expects to recover the carrying amount of the asset through use or sale. It can be difficult and subjective to assess whether recovery will be through use or through sale when the asset is measured using the fair value model in IAS 40, 'Investment property'. This amendment therefore introduces an exception to the existing principle for the measurement of deferred tax assets or liabilities arising on investment property measured at fair value. As a result of the amendments, SIC 21, 'Income taxes - recovery of revalued non-depreciable assets', will no longer apply to investment properties carried at fair value. The amendments also incorporate into IAS 12 the remaining guidance previously contained in SIC 21, which is withdrawn.	1 January 2012
Amendment to IAS 1, 'Financial statement presentation' regarding other comprehensive income	The main change resulting from these amendments is a requirement for entities to group items presented in 'other comprehensive income' (OCI) on the basis of whether they are potentially reclassifiable to profit or loss subsequently (reclassification adjustments). The amendments do not address which items are presented in OCI.	1 July 2012
Amendment to IAS 19, 'Employee benefits'	These amendments eliminate the corridor approach and calculate finance costs on a net funding basis.	1 January 2013
IFRS 9, 'Financial instruments'	IFRS 9 is the first standard issued as part of a wider project to replace IAS 39. IFRS 9 retains but simplifies the mixed measurement model and establishes two primary measurement categories for) financial assets: amortised cost and fair value. The basis of classification depends on the entity's business model and the contractual cash flow characteristics of the financial asset. The guidance in IAS 39 on impairment of financial assets and hedge accounting continues to apply.	1 January 2013
IFRS 10, 'Consolidated financial statements'	The objective of IFRS 10 is to establish principles for the presentation and preparation of consolidated financial statements when an entity controls one or more other entity (an entity that controls one or more other entities) to present consolidated financial statements. Defines the principle of control, and establishes controls as the basis for consolidation. Set out how to apply the principle of control to identify whether an investor controls an investee and therefore must consolidate the investee. Sets out the accounting requirements for the preparation of consolidated financial statements.	1 January 2013
IFRS 11, 'Joint arrangements'	IFRS 11 is a more realistic reflection of joint arrangements by focusing on the rights and obligations of the arrangement rather than its legal form. There are two types of joint arrangement: joint operations and joint ventures. Joint operations arise where a joint operator has rights to the assets and obligations relating to the arrangement and hence accounts for its interest in assets, liabilities, revenue and expenses. Joint ventures arise where the joint operator has rights to the net assets of the arrangement and hence equity accounts for its interest. Proportional consolidation of joint ventures is no longer allowed.	1 January 2013
IFRS 12, 'Disclosures of interests in other entities'	IFRS 12 includes the disclosure requirements for all forms of interests in other entities, including joint arrangements, associates, special purpose vehicles and other off balance sheet vehicles.	1 January 2013
IFRS 13, 'Fair value measurement'	IFRS 13 aims to improve consistency and reduce complexity by providing a precise definition of fair value and a single source of fair value measurement and disclosure requirements for use across IFRSs. The requirements, which are largely aligned between IFRSs and US GAAP, do not extend the use of fair value accounting but provide guidance on how it should be applied where its use is already required or permitted by other standards within IFRSs or US GAAP.	1 January 2013
IAS 27 (revised 2011), 'Separate financial statements'	IAS 27 (revised 2011) includes the provisions on separate financial statements that are left after the control provisions of IAS 27 have been included in the new IFRS 10.	1 January 2013
IAS 28 (revised 2011), 'Associates and joint ventures'	IAS 28 (revised 2011) includes the requirements for joint ventures, as well as associates, to be equity accounted following the issue of IFRS 11.	1 January 2013

GAAP UK Group Limited – Year ended 31 December 2011

Introduction – example annual report under UK GAAP

The example annual report that follows includes the consolidated financial statements of the GAAP UK Group Limited. The annual report has been prepared to show the disclosures and format that might be expected for a group of its size that prepares its financial statements in accordance with Schedule 1 and Schedule 6 to SI 2008/410 and subsequent Statutory Instruments.

GAAP UK Group Limited is a fictional, large private company that is incorporated in the UK.As part of a large private group, it has voluntarily adopted certain standards, such as FRS 22, 'Earnings per share'. Disclosures that are voluntary have been indicated by 'DV' in the margin. GAAP UK Group Limited has a number of UK and overseas investments, including subsidiaries and joint ventures. We acknowledge that GAAP UK Group Limited is not listed and perhaps would not adopt all the following standards; however, we have followed this course of action to show the disclosures necessary for those companies that do. GAAP UK Group Limited has adopted FRS 26 and the disclosure requirements of FRS 25, FRS 23 and FRS 29.

PwC guidance is presented in *italics*.

Further guidance and information

If you require further guidance on the UK law and accounting requirements affecting companies' financial statements, PricewaterhouseCoopers' *Manual of Accounting – UK GAAP 2011* may be of assistance.

This annual report does not show all conceivable disclosures. It should not therefore be used as a checklist. Neither is it a substitute for exercising judgement as to the fairness of presentation. These financial statements include many of the disclosure requirements contained in Financial Reporting Standards, Statements of Standard Accounting Practice, Urgent Issues Task Force Abstracts and Company Law applicable on or after 1 January 2011.

GAAP UK Group Limited is a private company; it is not required to include a directors' remuneration report or corporate governance report. It has not voluntarily included an operating and financial review.

Companies that present a report that purports to be an operating and financial review should comply with the ASB's statement of best practice, 'Reporting statement: Operating and financial review (OFR)'.

References to source material are given in the left-hand margin.

The suggested disclosure throughout is intended for guidance only and is not necessarily applicable to all groups or all companies. The names of the undertakings included in the annual report are used for illustration only; any resemblance to any existing undertaking is not intended.

Abbreviations

SI 2008/410 1 Sch 6	=	Statutory Instrument [year/number], Schedule [number], paragraph number.
s417	=	Companies Act 2006, section number.
APB 2002/2	=	Auditing Practices Board Bulletin, number
DV	=	Disclosure voluntary
FRS 3 p14	=	Financial Reporting Standard [number], paragraph number.
ISA (UK&I) 720 p11	=	International Standard on Auditing (UK and Ireland) [number], paragraph number.
SI 1996/189	=	Statutory Instrument [year/number].
SSAP 9 p14	=	Statement of Standard Accounting Practice [number], paragraph number.
UITF 38 p8	=	Urgent Issues Task Force Abstract [number], paragraph number.
Tech 24/03	=	Technical release [number], issued by the Institute of Chartered Accountants in England and Wales.

GAAP UK Group Limited

Example annual report for the year ended 31 December 2011

Contents

1

Directors' report

CA06 s415(2) **Directors' report for the year ended 31 December 2011**

CA06 s415(1) The directors present their report and the audited financial statements for the year ended 31 December 2011.

SI 2008/410 *Notes:*
7 Sch 1 *The directors' report must also comply with the relevant requirements of Schedule 7 to SI 2008/410.*

Various matters listed below may be included in the chairman's statement, or the notes to the financial statements provided there is a cross-reference in the directors' report to where the matter may be found.

Principal activities

CA06 *The narrative must cover the principal activities of the company and its subsidiary undertakings (note: it is also*
s416(1)(b),SI *appropriate to include any significant changes to activities) in the year. In addition, there must be an indication of the*
2008/410 7 *existence of branches (as defined in paragraph 7(1)(d) of Schedule 7 to SI 2008/410) outside the UK. (The disclosure of*
Sch 7(1)(d) *existence of branches outside the UK is only needed for those in the UK).*

Review of business

CA06 *The report must contain a fair review of the development and performance of the group's business during the year and*
s417(3)(a), (4) *of its position at the year end.*

DV *Where non-statutory numbers are disclosed, it should be clear that these differ from the statutory numbers. The equivalent statutory number must be disclosed, and there must be a reconciliation between the statutory and non-statutory numbers.*

The review of the business must include:

CA06 s417(3) *(a) a fair review of the business of the company; and*
(b) a description of the principal risks and uncertainties facing the company.

CA06 s417(4) *The review is required to give a balanced and comprehensive analysis of:*

(a) the development and performance of the business of the company during the financial year; and
(b) the position of the company at the end of the year,

consistent with the size and complexity of the business.

CA06 s417(6) *The review must, to the extent necessary for an understanding of the development, performance or position of the business of the company, include:*

(a) analysis using financial key performance indicators; and
(b) where appropriate, analysis using other key performance indicators, including information relating to environmental matters and employee matters.

CA06 s417(7) *Note: For medium-sized companies, where these indicators relate to non-financial information, disclosure is not required.*

CA06 s417(8) *The review must, where appropriate, include references to, and additional explanations of, amounts included in the financial statements of the company.*

CA06 s417(1) *This disclosure is required within the directors' report of all companies, with the exception of small companies, which are exempt.*

Future developments

SI 2008/410 The directors' report must contain an indication of the likely future developments in the company's/group's business.
7 Sch 7(1)(b)

Note: This disclosure is likely to fit well with the business review; it may therefore be appropriate to combine them.

Dividends

CA06 s416(3) *Disclosure of the recommended dividend is required.*

Research and development

SI 2008/410 ▪ *Provide an indication of the group's research and development activities.*
7 Sch 7(1)(c)
(see also SSAP
13 p30, 31 for
notes to
financial
statements)

DV
- *Comment on the profit and loss account charge for year (which must be separately disclosed in the notes to financial statements).*

Donations

SI 2008/410 7 Sch 3

If the company, and/or any of its subsidiaries, made any donations to a registered political party or other political organisation in the EU (including the UK), any independent election candidate, or incurred EU political expenditure exceeding £2,000 in aggregate in the financial year, disclose:

- *EU donations – name of political party and total amount given per party, by the company and each subsidiary that has donated individually.*
- *EU political expenditure – total amount incurred in the financial year, by the company and each subsidiary that has incurred such expenditure individually.*

SI 2008/410 7 Sch 4

Total contributions to non-EU political parties must be disclosed, for the group as a whole in aggregate. (There is no threshold for this disclosure.)

SI 2008/410 7 Sch 5

If the company, and/or any of its subsidiaries, has given money in excess of £2,000 in aggregate for charitable purposes during the year, disclose the total amount given for each such purpose.

Land and buildings

SI 2008/410 7 Sch 2

If significant, indicate the difference between market value and book value of land and buildings for the company or any of its subsidiary undertakings.

Financial instruments

SI 2008/410 7 Sch 6

Where material for the assessment of the assets, liabilities, financial position and profit or loss of the group, the directors' report must contain an indication of:

- *the financial risk management objectives and policies of the entity, including the policy for hedging each major type of forecasted transaction for which hedge accounting is used; and*
- *the exposure of the entity to price risk, credit risk, liquidity risk and cash flow risk.*

Post balance sheet events

SI 2008/410 7 Sch 7(1)(a), (see also FRS 21, p19-22 regarding disclosure in the notes)

The directors' report must include particulars of any important events affecting the company or group since the year end.

Directors

CA06 s416(1)(a)

Provide the names of all persons who were directors during any part of the period.

DV

Include changes in directors since the end of the financial year and the dates of any appointments and/or resignations of directors occurring during the financial year.

DV

Include information regarding the retirement of directors at the AGM and whether they offer themselves for election.

Directors' qualifying third party and pension indemnity provisions

CA06 s236(1–5)

Disclose whether:

(a) *at the time the report is approved, any qualifying third-party indemnity provision or qualifying pension scheme indemnity provision (whether made by the company or otherwise) is in place for the benefit of one or more of the directors or one or more directors of an associated company; or*

(b) *at any time during the year, any such provision was in force for the benefit of one or more persons who were then directors or directors of an associated company.*

Employees

SI 2008/410 7 Sch 11(1)

The requirements below only apply if the company employed on average 250 or more employees in the UK each week during the financial year.

SI 2008/410 7 Sch 11(3)

A statement is required describing the action that has been taken during the period to introduce, maintain or develop arrangements aimed at involving UK employees in the company's affairs. This statement must discuss the group's policy on:

- *systematic provision of relevant information to employees;*
- *regular consultation with employees or their representatives so that the employees' views may be taken into account in making decisions that are likely to affect their interests;*

- encouragement of employees' participation in the group's performance by employee share schemes or other means; and
- achieving awareness on the part of all employees of the financial and economic factors affecting the group's performance.

SI 2008/410
7 Sch 10(3)

A statement must be included as to the UK policy for giving full and fair consideration to applications for employment that disabled people make to the company, the policy for employment, training, career development and promotion of disabled people and for the continuing employment and training of employees who have become disabled while employed by the company.

Policy and practice on payment of creditors

SI 2008/410
7 Sch 12(2), (3)

Large companies that are public companies or are members of a group of which, at any time during the year, the parent company was a public company must disclose:

SI 2008/410
7 Sch 12(2)(a)

- in respect of some or all of its suppliers, it is the company's policy to follow any code or standard on payment practice and, if so, give the name of the code or standard and the place where information about the code or standard can be obtained; and/or

7 Sch 12(2)(b)

- in respect of some or all of its suppliers, it is the company's policy to settle the terms of payment with those suppliers when agreeing the terms of each transaction and to ensure that these suppliers are made aware of the terms of the payment and to abide by the terms of payment.

SI 2008/410
7 Sch 12(2)(c)

Where the statement does not cover all suppliers, the policy for the other suppliers needs to be disclosed.

SI 2008/410
7 Sch 12(3)

The number of creditor days in relation to trade creditors outstanding at the period end needs to be disclosed.

DV

Note: An additional statement regarding the group's policy and practice and number of days for the company and its UK subsidiaries, while not mandatory, is considered best practice.

Purchase of own shares and sales of treasury shares

SI 2008/410
7 Sch 8, 9

Where a company purchases or places a charge on its own shares, specific disclosures must be made. These disclosures include the number and nominal value of the shares, percentage of called-up share capital, aggregate consideration paid and the reasons for the purchase. See Schedule 7, paragraph 9 to SI 2008/410 for further details.

Health and safety

DV

This includes areas such as:

- Policy on health and safety.
- Risks faced by employees and controls in place.
- Health and safety goals and progress towards their achievement.
- The total cost of occupational injuries and illnesses suffered by staff in the reporting period.

Corporate social responsibility

DV

This includes areas such as:

- Whether the board takes regular account of the significance of social, environmental and ethical (SEE) matters to the group.
- Whether the board has identified and assessed the significant risks to the group's short- and long-term value arising from SEE matters, as well as the opportunities to enhance value that may arise from an appropriate response.
- Whether the board has received adequate training and information to make this assessment.
- Information on the SEE-related risks and opportunities identified and how they may impact the business.
- Whether the group has effective systems for managing significant risks which, where relevant, incorporate performance management systems and appropriate remuneration incentives.
- A description of the policies and procedures in place for managing short- and long-term risks arising from SEE matters (or, if there are none, that this is the case and the reason for this) and information about the group's level of compliance with these policies and procedures.
- A description of how the disclosures in respect of SEE matters are verified.

Statement of directors' responsibilities

The directors are responsible for preparing the annual report and the financial statements in accordance with applicable law and regulations.

Company law requires the directors to prepare financial statements for each financial year. Under that law, the directors have prepared the group and parent company financial statements in accordance with United Kingdom Generally Accepted Accounting Practice (United Kingdom Accounting Standards and applicable law).Under company law, the directors must not approve the financial statements unless they are satisfied that they give a true and fair view of the state of affairs of the group and the company, and of the profit or loss of the group for that period. In preparing these financial statements, the directors are required to:

- *select suitable accounting policies and then apply them consistently;*
- *make judgements and accounting estimates that are reasonable and prudent;*
- *state whether applicable UK Accounting Standards have been followed, subject to any material departures disclosed and explained in the financial statements; and*
- *prepare the financial statements on the going concern basis unless it is inappropriate to presume that the company will continue in business*

The directors are responsible for keeping adequate accounting records that are sufficient to show and explain the company's transactions, disclose with reasonable accuracy at any time the financial position of the company and the group, and enable them to ensure that the financial statements comply with the Companies Act 2006. They are also responsible for safeguarding the assets of the company and the group and hence for taking reasonable steps for the prevention and detection of fraud and other irregularities.

Statement of disclosure of information to auditors

CA06 s418(2) *The report must contain a statement to the effect that, in the case of each of the persons who are directors at the time when the report is approved:*

(a) as far as the director is aware, there is no relevant audit information of which the company's auditor is unaware; and
(b) he/she has taken all the steps that he ought to have taken as a director in order to make himself/herself aware of any relevant audit information and to establish that the company's auditor is aware of that information.

Independent auditors

DV (see also CA 06 s489(1), (2)) The auditors, PricewaterhouseCoopers LLP, have indicated their willingness to continue in office, and a resolution that they be reappointed will be proposed at the annual general meeting.

CA06 s419(1) By order of the board.

CA06 s419(1) AB Smith
Company secretary
12 March 2012

Notes:

CA06 s419(1) *(a) The directors' report must be signed by the company secretary or a director after it has been approved by the board of directors.*
(b) The copy of the directors' report that is delivered to the Registrar of Companies must be manually signed by the company secretary or a director.

Note: Where the financial statements are published on a website, the statement of directors' responsibilities may also include a statement that:

- *the directors are responsible for the maintenance and integrity of the web site; and*
- *legislation in the UK concerning the preparation and dissemination of financial statements may differ from legislation in other jurisdictions.*

Independent auditors' report to the members of GAAP UK Group Limited

Warning: Although this audit report was current at the date of going to press, it may not be the most up-to-date version. Therefore, it should not be used without checking that it is the appropriate version.

We have audited the group and parent company financial statements (the 'financial statements') of GAAP UK Group Limited for the year ended 31 December 2011. These comprise the consolidated profit and loss account, the statement of group total recognised gains and losses, the note of group historical cost profits and losses, the reconciliation of movements in group shareholders' funds, the group and company balance sheets, the consolidated cash flow statement, the accounting policies and related notes. The financial reporting framework that has been applied in their preparation is applicable law and United Kingdom Accounting Standards (United Kingdom Generally Accepted Accounting Practice).

Respective responsibilities of directors and auditors

As explained more fully in the Statement of directors' responsibilities set out on page 5, the directors are responsible for the preparation of the financial statements and for being satisfied that they give a true and fair view. Our responsibility is to audit and express an opinion on the financial statements in accordance with applicable law and International Standards on Auditing (UK and Ireland). Those standards require us to comply with the Auditing Practices Board's Ethical Standards for Auditors.

This report, including the opinions, has been prepared for and only for the company's members as a body in accordance with Chapter 3 of Part 16 of the Companies Act 2006 and for no other purpose. We do not, in giving these opinions, accept or assume responsibility for any other purpose or to any other person to whom this report is shown or into whose hands it may come save where expressly agreed by our prior consent in writing.

Scope of the audit of the financial statements

An audit involves obtaining evidence about the amounts and disclosures in the financial statements sufficient to give reasonable assurance that the financial statements are free from material misstatement, whether caused by fraud or error. This includes an assessment of: whether the accounting policies are appropriate to the group's and parent company's circumstances and have been consistently applied and adequately disclosed; the reasonableness of significant accounting estimates made by the directors; and the overall presentation of the financial statements. In addition, we read all the financial and non-financial information in the annual report to identify material inconsistencies with the audited financial statements. If we become aware of any apparent material misstatements or inconsistencies, we consider the implications for our report.

Opinion on financial statements

In our opinion the financial statements:

- give a true and fair view of the state of the group's and the parent company's affairs as at 31 December 2011 and of the group's profit and cash flows for the year then ended;
- have been properly prepared in accordance with United Kingdom Generally Accepted Accounting Practice; and
- have been prepared in accordance with the requirements of the Companies Act 2006.

Opinion on other matter prescribed by the Companies Act 2006

In our opinion, the information given in the Directors' report for the financial year for which the financial statements are prepared is consistent with the financial statements.

Matters on which we are required to report by exception

We have nothing to report in respect of the following matters where the Companies Act 2006 requires us to report to you if, in our opinion:

- adequate accounting records have not been kept by the parent company, or returns adequate for our audit have not been received from branches not visited by us; or
- the parent company financial statements are not in agreement with the accounting records and returns; or
- certain disclosures of directors' remuneration specified by law are not made; or
- we have not received all the information and explanations we require for our audit.

John Smith (Senior Statutory Auditor)
For and on behalf of PricewaterhouseCoopers LLP
Chartered Accountants and Statutory Auditors
London
12 March 2012

Consolidated profit and loss account

		Note	2011 £m	2011 £m	2010 £m	2010 £m
FRS 28 p6, CA06 s403(2)						
CA06 s404(1)) SI 2008/410 1 Sch Formats						
FRS 9 p21	Turnover (including share of joint ventures)					
FRS 3 p14,30	Continuing operations:					
FRS 3 p16	Existing		532.8	–	368.8	–
FRS 6 p23,28	Acquisitions					
	– Newsub plc		689.8	–	–	–
	– other		51.6	–	–	–
			–	1,274.2	–	368.8
FRS 3 p17	Discontinued operations		–	25.6	–	117.0
		2	–	1,299.8	–	485.8
FRS 9 p21, 27	Less: share of joint ventures' turnover Continuing operations:					
	– existing		(9.1)	–	(9.9)	–
	– acquisitions		(29.8)	(38.9)	–	(9.9)
SI 2008/410 1 Sch Formats	**Group turnover**	3	–	1,260.9	–	475.9
SI 2008/410 1 Sch Formats	Cost of sales	3	–	(1,083.9)	–	(342.4)
SI 2008/410 1 Sch Formats	Gross profit	3	–	177.0	–	133.5
SI 2008/410 1Sch 3	Net operating expenses	3	–	(70.8)	–	(30.1)
	Operating profit					
FRS 3 p14,30	Continuing operations		82.2	–	76.3	–
	Acquisitions (after £40.2m (2010 £nil) goodwill amortisation)					
FRS 6 p28	– Newsub plc		21.6	–	–	–
	– other		0.2	–	–	–
			–	104.0	–	76.3
FRS 3 p17	Discontinued operations		–	2.2	–	27.1
FRS 3 p14	**Group operating profit**	3	–	106.2	–	103.4
SI 2008/410 6 Sch 20(3)	Share of operating profit in joint ventures (after £0.9m (2010: £nil) goodwill amortisation)		–	2.8	–	1.2
	Total operating profit: group and share of joint ventures					
	Profit on sale of subsidiary	2	–	109.0	–	104.6
FRS 3 p20	– Discontinued operations	5	–	6.3	–	–
SI 2008/410 1 Sch Formats	Net interest (payable)/receivable					
	– Group	3a	(11.3)	–	3.6	–
FRS 9 p21, 27	– Joint ventures	3a	0.7	(10.6)	–	3.6
FRS 17 App (ii) p6 FRS 12 p48	Other finance income	3b	–	4.0	–	4.0
SI 2008/410 1 Sch 3	**Profit on ordinary activities before taxation**	4	–	108.7	–	112.2
SI 2008/410 1 Sch Formats, FRS 16 p17	Tax on profit on ordinary activities	6	–	(82.8)	–	(48.8)
SI 2008/410 1 Sch Formats	**Profit on ordinary activities after taxation**		–	25.9	–	63.4
SI 2008/410 6Sch 17 FRS 2 p36	Equity minority interests		–	(0.5)	–	(0.2)
SI 2008/410 1 Sch Formats	**Profit for the financial year**	25	–	25.4	–	63.2
FRS 22 p66, DV	Earnings per share expressed in pence per share	7				
	– Basic			2.23p		7.17p
	– Diluted			2.22p		7.03p
	Earnings per share from continuing operations expressed in pence per share	7				
	– Basic			1.55p		6.60p
	– Diluted			1.54p		6.48p

FRS 3 p27	**Statement of group total recognised gains and losses**[1]			

FRS 28 p6	**For the year ended 31 December**		**2011**	2010
		Note	**£m**	£m
FRS 3 p36(a)	Profit for the financial year:			
FRS 9 p21,28	– Group		**23.8**	62.8
	– Joint ventures		**1.6**	0.4
			25.4	63.2
FRS 3 p36(b), FRS 15 p63	Unrealised surplus on revaluation of properties	9	**5.4**	1.5
FRS 23 p52(b), FRS 3 p36(b)	Exchange adjustments offset in reserves (translation of overseas sales and foreign investments)	26	**(42.5)**	34.9
UITF 19 p9 FRS 16 p17	Tax on exchange adjustments offset in reserves	6, 25	**3.5**	2.8
FRS 17 p57	Actuarial (loss)/gain recognised in the pension scheme	34	**(22.2)**	2.7
FRS 16 p6	Current tax deductions allocated to actuarial losses	6	**3.6**	–
FRS 19 p35	Movement on deferred tax relating to pension asset	25	**2.8**	(0.1)
FRS 26 p55(b), FRS 29p20a(ii)	Movement on AFS investment reserve and other reserve	27	**(18.8)**	(14.5)
FRS 26p102(a)	Movement on hedging reserve	27	**7.4**	(16.6)
	Total recognised (losses)/gains for the year		**(54.9)**	73.9
FRS 9 p21,28	– Group		**(56.5)**	73.5
FRS 3 p27	– Joint ventures		**1.6**	0.4
	Total recognised (losses)/gains since last annual report		**(54.9)**	73.9

Notes:

FRS 3 p57	(a)	If the group has no recognised gains or losses other than its profit or loss for the period, a statement to this effect must be given immediately below the profit and loss account.

FRS 9 p28	(b)	Where an associate or joint venture has gains and losses reported in its STRGL, or has such gains and losses when its financial statements are restated on to the investor's GAAP, the investor's share of such gains and losses must be included in the investor's consolidated STRGL. The amounts must be shown separately under each heading, if material, either in the statement or in a note referred to in the statement.

FRS 3 p26	**Note of group historical cost profits and losses**

For the year ended 31 December	**2011**	2010
	£m	£m
Reported profit on ordinary activities before taxation	**108.7**	112.2
Realisation of property revaluation gains of previous years	**0.1**	0.1
Difference between historical cost depreciation charge and the actual depreciation charge of the year calculated on the revalued amount	**0.1**	–
Historical cost profit on ordinary activities before taxation	**108.9**	112.3
Historical cost profit for the year retained after taxation and minority interests	**25.6**	63.3

Note: The above note is only required if the difference is material. The difference is unlikely to be material in this example, but is shown for illustrative purposes.

[1] Companies with 31 December 2011 year ends will need to consider the impact of the reduction in tax rates in the Finance Act 2011 and whether this affects disclosure in the STRGL.

Reconciliation of movements in group shareholders' funds

FRS 3 p28	For the year ended 31 December	Note	2011 £m	2010 £m
	Profit for the financial year		25.4	63.2
	Dividends		(23.7)	(15.7)
	Other recognised gains and losses relating to the year (shown in STRGL)		(42.7)	10.7
	Proceeds of ordinary shares issued for cash	21	2.6	4.7
	Purchase of own shares	25	–	(23.1)
	Nominal value of ordinary shares issued for the acquisition of Newsub plc	21	4.8	–
	Premium (net of issue expenses) on ordinary shares issued for the acquisition of Newsub plc	27	913.6	–
	Goodwill recycled on disposal of subsidiary	32	3.9	–
	Adjustment in respect of employee share schemes	25	3.2	1.4
	Net change in shareholders' funds		**887.1**	41.2
	Opening shareholders' funds		167.0	125.8
	Closing shareholders' funds		**1,054.1**	167.0

Balance sheets

At 31 December 2011

			Group		Company	
		Note	**2011** **£m**	2010 £m	**2011** **£m**	2010 £m
Fixed assets						
Intangible assets		8	**1,078.7**	–	**–**	–
Tangible assets		9	**406.8**	91.3	**11.5**	9.7
Financial assets						
– Derivative financial instruments		19	**12.1**	4.9	**–**	–
– Available for sale investments		14	**523.1**	410.0	**–**	–
Investment in subsidiary undertakings		10	**–**	–	**419.2**	98.5
Interests in joint ventures		10				
– share of gross assets			**105.6**	7.2	**–**	–
– share of gross liabilities			**(96.7)**	(5.4)	**–**	–
– goodwill arising on acquisition			**7.6**	–	**–**	–
			16.5	1.8	**–**	–
			2,037.2	508.0	**430.7**	108.2
Current assets						
Stock		11	**33.8**	17.0	**–**	–
Financial assets						
– Derivative financial instruments		19	**8.6**	2.2	**–**	–
– Current asset investments		13	**25.3**	55.3	**–**	48.7
– Debtors		15	**290.6**	109.6	**68.3**	101.0
– Cash at bank and in hand			**74.8**	40.5	**7.0**	0.5
			433.1	224.6	**75.3**	150.2
Creditors – Amounts falling due within one year		16	**(401.2)**	(136.7)	**(99.8)**	(68.3)
Net current assets/(liabilities)			**31.9**	87.9	**(24.5)**	81.9
Total assets less current liabilities			**2,069.1**	595.9	**406.2**	190.1
Creditors – Amounts falling due after more than one year		17	**(865.5)**	(427.9)	**(240.5)**	(17.0)
Provisions for liabilities		20	**(163.0)**	(22.2)	**(0.1)**	(0.5)
Net assets excluding pension asset			**1,040.6**	145.8	**165.6**	172.6
Pension asset		34	**15.0**	22.0	**–**	–
Net assets including pension asset			**1,055.6**	167.8	**165.6**	172.6

Side references (left margin):
CA06 s403(2)
CA06 s404(1)
SI 2008/410 1Sch Formats
SI 2008/410 6 Sch 1(1), FRS 28 p6
SI 2008/410 1Sch Formats
SI 2008/410 1Sch Formats
SI 2008/410 1Sch Formats
FRS 25 p53, SI 2008/410 1Sch 3(3)
FRS 29p8(a)
SI 2008/410 1Sch Formats, FRS 29p8(d)
FRS 9 p21
FRS 9 p29
SI 2008/410 1Sch Formats
FRS 25p53, SI 2008/410 1Sch 3(3)
FRS 29p8(a)
SI 2008/410 1 Sch Formats, FRS 29p8(a)
1 Sch Formats, FRS 29p8(c)
SI 2008/410 1 Sch Formats, FRS 29p8
SI 2008/410 1 Sch Formats
SI 2008/410 1 Sch Formats
SI 2008/410 1 Sch Formats
SI 2008/410 1 Sch Formats
SI 2008/410 1 Sch Formats
FRS 17 p47

			Group		Company	
	Note	**2011** **£m**	2010 £m	**2011** **£m**	2010 £m
Capital and reserves						
Called up share capital	21	**13.8**	8.9	**13.8**	8.9
Share premium account	23	**10.8**	8.3	**10.8**	8.3
Revaluation reserve	24	**7.5**	2.5	**2.3**	0.8
Other reserves	27	**964.2**	5.8	**–**	–
Profit and loss reserve	25	**57.8**	141.5	**138.7**	154.6
Total shareholders' funds		**1,054.1**	167.0	**165.6**	172.6
Minority interests		**1.5**	0.8	**–**	–
Capital employed		**1,055.6**	167.8	**165.6**	172.6

SI 2008/410
1 Sch Formats
SI 2008/410
1 Sch Formats
SI 2008/410
1 Sch Formats
SI 2008/410
1 Sch Formats
SI 2008/410
1 Sch Formats
SI 2008/410
1 Sch Formats

FRS 2 p35, SI
2008/410 6Sch
17 (2)

FRS 21 p17   The financial statements on pages x to xwere approved by the board of directors on 26 February 2012 and were
CA06 s414   signed on its behalf by:

CD Jones
Director

Gaap UK Group Limited Registered number. xxyyzz

			Note	2011 £m	2011 £m	2010 £m	2010 £m
FRS 1 p7	**Net cash inflow from operating activities**		28	–	189.4	–	116.6
FRS 1 p7	Dividends received from joint ventures			–	0.1	–	0.2
FRS 1 p7	**Returns on investments and servicing of finance**						
FRS 1 p14(a)	Interest received			4.8	–	4.1	–
FRS 1 p15(a)	Interest paid			(25.7)	–	(1.1)	–
FRS 1 p15(b)	Issue costs of new bank loan			(5.3)	–	–	–
FRS 1 p15(c)	Interest element of finance lease payments			(1.0)	–	–	–
FRS 1 p15(e)	Dividends paid to minority interests			(0.1)	–	(0.1)	–
FRS 1 p15(d)	Preference share dividends paid to shareholders			(0.1)	–	(0.1)	–
	Net cash (outflow)/inflow from returns on investments and servicing of finance			–	(27.4)	–	2.8
FRS 1 p7	**Taxation**			–	(24.7)	–	(37.2)
FRS 1 p7	**Capital expenditure and financial investment**						
FRS 1 p21(a)	Purchase of tangible fixed assets			(106.1)	–	(34.5)	–
FRS 1 p20(a)	Sale of tangible fixed assets			4.2	–	6.7	–
	Net cash outflow for capital expenditure and financial investment			–	(101.9)	–	(27.8)
FRS 1 p7	**Acquisitions**						
FRS 6 p33, FRS 1 p24(a)	Purchase of subsidiary undertakings		31	(307.2)	–	(23.6)	–
FRS 1 p24(a)	Net overdrafts acquired with subsidiary undertakings		32	(15.1)	–	–	–
	Net cash outflow for acquisitions			–	(322.3)	–	(23.6)
FRS 1 p7	**Equity dividends paid to shareholders**			–	(23.7)	–	(15.7)
	Net cash (outflow)/inflow before use of liquid resources and financing			–	(310.5)	–	15.3
FRS 1 p7,52	**Management of liquid resources**		29	91.7	–	(21.9)	–
FRS 1 p27,28	Reduction/(increase) in short-term deposits with banks						
FRS 1 p28	Purchase of current asset investments		14	(100.0)	–	(400.0)	–
	Net cash outflow from management of liquid resources			–	(8.3)	–	(421.9)
FRS 1 p7	**Financing**						
FRS 1 p30(a)	Issue of ordinary share capital		23	2.6	–	4.7	–
FRS 1 p31(c)	Purchase of own shares			–	–	(23.1)	–
FRS 1 p31(d)	Expenses of share issue to acquire Newsub plc		29	(1.4)	–	–	–
FRS 1 p31(b)	Capital element of finance lease payments		31	(10.8)	–	–	–
FRS 1 p31(b)	Increase in borrowings		31	276.5	–	421.1	–
	Net cash inflow from financing			–	266.9	–	402.7
	Decrease in net cash			–	(51.9)	–	(3.9)
FRS 1 p33	**Reconciliation to net (debt)/cash**						
	Net cash at 1 January		29	–	33.2	–	39.0
	Decrease in net cash			–	(51.9)	–	(3.9)
	Borrowings net of short-term deposits acquired with subsidiaries			–	(57.1)	–	–
	Movement in liquid resources			–	8.3	–	421.9
	Movement in borrowings			–	(260.4)	–	(421.1)
FRS 1 p33(c)	Other non-cash changes			–	(2.1)	–	(3.0)
FRS 1 p33(d)	Exchange adjustments			–	44.5	–	0.3
	Net (debt)/cash at 31 December		29	–	(285.5)	–	33.2

Notes to the financial statements

1 Accounting policies

SI 2008/410 (1), FRS 18,58
The group financial statements have been prepared under the provision of the Large and Medium-sized Companies and Groups (Accounts and Reports) Regulations 2008 (SI 2008/410) and applicable accounting standards
The principal accounting policies applied in the preparation of these financial statements are set out below. These policies have been consistently applied to all the years presented unless otherwise stated. The financial statements are prepared under the historical cost convention modified to include the revaluation of certain financial assets and liabilities.

Note: Company disclosures should be given where appropriate. These have not been included in these financial statements.

CA06 s464
Note:
'Accounting standards' refers to those issued by bodies prescribed by regulations. The International Accounting Standards Board and the Accounting Standards Board are the only bodies so prescribed. Financial statements drawn up under UK GAAP should therefore only be prepared in accordance with the UK SSAPs and FRSs.

SI 2008/410 1 Sch (44), FRS 18 p55(a),56	*The accounting policies used for dealing with items that are judged material or critical in the context of the company's financial statements should be disclosed.*
	Where an accounting policy is prescribed by and fully described in an accounting standard, UITF Abstract or company's legislation, a succinct description of the policy should be given. Where an accounting policy is not prescribed by an accounting standard, a UITF Abstract or companies legislation, or an option permitted therein is used, a fuller description should be provided.
FRS 18 p55(b), 57	*A description should be given of those estimation techniques adopted that are significant — that is, where the range of reasonable amounts is so large that the use of a different amount from within the range could materially affect the view shown by the financial statements.*
FRS 18 p58	*Where a company falls within the scope of a SORP, the financial statements should state the name of the SORP and whether or not the company has complied with it. Where there is a departure from the SORP, further disclosure is required.*

SI 2008/410 6 Sch   **Consolidation**

FRS 6 p21	■ Basis of consolidation.
FRS 2 p23	■ Inclusion of all subsidiaries.
FRS 9 p20,26	■ Equity accounting for associates and gross equity accounting for joint ventures.
FRS 2 p40	■ Uniform accounting policies for group.
FRS 2 p39	■ Elimination of profits or losses on intra-group transactions.
FRS 9 p31(b)	■ Elimination of investor's shares of profits or losses on transactions with amounts and joint ventures.

CA06 s474   **Turnover**

| FRS 5 AppG | ■ Basis of income recognition and measurement for each principal income stream. |
| UITF 26 | ■ Barter transactions. |

SI 2008/410 1Sch 70   **Foreign currencies**

FRS 23 p23	■ Basis of translating foreign currency assets and liabilities.
FRS 23 p44	■ Basis of translating results of foreign subsidiaries.
	■ Treatment of exchange differences arising on the retranslation of opening net investments in subsidiary companies and translation of results (if at an average rate).
	■ Translation of all other exchange differences.
FRS 23 p53	■ Functional currency if different from presentation currency and reason why.
FRS 23 p54	■ Any change in the functional currency and reason why.
FRS 24 p39(b)	■ Method adopted for dealing with results of foreign subsidiaries operating in hyperinflationary economies.

Capitalisation of finance costs and interest

| FRS 15 p31, IAS 18 p56 | ■ Whether interest is capitalised or not. |
| | ■ If capitalised, basis of capitalisation of interest and other finance costs. |

FRS 15   **Tangible fixed assets**

FRS 18 p55(a), 56	■ Whether carried at cost or revalued amount.
FRS 15 p 42	■ Basis and frequency of revaluations.
UITF 24, UITF 29	■ What is included in cost.
FRS 15 p 100(a)	■ Methods of depreciation (for example, straight line or reducing balance).
FRS 15 p100(b)	■ Useful economic lives/depreciation rates.
FRS 15 p100(d), FRS 18 p55(d)	■ The reason for any change in the depreciation method, useful lives or residual values, if the effect is material.

FRS 10, UITF 27   **Goodwill and intangible assets**

FRS 10 p52	■ The method used to value intangible assets.
FRS 10 p55	■ The methods and periods of amortisation of goodwill and intangibles and the reasons for choosing those periods.
FRS 10 p71	■ Treatment of goodwill on disposal, including previously eliminated goodwill.
FRS 10 p56,57, FRS 18 p55(a)	■ The reason for any change in the amortisation method or period, if the effect is material.
FRS 10 p58	■ Where the period of amortisation exceeds 20 years, the grounds for rebutting the 20 year presumption.
UITF 27, 5	Where estimates of the useful economic lives of goodwill or intangible assets are revised, the carrying value should be amortised over the revised remaining useful economic life. This requirement applies equally where the presumption of a 20-year life has previously been rebutted as it does to other revisions of estimates of the useful economic lives of goodwill and intangible assets.
FRS 10 p64	■ Where negative goodwill exceeds the fair values of the non-monetary assets, the source of the excess negative goodwill and the periods in which it is being written back.

Investment properties

SSAP 19 p11	■ Basis of inclusion in the balance sheet.
SSAP 19 p13	■ Treatment of changes in value.

Research and development

SSAP 13 p30	■ Classification of expenditure.
	■ Treatment of expenditure.

FRS 11   Impairment of fixed assets and goodwill

FRS 11 p14	■ Basis for determining impairment write-down, by reference to higher of net realisable value and value in use.
FRS 11 p41	■ Use of discounting in determining value in use.
FRS 11 p45	■ Basis for using risk-free discount rate and method for adjusting cash flows for risk, where applicable.
FRS 11 p63	■ Treatment of impairment write-down on revalued assets.

SSAP 4 p17   Government grants

SSAP 4 p28(a)	■ Treatment of capital grants.
	■ Treatment of revenue based grants.
	■ Period over which the grants are credited to the profit and loss account.

FRS 29 p21   Accounting for financial assets

FRS 26 p14, 15, 39, 43, 45-47   ■ Basis of recognition and measurements (cost or valuation).

FRS 26 p58   ■ Recognition of impairments.

FRS 29appB5(a)- (f)   ■ For financial assets designated as at fair value through profit or loss:

    (i)   the nature of the financial assets or financial liabilities the entity has designated as at fair value through profit or loss;

    (ii)   the criteria for so designating such financial assets or financial liabilities on initial recognition; and

    (iii)   how the entity has satisfied the conditions in paragraphs 9, 11A or 12 of FRS 26 for such designation. For instruments designated in accordance with paragraph (b)(i) of the definition of a financial asset or financial liability at fair value through profit or loss in FRS 26, that disclosure includes a narrative description of the circumstances underlying the measurement or recognition inconsistency that would otherwise arise. For instruments designated in accordance with paragraph (b)(ii) of the definition of a financial asset or financial liability at fair value through profit or loss in FRS 26, that disclosure includes a narrative description of how designation at fair value through profit or loss is consistent with the entity's documented risk management or investment strategy.

■ the criteria for designating financial assets as available for sale;

■ when an allowance account is used to reduce the carrying amount of financial assets impaired by credit losses:

    (i)   the criteria for determining when the carrying amount of impaired financial assets is reduced directly (or, in the case of a reversal of a write- down, increased directly) and when the allowance account is used; and

    (ii)   the criteria for writing off amounts charged to the allowance account against the carrying amount of impaired financial assets.

■ how net gains or net losses on each category of financial instrument are determined, for example, whether the net gains or net losses on items at fair value through profit or loss include interest or dividend income;

■ the criteria the entity uses to determine that there is objective evidence that an impairment loss has occurred;

■ when the terms of financial assets that would otherwise be past due or impaired have been re-negotiated, the accounting policy for financial assets that are the subject of re- negotiated terms;

FRS 29p27(a)   ■ methods and, where a valuation technique is used, assumptions applied in determining fair values for each class of financial assets or financial liabilities; and

FRS 26 p9   ■ how assets are classified.

FRS 29p21   Derivative financial instruments and hedging activities

FRS 18 p14 FRS 29p21   Derivatives are initially accounted for and measured at fair value on the date a derivative contract is entered into and subsequently measured at fair value. The gain or loss on re- measurement is taken to the profit or loss account except where the derivative is a designated cash flow hedging instrument. The accounting treatment of derivatives classified as hedges depends on their designation, which occurs on the date that the derivative contract is committed to. The group designates derivatives as:

FRS 26 p86(a)	■ A hedge of the fair value of an asset or liability ('fair value hedge').
FRS 26 p86(b)	■ A hedge of the income/cost of a highly probable forecasted transaction or commitment ('cash flow hedge').
FRS 26 p86(c)	■ A hedge of a net investment in a foreign operation.

FRS 29p23,24   In order to qualify for hedge accounting, the group is required to document in advance the relationship between the item being hedged and the hedging instrument. The group is also required to document and demonstrate an assessment of the relationship between the hedged item and the hedging instrument, which shows that the hedge will be highly effective on an on- going basis. This effectiveness testing is re-performed at each period end to ensure that the hedge remains highly effective.

| FRS 26 p89 | Gains or losses on fair value hedges that are regarded as highly effective are recorded in the profit and loss account with the gain or loss on the hedged item attributable to the hedged risk. |

FRS 26 p95
FRS 26 p97-98 Gains or losses on cash flow hedges that are regarded as highly effective are recognised in equity. Where the forecast transaction results in a financial asset or financial liability, only gains or losses previously recognised in equity are reclassified to profit or loss in the same period as the asset or liability affects profit or loss. Where the forecasted transaction or commitment results in a non-financial asset or a non-financial liability, any gains or losses previously deferred in equity are included in the cost of the related asset or liability. If the forecasted transaction or commitment results in future income or expenditure, gains or losses deferred in equity are transferred to the profit and loss account in the same period as the underlying income or expenditure. The ineffective portions of the gain or loss on the hedging instrument are recognised in profit or loss.

FRS 26 p101 For the portion of hedges deemed ineffective or transactions that do not qualify for hedge accounting under FRS 26, any change in assets or liabilities is recognised immediately in the profit and loss account. Where a hedge no longer meets the effectiveness criteria, any gains or losses deferred in equity are only transferred to the profit and loss account when the committed or forecasted transaction is recognised in the profit and loss account. However, where an entity applied cash flow hedge accounting for a forecasted or committed transaction that is no longer expected to occur, the cumulative gain or loss that has been recorded in equity is transferred to the profit and loss account. When a hedging instrument expires or is sold, any cumulative gain or loss existing in equity at that time remains in equity and is recognised when the forecast transaction is ultimately recognised in the profit and loss account.

FRS 26 p102 Where the group hedges net investments in foreign operations through currency borrowings, the gains or losses on the translation of the borrowings are recognised in equity. If the group uses derivatives as the hedging instrument, the effective portion of the hedge is recognised in equity, with any ineffective portion being recognised in the profit and loss account. The group has not separated out the interest element of the fair value of the forward currency contract. Gains and losses accumulated in equity are included in the profit and loss account when the foreign operation is disposed of.

SSAP 9 p32 **Stocks, work in progress and long-term contracts**

SSAP 9 p32,
4 Sch 27
- Basis of amount stated at in the balance sheet (for example, lower of cost and NRV, FIFO).
- Methods of valuation (for example, average price, FIFO).
- Basis for inclusion of overheads.
- Basis of provision for obsolete, slow moving and defective stocks.
- Method of ascertaining turnover and attributable profit for long-term contracts.

FRS 29p21, **Trade debtors**

FRS
29appBp5(d)(f)
- When an allowance account is used to reduce the carrying amount of financial assets impaired by credit losses:

   (i) the criteria for determining when the carrying amount of impaired financial assets is reduced directly (or, in the case of a reversal of a write-down, increased directly) and when the allowance account is used; and
   (ii) the criteria for writing off amounts charged to the allowance account against the carrying amount of impaired financial assets.

- The criteria the entity uses to determine that there is objective evidence that an impairment loss has occurred.

FRS 26 p43,
46(a), 59
- When a financial asset or financial liability is recognised initially, an entity measures it at its fair value plus, in the case of a financial asset or financial liability not at fair value through profit or loss, transaction costs that are directly attributable to the acquisition or issue of the financial asset or financial liability.

FRS 29p21 **Trade creditors**

FRS 26p43, 47
- When a financial liability is recognised initially, an entity measures it at its fair value plus, in the case of a financial asset or financial liability not at fair value through profit or loss, transaction costs that are directly attributable to the acquisition or issue of the financial asset or financial liability.
- After initial recognition, an entity measures all financial liabilities at amortised cost using the effective interest method.

FRS 29p21 **Borrowings**

FRS 26p43, 47
FRS 25p18(a),
28, 33, FRS
29p27(a)
- When a financial liability is recognised initially, an entity measures it at its fair value plus, in the case of a financial liability not at fair value through profit or loss, transaction costs that are directly attributable to the acquisition or issue of the financial asset or financial liability.
- After initial recognition, an entity measures all financial liabilities at amortised cost using the effective interest method.
- The substance of a financial instrument, rather than its legal form, governs its classification on the entity's balance sheet.
- The issuer of a non-derivative financial instrument evaluates the terms of the financial instrument to determine whether it contains both a liability and an equity component. Such components are classified separately as financial liabilities, financial assets or equity instruments in accordance with paragraph 15 of FRS 25.

Own equity instruments

- If an entity reacquires its own equity instruments, those instruments ('treasury shares') are deducted from equity. No gain or loss is recognised in profit or loss on the purchase, sale, issue or cancellation of an entity's own equity instruments. Such treasury shares may be acquired and held by the entity or by other members of the consolidated group. Consideration paid or received is recognised directly in equity.
- The methods and, when a valuation technique is used, the assumptions applied in determining fair values of each class of financial assets or financial liabilities. For example, if applicable, an entity discloses information about the assumptions relating to prepayment rates, rates of estimated credit losses, and interest rates or discount rates.

Leases

SSAP 21 p57   As lessee:

- Basis of recognition of fixed assets held under finance leases in the balance sheet.
- Depreciation policy for assets held under finance leases.
- Treatment of the interest element of finance lease rental obligations.
- Treatment of payments for operating leases.

UITF 28 p14   - Treatment of incentives to take on operating leases (for example, rent free periods).

SSAP 21 p60   As lessor:

- Policy for operating leases.
- Policy for finance leases.
- Policy for finance lease income.
- Treatment of the costs of assets acquired for the purpose of letting under finance lease.

UITF 28 p15   - Treatment of lease incentives.

Leases include hire purchase contracts which have characteristics similar to operating or finance leases.

FRS 12   ### Provisions

FRS 12 p14   - Basis of accounting for each class of provision.
- Extent of use of discounting.

FRS 17, UITF 35   ### Pensions and post retirement benefits

- Type of scheme – defined contribution or defined benefit.
- For defined benefit schemes – valuation frequency and method.
- Method of charging to profit and loss account.
- Treatment of actuarial gains and losses for defined benefit schemes.
- Funding policy.

FRS 16
FRS 19
UITF 19
FRS 19 p61   ### Taxation including deferred tax

- Basis of charge for taxation.
- Policy adopted for providing for deferred taxation.
- Policy adopted regarding discounting.

FRS 20, UITF 32,
UITF 25, UITF 38   ### Share-based payment

- Basis of accounting.
- Basis of accounting for employee share ownership plans (ESOPs).
- Basis of recognition and measurement of the cost of share-based payments.
- Basis of accounting for employer NICs on employee share schemes.

FRS 25 p33   ### Treasury shares

- Basis of accounting.

Financial risk management

FRS 29 p31   The group's activities expose it to a variety of financial risks: market risk (including currency risk, fair value interest rate risk, cash flow interest rate risk and price risk), credit risk and liquidity risk. The group's overall risk management programme focuses on the unpredictability of financial markets and seeks to minimise potential adverse effects on the group's financial performance. The group uses derivative financial instruments to hedge certain risk exposures.

Risk management is carried out by a central treasury department (group treasury) under policies approved by the Board of Directors. Group treasury identifies, evaluates and hedges financial risks in close co-operation with the group's operating units. The Board provides written principles for overall risk management, as well as written policies covering specific areas, such as foreign exchange risk, interest rate risk, and credit risk, use of derivative financial instruments and non-derivative financial instruments, and investment of excess liquidity.

(a) Market risk

(i) Foreign exchange risk

FRS 29 p33(a) The group operates internationally and is exposed to foreign exchange risk arising from various currency exposures, primarily with respect to the US dollar and the euro. Foreign exchange risk arises from future commercial transactions, recognised assets and liabilities and net investments in foreign operations.

FRS 29 p33(b), FRS 29 p22(c) The management has set up a policy to require group companies to manage their foreign exchange risk against their functional currency. The group companies are required to hedge their entire foreign exchange risk exposure with the group treasury. To manage their foreign exchange risk arising from future commercial transactions and recognised assets and liabilities, entities in the group use forward contracts, transacted with group treasury. Foreign exchange risk arises when future commercial transactions or recognised assets or liabilities are denominated in a currency that is not the entity's functional currency.

FRS 26 p73 The group treasury's risk management policy is to hedge between 75% and 100% of anticipated cash flows (mainly export sales and purchase of inventory) in each major foreign currency for the next 12 months. Approximately 90% (2010: 95%) of projected sales in each major currency qualify as 'highly probable' forecast transactions for hedge accounting purposes.

FRS 29 p33(a)(b) FRS 29 p22(c) For segment reporting purposes, each subsidiary designates contracts with group treasury as fair value hedges or cash flow hedges, as appropriate. External foreign exchange contracts are designated at group level as hedges of foreign exchange risk on specific assets, liabilities or future transactions on a gross basis.

FRS 29 p40, IG36 The group has certain investments in foreign operations, whose net assets are exposed to foreign currency translation risk. Currency exposure arising from the net assets of the group's foreign operations is managed primarily through borrowings denominated in the relevant foreign currencies.

At 31 December 2011, if the pound had weakened/strengthened by 11% against the euro with all other variables held constant, post-tax profit for the year would have been £251,000 (2010: £220,000) higher/lower, mainly as a result of foreign exchange gains/losses on translation of euro-denominated trade receivables, financial assets at fair value through profit or loss and debt securities classified as available for sale. Equity would have been £1,913,000 (2010: £932,000) lower/higher, arising mainly from foreign exchange losses/gains on translation of euro- denominated borrowings designated as a hedge of the net investment in subsidiaries. The impact on equity in net investment hedges is netted by a corresponding credit/charge resulting from the translation of the hedged net investment. Equity is more sensitive to movement in pound/euro exchange rate in 2011 than 2010 because of the increased amount of euro-denominated borrowings designated as a hedge of the net investment and anticipated cash flows hedged in a cash flow hedge.

At 31 December 2011, if the pound had weakened/strengthened by 4% against the US dollar with all other variables held constant, post-tax profit for the year would have been £135,000 (2010: £172,000) lower/higher, mainly as a result of foreign exchange gains/losses on translation of US dollar-denominated trade receivables, financial assets at fair value through profit or loss, debt securities classified as available for sale and foreign exchange losses/gains on translation of US dollar-denominated borrowings.

(ii) Price risk

FRS 29 p33(a)(b) The group is exposed to equity securities price risk because of investments held by the group and classified on the consolidated balance sheet either as available for sale or at fair value through profit or loss. The group is not exposed to commodity price risk. To manage its price risk arising from investments in equity securities, the group diversifies its portfolio. Diversification of the portfolio is done in accordance with the limits set by the group.

The group's equity investments are publicly traded and are included in the FTSE-100.

FRS 29 p40, IG36 The table below summarises the impact of increases/decreases of the FTSE 100 on the group's post-tax profit for the year and on equity. The analysis is based on the assumption that the equity indexes had increased/decreased by 5% with all other variables held constant and all the group's equity instruments moved according to the historical correlation with the index:

	Impact on post-tax profit £m		Impact on equity £m	
	2011	2010	**2011**	2010
FTSE-100 UK	–	–	23	19

Post-tax profit for the year would increase/decrease as a result of gains/losses on equity securities classified as at fair value through profit or loss. Equity would increase/decrease as a result of gains/losses on equity securities classified as available for sale.

(b) Credit risk

FRS 29
p33(a)(b)
FRS 29 p34(a)

Credit risk is managed on a group basis. Credit risk arises from cash and cash equivalents, derivative financial instruments and deposits with banks and financial institutions, as well as credit exposures to wholesale and retail customers, including outstanding receivables and committed transactions. For banks and financial institutions, only independently rated parties with a minimum rating of 'A' are accepted. If wholesale customers are independently rated, these ratings are used. Otherwise, if there is no independent rating, risk control assesses the credit quality of the customer taking into account its financial position, past experience and other factors. Individual risk limits are set based on internal or external ratings in accordance with limits set by the Board. The utilisation of credit limits is regularly monitored. Sales to retail customers are settled in cash or using major credit cards.

The below table shows the credit rating and the utilisation of the credit facilities of the six major counterparties at the balance sheet date.

FRS 29 p36(c)

Counterparty	Rating	31 December 2011 Credit facility £m	31 December 2011 Utilised £m	31 December 2010 Credit facility £m	31 December 2010 Utilised £m
Bank A	AAA	750	739	450	414
Bank B	AA	60	53	30	25
Bank C	A	40	34	20	17
		850	826	500	456
Wholesaler Q	A	64	26	62	9
Wholesaler T	BBB	18	17	31	2
Wholesaler Z	BB	9	4	11	1
		91	47	104	12

No credit limits were exceeded during the reporting period, and management does not expect any losses from non-performance by these counterparties.

(c) Liquidity risk

FRS 29 p33,
39(b)
FRS 29 p34(a)

Prudent liquidity risk management includes maintaining sufficient cash and marketable securities, the availability of funding from an adequate amount of committed credit facilities and the ability to close out market positions. Due to the dynamic nature of the underlying businesses, group treasury maintains flexibility in funding by maintaining availability under committed credit lines.

Management monitors the group's liquidity reserves defined as follows:

Liquidity reserve as of 31 December 2011

	December 2011 £m	September 2011 £m	June 2011 £m	March 2011 £m	December 2010 £m
Cash at bank and on hand	74.8	84.7	106.1	73.5	40.5
Unused portion of committed long-term credit lines	212.0	207.0	196.0	224.0	253.0
Liquidity reserve	286.8	291.7	302.1	297.5	293.5

FRS 29
p34(a)

Cash flow forecasting is performed in the operating entities of the group in and aggregated by group finance. Group finance monitors rolling forecasts of the group's liquidity requirements to ensure it has sufficient cash to meet operational needs while maintaining sufficient headroom on its undrawn committed borrowing facilities (note 19) at all times so that the group does not breach borrowing limits or covenants (where applicable) on any of its borrowing facilities. Such forecasting takes into consideration the group's debt financing plans, covenant compliance, compliance with internal balance sheet ratio targets and, if applicable external regulatory or legal requirements – for example, currency restrictions.

FRS 29 p33,
39(c)
FRS 29 B11E

Surplus cash held by the operating entities, over and above balance required for working capital management are transferred to the group treasury. The group treasury invests surplus cash in interest-bearing current accounts, time deposits, money market deposits and marketable securities, choosing instruments with appropriate maturities or sufficient liquidity to provide sufficient head-room as determined by the above-mentioned forecasts.

FRS 29
p39(a)(b)

The table below analyses the group's non-derivative financial liabilities and net-settled derivative financial liabilities into relevant maturity groupings based on the remaining period at the balance sheet date to the contractual maturity date. Derivative financial liabilities are included in the analysis if their contractual maturities are essential for an understanding of the timing of the cash flows. The amounts disclosed in the table are the contractual undiscounted cash flows.

At 31 December 2011	Less than 1 month £m	Between 1 and 3 months £m	Between 3 and 12 months £m	Between 1 and 2 years £m	Between 2 and 5 years £m	Over 5 years £m
Bank borrowings	11.5	21.9	54.2	188.4	192.6	642.0
Trade and other payables (including net settled derivatives)	103.6	41.1	154.2	50.2	2.7	3.0
At 31 December 2010						
Bank borrowings	11.7	8.7	21.2	164.1	74.3	219.6
Trade and other payables (including net settled derivatives)	31.2	25.2	27.9	5.0	2.7	3.9

FRS 29 p39(a) AppxB15 The table below analyses the group's derivative financial instruments that will be settled on a gross basis into relevant maturity groupings based on the remaining period at the balance sheet to the contractual maturity date. The amounts disclosed in the table are the contractual undiscounted cash flows.

At 31 December 2011	Less than 1 month £m	Between 1 and 3 months £m	Between 3 and 12 months £m	Between 1 and 2 years £m	Between 2 and 5 years £m	Over 5 Years £m
Forward foreign exchange contracts – Cash flow hedges:						
– Outflow	940.1	836.7	1,082.7	–	–	–
– Inflow	942.3	835.2	1,086.4	–	–	–
At 31 December 2010						
Forward foreign exchange contracts – Cash flow hedges:						
– Outflow	287.1	321.4	198.2	–	–	–
– Inflow	287.2	323.2	195.2	–	–	–

(d) Cash flow and fair value interest rate risk

FRS 29 p33(a) As the group has no significant interest-bearing assets, the group's income and operating cash flows are substantially independent of changes in market interest rates.

FRS 29 p33(a)(b) FRS 29 p22(c) The group's interest rate risk arises from long-term borrowings. Borrowings issued at variable rates expose the group to cash flow interest rate risk. Borrowings issued at fixed rates expose the group to fair value interest rate risk. Group policy is to maintain approximately 60% of its borrowings in fixed rate instruments. During 2011 and 2010, the group's borrowings at variable rate were denominated in the pound and the euro.

FRS 29 p22(b)(c) The group analyses its interest rate exposure on a dynamic basis. Various scenarios are simulated taking into consideration refinancing, renewal of existing positions, alternative financing and hedging. Based on these scenarios, the group calculates the impact on profit and loss of a defined interest rate shift. For each simulation, the same interest rate shift is used for all currencies. The scenarios are run only for liabilities that represent the major interest bearing positions.

FRS 29 p22(b)(c) Based on the simulations performed, the impact on profit or loss of a 10 basis point shift would be a maximum increase of £41,000 (2010: £37,000) or decrease of £34,000 (2010: £29,000), respectively. The simulation is done on a quarterly basis to verify that the maximum loss potential is within the limit given by the management.

FRS 29 p22(b)(c) Based on the various scenarios, the group manages its cash flow interest rate risk by using floating-to-fixed interest rate swaps. Such interest rate swaps have the economic effect of converting borrowings from floating rates to fixed rates. Generally, the group raises long-term borrowings at floating rates and swaps them into fixed rates that are lower than those available if the group borrowed at fixed rates directly. Under the interest rate swaps, the group agrees with other parties to exchange, at specified intervals (primarily quarterly), the difference between fixed contract rates and floating-rate interest amounts calculated by reference to the agreed notional amounts.

FRS 29 p40 IG36 Occasionally the group also enters into fixed-to-floating interest rate swaps to hedge the fair value interest rate risk arising where it has borrowed at fixed rates in excess of the 60% target.

At 31 December 2011, if interest rates on pound-denominated borrowings at that date had been 10 basis points higher/lower with all other variables held constant, post-tax profit for the year would have been £22,000 (2010: £21,000) lower/higher, mainly as a result of higher/lower interest expense on floating rate borrowings; equity would have been £5,000 (2010: £3,000) lower/higher mainly as a result of a decrease/increase in the fair value of fixed rate financial assets classified as available for sale. At 31 December 2011, if interest rates on UK pound- denominated borrowings at that date had been 50 basis points higher/lower with all other variables held constant, post-tax profit for the year would have been £57,000 (2010: £38,000) lower/higher, mainly as a result of higher/lower interest expense on floating rate borrowings; equity would have been £6,000 (2010: £4,000) lower/higher mainly as a result of a decrease/ increase in the fair value of fixed rate financial assets classified as available for sale.

1p124(a)(b)
IG5
(e) Capital risk management

The group's objectives when managing capital are to safeguard the group's ability to continue as a going concern in order to provide returns for shareholders and benefits for other stakeholders and to maintain an optimal capital structure to reduce the cost of capital.

In order to maintain or adjust the capital structure, the group may adjust the amount of dividends paid to shareholders, return capital to shareholders, issue new shares or sell assets to reduce debt.

Consistent with others in the industry, the group monitors capital on the basis of the gearing ratio. This ratio is calculated as net debt divided by total capital. Net debt is calculated as total borrowings (including borrowings and trade and other payables, as shown in the consolidated balance sheet) less cash and cash equivalents. Total capital is calculated as equity, as shown in the consolidated balance sheet, plus net debt.

During 2011, the group's strategy, which was unchanged from 2010, was to maintain a gearing ratio over 40% and a BB credit rating. The gearing ratio has been over 40% and the BB rating maintained throughout the year. The gearing ratios at 31 December 2011 and at 31 December 2010 were as follows:

	2011 £m	2010 £m
Total borrowings	908.7	459.6
Less: cash at banks and in hand	(74.8)	(40.5)
Net debt	833.9	419.1
Total equity	1,055.6	167.8
Total capital	1,889.5	586.9
Gearing ratio	**44%**	71%

The decrease in the gearing ratio during 2011 resulted primarily from the issue of shares for the acquisition of Newsub plc (see note 32).

(f) Fair value estimation

The following table presents the group's assets and liabilities that are measured at fair value at 31 December 2011.

FRS 29p27B(a)

	Level 1 £m	Level 2 £m	Level 3 £m	Total balance £m
Assets				
Financial assets at fair value through profit or loss				
– Trading derivatives	–	4.9	–	4.9
Derivatives used for hedging	–	15.8	–	15.8
Available-for-sale financial assets				
– Equity securities	459.3	–	–	459.3
– Debt investments	39.2	–	24.6	63.8
Total assets	**498.5**	**20.7**	**24.6**	**543.8**
Liabilities				
Financial liabilities at fair value through profit or loss				
– Trading derivatives	–	2.2	–	2.2
Derivatives used for hedging	–	13.6	–	13.6
Total liabilities	**–**	**15.8**	**–**	**15.8**

The following table presents the group's assets and liabilities that are measured at fair value at 31 December 2010.

FRS 29p27B(a)

	Level 1 £m	Level 2 £m	Level 3 £m	Total balance £m
Assets				
Financial assets at fair value through profit or loss				
– Trading derivatives	–	3.1	–	3.1
Derivatives used for hedging	–	4.0	–	4.0
Available-for-sale financial assets				
– Equity securities	377.0	–	–	377.0
– Debt investments	21.1	–	11.9	33.0
Total assets	**398.1**	**7.1**	**11.9**	**417.1**
Liabilities				
Financial liabilities at fair value through profit or loss				
– Trading derivatives	–	3.3	–	3.3
Derivatives used for hedging	–	13.8	–	13.8
Total liabilities	**–**	**17.1**	**–**	**17.1**

The fair value of financial instruments traded in active markets is based on quoted market prices at the balance sheet date. A market is regarded as active if quoted prices are readily and regularly available from an exchange, dealer, broker, industry group, pricing service, or regulatory agency, and those prices represent actual and regularly occurring market transactions on an arm's length basis. The quoted market price used for financial assets held by the group is the current bid price. These instruments are included in Level 1. Instruments included in Level 1 comprise FTSE 100 equity investments classified as available for sale.

FRS 29p27   The fair value of financial instruments that are not traded in an active market (for example, over-the-counter derivatives) is determined by using valuation techniques. These valuation techniques maximise the use of observable market data where it is available and rely as little as possible on entity specific estimates. If all significant inputs required to fair value an instrument are observable, the instrument is included in Level 2.

If one or more of the significant inputs is not based on observable market data, the instrument would be included in Level 3.

The following table presents the changes in Level 3 instruments for the year ended 31 December 2011.

FRS 29p27B(c)

	Available for sale – Unlisted debt securities Total balance £m
Opening balance	11.9
Transfers into Level 3	–
Additions	9.7
Gains and losses recognised in the statement of total recognised gains and losses	3
Closing balance	**24.6**

The following table presents the changes in Level 3 instruments for the year ended 31 December 2010.

FRS 29p27B(c)

	Available for sale – Unlisted debt securities Total balance £m
Opening balance	–
Additions	11.9
Gains and losses recognised in the statement of total recognised gains and losses	–
Closing balance	**11.9**

Notes to the financial statements for the year ended 31 December 2011

		Turnover		Profit before tax	
		2011 **£m**	2010 £m	**2011** **£m**	2010 £m
SI 2008/410 1Sch 68(2)	**Geographical analysis**				
	UK	**576.9**	207.2	**34.6**	39.7
	Continental Europe				
FRS 9 p21, 27 SSAP 25 p36	– Group	**243.1**	98.8	**28.8**	28.8
	– Joint ventures (a)	**38.9**	9.9	**2.8**	1.2
	North America	**344.7**	91.6	**11.0**	10.4
	Asia Pacific and Africa	**96.2**	78.3	**31.8**	24.5
		1,299.8	485.8	**109.0**	104.6
	Profit on sale of subsidiary – UK			**6.3**	–
SSAP 25 p34	Net finance (cost)/income			**(6.6)**	7.6
	Total				
	– Group (b)	**1,260.9**	475.9	**105.2**	111.0
FRS 9 p21, 27	**– Joint ventures**	**38.9**	9.9	**3.5**	1.2
		1,299.8	485.8	**108.7**	112.2
SI 2008/410 1Sch 68(1))	**Business analysis**				
	Food products	**404.4**	175.1	**38.8**	37.7
	Personnel services	**125.7**	3.3	**(15.4)**	0.3
	Retail services	**113.8**	113.3	**35.8**	36.2
	Distribution services				
FRS 9 p21 SSAP 25 p36	– Group	**259.3**	11.9	**15.9**	4.6
	– Joint ventures (a)	**38.9**	9.9	**2.8**	1.2
	Property services	**154.3**	84.9	**18.8**	18.0
	Healthcare	**203.4**	87.4	**12.3**	6.6
		1,299.8	485.8	**109.0**	104.6

SSAP 25 p34   Analyses by business are based on the group's management structure. Turnover between segments is immaterial. Geographical analysis is based on the country in which the order is received. It would not be materially different if based on the country in which the customer is located

SSAP 25 p36   *Notes:*

(a) *The group's share of the profit before taxation and net assets of its joint ventures and associates should be separately disclosed on a segmental basis if any exceed 20% of the relevant total.*

(b) *Where non-statutory profit measures are shown, the statutory profit measure should be also shown.*

	Net assets	2011 £m	2010 £m
SSAP 25 p34(c)	**Geographical analysis**		
	UK	**465.3**	77.1
	Continental Europe		
FRS 9 p21, 27, SSAP 25 p26	– Group	**354.0**	34.5
	– Joint ventures	**16.5**	1.8
	North America	**505.7**	17.0
	Asia Pacific and Africa	**29.9**	20.2
		1,371.4	150.6
SSAP 25 p37	Central	**518.1**	439.3
	Net debt excluding liquid resources (note 30)	**(833.9)**	(422.1)
	Total		
FRS 9 p21, 27	**– Group**	**1,039.1**	166.0
	– Joint ventures	**16.5**	1.8
		1,055.6	167.8
SSAP 25 p34(c)	**Business analysis**		
	Food products	**199.2**	62.2
	Personnel service	**644.7**	0.1
	Retail services	**16.0**	33.2
	Distribution services		
FRS 9 p21 SSAP 25 p26	– Group	**420.1**	46.1
	– Joint ventures	**16.5**	1.8
	Property services	**37.3**	10.1
	Healthcare	**37.6**	(2.9)
		1,371.4	150.6
SSAP 25 p37	Central	**518.1**	439.3
	Net debt excluding liquid resources (note 30)	**(833.9)**	(422.1)
	Total		
	– Group	**1,039.1**	166.0
	– Joint ventures	**16.5**	1.8
		1,055.6	167.8

SSAP 25 p37   Central net assets comprise assets, partially offset by liabilities that cannot practicably be divided between the segments. These liabilities and assets are:

	2011 £m	2010 £m
AFS investment	**539.0**	410.0
Other central current assets	**39.3**	68.7
Corporation tax payable	**(60.2)**	(29.4)
	518.1	439.3

FRS 3 p15,53
FRS 6 p28

The above business analyses of turnover, profit before tax and net assets in 2011 includes contributions from Newsub plc:

Geographical analysis	Turnover £m	Profit £m	Net operating assets £m
UK	300.6	12.7	57.2
Continental Europe			
– Group	120.2	5.6	24.8
– Joint ventures	29.8	1.1	6.6
North America	234.0	4.7	20.1
Asia Pacific and Africa	5.2	0.3	21.7
	689.8	24.4	130.4
Net interest (including £0.7m in joint ventures)	–	(17.4)	–
Total			
– Group	**660.0**	**7.3**	**123.8**
– Joint ventures	**29.8**	**1.5**	**6.6**

Business analysis	Turnover £m	Profit £m	Net operating assets £m
Food products	214.7	14.0	31.1
Personnel services	121.7	(8.4)	18.1
Distribution services			
– Group	190.9	10.1	75.4
– Joint ventures	29.8	2.2	6.6
Property services	66.9	(0.7)	0.4
Healthcare	65.8	7.2	(1.2)
	689.8	24.4	130.4
Net interest (including £0.7m in joint ventures)		(17.4)	
Total			
– Group	**660.0**	**7.3**	**123.8**
– Joint ventures	**29.8**	**1.5**	**6.6**

FRS 3 p53

The segment analysis of turnover, profit before tax and net assets for the UK and Food Products includes £25.6m (2010: £117.0m) turnover, £2.2m (2010: £6.2m) profit before tax and £5.3m of net assets at 31 December 2010 in respect of H Limited, which was sold during the year.

2 Cost of sales, gross profit, distribution costs and administrative expenses

	2011 Continuing £m	2011 Acquisitions £m	2011 Discontinued £m	2011 Total £m	2010 Continuing £m	2010 Discontinued £m	2010 Total £m
Turnover	523.7	711.6	25.6	**1,260.9**	358.9	117.0	475.9
Cost of sales	408.4	613.5	(18.3)	**(1,040.2)**	(259.5)	(82.9)	(342.4)
Exceptional cost of sales	–	3.5	–	**(3.5)**	–	–	–
Goodwill amortisation	–	40.2	–	**(40.2)**	–	–	–
Total cost of sales	408.4	657.2	(18.3)	**(1,083.9)**	(259.5)	(82.9)	(342.4)
Gross profit	115.3	54.4	7.3	**177.0**	99.4	34.1	133.5
Distribution costs	9.1	4.7	–	**13.8**	–	–	–
Administrative expenses	26.5	18.8	5.1	**50.4**	25.1	7.0	32.1
Exceptional acquisition reorganisation costs	–	9.1	–	**9.1**	–	–	–
Total administrative expenses	35.6	32.6	5.1	**73.3**	25.1	7.0	32.1
Less: other operating income – Royalties	(2.5)	–	–	**(2.5)**	(2.0)	–	(2.0)
Net operating expenses	33.1	32.6	5.1	**70.8**	23.1	7.0	30.1
Group operating profit	82.2	21.8	2.2	**106.2**	76.3	27.1	103.4

FRS 3 p14

FRS 10 App 1 p16

SI 2008/410 1 Sch Formats

SI 2008/410 1 Sch Formats

FRS 6 p31

SI 2008/410 1 Sch Formats

SI 2008/410 1 Sch

3(a) Interest and similar items

		2011 £m	2010 £m
SI 2008/410 1 Sch 66 (1)	Interest payable on bank loans and overdrafts	(16.4)	(1.3)
	Amortisation of issue costs of bank loan	(1.1)	–
SI 2008/410 1 Sch 66(2)	Interest payable on other loans	(5.2)	(0.1)
SSAP 21 p53	Interest payable on finance leases	(1.2)	–
	Preference share dividends paid: 7p per £1 share	(0.1)	–
SI 2008/410 1 Sch Formats	Group interest and similar charges payable	(24.0)	(1.4)
FRS 9 p21	Share of joint venture interest payable	(0.5)	–
	Total interest and similar charges payable	(24.5)	(1.4)
SI 2008/410 1 Sch Formats	Group interest receivable	12.7	5.0
FRS 9 p21, 27	Share of joint venture interest receivable	1.2	–
SI 2008/410 1Sch Formats, FRS 29 p20(b)	Total interest receivable and similar income	13.9	5.0
	Net interest (payable)/receivable and similar items	(10.6)	3.6

SI 2008/410 1Sch 27(3), FRS 15 p31 *Note: If the group capitalises interest or other finance cost into assets, the total finance cost for the year should be shown in the above table and the amount capitalised shown as a deduction in arriving at the net amount shown in the profit and loss account. In addition, the rate of capitalisation should be given.*

3(b) Other finance income

		2011 £m	2010 £m
FRS 12 p48	Unwinding of discounts in provisions (note 20)	(0.4)	–
FRS 17 App(ii) p6	Other finance income (note 34)	4.4	4.0
		4.0	4.0

4 Profit on ordinary activities before taxation

		2011 £m	2010 £m
	Profit on ordinary activities before taxation is stated after charging/ (crediting):		
SI 2008/410 1 Sch Formats	Staff costs (note 33)	626.9	237.0
FRS 15 p100	Depreciation of tangible fixed assets		
	– Owned assets	68.5	22.9
SSAP 21 p50	– Under finance leases	2.6	–
	Amortisation of goodwill		
FRS 10 p53	– Subsidiaries	40.2	–
FRS 9 p27	– Joint ventures	0.9	–
FRS 3 p19	Loss/(profit) on disposal of fixed assets	6.6	(1.3)
SSAP 21 p55	Hire of machinery and equipment	12.2	1.2
SSAP 21 p55	Other operating lease rentals	5.2	5.6
FRS 29 p20(e)	Trade debtors impairment	21.8	18.4
FRS 3 p19	Costs of product remediation (see below)	3.5	–
FRS 6 p31, SI 2008/410 1 Sch 69(3), FRS 3 p19	Costs incurred in reorganising acquired businesses (see below)	9.1	–
FRS 23 p 52(a)	Net exchange differences on foreign currency borrowings less deposits	5.4	2.3
SI 2008/410 55(2)	Net fair value gains on open forward foreign exchange contracts	4.1	–

SI 2008/489
ICAEW Tech
06/ 06
(Revised)

Services provided by the company's auditors and its associates

During the year the group (including its overseas subsidiaries) obtained the following services from the company's auditors and its associates:

	2011 £m	2010 £m
Fees payable to company auditors for the audit of parent company and consolidated financial statements	0.7	0.6
Fees payable to the company's auditors and its associates for other services:		
The audit of company's subsidiaries pursuant to legislation	0.9	0.5
Other services pursuant to legislation	0.3	–
Tax services	0.1	0.1
	2.0	1.2

	2011 £m	2010 £m
Fees in respect of the GAAP UK Group Limited pension scheme:		
Audit	0.2	0.2
Other services pursuant to legislation	0.1	–
	0.3	0.2

SI 2008/489

The requirements in the Companies (Disclosure of Auditor Remuneration and Liability Limitation Agreements) Regulations 2008 on disclosure of auditor remuneration, apply to all financial statements with the following exceptions:

PwC commentary

A new statutory instrument has just been published (SI 2011/2198) which will change this disclosure. However, its implementation date is financial periods beginning on or after 1 October 2011, so it is not effective for this period

- Where a parent company is required to (and does) prepare consolidated financial statements, there is no requirement to disclose, in addition to the group audit fee, the audit fee for the company.
- The disclosures in respect of fees for 'Other services' are not required to be given by:
  - small or medium companies or groups (reduced disclosure requirements apply);
  - subsidiary companies in their individual financial statements, whose parents are required to, and do, prepare consolidated financial statements in accordance with the Companies Act 2006 and the subsidiary company is included in the consolidation; or
  - parent companies in their individual financial statements, where the company is required to, and does, prepare consolidated financial statements in accordance with the Companies Act 2006.
- The disclosure in respect of fees for 'Other services' provided by a distant associate of the company's auditor are not required if the total remuneration receivable for all of those services supplied by that associate does not exceed £10,000 or, if higher, 1% of the total audit remuneration received by the company's auditor in the most recent financial year of the auditor.

The statutory requirements in relation to auditors' remuneration are supported by guidance published by the ICAEW in Tech 06/06 (Revised), 'Disclosure of Auditors' Remuneration', which also provides example disclosures.

Disclosure is required of:

- any remuneration receivable by the company's auditors for the auditing of the financial statements (parent company and group financial statements); and
- any remuneration receivable by the company's auditors or 'its associates' for the supply of other services to the company or 'its associates'.

Separate disclosure is required in the parent company's group and individual financial statements in respect of fees paid to the 'Auditor and its associates' by the 'Company and its associates' (including that of countries and territories outside Great Britain) in the following categories:

- fees payable for the audit of the group financial statements (including the audit of the company's subsidiaries for consolidation purposes only); and
- fees for other services including:
  - audit of company's subsidiaries (excluding consolidation work);
  - other services supplied pursuant to legislation;
  - other services relating to taxation;
  - services relating to information technology;
  - internal audit services;
  - valuation and actuarial services;
  - services relating to litigation;
  - services relating to recruitment and remuneration;

- services relating to corporate finance transactions entered into or proposed to be entered into by or on behalf of the company or any of its associates; and
- all other services.

Separate disclosure is required of:

- fees in respect of the company and its subsidiaries; and
- fees in respect of company pension schemes.

The 'Company and its associates' refers to the subsidiaries of the company, and not to its associates as defined in FRS 9, 'Associates and joint ventures'. Similarly, references to the 'Auditor and its associates' refer to members of the same network of firms as the company's auditor.

Where fees for services performed by other parts of the audit firm that assist in the audit are invoiced either as part of, or separately from, the audit fee, those fees are included within the audit fees disclosed.

The above disclosure requirements will still apply to parent company's individual financial statements where it chooses to take advantage of section 401 Companies Act 2006 exemption from consolidation for intermediate holding companies within a group headed by a non-EEA parent company (where the financial statements are drawn up in accordance with the Insurance Accounts Directive or in an equivalent manner).

Exceptional items

SI 2008/410
1 Sch 69(3)
FRS 3 p19

During the year, a few batches of one of the group's food products were found to have been contaminated with small pieces of glass. As a precaution, the group recalled all batches of this product made within six weeks of the contamination being discovered. The exceptional charge to cost of sales represents the cost of correcting the defective machinery, replacing the withdrawn product and meeting product liability claims.

FRS 3 p46
FRS 6 p31

The costs of £9.1m incurred in reorganising the businesses of Newsub plc arise from the integration and streamlining of the food products and health care divisions within the group's existing businesses. These costs relate to the project identified and controlled by management as part of the integration programme set up at the time of Newsub plc's acquisition.

5 Profit on sale of subsidiary

	2011 £m	2010 £m
Discontinued operations		
Gain on disposal of subsidiary's net tangible fixed assets (note 32c)	10.2	–
Goodwill previously eliminated against reserves (note 32c)	(3.9)	–
Profit on sale of subsidiary (note 34c)	6.3	–
Taxation	0.7	–

FRS 10
p71(c)(ii)

FRS 3 p20

SI 2008/410
1 Sch 67(1)
FRS 3 p20

FRS 3 p24
SI 2008/410
1 Sch 69(3)

On 1 December 2011, the group sold H Limited, a wholly-owned subsidiary, for £15.7m in cash. The consideration is due to be received in March 2011. H Limited was the group's only poultry product manufacturing operation, and the disposal completed the exit from these activities. As a result of the material change in the nature and focus of the group's operations that this disposal represented, it has been treated as a discontinued operation in the profit and loss account.

6 Tax on profit on ordinary activities — analysis of charge in year

		2011 £m	2010 £m
	Current tax		
SI 2008/410 1 Sch 67(2)	**United Kingdom**		
FRS 16 p17(a)	Corporation tax at 26.5% (2010: 28%)	20.2	31.5
FRS 16 p17	Double tax relief	(0.9)	(13.1)
		19.3	18.4
	Foreign tax		
FRS 16 p17(b)	Corporation taxes	22.8	18.5
	Other current tax		
FRS 16 p17	Adjustment in respect of prior years	1.6	5.3
FRS 9 p21	Share of joint ventures	1.9	0.8
	Total current tax	45.6	43.0
FRS 19 p60(a)(i)	**Deferred tax**		
	Origination and reversal of timing differences:		
	– UK	18.1	2.5
	– Foreign tax	19.1	3.3
	Impact of change in tax rate[1]	–	–
FRS 19 p60	Total deferred tax (note 20)	37.2	5.8
	Tax on profit on ordinary activities	82.8	48.8

		2011 £m	2010 £m
FRS 16 p17	**Tax on recognised gains and losses not included in the profit and loss account (note 25)**		
	UK corporation tax at 26.5% (2010: 28%)		
	Current tax credit allocated to actuarial losses	3.6	–
	Current tax credit/(charge) on exchange movements offset in reserves	3.5	2.8
	Other deferred tax movement relating to pension scheme	2.8	(0.8)
	Impact of change in tax rate[2]	–	–
		9.9	2.7

FRS 19 p64(a) The tax for the period is higher (2010: higher) than the standard effective rate of corporation tax in the UK for the year ended 31 December 2011 of 26.5% (2010: 28.0%). The differences are explained below:

	2011 £m	2010 £m
Profit on ordinary activities before tax	108.7	112.2
Profit on ordinary activities multiplied by standard rate of corporation tax in the UK of 26.5% (2010: 28%)	28.8	31.4
Effects of:		
– Adjustments in respect of prior years	1.6	5.3
– Adjustment in respect of foreign tax rates	6.4	5.9
– Pension cost charge in excess of pension cost relief	–	1.3
– Capital allowances in excess of depreciation	(40.4)	(4.8)
– Other short-term timing differences	3.2	(2.3)
– Expenses not deductible for tax purposes	46.0	6.2
– Remeasurement of deferred tax – change in UK tax rate[2]	–	–
Total current tax	45.6	43.0

Factors affecting current and future tax charges

During the year, the relevant deferred tax balances have been re-measured[2] as a result of the change in the UK main corporation tax rate to 26%, which was substantively enacted on 29 March 2011 and will be effective from 1 April 2011; and to 25%, which was substantively enacted on 5 July 2011 and will be effective from 1 April 2012.

Further reductions to the UK corporation tax rate were announced in the March 2011 Budget. The changes, which are expected to be enacted separately each year, propose to reduce the rate by 1% per annum to 23% by 1 April 2014. The changes had not been substantively enacted at the balance sheet date and therefore are not recognised in these financial statements[3].

---

[1] The line item for 'Impact of change in tax rate' is shown for illustrative purposes. Companies with 31 December 2011 year ends will need to consider the impact of the reductions in tax rates in the Finance Act 2011.

[2] The line item for the change in UK tax rate is shown for illustrative purposes. Companies with 31 December 2011 year ends will need to consider the impact of the reductions in tax rates in the Finance Act 2011.

[3] If the effect of the proposed changes is material, disclosure should be given of the effect of the changes, either as disclosure of events after the reporting period (if applicable) or as factors affecting current and future tax charges.

7 Earnings per share

FRS 22 p10
FRS 22 p20, DV
Basic earnings per share is calculated by dividing the earnings attributable to ordinary shareholders by the weighted average number of ordinary shares outstanding during the year, excluding those held in the employee share trust (note 25), which are treated as cancelled.

FRS 22 p31
For diluted earnings per share, the weighted average number of ordinary shares in issue is adjusted to assume conversion of all dilutive potential ordinary shares. The group has two classes of dilutive potential ordinary shares: those share options granted to employees where the exercise price is less than the average market price of the company's ordinary shares during the year, and the contingently issuable shares under the group's long-term incentive plan. At 31 December 2011, the performance criteria for the vesting of the awards under the incentive scheme had not been met and consequently the shares in question are excluded from the diluted EPS calculation.

FRS 22 p70(a)
FRS 22 p70(b)
Reconciliations of the earnings and weighted average number of shares used in the calculations are set out below.

	2011 Number of shares (millions)	2010 Number of shares (millions)
FRS 22 p70(b) Weighted average ordinary shares in issue	1,137.8	881.6
FRS 22 p70(b) Options	5.0	17.2
FRS 22 p70(b) Diluted number of shares	1,142.8	898.8

	2011			2010		
	Continuing	Discontinued	Total	Continuing	Discontinued	Total
FRS 22 p70(a) Earnings (£m)	17.6	7.8	25.4	58.2	5.0	63.2
Earnings per share – Basic (p)	1.55	0.68	2.23	6.6	0.57	7.17
– Diluted (p)	1.54	0.68	2.22	6.48	0.55	7.03

8 Intangible fixed assets

	Goodwill £m
SI 2008/410 1 Sch Formats **Group**	
SI 2008/410 1 Sch 51(1) **Cost**	
FRS 10 p53(a) At 1 January 2011	–
FRS 10 p53(c) Additions (note 32)	1,151.5
Exchange adjustments	(32.6)
FRS 10 p53(a) **At 31 December 2011**	**1,118.9**
SI 2008/410 1 Sch 51(3) **Accumulated amortisation**	
FRS 10 p53(b) At 1 January 2011	–
FRS 10 p53(c) Charge for the year	40.2
FRS 10 p53(b) **At 31 December 2011**	**40.2**
FRS 10 p53(d) **Net book amount at 31 December 2011**	**1,078.7**
FRS 10 p53(d) Net book amount at 31 December 2010	–

9 Tangible assets

SI2008/410 1 Sch Formats	Group	Land and buildings short leasehold £m	Land and buildings freehold and long leasehold £m	Fit-out, plant and equipment £m	Vehicles and office equipment £m	Total £m
SI 2008/410 1 Sch 51(3)	**Cost or valuation**					
FRS 15 p100(e)	At 1 January 20010	–	20.7	85.2	77.2	183.1
FRS 15 p100(g)	Exchange adjustments	–	(3.2)	(14.7)	(9.3)	(27.2)
	Additions at cost	1.2	10.9	54.3	30.4	96.8
	Acquisitions (note 32)	4.2	64.7	181.6	61.9	312.4
	Surplus on revaluation	–	3.1	–	–	3.1
FRS 15 p100(e)	**At 31 December 2011**	**5.4**	**96.0**	**278.9**	**135.4**	**515.7**
SI 2008/410 1 Sch 51 (1)	**Accumulated depreciation**					
FRS 15 p100(f)	At 1 January 2011	–	2.4	52.8	36.6	91.8
FRS 15 p100(g)	Exchange adjustments	–	(0.3)	(5.5)	(4.2)	(10.0)
FRS 15 p100(c)	Charge for the year	2.0	4.4	39.5	25.2	71.1
	Revaluation	–	(2.3)	–	–	(2.3)
	Disposals	–	(0.2)	(24.6)	(16.9)	(41.7)
FRS 15 p100(f)	**At 31 December 2011**	**2.0**	**4.0**	**62.2**	**40.7**	**108.9**
FRS 15 p100(g)	**Net book amount at 31 December 2011**	**3.4**	**92.0**	**216.7**	**94.7**	**406.8**
FRS 15 p100(g)	Net book amount at 31 December 2010	–	18.3	32.4	40.6	91.3

SSAP 21 p49,50 Assets held under finance leases, capitalised and included in tangible fixed assets:

	2011 £m	2010 £m
Cost	21.2	–
Accumulated depreciation	(2.6)	–
Net book amount	18.6	–

SI 2008/410 1 Sch 27 (3)(b) FRS 15 p31(b), (c), (e)

Note:

If the group capitalises finance costs directly attributable to tangible fixed assets, the amount added in the year and the cumulative total of such interest included at the balance sheet date should be disclosed. In addition, disclosure of the rate of capitalisation is required.

SI 2008/410 1 Sch Formats	Company	Land and buildings short leasehold £m	Land and buildings freehold and long leasehold £m	Total £m
SI 2008/410 1 Sch 51(1) FRS 15 p100(e)	**Cost or valuation**			
	At 1 January 2011	–	10.9	10.9
FRS 15 p100(g)	Additions at cost	0.1	0.6	0.7
	Surplus on revaluation	–	1.1	1.1
	Disposals	–	(0.3)	(0.3)
FRS 15 p100(e)	**At 31 December 2011**	**0.1**	**12.3**	**12.4**
SI 2008/410 1 Sch 51(3) FRS 15 p100(f)	**Accumulated depreciation**			
	At 1 January 2011	–	1.2	1.2
FRS 15 p100(g)	Charge for year	–	0.3	0.3
	Revaluation	–	(0.4)	(0.4)
	Disposals	–	(0.2)	(0.2)
FRS 15 p100(f)	**At 31 December 2011**	**–**	**0.9**	**0.9**
FRS 15 p100(g)	**Net book amount at 31 December 2011**	**0.1**	**11.4**	**11.5**
FRS 15 p100(g)	Net book amount at 31 December 2010	–	9.7	9.7

SI 2008/410
1 Sch 34 (2),
SI 2008/410 1
Sch 52(a),
FRS 15
p74(a)(ii)(iii),
FRS 15
p74(a)(i), (v)

The group's freehold properties and long leasehold properties were revalued at 30 November 2011, on the basis of existing use value by independent qualified valuers. The valuations were undertaken in accordance with the Appraisal and Valuation Manual of the Royal Institution of Chartered Surveyors in the United Kingdom by Surveyor & Son, a firm of independent Chartered Surveyors and overseas by valuers having equivalent professional qualifications.

FRS 15
p74(a)(i)

These valuations have been incorporated into the financial statements; the resulting revaluation adjustments have been taken to the revaluation reserve. The revaluations during the year ended 31 December 2011 resulted in a revaluation surplus of £5.4m (note 24).

FRS 19 p15

No deferred tax is provided on timing differences arising from the revaluation of fixed assets unless, by the balance sheet date, a binding commitment to sell the asset has been entered into and it is unlikely that any gain will be rolled over.

		Group		Company	
		2011 £m	2010 £m	2011 £m	2010 £m
SI 2008/410 1 Sch 53	**Analysis of net book value of land and buildings – freehold and long leasehold**				
	Freehold	87.1	18.3	10.8	9.7
SI 2008/410 10 Sch 7	Leasehold: (over 50 years unexpired)	4.9	–	0.6	–
		92.0	18.3	11.4	9.7

If the revalued assets were stated on the historical cost basis, the amounts would be as follows:

Freehold and long leasehold land and buildings

		Group		Company	
		2011 £m	2010 £m	2011 £m	2010 £m
	At cost	88.8	17.1	10.5	9.1
	Aggregate depreciation	(4.3)	(1.3)	(0.5)	(0.2)
SI 2008/410 1 Sch 34 (3),(4), FRS 15 p74(a)(iv)	Net book value based on historical cost	84.5	15.8	10.0	8.9

SI 2008/410
1 Sch Formats,
FRS 29 p29(b),
SI 2008/410 1
Sch 51(1)

10 Investments in subsidiaries and joint ventures

	Group		Company	
	2011 **£m**	2010 £m	**2011** **£m**	2010 £m
Shares in group undertakings				
At 1 January	–	–	**98.5**	95.0
Additions in year	–	–	**320.7**	3.5
At 31 December	–	–	**419.2**	98.5

SI 2008/410
6 Sch 20(2)

FRS 9 p29

Interests in joint ventures				
At 1 January				
– Net assets	**1.8**	1.5	–	–
– Goodwill	–	–	–	–
	1.8	1.5	–	–
Exchange adjustments	**(0.9)**	(0.1)	–	–
Additions				
– Net assets	**5.5**	–	–	–
– Goodwill	**8.5**	–	–	–
Share of profits retained	**2.5**	0.4	–	–

FRS 9 p29

At 31 December				
– Net assets	**8.9**	1.8	–	–
– Goodwill	**8.5**	–	–	–
	17.4	1.8	–	–
Accumulated amortisation of goodwill				
At 1 January	–	–	–	–
Charge for the year	**(0.9)**	–	–	–
At 31 December	**(0.9)**	–	–	–

FRS 9 p29

Net book amount at 31 December				
– Net assets	**8.9**	1.8	–	–
– Goodwill	**7.6**	–	–	–
Total fixed asset investments	**16.5**	1.8	419.2	98.5

FRS 9 p57,58 *Note:*

Further disclosures are required for associates and joint ventures if the 15% and/or 25% thresholds are exceeded.

CA06 s410
(1),(2),(3)

Investments in group undertakings are stated at cost. As permitted by section 615 of the Companies Act 2006, where the relief afforded under section 612 of the Companies Act 2006 applies, cost is the aggregate of the nominal value of the relevant number of the company's shares and the fair value of any other consideration given to acquire the share capital of the subsidiary undertakings. The directors consider that to give full particulars of all subsidiary undertakings would lead to a statement of excessive length. A list of principal subsidiary undertakings and joint ventures is given on page 62. A full list of subsidiary undertakings and joint ventures at 31 December 2011 will be annexed to the company's next annual return.

FRS 10 p55

The goodwill arising on the joint ventures acquired with Newsub plc is being amortised on a straight-line basis over five years. This is the period over which the directors estimate that values of the underlying businesses are expected to exceed the values of the underlying assets.

SI 2008/410
1 Sch Formats

11 Stocks

	Group		Company	
	2011 **£m**	2010 £m	**2011** **£m**	2010 £m
Raw materials and consumables	**6.1**	4.3	–	–
Work in progress	**3.0**	0.8	–	–
Finished goods	**24.7**	11.9	–	–
	33.8	17.0	–	–

SSAP 9 p27
SI 2008/410
1 Sch Formats

SI 2008/410
1 Sch 28(3),(4)

Note:

If there is a material difference between the balance sheet amount of stock and its replacement cost, the latter amount should be disclosed.

FRS 29 p6   **12 Financial instruments by category**

The accounting policies for financial instruments on pages 15 to 24 have been applied to the line items below:

Group	Loans and receivables £m	Assets at fair value through profit and loss £m	Derivatives used for hedging £m	Available for sale £m	Total £m
Assets at 31 December 2011					
Available-for-sale investments	–	–	–	523.1	523.1
Derivative financial instruments	–	4.9	15.8	–	20.7
Current asset investments	25.3	–	–	–	25.3
Debtors	290.6	–	–	–	290.6
Cash at bank and in hand	74.8	–	–	–	74.8
	390.7	**4.9**	**15.8**	**523.1**	**934.5**
Assets at 31 December 2010					
Available-for-sale investments	–	–	–	410.0	410.0
Derivative financial instruments	–	3.1	4.0	–	7.1
Current asset investments	55.3	–	–	–	55.3
Debtors	109.6	–	–	–	109.6
Cash at bank and in hand	40.5	–	–	–	40.5
	205.4	**3.1**	**4.0**	**410.0**	**622.5**

Group	Liabilities at fair value through profit and loss £m	Derivatives used for hedging £m	Other financial liabilities £m	Total £m
Liabilities at 31 December 2011				
Borrowings	–	–	908.7	908.7
Derivative financial instruments	13.6	2.2	–	15.8
	13.6	**2.2**	**908.7**	**924.5**
Liabilities at 31 December 2010				
Borrowings	–	–	459.6	459.6
Derivative financial instruments	13.8	3.3	–	17.1
	13.8	**3.3**	**459.6**	**476.7**

Company

All financial assets of the company were categorised as loans and receivables at both 31 December 2011 and 31 December 2010. All financial liabilities of the company were categorised as other financial liabilities at both 31 December 2011 and 31 December 2010.

SI 2008/410
1 Sch Formats,
FRS 29 p29(b)   **13 Current asset investments**

	Group		Company	
	2011 £m	2010 £m	2011 £m	2010 £m
Short-term deposits	25.3	55.3	–	48.7

FRS 29 p6   Short-term deposits are with major UK banks. The credit risk associated with these investments is considered to be low.

FRS 29p8(d),
25   **14 Available-for-sale investments**

	Group		Company	
	2011 £m	2010 £m	2011 £m	2010 £m
At 1 January	410.0	12.8	–	–
Exchange differences (note 27)	2.0	1.2	–	–
Additions	100.0	400.0	–	–
Disposals	(2.0)	–		
Revaluation surplus/(deficit) transfer to equity (note 27)	13.1	(4.0)	–	–
At 31 December	523.1	410.0	–	–

SI 2008/410
1Sch 40

		2011 £m	2010 £m

FRS 29 p16 There were no impairment provisions on the available-for-sale investments in 2011 or 2010.

SI 2008/410 1 Sch 23-26, FRS 29p27(b), 31, 34(c) Available-for-sale financial assets include the following:

	2011 £m	2010 £m
Listed securities:		
– Equity securities – UK	459.3	377.0
– Debentures with fixed interest of 6.5% and maturity date of 12 August 2011[1]	39.2	21.1
Unlisted securities:		
– Debt securities traded on inactive markets	24.6	11.9
	523.1	410.0

FRS 29 p27(a) The fair values of unlisted securities are based on cash flows discounted using a rate based on the market interest rate and the risk premium specific to the unlisted securities 2011: 6% (2010: 5.8%).

	2011 £m	2010 £m
Listed securities:		
– Equity securities - UK	443.2	367.0
– Debentures with fixed interest of 6.5% and maturity date of 12 August 2011	35.2	21.1
Unlisted securities:		
–Debt securities	21.6	11.9
	500.0	400.0

SI 2008/410 1 Sch Formats ## 15 Debtors

	Group		Company	
	2011 £m	2010 £m	2011 £m	2010 £m
	Amounts falling due within one year:			
FRS 29p36 Trade debtors	230.2	100.6	–	–
Less: Provision for impairment of receivables	(8.0)	(7.0)	–	–
	222.2	93.6	–	–
Amounts owed by group undertakings	–	–	67.1	55.4
FRS 9 p55 Amounts owed by joint ventures (*all trading balances*)	1.3	1.5	–	–
Amount due on sale of subsidiary (note 32(c))	15.7	–	–	–
Other debtors (see below)	39.4	5.8	–	–
SI 2008/410 1 Sch Formats Prepayments and accrued income	12.0	8.7	–	–
Dividends due from group undertakings	–	–	1.2	45.6
	290.6	109.6	68.3	101.0

FRS 29p25, 29(a) The carrying amount of debtors is a reasonable approximation to fair value.

SI 2008/410 1 Sch Formats *Notes:*
The amount falling due after more than one year must be shown separately for each item included within debtors.

UITF 4 p3 *Debtors due after one year must be disclosed separately on the face of the balance sheet if material to net current assets.*

Other debtors at 31 December 2011 include £7,000 in respect of loans to two officers of the company.

	2011 £m	2010 £m
3 to 6 months past due	8.5	7.3
Over 6 months past due	1.5	1.9
	10.0	9.2

FRS 29 p37(b) The debtors determined as individually impaired were mainly wholesalers, which are in unexpected difficult economic situations; it was assessed that not all of the debtor balance may be recovered.

FRS 29 p37(a) FRS 29 p36 Trade debtors that are less than three months past their due date are not considered impaired. As of 31 December 2011, trade debtors of carrying value of £7.0m (2010: £5.8m) were past their due date but not impaired. These are balances from a number of independent customers and there is no history of defaults for these customers recently. The ageing of the trade debtors, which are past due but not impaired is the following:

[1] Effective interest rate was 7.3%.

	2011 £m	2010 £m
Up to 3 months past due	2.6	2.2
3 to 6 months past due	0.9	0.7
Over 6 months past due	3.5	2.9
	7.0	5.8

FRS 29 p31 Concentration of credit risk with respect to trade receivables is limited due to the group's customer base being large and unrelated. Management therefore believes there is no further credit risk provision required in excess of normal provision for doubtful receivables.

FRS 29 p36(c)) The credit quality of trade debtors that are neither past due nor impaired is assessed by reference to external credit ratings where available. Where no external credit rating is available, historical information about counterparty default rates is used.

Trade debtors that are neither past due nor impaired are shown by their credit risk below.

	2011 £m	2010 £m
Counterparties with external credit rating:		
A	56.7	20.3
BB	17.0	4.8
BBB	40.9	7.3
	114.6	32.4
Counterparties with no external credit rating:		
New customers (less than 6 months)	23.4	13.9
Existing customers with no defaults in the past	49.5	26.7
Existing customers with some defaults in the past	25.7	12.6
	98.6	53.2
Total neither past due nor impaired	213.2	85.6

FRS 29 p36(d) None of those trade debtors that are neither past due nor impaired have had their terms re- negotiated.

FRS 29 p31, 34(c) The carrying amounts of the group's debtors are denominated in the following currencies:

	2011 £m	2010 £m
Pounds	210.6	78.7
Euros	19.6	9.7
US dollars	50.4	15.2
Other currencies	10.0	6.0
	290.6	109.6

FRS 29 p16 Movements on the provision for impairment of trade debtors are as follows:

	2011 £m	2010 £m
At 1 January	7.0	6.0
FRS 29 p20(e) Provision for debtors impairment	22.3	18.6
Debtors written off during the year as uncollectible	(20.8)	(17.4)
Unused amounts reversed	(0.5)	(0.2)
At 31 December	**8.0**	7.0

FRS 29 p16 The other classes within debtors do not contain impaired assets nor items past due date. Of the amounts due in other classes, £34.6m (2010: £4.4m) have a credit rating of BB or better. The remaining £11.8m (2010: £2.9m) do not have external credit ratings but are long established customers of the company with no history of default.

SI 2008/410
1 Sch Formats,
FRS 29 p8(f)

16 Creditors – Amounts falling due within one year

	Group		Company	
	2011	2010	2011	2010
	£m	£m	£m	£m
Bank and other borrowings (note 18)	92.2	41.7	53.4	43.6
Trade creditors	55.7	15.3	–	–
Amounts owed to group undertakings	–	–	45.0	24.7
Amounts owed to joint ventures (all trading balances)	2.4	1.8	–	–
Corporation tax	60.2	29.4	1.4	–
Taxation and social security	38.7	20.5	–	–
Other creditors	45.7	7.4	–	–
Derivative financial instruments (note 19)	10.1	(10.7)	–	–
Accruals and deferred income	96.2	9.9	–	–
	401.2	136.7	99.8	68.3

FRS 9 p55 (Amounts owed to group undertakings)
SI 2008/410 1 Sch Formats (Corporation tax)
SI 2008/410 1 Sch Formats (Other creditors)
FRS 29 p8(e) (Derivative financial instruments)
FRS 12 p11(b) (Accruals and deferred income)

FRS 9 p55

Note:

Amounts owed to (or owing from) an associate or joint venture should be analysed between loans and trading balances, if applicable.

SI 2008/410
1 Sch Formats

17 Creditors – Amounts falling due after more than one year

	Group		Company	
	2011	2010	2011	2010
	£m	£m	£m	£m
Bank and other borrowings (note 18)	816.5	417.9	240.5	17.0
Deferred consideration for acquisitions	0.8	0.6	–	–
Derivative financial instruments (note 19)	5.7	6.4	–	–
Other creditors	42.5	3.0	–	–
	865.6	427.9	240.5	17.0

FRS 29 p8(e) (Derivative financial instruments)

FRS 9 p55

Note:

Amounts owed to (or owing from) an associate or joint venture should be analysed between loans and trading balances, if applicable.

18 Bank and other borrowings

	Group		Company	
	2011	2010	2011	2010
	£m	£m	£m	£m
Due within one year or on demand:				
Bank loans and overdrafts				
Secured (a)	21.2	–	–	–
Unsecured (b)	66.4	41.6	53.4	43.6
	87.6	41.6	53.4	43.6
Unsecured debenture loans due within one year (c)	1.3	0.1	–	–
Finance lease obligations	3.3	–	–	–
	92.2	41.7	53.4	43.6
Due after more than one year				
Bank loans:				
Secured (a)	0.1	–	–	–
Unsecured (b)	738.6	414.0	237.5	14.0
	738.7	414.0	237.5	14.0
Debenture loans (d)	65.0	–	–	–
Other unsecured loans	–	0.9	–	–
Finance lease obligations	9.8	–	–	–
Cumulative preference shares of £1 each 2,000,000 shares	3.0	3.0	3.0	3.0
	816.5	417.9	240.5	17.0
Total borrowings	908.7	459.6	293.9	60.6

SI 2008/410 1 Sch 61(4) (Secured (a) within one year)
SSAP 21 p51 (Finance lease obligations within one year)
SI 2008/410 1 Sch 61 (4) (Secured (a) after one year)
SSAP 21 p51 (Finance lease obligations after one year)

**SI 2008/410
1 Sch 61(4)**

(a) The secured bank loans and overdrafts are secured by a fixed charge over the group's freehold property in Exeter and by floating charges over the remaining assets of GAAP UK Group Limited.

(b) Group and company unsecured bank loans are stated net of unamortised issue costs of £4.2m (2010: £nil). The company incurred total issue costs of £5.3m in respect of the five-year committed multi-option facility entered into in June 2011 under which amounts have been drawn down to fund the acquisition of Newsub plc. These costs together with the interest expense are allocated to the profit and loss account over the five year term of the facility. Interest is calculated using the effective interest rate method.

(c) Debenture loans represents 6.5% unsecured loan stock, which is redeemable at par on 1 July 2014. Debenture loans issued during the year are stated at net proceeds.

(d) The debenture loans represent US$110m 7% bonds due 2013.

**SI 2008/410
1 Sch 61(2)**

Bank loans are denominated in a number of currencies and bear interest based on LIBOR or foreign equivalents, or government bond rates appropriate to the country in which the borrowing is incurred. In June 2011, as part of the interest rate management strategy, the company entered into one interest rate swap (2010: none) for a notional principal amount of £100m maturing in 2015. Under this swap, the company receives interest on a variable basis and pays interest fixed at a rate of 8.8%.

The group's borrowing limit at 31 December 2011 calculated in accordance with the Articles of Association was £973m (2010: £331m).

FRS 29 p31

The exposure of the group's borrowings to interest rate changes and the contractual repricing dates at the balance sheet are as follows.

	2011 £m	2010 £m
6 months or less	85.1	40.0
6-12 months	3.8	1.7
1-5 years	457.1	62.3
Over 5 years	362.7	355.6
	908.7	459.6

FRS 29 p25

The carrying amounts and fair value of the borrowings due after more than one year are as follows:

	Group carrying amount 2011 £m	Group carrying amount 2010 £m	Group fair value 2011 £m	Group fair value 2010 £m
Bank borrowings	738.7	417.9	730.2	411.7
Preference shares	3.0	–	2.9	–
Debentures and other loans	74.8	–	73.9	–
	816.5	417.9	807.0	411.7

	Company 2011 Book value £m	Company 2011 Fair value £m	Company 2010 Book value £m	Company 2010 Fair value £m
Long-term borrowings	(237.5)	(205.6)	(14.0)	(12.6)
Preference shares	(3.0)	(2.9)	(3.0)	(2.9)
	(240.5)	(208.5)	(17.0)	(15.5)

FRS 29 p27(a) The fair values are based on cash flows discounted using a rate based on the borrowing rate of 7.5% (2010: 7.2%).

FRS 29 p25 The carrying amounts of short-term borrowings approximate their fair value.

**FRS 29 p31,
34(c)** The carrying amounts of the group's borrowings are denominated in the following currencies:

	2011 £m	2010 £m
Pounds	762.4	364.8
US dollars	71.3	8.1
Euros	53.4	54.0
Other currencies	21.6	32.7
	908.7	459.6

Borrowing facilities

DV FRS 29 p50(a)
The group has the following undrawn committed borrowing facilities available at 31 December 2011 in respect of which all conditions precedent had been met at that date.

| | 2011 | | |
	Floating rate £m	Fixed rate £m	Total £m
Expiring within 1 year	110.5	–	110.5
Expiring between 1 and 2 years	199.1	323.5	522.6
Expiring in more than 2 years	100.0	–	100.0
	409.6	**323.5**	**733.1**

The facilities expiring within one year are annual facilities subject to review at various dates during 2012. The other facilities have been arranged to help finance the proposed expansion of the group's activities into Continental Europe. All these facilities incur commitment fees at market rates.

Note:
Where a company has issued convertible debt, that debt should be shown separately from other liabilities. Where such convertible debt is not shown separately on the face of the balance sheet but instead is shown separately in the notes, the relevant caption for liabilities in the balance sheet should state that convertible debt is included.

Preference share capital – authorised, issued and fully paid

| | | 2011 | |
Group and company		Shares	£m
FRS 25 p 15 7% cumulative preference shares of £1 each at 1 January		2,000,000	3.0
FRS 25 p 18(a) At 31 December SI 2008/410 1 Sch 47(2)		2,000,000	3.0

The 7% cumulative preference shares, which do not carry any voting rights, were issued in 2005 at £1.50 per share and are redeemable at £1.50 at the option of the shareholders on 1 June 2015. Shareholders are entitled to receive dividends at 7% per annum on the par value of these shares on a cumulative basis; these dividends are payable on 22 December each year. On winding up, the preference shareholders rank above ordinary shareholders and are entitled to receive £1 per share and any dividends accrued but unpaid in respect of their shares. In the event that dividends on the preference share are in arrears for six months or more, holders of the preference shares become entitled to vote at general meetings of members.

SSAP 21 p 51, 52
The minimum lease payments under finance leases fall due as follows:

	2011 £m	2010 £m
Less than one year	3.3	4.4
Later than one year but no more than two	3.7	2.0
In more than two years but no more than five years	6.1	1.0
	13.1	7.4
SSAP 21 p53 Future finance charges on finance leases	–	–
Present value of finance lease liabilities	13.1	7.4

**FRS
29p39(a),(b)**

Maturity of financial liabilities

The maturity profile of the carrying amount of the group's liabilities, at 31 December was as follows:

	Debt £m	Finance leases £m	Other financial liabilities £m	2011 Total £m	2010 Total £m
Less than one year	88.9	3.3	–	**92.2**	41.7
In more than one year but no more than two years	94.0	3.7	–	**97.7**	10.0
In more than two years but no more than five years	347.0	6.1	–	**353.1**	52.3
In more than five years	362.7	–	3.0	**365.7**	355.6
	892.6	13.1	3.0	**908.7**	459.6

Company	2011 £m	2010 £m
Between two and five years	**237.5**	205.5
In more than five years	**3.0**	3.0
	240.5	208.5

	2011 £m	2010 £m
Amounts repayable otherwise than by instalment after more than five years	**250.0**	–

19 Derivative financial instruments

	2011		2010	
	Assets £m	Liabilities £m	Assets £m	Liabilities £m
At 31 December				
Interest rate swaps	**4.9**	**(7.9)**	3.1	(7.4)
Cross-currency swap – net investment hedge	**7.2**	**–**	1.8	–
Forward foreign currency contracts – cash flow hedge	**8.6**	**(2.2)**	2.2	(3.3)
Embedded derivative – operating lease renewal option	**–**	**(5.7)**	–	(6.4)
	20.7	**(15.8)**	7.1	(17.1)
Current portion	**8.6**	**(10.1)**	2.2	(10.7)
Non-current portion	**12.1**	**(5.7)**	4.9	(6.4)

In accordance with FRS 26, 'Financial instruments: Recognition and measurement', GAAP UK Group Limited has reviewed all contracts for embedded derivatives that are required to be separately accounted for if they do not meet certain requirements set out in the standard. In relation to the group head office, there is a renewal clause that determines the rent the group will pay from 2011 to 2020 based on a measure of the performance of construction companies as recorded in the London Stock Exchange. This is not cancellable or alterable without the payment of a significant penalty, which the directors believe would not be in the interests of the shareholders to pay. As at 1 January 2011, the fair value of this embedded derivative was a liability of £3.7m. This derivative is fair valued based on discounted future cash flows with gains and losses passing through the profit and loss account as hedge accounting is not available. Amounts recorded in the profit and loss account are shown below.

	2011 £m	2010 £m
Gain/(loss) in profit and loss	**0.7**	(2.7)

**FRS 29
p24(b,c)**

The ineffective portion recognised in the profit or loss that arose from cash flow hedges was not material in either 2011 or 2010. There was no ineffectiveness to be recorded from net investment in foreign operation hedges.

**FRS 29p23(a)
SI 2008/410
1 Sch 55(2)(b)**

The net fair value gains at 31 December 2011 on open forward foreign exchange contracts that hedge the foreign currency risk of anticipated future sales are £4.1m (2010: £2.3m). These will be transferred to the profit and loss account when the forecast sales occur over the next four months. There were no derivatives outstanding at the balance sheet date that were designated as fair value hedges.

Interest rate swaps

FRS 29p31

The notional principal amount of the outstanding interest rate swap contracts at 31 December 2011 was £100m (2010: £87m).

**FRS
29p23(a),22**

At 31 December 2011, the fixed interest rates vary from 3.3% to 8.8% and floating rates are 6.5% (LIBOR plus 275 basis points), 3.9% (US PRIME plus 215 basis points) and 4.5% (EUROBOR plus 200 basis points).

Hedge of net investment in foreign entity

FRS 29p22
SI 2008/410
1 Sch 35

The group has both dollar- and euro- denominated borrowings, which it has designated as a hedge of the net investment in its subsidiaries in the US and France. The fair value of the dollar borrowings at 31 December 2011 was £130.0m (2010: £120m), and the euro borrowings £32.1m (2010: £27.1m)

FRS 29p31

Fair values of non-derivative financial assets and financial liabilities

Where market values are not available, fair values of financial assets and financial liabilities have been calculated by discounting expected future cash flows at prevailing interest rates and by applying year end exchange rates. The carrying amounts of short-term borrowings approximate to book value.

SI 2008/410
1 Sch Formats

20 Provisions for liabilities

Group	Vacant properties £m	Restructuring £m	Environment £m	Deferred tax £m	Total £m
FRS 12 p89(a), At 1 January 2011 as previously reported	5.7	2.7	–	13.8	22.2
SI 2008/410 1 Sch 59(2)(a)					
FRS 6 p32 On acquisition (note 32)	68.1	3.8	18.3	22.5	112.7
Exchange adjustments (note 26)	(2.0)	(0.4)	–	–	(2.4)
FRS 12 p89(b) Charged to the profit and loss account	–	13.1	–	–	13.1
Utilised in year					
FRS 12 p89(c) – Existing	(0.5)	(15.2)	–	–	(15.7)
FRS 6 p32 – Acquired	(3.8)	(0.7)	–	–	(4.5)
FRS 12 p89(e) Amortisation of discount	0.3	–	0.1	–	0.4
FRS 19 p61 (c), Charged to the profit and loss account	–	–	–	37.2	37.2
SI 2008/410 1 Sch 59(2)(b)					
SI 2008/410 At 31 December 2011	67.8	3.3	18.4	73.5	163.0
1 Sch 59(2)(a), FRS 12 p89(a)					
Company					
SI 2008/410 At 1 January 2011	–	–	–	0.5	0.5
1 Sch 59					
FRS 19 p61(c), Charged to the profit and loss account	–	–	–	(0.4)	(0.4)
SI 2008/410 1 Sch 59(2)(b)					
At 31 December 2011	–	–	–	0.1	0.1

Vacant properties

FRS 12 p90(a), (b) Prior to the acquisition of Newsub plc, the group's vacant leasehold properties comprised the old Food Product's divisional head office in Swindon and a disused warehouse in Cleveland, Ohio. Full provision had been made for the residual lease commitments, together with other outgoings for the remaining period of the leases, which at 31 December 2011 is approximately 12 years. It is not expected that these premises will be sub-let.

FRS 12 p90(b) With the acquisition of Newsub plc, the group has inherited a substantial number of vacant and partly sub-let leasehold properties arising from the significant downsizing and retrenchment undertaken by Newsub plc in the early part of the decade. The properties are primarily located in London and Bradford in the UK, and Los Angeles in the US. Provision has been made for the residual lease commitments, together with other outgoings, after taking into account existing sub-tenant arrangements. It is not assumed that the properties will be able to be sub-let beyond the periods in the present sub-lease agreements. This has resulted in increasing the provision already made by Newsub plc to bring its provisioning policy in line with the group's and has been reflected as a fair value adjustment. Investigations are still being made as to the extent that there might be other contractual arrangements separate from the sub-lease agreements that enable the sub-lessees to terminate their leases early. Should the investigations prove this to be the case, it may be necessary to increase the amount of the provision. In determining the provision for Newsub plc's properties, the cash flows have been discounted on a pre-tax basis using appropriate government bond rates.

Maturity profile of provisions	2011 £m	2010 £m
Within 1 year	8.4	0.5
Between 1 and 2 years	16.8	1.0
Between 2 and 5 years	13.8	1.0
Over 5 years	28.8	3.2
	67.8	5.7

FRS 12 p90   **Restructuring**

FRS 12 p90(b) The £3.8m provision in 2011 arises in respect of a re-organisation commenced by Newsub plc in November 2010 of its healthcare activities. The restructuring of the healthcare activities involves the loss of 125 jobs at two factories and the closure of the site at Newark, New Jersey. Agreement had been reached in October 2010 with the local union representatives that specified the number of staff involved and quantified the amounts payable to those made redundant and customers and suppliers of the Newark site were informed in early November 2010. The associated impairment charge for the write-down of the property and other fixed assets at the Newark site was recognised in Newsub plc's financial statements for its year ended 31 March 2011, prior to the acquisition. As indicated in note 32, the level of provision at the date of Newsub plc's acquisition was reviewed and considered insufficient to cover the costs envisaged in the plans drawn up by Newsub plc's management. Consequently, an adjustment was made as part of the fair value exercise. The provision is expected to be fully utilised during the first half of 2012.

FRS 12 p90 A group company, UK GAAP Limited, announced on 11 December 2011 a rationalisation of product processes at two of its factories. A provision of £0.1m has been raised in respect of the redundancies that will occur over the next few months.

FRS 12 p90   **Environmental**

As part of the group's normal acquisition review procedures, Environmental Appraisers, Inc of San Francisco have been commissioned to ascertain the extent of land contamination of Newsub plc's operational sites in the US. The interim report received from the appraisers indicates that four sites require remediation to deal with chemical spills that have occurred over the last decade. A provisional estimate of the cost of the remediation has been made as part of the fair value exercise on the acquisition of Newsub plc (note 32). It is expected that the decontamination work will take three years to complete. In determining the provision, the cash flows have been discounted on a pre-tax basis using appropriate US Treasury bill rates.

Deferred tax

	Group		Company	
	2011	2010	2011	2010
	£m	£m	£m	£m
FRS 19 p61 Provision for deferred tax comprises:				
Accelerated capital allowances	**96.5**	10.8	**0.1**	0.6
Short-term timing differences	**(23.0)**	3.0	**–**	(0.1)
Deferred tax provision	**73.5**	13.8	**0.1**	0.5
Deferred tax liability on pension asset (note 34)	**5.8**	8.6	**–**	–
Provision at end of year including deferred tax on pension asset	**79.3**	22.4	**0.1**	0.5
Deferred tax liability relating to pension surplus				
1 January			**8.6**	9.8
Deferred tax charged/(credited) to profit and loss account			**–**	(1.3)
Deferred tax charged/(credited) to the statement of total recognised gains and losses:				
–on actuarial loss			**(2.8)**	0.1
– change in tax rate[1]			**–**	–
31 December			**5.8**	8.6

The deferred tax liability of £5.8m (2010: £8.6m) has been deducted in arriving at the net pension surplus on the balance sheet.

Factors that may affect future tax charges

In addition to the factors disclosed in note 6, the following factors may affect future tax charges.

FRS 19 p64(b) ■ No provision has been made for deferred tax on gains recognised on revaluing property to its market value or on the sale of properties where potentially taxable gains have been rolled over into replacement assets. Such tax would become payable only if the property were sold without it being possible to claim rollover relief. The total amount unprovided for is £5.8m. At present it is not envisaged that any such tax will become payable in the foreseeable future.

■ No deferred tax is recognised on the unremitted earnings of overseas subsidiaries, associates and joint ventures. As the earnings are continually reinvested by the group, no tax is expected to be payable on them in the foreseeable future. If tax were to be recognised, a provision of approximately £50m (2010: £40m) would have been required.

[1] The line item for change in tax rate is shown for illustrative purposes. Companies with 31 December 2011 year ends will need to consider the impact of the reductions in tax rates in the Finance Act 2011.

21 Called-up share capital

	Group and Company	
	2011	2010
SI 2008/410 1 Sch 47(1)(a) **Allotted, and fully paid**	**£m**	£m
SI 2008/410 1 Sch 47(1)(a) **Ordinary shares of 1p each**		
SI 2008/410 1 Sch Formats At 1 January – 887,125,690	**8.9**	8.8
SI 2008/410 1 Sch 48(b)(c) Allotted under share option schemes (10,008,001 shares)	**0.1**	0.1
SI 2008/410 1 Sch 48(b)(c) Allotted on acquisition of Newsub plc (486,586,318 shares)	**4.8**	–
At 31 December – 1,383,898,437 shares[1]	**13.8**	8.9

From 1 October 2009, the Companies Act 2006 abolished the requirement for a company to have an authorised share capital. Shareholders wishing to restrict the number of shares that can be issued by a company need to address this issue in the company's articles.

Potential issues of ordinary shares

SI 2008/410 1 Sch 49(1) FRS 20 p45(d)   Certain senior executives hold options to subscribe for shares in the company at prices ranging from 26.0p to 223.5p under the share option schemes approved by shareholders in October 2011 and September 2010. Options on 10,008,001 shares were exercised in 2011 and 70,300 options lapsed. The number of shares subject to options, the periods in which they were granted and the periods in which they may be exercised are given below.

Year of grant	Exercise price (pence)	Exercise period	2011 Numbers	2010 Numbers
2003	26.00	2004 – 2011	**197,777**	10,205,778
2005	50.00	2008 – 2012	**1,152,500**	1,152,500
2007	136.25	2010 – 2014	**3,182,866**	3,182,866
2010	185.75	2010 – 2015	**7,451,486**	7,451,486
2011	223.50	2011 – 2016	**8,630,316**	–
			20,614,945	21,992,630

SI 2008/410 1 Sch 49(1)   Under the group's long-term incentive plan for executive directors and former directors, such individuals hold rights over ordinary shares which may result in the issue of up to 466,439 1p ordinary shares by 2012.

22 Share-based payments

FRS 20 p45(a) FRS 20 p47(a)(i), FRS 20 p47(a)(iii)   The Executive Share Option Plan (ESOP) was introduced in January 2011. Under the ESOP the remuneration committee can grant options over shares in the company to employees of the group. Options are granted with a fixed exercise price equal to the market price of the shares under option at the date of grant. The contractual life of an option is 10 years. Awards under the ESOP are generally reserved for employees at senior management level and above; and 107 employees are currently eligible to participate in this group. There are no reload features. The company has made annual grants on 1 January each year since January 2010. Options granted under the ESOP will become exercisable on the third anniversary of the date of grant, subject to the growth in earnings per share over that period exceeding an average of inflation plus 3% (for awards in January 2010 and January 2011, 4%). Exercise of an option is subject to continued employment. Options were valued using the Black-Scholes option-pricing model. No performance conditions were included in the fair value calculations. The fair value per option granted and the assumptions used in the calculation are as follows:

FRS 20 p46 Grant date	01 Jan 2011	01 Jan 2010
Share price at grant date	**£2.235**	£1.8575
Exercise price	**£2.235**	£1.8575
Number of employees	**107**	85
Shares under option	**8,630,316**	7,451,486
Vesting period (years)	**3**	3
Expected volatility	**40%**	40%
Option life (years)	**10**	10
Expected life (years)	**5**	5
Risk-free interest rate	**4.80%**	4.80%
Expected dividends expressed as a dividend yield	**2.50%**	2.50%
Fair value per option	**£0.73**	£0.85

FRS 20 p47(a)(ii)   The expected volatility is based on historical volatility over the last three years. The expected life is the average expected period to exercise. The risk-free rate of return is the yield on zero-coupon UK government bonds of a term consistent with the assumed option life. A reconciliation of option movements over the year to 31 December 2011 is shown below:

[1] Included in the total are 178,428 1p ordinary shares allotted to directors under the group's long-term incentive plan (2010: 148,447 1p ordinary shares) with a nominal value of £1,784 (2010: £1,484). [SI 2008/410 1 Sch 48(b)(c)].

		2011		2010	
		Number (000)	Weighted average exercise price	Number (000)	Weighted average exercise price
FRS 20 p45(b)(i)	Outstanding at 1 January	21,993	£0.97	21,698	£0.49
FRS 20 p45(b)(ii)	Granted	8,630	£2.23	7,541	£1.86
FRS 20 p45(b)(iii)	Forfeited	–	–	(6,112)	£0.46
FRS 20 p45(b)(iv)	Exercised	(10,008)	£0.26	(1,134)	£0.50
FRS 20 p45(b)(vi)	Outstanding at 31 December	20,615	£1.85	21,993	£0.97
FRS 20 p45(b)(vii)	Exercisable at 31 December	1,350	£0.46	10,206	£0.26

FRS 20 p47(a) The weighted average fair value of options granted in the year was £6.3m (2010: £6.4m).

FRS 20 p45(d)

		2011				2010		
Range of exercise prices	Weighted average exercise price	Number of shares ('000)	Weighted average remaining life:		Weighted average exercise price	Number of shares ('000)	Weighted average remaining life:	
			Expected	Contrac-tual			Expected	Contrac-tual
£0.00 – £1.50	£1.37	4,246	1.5	7.0	£0.35	10,254	2.2	7.7
£1.50 – £2.50	£1.97	16,369	2.8	8.8	£1.58	11,739	3.3	9.3

FRS 20 p45(c),50,51(a) The weighted average share price during the period for options exercised over the year was £0.46 (2010: £0.26). The total charge for the year relating to employee share-based payment plans was £3.2m (2010: £1.4m), all of which related to equity-settled share-based payment transactions. After deferred tax, the total charge was £1.8m (2010: £2.2m).

23 Share premium account

	Group and Company	2011 £m	2010 £m
SI 2008/410 1 Sch 59	At 1 January	8.3	3.7
	Premium on shares issued during the year under the share option schemes	2.5	4.6
	At 31 December	10.8	8.3

24 Revaluation reserve

		Group £m	Company £m
SI 2008/410 1 Sch 5	At 1 January 2011	2.5	0.8
	Exchange adjustments	(0.2)	–
FRS 29 20(a)(ii)	Revaluation in year	5.4	1.5
	Transfer to profit and loss account	(0.2)	–
	At 31 December 2011	7.5	2.3

25 Profit and loss account

		Group £m	Company £m
	At 1 January 2011	141.5	154.6
	Net exchange adjustments	(80.4)	(1.4)
UITF 19 p9	Tax on exchange adjustments	3.5	–
	Profit for the financial year	25.4	9.2
	Dividend	(23.7)	(23.7)
	Adjustment in respect of employee share schemes	3.2	–
	Goodwill recycled on disposal of subsidiary	3.9	–
SI 2008/410 1 Sch 59(2)(b)	Transfer from revaluation reserve(note 24)	0.2	–
	Actuarial loss on pension scheme(note 34)	(22.2)	–
	Current tax deductions allocated to actuarial losses	3.6	–
	Movement on deferred tax relating to pension asset	2.8	–
	At 31 December 2011	57.8	138.7

SI 2008/410 6 Sch 14 FRS 10 p71(a)(ii) Cumulative goodwill relating to acquisitions made prior to 1999, which has been eliminated against reserves, amounts to £172.2m (2010: £176.1m).

FRS 2 p53 The reserves of subsidiary undertakings have generally been retained to finance their businesses. The ability to distribute £0.7m (2010: £1.2m) of consolidated retained profits of the group is restricted by exchange controls in certain countries.

Included in net exchange adjustments are exchange gains of £16.9m (2010: £2.4m) arising on borrowings denominated in, or swapped into, foreign currencies designated as hedges of net investments overseas.

26 Reconciliation of exchange differences recognised through the statement of total recognised gains and losses

FRS 23 p52(b)

	Note	2011 £m	2010 £m
Opening balance of cumulative exchange difference		8.9	(26.0)
Exchange adjustments on intangibles	8	32.6	26.3
Exchange adjustments on tangible fixed assets	9	27.2	24.1
Exchange adjustments on tangible fixed assets accumulated depreciation	9	(10.0)	(9.0)
Exchange adjustments on interests in joint ventures	10	0.9	1.5
Exchange adjustments on AFS investment	14	(2.0)	(1.2)
Exchange adjustments on provisions	19	(2.4)	(1.0)
Exchange adjustments on overseas subsidiaries		(69.4)	(5.8)
Closing balance of cumulative exchange differences		**(14.2)**	**8.9**

27 Other reserves

	Merger reserve £m	Other reserve £m	AFS revaluation reserve £m	Hedging reserve £m	Total £m
SI 2008/410 1 Sch 59, 40, 41 As at 1 January 2011	–	(4.2)	10.0	–	5.8
SI 2008/410 1 Sch 55(2)(b) Shares issued on acquisition of Newsub plc	933.6	–	–	–	933.6
Issue expenses	(1.4)	–	–	–	(1.4)
Exchange adjustments	–	(1.9)	2.0	–	0.1
FRS 29 p20(a)(ii) Net revaluation to AFS investments	–	–	13.1	–	13.1
Net movement on foreign currency cash flow hedge	–	–	–	4.5	4.5
Net movement on cross currency net investment hedge	–	–	–	5.0	5.0
Movement on other reserve	–	7.6	–	–	7.6
Net movement on interest rate swap	–	–	–	(2.1)	(2.1)
As at 31 December 2011	**932.2**	**1.5**	**23.1**	**7.4**	**964.2**

28 Cash flow from operating activities

FRS 1 p12 Reconciliation of operating profit to net cash inflow from operating activities:

	Group	
Continuing operations	2011 £m	2010 £m
Operating profit	104.0	76.3
Depreciation charge (net of profit on disposals)	77.7	15.5
Goodwill amortisation	40.2	–
Difference between pension charge and cash contributions	(8.0)	9.3
(Increase) in stocks	(2.7)	(3.3)
Decrease/(increase) in debtors	15.0	(3.1)
(Decrease) in creditors	(47.5)	(13.5)
Other non-cash changes	3.2	1.7
Net cash inflow from continuing operations	**181.9**	**82.9**
Discontinued operations		
Operating profit	2.2	27.1
Depreciation charge	5.8	6.2
Decrease in stocks	1.0	2.0
(Increase) in debtors	(3.8)	(4.9)
Increase in creditors	2.3	3.3
Net cash inflow from discontinued operations	**7.5**	**33.7**
Total net cash inflow from operating activities	**189.4**	**116.6**

29 Analysis of net debt

	As at 1 January 2011 £m	Cash flow £m	Acquisition (excluding Cash and overdrafts) £m	Other non-cash changes £m	Exchange movements £m	At 31 December 2011 £m
Cash in hand and at bank	40.5	40.1	–	–	(5.8)	74.8
Overdrafts	–	(92.0)	–	–	5.0	(87.0)
Debt due after 1 year	(417.9)	(328.3)	(65.8)	(1.1)	9.4	(803.7)
Debt due within 1 year	(41.7)	57.1	(17.5)	–	0.2	(1.9)
Finance leases due after 1 year	–	–	(17.8)	8.0	–	(9.8)
Finance leases due within 1 year	–	10.8	(6.1)	(8.0)	–	(3.3)
Liquid resources	455.3	8.3	50.1	(1.0)	35.7	548.4
Preference shares	(3.0)	–	–	–	–	(3.0)
	33.2	(304.0)	(57.1)	(2.1)	44.5	(285.5)

FRS 1 p33 — left margin reference for the table.

FRS 1 p26

Liquid resources comprise short-term deposits with banks which mature within 12 months of the date of inception and current asset investments that are traded in an active market.

Non-cash charges comprise amortisation of issue costs relating to debt issues and transfers between categories of finance leases.

Movement in borrowings	£m	£m
Debt due within 1 year:		
Repayment of part of bank loan	–	(57.1)
Debt due after 1 year:		
New secured bank loan	321.2	–
New unsecured bank loan	100.0	–
Repayment of part of bank loan	(87.6)	333.6
Increase in borrowings	–	276.5
Issue costs of new bank loan	–	(5.3)
	–	271.2
Capital element of finance lease payment	–	(10.8)
Cash inflow	–	260.4

30 Cash flow relating to exceptional items

FRS 1 p37

Operating cash flows include under continuing operations an outflow of £8.5m which relates to the reorganisation costs of £9.1m incurred in integrating Newsub plc. The balance of £0.6m was paid in January 2012. In addition, operating cash flows from continuing operations includes an outflow of £3.5m in respect of product remediation costs.

31 Major non-cash transactions

FRS 1 p46

Part of the consideration for the purchase of Newsub plc comprised shares. Further details of the acquisition are set out in note 32.

32 Acquisitions and disposals

(a) Acquisition of Newsub plc

SI 2008/410 6 Sch 13(2) FRS 6 p21

The group purchased three companies during the year for a total consideration of £1,239.4m, of which £1,234.7m was in respect of the acquisition on 30 June 2011 of Newsub plc. The total adjustments required to the book values of the assets and liabilities of the companies acquired in order to present the net assets of those companies at fair values in accordance with group accounting principles were £106.2m, of which £105.5m related to Newsub plc, details of which are set out together with the resultant amount of goodwill arising. All of these purchases have been accounted for as acquisitions.

FRS 6 p29 FRS 1 p45

Newsub plc contributed £77.0m to the group's net operating cash flows, paid £17.4m in respect of interest, £8.6m in respect of taxation and utilised £63.4m for capital expenditure.

FRS 6 p35 In its last financial year to 31 March 2011, Newsub plc made a profit after tax and minority interests of £56.6m. For the period since that date to the date of acquisition, Newsub plc management accounts show the following:

	£m
FRS 6 p36,83 Turnover	94.3
Operating profit	4.0
Profit before taxation	2.9
Taxation and minority interests	(1.2)
Profit attributable to shareholders	1.7
Exchange adjustments	(0.3)
Total recognised gains for the period	1.4

SI 2008/410 6 Sch 13 (4)	Newsub plc acquisition	Book value £m	Revaluations £m	Consistency of accounting policy £m	Other £m	Provisional fair value £m
FRS 6 p25	Intangible fixed assets	7.9	–	(7.9)	–	–
	Tangible fixed assets	330.5	(18.1)	–	–	312.4
	Investments in joint ventures	17.5	(1.9)	(1.6)	–	14.0
	Stocks	15.3	(1.7)	–	–	13.6
	Debtors	206.9	6.9	(0.3)	–	213.5
	Creditors	(244.2)	–	(3.4)	(30.9)	(278.5)
	Provisions:					
	– Vacant property	(13.9)	–	(54.2)	–	(68.1)
	– Environmental	–	–	–	(18.3)	(18.3)
	– Pre-acquisition restructuring	(1.0)	–	–	(2.8)	(3.8)
	Taxation					
	– Current	(6.2)	–	–	–	(6.2)
	– Deferred	(53.9)	–	–	31.4	(22.5)
	Cash	10.3	–	–	–	10.3
	Overdrafts	(25.7)	–	–	–	(25.7)
	Loans net of deposits	(54.0)	(3.1)	–	–	(57.1)
		189.5	(17.9)	(67.4)	(20.6)	83.6
	Minority interests	(0.8)	0.4	–	–	(0.4)
	Net assets acquired	188.7	(17.5)	(67.4)	(20.6)	83.2
	Goodwill					1,151.5
	Consideration					1,234.7

SI 2008/410 6 Sch 13(3)	**Consideration satisfied by:**	
FRS 6 p24	Shares issued (net of issue costs of £1.4m	932.2
FRS 1 p45	Cash	302.5
		1,234.7

FRS 6 p25
SI 2008/410
6 Sch 13(4)
FRS 6 p27

The book values of the assets and liabilities have been taken from the management accounts of Newsub plc at 30 June 2011 (the date of acquisition) at actual exchange rates on that date. The fair value adjustments contain some provisional amounts, as indicated below, which will be finalised in the 2012 financial statements when the detailed acquisition investigation has been completed.

Revaluation adjustments in respect of tangible fixed assets comprise the valuations of certain freehold properties.

Revaluations of investments and stocks reflect the write-down to estimated realisable value. The revaluation adjustment to debtors includes a revision to the bad debt provision to reflect an adjustment for an amount distributed in respect of a customer in receivership.

The revaluation of loans relates to an adjustment of £3.1m in order to reflect current market rate of interest on the Newsub plc US-dollar bond. Other adjustments to creditors of £30.9m relate to liabilities that were not fully reflected in the balance sheet of Newsub plc at the date of acquisition. These include adjustments to increase the creditor amounts for certain insurance and legal claims to reflect their final settlement shortly after 30 June 2011.

The fair value adjustment for alignment of accounting policies reflects the restatement of assets and liabilities in accordance with the group's policies including: the removal of capitalised in- store marketing costs (£7.9m); provision for the group's share of deferred consideration payable by an associated company for the acquisition of a business (£1.6m); establishing a creditor for outstanding holiday pay entitlement of employees and the alignment of general bad debt provisioning policy.

A provisional adjustment (£18.3m) has been made for the remediation of Newsub plc operational sites in the US. The final report from Environment Appraisers, Inc. will not be available until April 2011 and further provision may be required.

The book values of the net assets acquired included provisions for reorganisation and restructuring costs amounting to £1.0m. These provisions were established by Newsub plc in November 2011 and relate to an irrevocable reorganisation commenced by Newsub plc management before the acquisition. However, on review at the time of acquisition, the provisions were considered to be insufficient to cover the expected costs and have been increased by £2.8m. The adjustment in respect of vacant property is discussed in note 20.

No deferred tax has been recognised on fair value adjustments on non-monetary fixed assets as there is no intention to sell the assets concerned. However, the book value of deferred tax liability of £53.9m was reduced by a net deferred asset of £31.4m in respect of various fair value adjustments arising on the acquisition in accordance with FRS 19.

(b) Other acquisitions

	£m
Book value of net assets acquired (includes £0.3m cash)	0.2
Fair value adjustments	(0.7)
Goodwill	5.2
Consideration satisfied by cash	4.7

FRS 6 p21
SI 2008/410 6 Sch 13(2)

Co Limited and Sub SA were acquired by GAAPsub Ltd on 6 May 2011 and 12 July 2011 respectively. Fair value adjustments of £0.7m were made to align accounting policies in respect of fixed assets (£0.2m), stock (£0.2m) and creditors (£0.3m).

SI 2008/410 6 Sch 15

(c) Disposal of H Limited

	£m
Tangible fixed assets	1.4
Stocks	2.5
Debtors	6.5
Creditors	(4.9)
Goodwill previously written off to reserves	3.9
	9.4
Profit on disposal (note 5)	6.3
Deferred cash consideration	15.7

FRS 2 p47

FRS 10 p71(c)(ii)

FRS 10 p54

FRS 1 p45

FRS 1 p45

H Limited contributed £7.5m to the net operating cash flows, and paid £0.8m in respect of net returns on investments and servicing of finance and £0.9m in respect of taxation.

33 Employees and directors

CA06 s411(5)

Staff costs for the group during the year	2011 £m	2010 £m
Wages and salaries	544.3	203.7
Social security costs	62.0	22.3
Other pension costs (note 34)	17.2	9.3
Defined contribution pension cost (note 34)	0.2	–
Cost of employee share schemes (note 22)	3.2	1.7
	626.9	237.0

FRS 20 p51(a) Cost of employee share schemes (note 22)

CA06 s411

Average monthly number of people (including executive directors) employedby the group	2011 number	2010 number
By business group		
Food products	18,630	7,602
Personnel services	5,789	138
Retail services	5,241	4,758
Distribution services	13,735	915
Property services	7,107	3,565
Health care	9,368	3,499
	59,870	20,477

47

		2011 £	2010 £
SI 2008/410 5 Sch 2(1)	Aggregate emoluments, gains on share options exercised and benefits under long-term incentive schemes	**200,000**	180,000
SI 2008/410 5 Sch 2(2) (a)(b)	Defined benefit scheme:		
	– Accrued pension at end of year	**30,000**	25,000
	– Accrued lump sum at end of year	**60,000**	50,000

SI 2008/410 5 Sch 2(3) (a)(b) The highest paid director exercised share options during the year and received shares under the executive long-term incentive scheme.

Notes:
Details should be given of all transactions or arrangements with the company or any subsidiary of it in which a person who was a director of the company or its holding company had a material interest.

SI 2008/410 5 Sch 3 *Details should be given of any excess retirement benefits of directors and past directors.*

SI 2008/410 5 Sch 4 *Details should be given of the aggregate of compensation paid to directors or past directors for loss of office, including retirement.*

SI 2008/410 5 Sch 5 *Details should be given of the aggregate of any consideration paid to or receivable by third parties for making available the services of any person while a director. This includes benefits other than in cash.*

34 Pension commitments

FRS 17 p77(a) SI 2008/410 1 Sch 63(4) The group has established a number of pension schemes around the world covering many of its employees. The principal funds are those in the UK: the GAAP UK Group Limited staff pension plan, the UK GAAP Limited pension scheme and the Newsub plc pension plan. The GAAP UK Group Limited staff pension plan and the UK GAAP Limited pension scheme are funded schemes of the defined benefit type, with assets held in separate trustee administered funds. The Newsub plc pension plan and schemes outside the UK are predominantly of the defined contribution type.

FRS 17 p77(a) The most recent actuarial valuations of the GAAP UK Group Limited staff pension plan and the UK GAAP Limited pension scheme were at 31 December 2011. The valuations of both schemes used the projected unit method and were carried out by Actuary & Actuary, professionally qualified actuaries. The principal assumptions for both plans made by the actuaries were as follows:

	2011 %	2010 %
FRS 17 p77(m) Rate of increase in pensionable salaries	**3.6**	3.0
FRS 17 p77(m) Rate of increase in pensions in payment and deferred pensions	**3.0**	4.0
FRS 17 p77(m) Discount rate	**6.0**	5.5
FRS 17 p77(m) Inflation assumption	**3.6**	3.3

FRS 17 p77(m) The mortality assumptions used in the group's actuarial valuations have been amended to assume that pensioners have a longer life expectancy. The mortality assumptions used in the valuation of the defined benefit pension liabilities of the group's UK plans are summarised in the table below and have been selected to reflect the characteristics and experience of the membership of those plans. This has been done by adjusting standard mortality tables which reflect recent research into mortality experience in the UK (PA 92 tables combined with the 2002 short cohort improvement factors) and the US (UP-94 tables using projection scale AA). In addition, the UK assumptions have been further adjusted to reflect the latest available trend information, which indicates that mortality relating in particular to blue-collar workers may not be improving as quickly as indicated by the standard tables. Based on an analysis of the mix of blue- and white-collar workers in the group's plan, the UK assumptions have been adjusted (using a scaling factor of 118.75%) to reflect a lower level of longevity amongst the blue collar membership.

	UK	
	2011 Years	2010 Years
Longevity at age 65 for current pensioners		
– Men	**20**	18
– Women	**22**	21
Longevity at age 65 for future pensioners		
– Men	**20**	19
– Women	**23**	22

The assets of the schemes and the weighted average expected rate of return were as follows:

	Long-term rate of return expected 31 December 2011 %	Value at 31 December 2011 £m	Long-term rate of return expected 31 December 2010 %	Value at 31 December 2010 £m
FRS 17 p77(i) Equities	7.9	140.6	8.4	116.6
FRS 17 p77(i) Bonds	5.4	94.2	5.6	81.0
Total market value of assets		234.8		197.6
Present value of scheme liabilities		(214.0)		(167.0)
FRS 17 p77(e) Surplus in the scheme		20.8		30.6
Related deferred tax liability[1]		(5.8)		(8.6)
FRS 17 p77(e) **Net pension asset**	15.0	22.0		

FRS 17 p77(b) Reconciliation of present value of scheme liabilities

	2011 £m	2010 £m
1 January	167.0	136.9
Current service cost	17.2	8.3
Past service cost	–	1.0
Interest cost	10.0	7.8
Benefits paid	(49.5)	(32.7)
Actuarial loss	69.3	45.7
31 December	214.0	167.0

Best Practice Sensitivity analysis of scheme liabilities

The sensitivity of the present value of scheme liabilities to changes in the principle assumptions used is set out below.

	Change in assumption	Impact on scheme liabilities
Discount rate	Increase/decrease by 1%	Increase/decrease by 9.5%
Rate of inflation	Increase/decrease by 1%	Increase/decrease by 4.5%
Rate of increase in salaries	Increase/decrease by 1%	Increase/decrease by 4.0%
Rate of increase in pensions in payment	Increase/decrease by 1%	Increase/decrease by 3.5%
Mortality	Increase by 1 year	Increase by 5.0%

FRS 17 p77(d) Reconciliation of fair value of scheme assets

	2011 £'000	2010 £'000
1 January	197.6	170.1
Expected return on scheme assets	14.4	11.8
Actuarial gains	47.1	48.4
Benefits paid	(49.5)	(32.7)
Contributions paid by employer	25.2	–
31 December	234.8	197.6

FRS 17 p77(j) Scheme assets do not include any of GAAP UK Group Limited own financial instruments or any property occupied by GAAP UK Group Limited.

FRS 17 p77(k) The expected return on scheme assets is determined by considering the expected returns available on the assets underlying the current investment policy. Expected yields on fixed interest investments are based on gross redemption yields as at the balance sheet date. Expected returns on equity investments reflect long-term real rates of return experienced in the respective markets.

FRS 17 p77(l) The actual return on scheme assets in the year was £61.5m (2010: £61.0m).

---

[1] The tax figures shown are for illustrative purposes only and do not reflect the actual tax rates or any remeasurement as a result of the change in tax rates in the Finance (No. 2) Act 2010.

FRS 17 p77(f) The amounts recognised in the profit or loss account are as follows:

	2011 £m	2010 £m
Current service cost	17.2	8.3
Past service cost	–	1.0
Expected return on pension scheme assets	(14.4)	(11.8)
Interest on pension scheme liabilities	10.0	7.8
Total charge	**12.8**	**5.3**

£12.6m (2010: £6.3m) of the current service cost is included within cost of sales, and £4.6m (2010: £2.0m) is included within administrative expenses.

FRS 17 p77(o) **Amounts for current period and previous four periods**

	2011	2010	2009	2008	2007
Defined benefit obligation	(214.0)	(167.0)	(136.9)	(120.0)	(115.8)
Plan assets	234.8	197.6	170.1	165.0	156.7
Surplus/(Deficit)	20.8	30.6	33.2	45.0	40.9
Experience adjustments on plan assets					
Amount (£m)	47.1	48.4	40.6	40.4	20.6
Experience adjustments on plan liabilities					
Amount (£m)	(12.3)	(14.7)	(15.9)	2.9	5.2

FRS 17 p77(g) **Total actuarial gains and losses recognised in statement of total recognised gains and losses**

	2011	2010	2009	2008	2007
Amount (£m)	(22.2)	2.7	7.8	6.3	(3.8)

FRS 17p75 The Newsub plc pension plan is a defined contribution plan. The contributions made to the plan from the date of acquisition were £242,000. (2010: £nil). At the end of the year, contributions of £21,000 (2010: £nil), representing the unpaid contributions for December 2011, were outstanding.

GAAP UK Group Limited has no employees (the members of the group defined benefit scheme are or were employed by subsidiaries of GAAP UK Group Limited); consequently, no defined benefit scheme disclosures are given for the company.

FRS 17 p77(p) The valuation at 31 December 2011 showed a decrease in the surplus from £30.6m to £20.8m. Improvements in benefits of £1m were made in 2010, and no additional improvements in benefits were made in 2011. From 1 January 2011, contributions were made to the pension scheme at a rate of 5% of pensionable salaries. It has been agreed with the trustees that contributions will remain at that level for the next three years.

35 Operating lease commitments

At 31 December 2011, the group has lease agreements in respect of properties, vehicles, plant and equipment, for which the payments extend over a number of years.

	2011 Property £m	2011 Vehicles, plant and equipment £m	2010 Property £m	2010 Vehicles, plant and equipment £m
SSAP 21 p56 **Annual commitments under non-cancellable operating leases expiring:**				
Within one year	1.1	0.6	0.3	0.3
Within two to five years	6.1	3.5	1.0	2.5
After five years	6.9	0.5	0.6	1.2
	14.1	4.6	1.9	4.0

36 Contingent liabilities

FRS 12 p91
SI 2008/410 1 Sch 73
FRS 9 p53 The company has guaranteed bank and other borrowings of subsidiary undertakings and, jointly with its co-investors, of joint ventures amounting to £2.7m (2010: £0.4m) and £3.7m (2010: £0.7m) respectively.

SI 2008/410 1 Sch 63(2)
FRS 12 p91 At 31 December 2011, the group was in dispute with one of its food suppliers over surcharges invoiced above the original contracted price for specialist ingredients. The directors are strongly resisting the payment of the surcharges and it is unlikely that the outcome of this dispute will have a material effect on the group's financial position.

37 Capital and other financial commitments

FRS 9 p53		Share of joint ventures		Group		Company	
		2011	2010	2011	2010	2011	2010
		£m	£m	£m	£m	£m	£m
SI 2008/410 1 Sch 63(3)	Contracts placed for future capital expenditure not provided in the financial statements	2.1	0.7	12.9	2.4	0.1	0.1
SSAP 21 p54	Commitments under finance leases entered into, but not yet provided for	1.0	–	6.7	–	–	–

38 Related-party transactions

FRS 8 p6,19
FRS 9 p55

During the year the group purchased food products from two joint ventures, ABC AG and DEF AG to the value of £19.5m (2010: £16.7m). At 31 December 2011 £2.4m (2010: £1.8m) was payable in respect of these purchases. During the year, the group sold healthcare products totalling £11.2m (2010: £13.4m) to HIJ SpA, a joint venture. At 31 December 2011 the outstanding balances receivable from HIJ SpA were £1.3m (2010: £1.5m).

CA06
s255(2)(5)
FRS 8 p6

Mrs S James, wife of Mr F James, a main board director and managing director of the healthcare division, owns the entire share capital of LMN Ltd. The nature of the business of the healthcare division necessitates the exporting of products to Saudi Arabia. LMN Ltd acts as an export agency on behalf of a group subsidiary company, OPQ Ltd. Throughout the year, CPS Inter Ltd has traded under the same terms as those available to other customers in the ordinary course of business. The value of export work performed during the year ended 31 December 2011 for OPQ Ltd amounted to £9.7m (2010: £8.4m). The amount owed to LMN Ltd at the year end amounted to £0.9m (2010: £0.8m).

39 Post balance sheet events

FRS 21 p21,
SI 2008/410
1 Sch 12(b)

On 15 February 2012, the company completed the purchase of RST, Inc for a total consideration of £75.1m. The company operates in North America providing healthcare services. At the date of acquisition it had estimated net assets of US$40m (£25m).

CA06 s409

40 Principal subsidiaries, joint ventures and associates

Subsidiary undertakings

Management should disclose the following:

SI 2008/410
4 Sch 1

Particulars of subsidiary undertaking:

(a) Name.

SI2008/410
4 Sch 17

(b) Country of incorporation, if incorporated outside Great Britain.

(c) If unincorporated, address of principal place of business.

SI2008/410 4
Sch 16(2)
SI2008/410 4
Sch 16(3)

(d) Description and proportion of the nominal value of the shares of each class distinguishing between shares held by the parent undertaking and those held by the group.

(e) Whether or not included in the consolidation and explain if not.

FRS 2 p34

(f) The specific definition of subsidiary undertaking that makes the undertaking a subsidiary – this need not be given if the reason is that the parent holds a majority of the voting rights and the proportion of shares and voting rights held are the same.

FRS 2 p33

(g) Where a subsidiary undertaking is consolidated on the basis of a participating interest with actual dominant influence, the basis of dominant influence.

(h) Proportion of voting rights held by group.

(i) Indication of nature of business.

Joint ventures and associates

For joint ventures and associates included in the group financial statements, give:

SI 2008/410
4 Sch 19
FRS 9 p52

(a) Name.

(b) Country of incorporation, if incorporated outside Great Britain.

(c) If unincorporated, address of principal place of business.

FRS 9 p52(a)

(d) The identity and proportion of each class of shares held by the parent company and by the group, indicating any special rights or constraints attaching to them.

FRS 9 p52(c)

(e) Indication of nature of business.

FRS 9 p52(b)

(f) The accounting period or date of the financial statements used if they differ from the group's.

FRS 9 p56

Notes:
An explanation should be given to each case where either of the following presumptions is rebutted:

(a) An investor holding 20% or more of the voting rights has significant influence.
(b) An investor holding 20% or more of the shares of another entity has a participating interest.

FRS 9 p53 *Disclosure should be made of any notes or matters that should have been noted, had the investor's accounting policies been applied, that are material to understanding the effect on the investor of its investments, particularly in respect of contingent liabilities and capital commitments.*

41 Ultimate parent company

FRS 8, 5, Sch 4, 8, 9 The directors regard UVW-US Inc, a company incorporated in the US, as the immediate and ultimate parent company and ultimate controlling party[1]. Copies of the consolidated financial statements of UVW-US Inc can be obtained from The Company secretary, UVW-US Inc, 589 Fourth Avenue, New York 59361.

FRS 8p3 Advantage has been taken of the exemption in FRS 8 not to disclose transactions with entities that are part of the UVW-Inc group.

---

[1] Where the entity is itself a subsidiary, whether consolidated accounts are required to be prepared or not, will depend of on whether the exemptions in the Companies Act 2006, section 401, have been satisfied. For the purposes these financial statements, we have assumed that the exemption criteria have not be satisfied.

UK GAAP Limited – Year ended 31 December 2011

The example annual report that follows includes the financial statements of UK GAAP Limited, a wholly-owned private subsidiary company. Although UK GAAP Limited meets the size criteria for a medium-sized company, it is ineligible due to its ultimate parent company, GAAP UK plc, being a plc, and therefore it does not qualify as a medium-sized company.

UK GAAP Limited is a fictitious company. The annual report has been prepared for illustrative purposes only and shows the disclosures and formats that might be expected for a company of its size that prepares its financial statements in accordance with the requirements of Part 15 of the Companies Act 2006 and 'The Large and Medium-sized Companies and Groups (Accounts and Reports) Regulations 2008' (SI 2008/410). The intention is not to show all conceivable disclosures and this annual report should not, therefore, be used as a checklist. The suggested disclosures are not necessarily applicable for all private companies. These financial statements include many of the disclosure requirements contained in current Financial Reporting Standards, Statements of Standard Accounting Practice, Urgent Issues Task Force Abstracts and Company Law, effective from 1 January 2011. Proposals included in exposure drafts at that date are not yet standard practice and have, therefore, not been reflected in these financial statements.

This illustrative annual report does not cover (amongst other items):

- Discontinued activities.
- Exceptional items.
- ESOP and similar share-based payment schemes where the entity's employees are recipients.
- Long-term contracts.
- Government grants.
- Investment properties.
- Sophisticated capital instruments.
- Impairment of fixed assets.
- Acquisition of a business.
- A cash flow statement.
- Share-based payment.

UK GAAP Limited does not apply the fair value accounting rules and therefore has not adopted FRS 23, FRS 26, FRS 29 or paragraphs 51 to 95 of FRS 25.

The GAAP UK Group Limited example financial statements are consolidated financial statements for a group of companies that include many of these items.

UK GAAP Limited

Example annual report for the year ended 31 December 2011

Contents

Directors' report

Directors' report for the year ended 31 December 2011

The directors present their report and the audited financial statements of the company for the year ended 31 December 2011.

Principal activities

The company's principal activity during the year was the manufacture and sale of processed foods and bakery products. The company's entire product areas continued to expand during the year but, because of difficult trading conditions, suffered a fall in profitability.

At the year end, the company was in a strong position to take advantage of suitable expansion opportunities that may arise.

Business review

The review should cover the following:

(a) a fair review of the company's business; and
(b) a description of the principal risks and uncertainties facing the company.

The review required is a balanced and comprehensive analysis of:

(a) the development and performance of the company's business during the financial year; and
(b) the company's position at the end of that year, consistent with the business size and complexity.

The review must, to the extent necessary for an understanding of the development, performance or position of the business, include:

(a) analysis using financial key performance indicators; and
(b) where appropriate, analysis using other key performance indicators, including information relating to environmental matters and employee matters.

Notes:

(a) Section 417 of the Companies Act requires this disclosure within the directors' report of all companies with the exception of small companies, which are exempt.
(b) For medium-sized companies, where these indicators relate to non-financial information, disclosure is not required. Where advantage has been taken of this exemption, this fact should be disclosed in the directors' report.

The review must, where appropriate, include references to, and additional explanations of, amounts included in the annual financial statements of the company.

Political and charitable contributions

If the company has made any political donation to any political party or other political organisation, any political donation to any independent election candidate or incurred any political expenditure and the amount of the donation/expenditure exceeded £2,000, disclose:

- the name of each political party, organisation, or independent election candidate to whom any such donation has been made;
- the total amount given to that party, organisation or candidate by way of such donations in the financial year; and
- the total amount incurred in respect of political expenditure in the financial year.

Wholly-owned subsidiaries of companies incorporated in the UK are exempt.

[7Sch 3]

If the company or its subsidiaries have made any contributions to a non-EU political party disclose:

- the amount of the contribution; or
- if it has made two or more contributions in the year, a statement of the total amount of the contribution.

A non-EU political party means any political party that carries on, or proposes to carry on, activities wholly outside Member States.

Wholly-owned subsidiaries of companies incorporated in the UK are exempt.

[7Sch 4]

If the company or its subsidiaries have given money for charitable purposes and the money given by the company and its subsidiaries exceeds £2,000 in amount, disclose in the case of each of the purposes for which the money was given, the amount of money given for that purpose.

Wholly-owned subsidiaries of companies incorporated in the UK are exempt.

Money given for charitable purposes to a person who, when it was given, was ordinarily resident outside of the UK is excluded from disclosure.

[7Sch5]

Shares

Where shares in a company are purchased or acquired by forfeiture or surrender in lieu of forfeiture, or in pursuance of s659 of the Act or s662(1) or where shares are subject to lien or charge under s670(2) or (4), disclose:

■ the number, nominal value and percentage of the called-up shares of that class of shares acquired or charged during the period and, if acquired by purchase, the consideration paid and reasons for purchase;

■ the maximum number, nominal value and percentage of the called-up shares of that class held or charged at any time during the period;

■ the number, nominal value and percentage of the called-up shares of that class so acquired or charged that have been disposed of or cancelled during the period, and the amount of the proceeds of disposal, if any and;

■ Where any shares have been so charged, the amount of the charge.

[7Sch8,9]

Future developments

An indication should be given of the likely future developments in the business of the company.

Financial risk management

The company's operations expose it to a variety of financial risks that include the effects of changes in debt market prices, credit risk, liquidity risk and interest rate risk. The company has in place a risk management programme that seeks to limit the adverse effects on the financial performance of the company by monitoring levels of debt finance and the related finance costs.

In order to ensure stability of cash out flows and hence manage interest rate risk, the company has a policy of maintaining 90 per cent of its debt (2010: 90 per cent) at fixed rate. The company seeks to minimise the risk of uncertain funding in its operations by borrowing within a spread of maturity periods. Given the size and nature of operations, the company's policy is to operate with 50 per cent of its debt being repayable within one year. At the year end, 52 per cent (2010: 43 per cent) of debt was repayable within one year. The company does not use derivative financial instruments to manage interest rate costs and as such, no hedge accounting is applied.

Given the size of the company, the directors have not delegated the responsibility of monitoring financial risk management to a sub-committee of the board. The policies set by the board of directors are implemented by the company's finance department. The department has a policy and procedures manual that sets out specific guidelines to manage interest rate risk, credit risk and circumstances where it would be appropriate to use financial instruments to manage these.

Price risk

The company is exposed to commodity price risk as a result of its operations. However, given the size of the company's operations, the costs of managing exposure to commodity price risk exceed any potential benefits. The directors will revisit the appropriateness of this policy should the company's operations change in size or nature.

Credit risk

Credit risk arises from cash and cash equivalents, and deposits with banks and financial institutions, as well as credit exposures to wholesale and retail customers, including outstanding receivables and committed transactions. For banks and financial institutions, only independently rated parties with a minimum rating of 'A' are accepted. If wholesale customers are independently rated, these ratings are used. If there is no independent rating, risk control assesses the credit quality of the customer, taking into account its financial position, past experience and other factors. Individual risk limits are set based on internal or external ratings in accordance with limits set by the board. The utilisation of credit limits is regularly monitored. The amount of exposure to any individual counterparty is subject to a limit, which is reassessed annually by the board.

Liquidity risk

The company actively maintains a mixture of long-term and short-term debt finance that is designed to ensure the company has sufficient available funds for operations and planned expansions.

Interest rate cash flow risk

The company has both interest-bearing assets and interest-bearing liabilities. Interest-bearing assets include only government securities and cash balances, all of which earn interest at fixed rate. The company has a policy of maintaining debt at fixed rate to ensure certainty of future interest cash flows. The directors will revisit the appropriateness of this policy should the company's operations change in size or nature.

Note: This disclosure is required by Schedule 7(6) to SI 2008/410. It is not required where such information is not material for the assessment of the entity's assets, liabilities, financial position and profit or loss. In addition, an exemption from making these disclosures is available to small companies.

Results and dividends

The company's profit for the financial year is £243,000 (2010: £519,000). An interim dividend of 3.51p (2010: 2.57p) per ordinary share, amounting to £71,000 (2010: £52,000) was paid on 1 September 2011. A final dividend of 5.0p (2010: 3.32p) per ordinary share amounting to £102,000 (2010: £67,000) is proposed and, if approved, will be paid on 6 April 2011. The company also paid a preference dividend amounting to £2,625 (2010: £2,625). The aggregate dividends on the ordinary shares recognised as an expense during the year amounts to £138,000 (2010: £52,000) excluding proposed dividends that have yet to be approved by the balance sheet date.

Directors

The directors who held office during the year and up to the date of signing the financial statements are given below:

C D Jones   (Chairman)
E F Logan (resigned 6 July 2011)
J F King
I D Davies (appointed 31 July 2011)

Qualifying third-party and pension scheme indemnity provisions

The directors' report should disclose whether:

(a) *at the time the report is approved any qualifying third-party indemnity provision and/or qualifying pension scheme indemnity provision (whether made by the company or otherwise) is in place for the benefit of one or more of the directors or one or more directors of an associated company; or*

(b) *at any time during the year any such provision was in force for the benefit of one or more persons who were then directors or directors of an associated company.*

Research and development

The company is currently undertaking research and development into a new form of processed food based on soya beans.

Note: It is good practice to comment on the charge in the profit and loss account.

Differences between market and balance sheet value of land

In the opinion of the directors, the difference between the market value and balance sheet value of land is not significant.

Note: For the purpose of this disclosure, 'land' includes the buildings and other structures. Where there is a significant difference, it should be shown with such degree of precision as is practicable.

Post balance sheet events

Particulars of any important events affecting the reporting entity that have occurred since the end of the financial year must be disclosed.

Purchase of own shares and sale of treasury shares

Where the company has an interest in its own shares, the directors' report should provide a number of disclosures, including:

- *the number and nominal value of shares purchased;*
- *the percentage of the called-up share capital which those shares represent;*
- *the aggregate consideration paid; and*
- *the reason for the purchase.*

Employees

Applications for employment by disabled persons are always fully considered, bearing in mind the respective aptitudes and abilities of the applicant concerned. In the event of members of staff becoming disabled, every effort is made to ensure that their employment with the company continues and the appropriate training is arranged. It is the policy of the company that the training, career development and promotion of a disabled person should, as far as possible, be identical to that of a person who does not suffer from a disability.
Note: This disclosure is required if the average number of employees during the year and working within the UK exceeds 250.

Consultation with employees or their representatives has continued at all levels, with the aim of ensuring that their views are taken into account when decisions are made that are likely to affect their interests and that all employees are aware of the financial and economic performance of their business units and of the company as a whole. Communication with all employees continues through the in-house newspaper and newsletters, briefing groups and the distribution of the annual report.

Note: Where employee involvement in the company's performance is encouraged through an employee share scheme or some other means, details should be provided.

This disclosure is required if the average number of employees during the year and working within the UK exceeds 250.

Policy and practice on payment of creditors

The company is a registered supporter of the Better Payment Practice Group's 'Better Payment Practice Code' to which it subscribes when dealing with all of its suppliers. Copies of the Better Payment Practice Group's code are available from the Department for Business, Innovation & Skills (BIS). Trade creditors at the year end represented 34 days (2010: 34 days) of purchases. It is the company's policy in respect of all suppliers to agree payment terms in advance of the supply of goods and to adhere to those payment terms.

Note: This disclosure is voluntary for UK GAAP Limited because a company that is medium in size under Section 465 of the 2006 Act, within a group of which the parent is a public company is exempt under paragraph 12(1)(b) of Schedule 7 to SI 2008/410, is exempt from this disclosure requirement. This disclosure is, however, required for any company that was at any time within the financial year a public company or a large private subsidiary of a plc. Large private companies are those that exceed the limits in section 465 of the Companies Act 2006.

Statement of directors' responsibilities

The directors are responsible for preparing the directors' report and the financial statements in accordance with applicable law and regulations.

Company law requires the directors to prepare financial statements for each financial year. Under that law, the directors have prepared the financial statements in accordance with United Kingdom Generally Accepted Accounting Practice (United Kingdom Accounting Standards and applicable law). Under company law, the directors must not approve the financial statements unless they are satisfied that they give a true and fair view of the state of affairs of the company and of the profit or loss of the company for that period. In preparing these financial statements, the directors are required to:

- select suitable accounting policies and then apply them consistently;
- make judgements and accounting estimates that are reasonable and prudent;
- state whether applicable UK Accounting Standards have been followed, subject to any material departures disclosed and explained in the financial statements; and
- prepare the financial statements on the going concern basis unless it is inappropriate to presume that the company will continue in business.

The directors are responsible for keeping adequate accounting records that are sufficient to show and explain the company's transactions and disclose with reasonable accuracy at any time the financial position of the company and enable them to ensure that the financial statements comply with the Companies Act 2006. They are also responsible for safeguarding the assets of the company and hence for taking reasonable steps for the prevention and detection of fraud and other irregularities.

Disclosure of information to auditors

Note: Section 418(1) to (4) of the Companies Act 2006 requires this disclosure within the directors' report. This section is applicable unless the directors have taken advantage of the exemption conferred by section 477(1) or 480(1). The report must contain a statement to the effect that, in the case of each of the persons who are directors at the time when the report is approved, the following applies:

- *so far as the director is aware, there is no relevant audit information of which the company's auditor is unaware; and*
- *he has taken all the steps that he ought to have taken as a director in order to make himself aware of any relevant audit information and to establish that the company's auditor is aware of that information.*

Independent auditors

The auditors, PricewaterhouseCoopers LLP, have indicated their willingness to continue in office and a resolution concerning their re-appointment will be proposed at the Annual General Meeting.

By order of the board

J F King
Company secretary 12 March 2012

Independent auditors' report to the members of UK GAAP Limited

Warning – *This audit report was current at the date of going to press. However, it may not be the most up-to-date version. It should not be used without checking that it is the appropriate version.*

We have audited the financial statements of UK GAAP Limited for the year ended 31 December 2011, which comprise the profit and loss account, the balance sheet, the statement of total recognised gains and losses and the related notes. The financial reporting framework that has been applied in their preparation is applicable law and United Kingdom Accounting Standards (United Kingdom Generally Accepted Accounting Practice).

Respective responsibilities of directors and auditors

As explained more fully in the statement of directors' responsibilities set out in the directors' report, the directors are responsible for the preparation of the financial statements and for being satisfied that they give a true and fair view. Our responsibility is to audit and express an opinion on the financial statements in accordance with applicable law and International Standards on Auditing (UK and Ireland). Those standards require us to comply with the Auditing Practices Board's Ethical Standards for Auditors.

This report, including the opinions, has been prepared for and only for the company's members as a body in accordance with Chapter 3 of Part 16 of the Companies Act 2006 and for no other purpose. We do not, in giving these opinions, accept or assume responsibility for any other purpose or to any other person to whom this report is shown or into whose hands it may come save where expressly agreed by our prior consent in writing.

Scope of the audit of the financial statements

An audit involves obtaining evidence about the amounts and disclosures in the financial statements sufficient to give reasonable assurance that the financial statements are free from material misstatement, whether caused by fraud or error. This includes an assessment of: whether the accounting policies are appropriate to the company's circumstances and have been consistently applied and adequately disclosed; the reasonableness of significant accounting estimates made by the directors; and the overall presentation of the financial statements. In addition, we read all the financial and non-financial information in the Annual Report to identify material inconsistencies with the audited financial statements. If we become aware of any apparent material misstatements or inconsistencies we consider the implications for our report

Opinion on financial statements

In our opinion the financial statements:

- give a true and fair view of the state of the company's affairs as at 31 December 2011 and of its profit for the year then ended;
- have been properly prepared in accordance with United Kingdom Generally Accepted Accounting Practice; and
- have been prepared in accordance with the requirements of the Companies Act 2006.

Opinion on other matter prescribed by the Companies Act 2006

In our opinion, the information given in the directors' report for the financial year for which the financial statements are prepared is consistent with the financial statements.

Matters on which we are required to report by exception

We have nothing to report in respect of the following matters where the Companies Act 2006 requires us to report to you if, in our opinion:

- adequate accounting records have not been kept, or returns adequate for our audit have not been received from branches not visited by us; or
- the financial statements are not in agreement with the accounting records and returns; or
- certain disclosures of directors' remuneration specified by law are not made; or
- we have not received all the information and explanations we require for our audit.

John Smith (Senior Statutory Auditor)
For and on behalf of PricewaterhouseCoopers LLP
Chartered Accountants and Statutory Auditors
London
12 March 2012

Notes:

- *Where the financial statements are published on the company's website, include these notes unless the statement of directors' responsibilities clearly:*

    - *states the directors' responsibility for the maintenance and integrity of the website; and*

    - *refers to the fact that uncertainty regarding legal requirements is compounded as information published on the internet is accessible in many countries with different legal requirements relating to the preparation and dissemination of financial statements.*

(a) *The maintenance and integrity of the [name of entity] website is the responsibility of the directors; the work carried out by the auditors does not involve consideration of these matters and, accordingly, the auditors accept no responsibility for any changes that may have occurred to the financial statements since they were initially presented on the website.*

(b) *Legislation in the United Kingdom governing the preparation and dissemination of financial statements may differ from legislation in other jurisdictions.*

Profit and loss account for the year ended 31 December 2011

Continuing operations	Note	2011 £'000	£'000	2010 £'000	£'000
Turnover	3	–	11,275	–	10,010
Cost of sales		–	(8,734)	–	(7,305)
Gross profit		–	2,541	–	2,705
Distribution costs		–	(434)	–	(590)
Administrative expenses		–	(1,536)	–	(1,220)
Other operating income		–	13	–	11
Operating profit	4	–	584	–	906
Income from fixed asset investments			17		9
Profit on ordinary activities before interest and taxation		–	601	–	915
Interest receivable and similar income		21	–	13	–
Interest payable and similar charges	7	(166)	–	(97)	–
Other finance income	23	45	–	94	–
			(100)		10
Profit on ordinary activities before taxation		–	501	–	925
Tax on profit on ordinary activities	8	–	(258)	–	(406)
Profit for the financial year		–	243	–	519

Note: The above presentation of the profit and loss account follows format 1 as outlined in Schedule 1 to SI 2008/410. Alternatively, a company may present its profit and loss account such that expenses are classified by type using, for example, format 2. An example of presentation of expenses by type in line with format 2 using the above profit and loss account balances is shown below:

Continuing operations	Note	2011 £'000	£'000	2010 £'000	£'000
Turnover	3	–	11,275	–	10,010
Change in stocks of finished goods and work in progress		–	76	–	74
Own work capitalised		–	11	–	9
Other operating income		–	13	–	11
		–	11,375	–	10,104
Raw materials and consumables		(6,519)	–	(5,537)	–
Other external charges		(293)	–	(278)	–
Staff costs	4	(3,277)	–	(2,921)	–
Depreciation		(202)	–	(200)	–
Other operating charges		(500)	–	(262)	–
		–	(10,791)	–	(9,198)
Operating profit		–	584	–	906

Statement of total recognised gains and losses for the year ended 31 December 2011

		2011 £'000	2010 £'000
Profit for the financial year		243	519
Actuarial losses on pension scheme	23	(131)	(124)
Current tax deductions allocated to actuarial losses		17	35
Movement on deferred tax relating to pension deficit	18	22	2
Total recognised gains and losses relating to the year		151	432

There are no material differences between the profit on ordinary activities before taxation and the profit for the financial year stated above and their historical cost equivalents.

Balance sheet as at 31 December 2011

	Note	2011 £'000	£'000	2010 £'000	£'000
Fixed assets					
Tangible assets	10	2,385	–	2,031	–
Investments	11	56	–	76	–
		–	2,441	–	2,107
Current assets					
Stocks	12	1,908	–	1,779	–
Debtors (including £205,000 (2010: £56,000) due after one year)*	13	2,015	–	1,509	–
Investments	14	50	–	125	–
Cash at bank and in hand		91	–	159	–
			4,064		3,572
Creditors – amounts falling due within one year	15	–	(2,232)	–	(1,959)
Net current assets		–	1,832	–	1,613
Total assets less current liabilities		–	4,273	–	3,720
Creditors – Amounts falling due after more than one year	16	–	(794)	–	(524)
Provisions for liabilities	18	–	(234)	–	(48)
Net assets excluding pension deficit		–	3,245	–	3,148
Pension deficit	23	–	(150)	–	(93)
Net assets including pension deficit		–	3,095	–	3,055
Capital and reserves					
Called-up share capital	19	–	508	–	505
Share premium account	20	–	144	–	120
Revaluation reserve	20	–	172	–	177
Profit and loss account	20	–	2,271	–	2,253
Total shareholders' funds	21	–	3,095	–	3,055

Notes:

*Debtors due after one year must be disclosed separately if material compared to net current assets.

The financial statements on pages 7 to 20 were approved by the board of directors on 12 March 2012 and were signed on its behalf by:

C D Jones

UK GAAP Limited Registered number xxyyzz

Notes to the financial statements for the year ended 31 December 2011

1 Accounting policies

These financial statements are prepared on a going concern basis, under the historical cost convention, as modified by the revaluation of certain tangible fixed assets and in accordance with the Companies Act 2006 and applicable accounting standards in the United Kingdom.
The principal accounting policies are set out below and have been applied consistently throughout the year.

Note: A description of each of the accounting policies that is material in the context of the entity's financial statements should be disclosed. The policies must be the most appropriate. Where an accounting policy is prescribed by and fully described in an accounting standard, UITF Abstract or companies legislation, a succinct description of the policy should be given. Where an accounting policy is not prescribed by an accounting standard, a UITF Abstract or companies legislation, or an entity uses an option therein, a further description should be provided. In addition, there should be a description of those estimation techniques adopted that are significant (those where the range of reasonable amounts is so large that the use of a different amount from within the range could materially affect the view shown by the financial statements). The list of areas where companies might reasonably be expected to disclose accounting policies is not exhaustive.

- *Capital instruments.*
- *Deferred taxation.*
- *Depreciation and amortisation.*
- *Finance costs.*
- *Financial instruments.*
- *Fixed assets.*
- *Foreign currencies.*
- *Goodwill and intangible assets.*
- *Government grants.*
- *Impairment and provisions.*
- *Interest capitalisation.*

- *Investment properties.*
- *Leases.*
- *Long-term contracts.*
- *Pensions.*
- *Post-retirement benefits.*
- *Provisions.*
- *Research and development.*
- *Revaluation of fixed assets.*
- *Stocks and work in progress.*
- *Revenue recognition.*

2 Cash flow statement and related party disclosures

The company is a wholly-owned subsidiary of GAAP UK plc and is included in the consolidated financial statements of GAAP UK plc, which are publicly available. Consequently, the company has taken advantage of the exemption from preparing a cash flow statement under the terms of FRS 1 (revised 1996). The company is also exempt under the terms of FRS 8 from disclosing related-party transactions with entities that are part of the GAAP UK plc group or investees of the GAAP UK plc group. For details of other related-party transactions see note 26.

3 Segment reporting

The company's activities consist solely of the processing and sale of food in the United Kingdom.

4 Operating profit

	2011 £'000	2010 £'000
Operating profit is stated after charging		
Wages and salaries	2,661	2,391
Social security costs	515	436
Other pension costs (note 23)	101	94
Staff costs	**3,277**	**2,921**
Depreciation of tangible fixed assets:		
– Owned assets	159	158
– Leased assets	43	42
Operating lease charges:		
– Plant and machinery	42	34
– Other	55	48
Own work capitalised	11	9
Research and development – current year	15	18
Services provided by the company's auditor		
Fees payable for the audit	13	13
Fees payable for other services – tax compliance	5	5

5 Directors' emoluments

	2011 £'000	2010 £'000
Aggregate emoluments	210	206
Aggregate amounts (excluding shares) receivable under long-term incentive schemes	5	7
Sums paid to third parties for directors' services	2	–

Retirement benefits are accruing to three (2010: two) directors under a defined benefit scheme.

Notes:

(a) *If the company has a defined contribution scheme, a separate figure is to be disclosed showing the aggregate value of any company contributions paid or treated as paid to a pension scheme in respect of money purchase benefits. The number of directors to whom retirement benefits are accruing under each of money purchase and defined benefit schemes must also be disclosed.*

(b) *For unlisted companies, the net value of assets received or receivable under a long-term incentive scheme excludes shares and, hence, such companies must disclose the number of directors entitled to shares under a long-term incentive scheme, if applicable.*

(c) *The aggregate amount of excess retirement benefits and the aggregate amount of compensation for loss of office must also be disclosed, where applicable.*

Highest paid director

	2011 £'000	2010 £'000
Total amount of emoluments and amounts (excluding shares) receivable under long-term incentive schemes	75	70
Defined benefit pension scheme:		
– Accrued pension at end of year	38	36
– Accrued lump sum at the end of the year	50	45

Note: Where the highest paid director exercised any share options, and where any shares under a long-term incentive scheme were receivable by him, these facts must be disclosed (Companies Act 2006 5 Sch 2(3)). Where he is a member of a defined contribution scheme, the amount of company contributions in respect of him must be disclosed.

6 Employee information

The average monthly number of persons (including executive directors) employed by the company during the year was:

By activity	2011 £'000	2010 £'000
Production	166	170
Selling and distribution	32	30
Administration	55	55
	253	255

7 Interest payable and similar charges

	2011 £'000	2010 £'000
Interest payable on overdrafts and bank loans	109	33
Interest payable on other loans	18	23
Preference share dividend paid: 3.5p (2010 :3.5p) per £1 share	3	3
Finance lease interest	36	38
	166	97

8 Tax on profit on ordinary activities

	2011 £'000	2010 £'000
Current tax:		
– UK corporation tax on profits of the year	211	339
– Adjustment in respect of previous years	25	36
Total current tax	236	375
Deferred tax:		
– Origination and reversal of timing differences	22	31
– Impact of change in tax rate[1]	–	–
Total deferred tax (note 18)	22	31
Tax on profit on ordinary activities	258	406

The tax assessed for the period is higher (2010: higher) than the standard effective rate of corporation tax in the UK for the year ended 31 December 2011 of 26.5% (2010: 28%). The differences are explained below:

	2011 £'000	2010 £'000
Profit on ordinary activities before tax	501	925
Profit on ordinary activities multiplied by standard rate in the UK 26.5% (2010: 28%)	133	259
Effects of:		
– Expenses not deductible for tax purposes	100	109
– Accelerated capital allowances and other timing differences	(22)	(29)
– Adjustments to tax charge in respect of previous years	25	36
– Remeasurement of deferred tax-change in UK tax rate[2]	–	–
Current tax charge for the year	236	375

Tax on recognised gains and losses not included in the profit and loss account

	2011 £m	2010 £m
UK corporation tax at 26.5% (2010: 28%)		
Current tax deductions allocated to actuarial losses	(17)	(35)
Origination and reversal of timing differences relating to pension scheme	(22)	(2)
Impact of change in tax rate[1]	–	–
	(39)	(37)

Factors affecting current and future tax charges

During the year, as a result of the changes in the UK main corporation tax rate to 26% that was substantively enacted on 29 March 2011 and that will be effective from 1 April 2011, and to 25% that was substantively enacted on 5 July 2011 and that will be effective from 1 April 2012, the relevant deferred tax balances have been re-measured[3].

Further reductions to the UK corporation tax rate were announced in the March 2011 Budget. The changes, which are expected to be enacted separately each year, propose to reduce the rate by 1% per annum to 23% by 1 April 2016. The changes had not been substantively enacted at the balance sheet date and, therefore, are not recognised in these financial statements[4].

Based on current capital investment plans, the company expects to continue to be able to claim capital allowances in excess of depreciation in future years at a similar level to the current year.

No provision has been made for deferred tax on gains recognised on revaluing property to its market value. Such tax would become payable only if the property was sold without it being possible to claim rollover relief. The total amount unprovided for is £53,100 (2010: £53,100).

Deferred tax liabilities have not been discounted.

[1] The line item for 'Impact of change in tax rate' is shown for illustrative purposes. Companies with 31 December 2011 year ends will need to consider the impact of the reduction in tax rates in the Finance) Act 2011.
[2] The line item for the change in UK tax rate is shown for illustrative purposes. Companies with 31 December 2011 year ends will need to consider the impact of the reduction in tax rates in the Finance Act 2011.
[3] If the effect of the substantively enacted changes is material, disclosure should be given of the effect of on the profit and loss account and on the STRGL.
[4] If the effect of the proposed changes is material, disclosure should be given of the effect of the changes, either as disclosure of events after the reporting period (if applicable) or as factors affecting current and future tax charges.

9 Dividends

	2011 £'000	2010 £'000
Equity – Ordinary		
Interim paid: 3.51p (2010: 2.57p) per £0.25 share	71	52
Final paid (2010): 3.32p per £0.25 share	67	–
	138	52

The directors have proposed a final dividend for the year ended 31 December 2011 of 5.0p per share, which is a total of £102,000. This dividend has not been accounted for within the current year financial statements as it has yet to be approved.

10 Tangible assets

	Land and buildings £'000	Plant and machinery £'000	Total £'000
Cost or valuation			
At 1 January 2011	1,291	1,561	2,852
Additions	246	426	672
Disposals	(24)	(106)	(130)
At 31 December 2011	**1,513**	**1,881**	**3,394**
Accumulated depreciation			
At 1 January 2011	211	610	821
Charge for the year	45	157	202
Disposals	(6)	(8)	(14)
At 31 December 2011	**250**	**759**	**1,009**
Net book amount			
At 31 December 2011	**1,263**	**1,122**	**2,385**
At 31 December 2010	1,080	951	2,031

Analysis of land and buildings

	2011 £'000	2010 £'000
Analysis of land and buildings at cost or valuation		
At cost	1,224	1,002
At valuation	289	289
	1,513	1,291

The Company has taken advantage of the transitional arrangements in FRS 15 'Tangible fixed assets', and retained the book values of certain freehold properties that were revalued prior to implementation of that standard. Where an asset that was previously revalued is disposed of, its book value is eliminated and an appropriate transfer made from the revaluation reserve to the profit and loss reserve.

The transition rules set out in FRS 15 were adopted as at 31 December 1999; book values of property assets were frozen accordingly.

	2011 £'000	2010 £'000
The net book amount of land and buildings comprises		
Freehold	1,216	1,031
Long leaseholds	36	37
Short leaseholds	11	12
	1,263	1,080

If land and buildings had not been revalued, they would have been included at the following amounts:

	Land and buildings	
	2011	2010
	£'000	£'000
Cost	1,326	1,104
Aggregate depreciation	(235)	(201)
Net book amount	1,091	903

	2011	2010
	£'000	£'000
Assets held under finance leases and capitalised in plant and machinery		
Cost	349	396
Aggregate depreciation	(116)	(132)
Net book amount	233	264

11 Fixed asset investments

	£'000
At 1 January 2011	76
Disposals	(20)
At 31 December 2011	56

Fixed asset investments comprise equity shares in a trade investment with a cost of £56,000 (2010: £76,000). These are listed on the London Stock Exchange and had a market value of £145,000 (2010: £170,000) at 31 December 2011.

12 Stocks

	2011	2010
	£'000	£'000
Raw materials and consumables	873	820
Work in progress	209	182
Finished goods and goods for resale	826	777
	1,908	1,779

£200,000 (2010: £100,000) of finished goods included above are consignment stocks that are held on a sale or return basis from the manufacturer. Title to these stocks passes at the earlier of when they are sold and nine months from delivery date. On delivery a deposit of 30% is payable. The balance is included in trade creditors and bears interest at LIBOR plus 1.75% and becomes payable when title passes.

The replacement cost of stocks exceeds balance sheet values as follows:

	2011	2010
	£'000	£'000
Raw materials and consumables	40	19

13 Debtors

	2011	2010
	£'000	£'000
Trade debtors	1,533	1,067
Amounts owed by group undertakings	389	367
Other debtors	32	21
Prepayments and accrued income	61	54
	2,015	1,509

Trade debtors include £205,000 (2010: £56,000) falling due after more than one year. Amounts owed by group undertakings are unsecured, interest free, have no fixed date of repayment and are repayable on demand.

14 Current asset investments

	2011 £'000	2010 £'000
Government securities	50	125

The market value of the government securities is not materially different from their carrying amount.

15 Creditors – amounts falling due within one year

	2011 £'000	2010 £'000
Debenture loans (note 17)	349	12
Bank loans and overdrafts (note 17)	388	319
Trade creditors	876	1,005
Amounts owed to group undertakings	241	180
Finance leases (note 17)	27	31
Taxation and social security	243	291
Other creditors	15	12
Accruals and deferred income	93	109
	2,232	1,959

Amounts due to group undertakings are unsecured, interest free and repayable on demand.

16 Creditors – amounts falling due after more than one year

	2011 £'000	2010 £'000
Debenture loans (note 17)	175	107
Bank loans (note 17)	166	52
Finance leases (note 17)	283	250
Cumulative preference shares of £1 each – 75,000 (note 17)	75	75
Other creditors	95	40
	794	524

17 Loans and other borrowings

	2011 £'000	2010 £'000
7% unsecured loan stock 2011/2012	349	12
10% unsecured loan stock 2016/2017	175	107
Bank loans and overdrafts	554	371
Finance leases	310	281
Cumulative preference shares of £1 each – 75,000	75	75
	1,463	846

Maturity of financial liabilities		
In one year or less, or on demand	764	362
In more than one year, but not more than two years	218	102
In more than two years, but not more than five years	211	168
In more than five years	270	214
	1,463	846

Note: The maturity time bandings are derived from paragraph 67 of FRS 25. This disclosure is suggested best practice for those companies that are not applying the disclosure requirements of FRS 25 as the equivalent disclosure requirements in FRS 4 have been deleted.

The 7% unsecured loan stock 2011/2012 is redeemable at par between 1 January 2011 and 31 December 2012. The 10% unsecured loan stock 2016/2017 is redeemable at par between 1 January 2016 and 31 December 2017.

Included in the bank loans is an amount of £300,000, which is payable in two annual instalments commencing 1 January 2010 and carries interest at 11% fixed. The balance of £80,000 carries interest at LIBOR plus 3% and is repayable in six quarterly instalments commencing 1 February 2012.

Finance leases

Future minimum payments under finance leases are as follows:

	2011 £'000	2010 £'000
Within one year	31	35
In more than one year, but not more than five years	302	243
After five years	25	37
Total gross payments	358	315
Less finance charges included above	(48)	(34)
	310	281

The total value of leases repayable by instalments any part of which falls due after more than five years is £24,184 (2010: £35,875).

Debentures issued

The company issued the following debentures during the year.

Class	Amount issued £'000	Consideration received £'000
7% unsecured redeemable 2011/2012	337	337
10% unsecured redeemable 2016/2017	68	68

Preference share capital issued and fully paid	2011	2010
75,000: 3.5% cumulative preference shares of £1 each at 1 January 2011	75	75

The 3.5% cumulative preference shares carry a fixed cumulative preferential dividend at the rate of 3.5% per annum, payable half yearly in arrears on 31 December and 30 June. The shares have no redemption entitlement. On a winding-up, the holders have priority before all other classes of shares to receive repayment of capital plus any arrears of dividend. The holders have no voting rights unless the dividend is in arrears by six months or more.

Note: Although not applicable for UK GAAP Limited, companies that elect not to adopt fair value accounting for certain financial instruments must give additional disclosures relating to their derivative financial instruments. The following disclosure is required for each class of derivative financial instrument:

- *the fair value of the derivatives in that class, if such a value can be determined; and*
- *the extent and nature of the derivatives.*

[SI 2008/410 1 Sch 56 (a), (b)].

In addition, where:

- *a company has financial fixed assets that could be included at fair value;*
- *the amount at which those assets are included in the financial statements is in excess of their fair value; and*
- *the company has not made provision for diminution in value of those assets.*

The following disclosure must be made:

- *The amount at which either the individual assets or appropriate groupings of those individual assets is stated in the company's financial statements.*
- *The fair value of those assets or groupings.*
- *The reasons for not making a provision for diminution in value of those assets, including the nature of the evidence that provides the basis for the belief that the amount at which they are stated in the financial statements will be recovered.*

[SI 2008/410 1 Sch 57 (1), (2)].

18 Provisions for liabilities

	Pending litigation £'000	Reorganisation provision £'000	Environmental provision £'000	Deferred tax provision £'000	Total £'000
1 January 2011	–	–	–	48	48
Charged to the profit and loss account	15	153	72	22	262
Utilised during the year	–	(42)	(34)	–	(76)
31 December 2011	**15**	**111**	**38**	**70**	**234**

Pending litigation

In December 2011, the company received a claim from Customer Limited that green colouring had been found in a batch of bread. A provision of £15,000 has been made for the costs of product recall and loss of profit claim from Customer Limited. The claim is expected to be fully resolved in early 2012.

Reorganisation

A rationalisation of product processes at the company's two factories in London and Bradford was announced on 11 December 2011. This rationalisation involving the introduction of new technology will result in the loss of 15 jobs in total over the next few months. The provision is expected to be fully utilised by 31 December 2012.

Environmental

In April 2011 a spillage of cleaning chemicals contaminated land surrounding the Bradford factory. The company is committed to a policy of environmental protection and immediate action is being taken to deal with the contamination. A provision of £72,000 has been recognised for those clean-up costs, which are expected to be incurred over an eighteen-month period.

Provision for deferred tax	2011 £'000	2010 £'000
Accelerated capital allowances	65	40
Other timing differences	5	8
Total provision for deferred tax	**70**	**48**
1 January	48	21
Deferred tax charged in profit and loss account (note 8)	22	27
31 December	**70**	**48**

Deferred tax asset relating to pension deficit	2011 £'000	2010 £'000
1 January	36	38
Deferred tax credit charged in profit and loss account	–	(4)
Deferred tax credited/(charged) to the statement of total recognised gains and losses:		
–On actuarial loss	22	3
–Change in tax rate[1]	–	–
31 December	**58**	**36**

The deferred tax asset of £58,000 (2010: £36,000) has been deducted in arriving at the net pension deficit on the balance sheet.

19 Called-up share capital

	2011 £'000	2010 £'000
Allotted and fully paid		
2,032,000 (2010: 2,020,000) ordinary shares of £0.25 each	508	505

From 1 October 2010, the Companies Act 2006 abolished the requirement for a company to have an authorised share capital. Shareholders wishing to restrict the number of shares that can be issued by a company need to address this issue in the company's articles.

[1] The line item for change in tax rate is shown for illustrative purposes. Companies with 31 December 2011 year ends will need to consider the impact of the reduction in tax rates in the Finance Act 2011.

On 3 May 2011 12,000 ordinary shares were issued for cash. The nominal value of these shares was £3,000, and the consideration received was £27,000 after deducting expenses of £1,000.

20 Reserves

	Share premium account £'000	Revaluation reserve £'000	Profit and loss account £'000
1 January 2011	120	177	2,253
Premium on ordinary shares issued (net of £1,000 expenses)	24	–	–
Retained profit for the financial year (note 21)	–	–	105
Actuarial losses on pension scheme	–	–	(92)
Transfer to profit and loss reserve	–	(5)	5
31 December 2011	**144**	**172**	**2,271**
Pension deficit	–	–	(150)
Profit and loss reserve excluding pension deficit	–	–	2,421

21 Reconciliation of movements in shareholders' funds

	2011 £'000	2010 £'000
Profit for the financial year	243	519
Dividends	(138)	(52)
Retained profit for the financial year	105	467
Net proceeds of issue of ordinary share capital (note 19)	27	50
Actuarial losses on pension scheme net of tax	(92)	(87)
Net addition to shareholders' funds	40	430
Closing shareholders' funds	3,095	3,055

22 Contingent liabilities

The company has given a guarantee in respect of the bank borrowings of a fellow subsidiary, which amounted to £35,000 at 31 December 2011 (2010: £25,000).

An overseas customer has commenced an action against the company in respect of equipment claimed to be defective. It has been estimated that the liability should the action be successful is £2,000. A trial date has not yet been set; therefore it is not therefore practical to state the timing of any payment.

The company has been advised by Counsel that it is possible, but not probable, the action will succeed; accordingly no provision for any liability has therefore been made in these accounts.

23 Pension commitments

The company operates a defined benefit pension scheme with assets held in a separately administered fund. The scheme provides retirement benefits on the basis of members' final salary. On 1 January 2010, the defined benefit pension scheme was closed to new entrants. At the same time, the company established a defined contribution scheme to provide benefits to new employees.

Defined benefit scheme

An actuarial valuation of the UK GAAP Limited pension scheme, using the projected unit basis, was carried out at 31 December 2011 by Actuary and Actuary, independent consulting actuaries. The major assumptions used by the actuary were:

	2011 %	2010 %
Rate of increase in salaries	4.3	4.0
Rate of increase in pensions in payment	3.0	4.0
Discount rate	5.2	5.0
Rate of inflation	2.8	2.5

The mortality assumptions used were as follows:

	2011 years	2010 years
Longevity at age 65 for current pensioners:		
– Men	19.7	18.4
– Women	22.4	21.3
Longevity at age 65 for future pensioners:		
– Men	20.4	19.3
– Women	23.1	22.3

The assets in the scheme and the expected rates of return were:

	Long-term rate of return expected 31 December 2011 %	Value at 31 December 2011 £000	Long-term rate of return expected at 31 December 2010 %	As restated value at 31 December 2010 £000
Equities	8.2	5,852	8.4	5,341
Bonds	4.9	1,600	5.6	1,500
Total market value of assets		7,452		6,841
Present value of scheme liabilities		(7,660)		(6,970)
Deficit in scheme		**(208)**		**(129)**
Related deferred tax asset[1]		58		36
Net pension deficit		**(150)**		**(93)**

The equity investments and bonds that are held in plan assets are quoted and are valued at the current bid price following the adoption of the amendment to FRS 17. These were previously valued at mid price. The effect of this change is that the value of assets at 31 December 2010 has been restated from £6,875,000 to £6,841,000, a decrease of £34,000.

Reconciliation of present value of scheme liabilities

	2011 £'000	2010 £'000
1 January	6,970	6,315
Current service cost	84	90
Past service cost	5	–
Interest cost	505	489
Benefits paid	(51)	(63)
Actuarial loss	147	139
31 December	**7,660**	**6,970**

Sensitivity analysis of scheme liabilities

The sensitivity of the present value of scheme liabilities to changes in the principle assumptions used is set out below.

	Change in assumption	Impact on scheme liabilities
Discount rate	Increase/decrease by 1%	Increase/decrease by 8.5%
Rate of inflation	Increase/decrease by 1%	Increase/decrease by 5.0%
Rate of increase in salaries	Increase/decrease by 1%	Increase/decrease by 3.5%
Rate of increase in pensions in payment	Increase/decrease by 1%	Increase/decrease by 3.0%
Mortality	Increase by 1 year	Increase by 4.5%

[1] The tax figures shown are for illustrative purposes and do not reflect the tax notes or any remeasurement as a result of change in the tax note in the Finance Act 2011.

Reconciliation of fair value of scheme assets

	2011 £'000	2010 £'000
1 January	6,841	6,190
Expected return on scheme assets	550	583
Actuarial gains	16	15
Benefits paid	(51)	(63)
Contributions paid by employer	96	116
31 December	7,452	6,841

Scheme assets do not include any of UK GAAP Limited's own financial instruments or any property occupied by UK GAAP Limited.

The expected return on scheme assets is determined by considering the expected returns available on the assets underlying the current investment policy. Expected yields on fixed interest investments are based on gross redemption yields as at the balance sheet date. Expected returns on equity investments reflect long-term real rates of return experienced in the respective markets.

The actual return on scheme assets in the year was £566,000 (2010: £598,000).

Analysis of the amount charged to profit or loss is as follows:

	2011 £'000	2010 £'000
Current service cost	84	90
Past service cost	5	–
Expected return on pension scheme assets	(550)	(583)
Interest on pension scheme liabilities	505	489
Total	44	(4)

Of the total current and past service cost, £63,000 (2010: £65,000) is included within cost of sales, and £26,000 (2010: £25,000) is included within administrative expenses.

Actuarial gains and losses

The cumulative amount of actuarial losses recognised in the statement of recognised gains and losses is £536,000.

Actuarial valuation

The full actuarial valuation at 31 December 2011 showed an increase in the deficit from £135,000 to £215,000. It has been agreed with the trustees that contributions for the next two years will be increased by £100,000 to make good the deficit. The total contributions expected to be made to the scheme by UK GAAP Limited in the year to 31 December 2012 is therefore £195,000. Further to this, as the scheme is closed to new entrants, the current service cost will increase as members approach retirement.

Amounts for current and previous four years

	2011 £'000	2010 £'000	2009 £'000	2008 £'000	2007 £'000
Defined benefit obligation	(7,660)	(6,970)	(6,315)	(6,115)	(5,987)
Plan assets	7,445	6,835	6,190	5,990	5,780
Deficit	(215)	(135)	(125)	(125)	(207)
Experience adjustments on plan assets:					
– Amount	16	15	50	41	(33)
Experience adjustments on plan liabilities:					
– Amount	(22)	21	98	45	66
Total amount recognised in the statement of total recognised gains and losses:	131	124	150	245	160

Defined contribution scheme

The cost of contributions to the defined contribution scheme amounts to £12,000 (2010: £4,000).

24 Capital and other commitments

	2011 £'000	2010 £'000
Contracts placed for future capital expenditure not provided in the financial statements	145	226

25 Financial commitments

At 31 December 2011, the company had annual commitments under non-cancellable operating leases for assets other than land and buildings expiring as follows:

	2011 £'000	2010 £'000
Within one year	12	20
Within two to five years	23	12
After five years	95	65
	130	97

26 Other related-party transactions

Note: Information concerning transactions with related parties should be disclosed here, if they are not disclosed elsewhere within the financial statements. Information concerning transactions with directors and loans, etc, to officers should also normally be disclosed here.

27 Ultimate parent undertaking

The immediate parent undertaking is GAAP UK Intermediate Holdings Limited.

The ultimate parent undertaking and controlling party is GAAP UK plc, which is the parent undertaking of the smallest and largest group to consolidate these financial statements. Copies of GAAP UK plc consolidated financial statements can be obtained from the Company Secretary at GAAP Towers, 2 The Square, London EC4Y 2DE.